A
Pictorial History of
New England

A
Pictorial History of
New England

BY EDWARD WAGENKNECHT

Picture Editor: Anita Duncan

CROWN PUBLISHERS, INC. NEW YORK

RECENT BOOKS BY EDWARD WAGENKNECHT

Nathaniel Hawthorne, Man and Writer (New York, 1961)
Mark Twain: The Man and His Work (Norman, 1961, 1967)
Washington Irving: Moderation Displayed (New York, 1962)
The Movies in the Age of Innocence (Norman, 1962)
Edgar Allan Poe: The Man Behind the Legend (New York, 1963)
Chicago (Norman, 1964)
Seven Daughters of the Theater (Norman, 1964)
Harriet Beecher Stowe: The Known and the Unknown (New York, 1965)
Dickens and the Scandalmongers: Essays in Criticism (Norman, 1965)
The Man Charles Dickens: A Victorian Portrait (Norman, 1966)
Henry Wadsworth Longfellow: Portrait of an American Humanist (New York, 1966)
Merely Players (Norman, 1966)
John Greenleaf Whittier, A Portrait in Paradox (New York, 1967)
The Personality of Chaucer (Norman, 1968)
As Far as Yesterday: Memories and Reflections (Norman, 1968)
The Supernaturalism of New England, by John Greenleaf Whittier, edited by E. W.
   (Norman, 1969)
William Dean Howells: The Friendly Eye (New York, 1969)
Marilyn Monroe: A Composite View, edited by E. W. (Philadelphia, 1969)
The Personality of Milton (Norman, 1970)
James Russell Lowell: Portrait of a Many-Sided Man (New York, 1971)
Ambassadors for Christ: Seven American Preachers (New York, 1972)
The Personality of Shakespeare (Norman, 1972)
Ralph Waldo Emerson: Portrait of a Balanced Soul (New York, 1974)
The Letters of James Branch Cabell, edited by E. W. (Norman, 1974)
The Films of D. W. Griffith, with Anthony Slide (New York, 1975)

Library of Congress Cataloging in Publication Data

Wagenknecht, Edward Charles, 1900-
   A pictorial history of New England.

   Bibliography: p.
   Includes index.
   1. New England—History.   I. Title.
F4.W3   1976   974   76-3669
ISBN 0-517-52346-9

For My Wife

*"More is thy due than more
than all can pay."*

Contents

Introduction

To provide the text for a popular pictorial history of New England in a single volume involves many problems. Intense selectivity must rule at every point, and the author can hardly hope for a single reader who will not at some point lament that what interests him most has been left out!

The volume in hand combines chronological with topical methods. The opening chapter is confined to the colonial period, but Chapters 2 through 5 range widely. Chapter 2 deals with four cities and Chapter 3 with five towns. Chapter 4 attempts a survey of New England literature in what has traditionally been regarded as its "golden" or "classical" period, while Chapter 5 presents miniature portraits or vignettes of nine famous New Englanders.

In Chapter 4 the material was relatively predetermined, but in all other cases more or less arbitrary choices had to be made. Chapter 3 is more arbitrary than Chapter 2, however. In Chapter 2 the idea was to choose cities representative of the various states, and since I had to fight all along the line to prevent Massachusetts from running away with the book, I could not, having included Boston, consider using either Springfield or Worcester. In Chapter 3 my range of choice was much wider. Here I had to content myself with lining up an array of towns that would illustrate different types of settlement in different regions, and if anyone objects that I might just as well have chosen This as That, I can only admit the soft impeachment. I am aware too that places which call themselves cities and operate under the city form of government may very well object to being called towns, but I had to find some way to distinguish between the larger centers of population in Chapter 2 and the smaller in Chapter 3. The word town has had a long and varied and honorable history in New England, and the form of local government adopted does not anywhere depend absolutely upon size. Oak Park, Illinois, for example, is quite large enough to be a city, but it remains, by its own fiat, the Village of Oak Park, the largest village, they say, in the world. In my biographical Chapter 5, of course, my range of choice widened out almost indefinitely; if I could have written a hundred sketches, I might have given an adequate idea of the range of New England character. For the nine I finally chose I can only claim that I do think them reasonably representative within the limitations imposed.

Chapters 6, 7, and 8 deal with New England from the Revolution to the present time and combine chronological and topical methods. It must be remembered, however, that much that belongs to the national period has been anticipated in Chapters 2 through 5 and also that New England is now a less self-contained entity than she was in colonial times. I cannot quite go along with the writer of a leading Massachusetts handbook who asserts that, during the early years, the history of Massachusetts and that of the country were virtually one and the same (Virginia, I am sure, would be interested to know this!), for the statement reflects a degree of provincialism that seems to belong less to our own time than to the days when George Edward Woodberry recorded that he found the biography of Poe an interesting problem because his was "a life led outside of New England." But even if one cavils at the "aloofness," one still remembers that James Truslow Adams decided to end his history of New England at 1850 because after that date,

New England became linked with the other sections. Geographic factors were still of influence, it is true, and the section has always maintained a certain aloofness from national interest and the national life, but from the middle of the nineteenth century on its history becomes rather that of a mere section than of a distinct unit of the nation.

Even the author of a history of New England much longer and more pretentious than mine would have to draw the line at permitting his work to expand, elephantiasis-like, to a history of the United States, while at the same time he would have to remember that though New England continued to experience, and struggle with, its local problems after having become a part of these United States, much of this local material is no longer of great interest to anybody outside her own borders or, for that matter, to many within them.

Much of my manuscript was read by my friend, Robert E. Moody, Professor Emeritus of History and former Librarian at Boston University, who made many valuable suggestions, most of which I have adopted. Portions of the manuscript have also been read by Charles G. Bennett, Librarian of the Genealogical Library of The Bennington Museum, as well as his colleague Eugene R. Kosche and Alexander R. Drysdale; Marian B. (Mrs. Hans W.) Miller, of the Concord Antiquarian Society; Marcia E. Moss, of the Concord Public Library; Dorothy M. (Mrs. Charles A.) Potter, Librarian of the Essex Institute; William L. Warren; James E. White, Professor in Rhode Island College, and his colleague, Chester E. Smolski; and Ola Elizabeth Winslow. Some of these people are friends; most of them I have never seen. I am grateful to all of them, but it must be understood that responsibility for what I have written is mine alone. Finally, I should like to express my appreciation of the work of the picture editor, Miss Anita Duncan, who collected and largely captioned the multitudinous illustrations in this volume.

EDWARD WAGENKNECHT

West Newton, Massachusetts

Chapter 1

"In the Old Colony Days"

The breaking waves dashed high
On a stern and rock-bound coast,
And the woods, against a stormy sky,
Their giant branches tossed;

And the heavy night hung dark
The hills and waters o'er,
When a band of exiles moored their bark
On the wild New England shore.

MRS. HEMANS was an English poet, and we should not blame her for not knowing that the coast at Plymouth, Massachusetts, is not "rock-bound" but sandy beach. This was not the only thing she got wrong in "The Landing of the Pilgrim Fathers in New England," and it is said that when her errors were pointed out to her, she was so distressed that she burst into tears. But geographical accuracy was not the heart of what she had to offer. She concluded her composition thus:

What sought they thus afar?
Bright jewels of the mine?
The wealth of seas, the spoils of war?—
They sought a faith's pure shrine!

Ay, call it holy ground,
The soil where first they trod!
They have left unstained what there they found—
Freedom to worship God!

Even second-rate art often exercises a power over men's hearts which is denied to first-rate history, and untold thousands of Americans still travel every year to stand reverently before the "Plymouth Rock" upon which the Pilgrims never landed. For all that, there may still be more truth in art than in "the low-down facts." Was Mrs. Hemans a true interpreter of the "Pilgrim Fathers" or was she merely a sentimental eulogist? The answer is not simple, but we may hope that it will emerge, at least in part, from the ensuing discussion.

Though Governor Bradford's great history *Of Plymouth Plantation* (not published until 1856) does apply the term pilgrim in its religious sense (Hebrews 11:13) to the Plymouth colonists, they never called themselves "the Pilgrims" nor has the term been generally applied to them for more than the last century and a half. The Pilgrim colony was neither the first attempted settlement in New England nor the most important English

1

Aerial view taken from a point about two miles south of Plymouth center, looking northward. The beach is in the upper right quarter. The photograph was taken before Plimoth Plantation was built, but its site lies in the center of the picture, between the two highways, where a large house can be seen and a field sloping toward the water and down to the further highway. Photograph for Plimoth Plantation by Eastern Aerial Surveys, Inc.

Plymouth Rock, Plymouth, Mass. U. S. Bureau of Public Roads, National Archives

settlement achieved; its resources were insignificant and its people few, poor, and humble compared to those of the Massachusetts Bay Colony which, in 1691, finally swallowed it up. Its modern fame it owes to a number of circumstances: Bradford's history itself; the bicentennial celebration in 1820; Longfellow's poem, *The Courtship of Miles Standish*; its establishment of an annual Thanksgiving Day (not a national holiday until President Lincoln made it one in 1863, shifting its observance from October to November); and a widespread impression that the people of Plymouth were gentler, more "human," and even more democratic than those of Boston. As we shall see, there is some justification for this. Certainly nothing could be more winning than the spirit of the Pilgrim pastor, John Robinson, who did not live to come to America, but who believed that "the Lord had more truth and light yet to break forth out of his holy word," and who urged his hearers "to follow him no further than he followed Christ." But the general impression must still be subjected to many qualifications.

Puritans never wore the absurd costumes which modern artists have designed for them; their habiliments may have been plain by aristocratic standards, but in design their garments did not differ from those of their contemporaries, and both men and women were fond of bright colors. Of course they lacked a great many things that we take for granted, and of course there were terrible hardships in the beginning. At the end of the first winter in Plymouth, half the *Mayflower* passengers were dead, and at one time only William Brewster, Miles Standish, and five others were on their feet

The Plimoth Seal. Courtesy Plimoth Plantation

The Departure of the Pilgrim Fathers. Engraving by John Burnet after painting by Lucy, 1847. Library of Congress

and able to tend the sick. "It is not with us," said Brewster, "as with men whom small things can discourage or small discontentments cause to wish themselves at home again," which was surely, under the circumstances, one of the world's great moving utterances of heroism, and almost sufficient to justify the arrogance of William Stoughton's election sermon of 1688, in which he declared that "God sifted a whole nation, that He might send choice grain into the wilderness" (Archbishop Laud had had other ideas; to him all Puritans were "swine which rooted out God's vineyard"). There must have been many even in Plymouth who could not rise to Brewster's level, however. William Bradford's own young wife, Dorothy, was drowned from the deck of the *Mayflower* in Plymouth harbor, and nobody knows whether it was accident or suicide. But there are suicides too in rich, modern America, and though the Puritans might well have regarded our modern preoccupation with happiness as degenerate, once the colonies had been reasonably established, they were probably no less nor no more happy than we are ourselves.

It is sometimes carelessly assumed that the Plymouth people were "Pilgrims" while those who settled in Boston were "Puritans"; this of course is nonsense. The Massachusetts Bay people have never been called Pilgrims, but both groups were thoroughly Puritan. In its larger sense, puritanism, though less prevalent than impuritanism, represents a permanent attitude toward life. There was puritanism in ancient Rome, and Catholic Ireland is arguably the most puritan country in the

world today. In its specific application to sixteenth and seventeenth century England, however, the term Puritan indicates those who believed that the English Reformation had not gone far enough. There were some nobles and aristocrats among them and many country gentlemen and wealthy merchants, and the Puritan movement had great strength at Cambridge. Not many Puritans wished to break with the Established Church, however. Some would have preferred the presbyterian form of church government by elders (laymen) to the episcopal government by bishops but not all went even that far. What they did want was to "purify" the service, to stress preaching and unstress ritual, and to throw out everything suggestive of "Romanism." If they were Calvinists, it was only because they regarded Calvin as a sound interpreter of the Bible, which was their supreme authority in religion. They had fallen in love with the primitive church, and they would have liked to re-create it in England. When this turned out to be impossible, they thought they saw a chance in America, with those who continued to love Mother Church, even thinking of themselves as preserving her light afar and cherishing the hope that ultimately the daughter might come to the mother's aid and deliver her.

The real religious radicals or "come-outers" were the Separatists or Brownists, who did wish to leave the church and to organize their "gathered" conventicles upon a strictly congregational basis. Robert Browne himself turned out to be a broken reed; he recanted as early as 1588 and accepted a living in the Church of England. Shakespeare mentions Brownists in *Twelfth Night*, where the imbecilic Sir Andrew Aguecheek, who sometimes thinks he has "no more wit than a Christian or an ordinary man," and who would be willing to beat Malvolio like a dog if he thought him a Puritan, would yet "as lief be a Brownist as a politician." There was a Separatist church in Norwich in 1580, and William Brewster, John Robinson, and the seventeen-year-old William Bradford were members of the Separatist group organized in the drawing room of Scrooby Manor in 1606.

In America, however, as John Robinson had foretold, the differences between Separatist and non-Separatist tended quickly to disappear, partly because of distance (bishops could not ordain where bishops did not exist) and partly because of the spirit of independence toward English institutions in general which appeared in the colonies at a very early date. Plymouth was without a pastor for long periods, and since Elder Brewster could not administer the sacraments, marriage became a civil contract, while baptism, which Calvin had not considered necessary to salvation, was, for the time being, omitted. John Lyford, a Church of England clergyman, was driven from the colony after he had administered the sacraments and conducted service according to the Prayer Book. Bradford called him "a vile man and an enemy to the plantation," which he may well have been, but his fate would probably have been the same whatever his personal qualities. Those who settled at Salem had certainly not been Separatists in the Old World, yet when the first church was organized there, the clergymen, Samuel Skelton and Francis Higginson, consecrated each other and Plymouth's good fellowship was sought, and when objections were raised to these procedures, Governor Endicott (or Endecott) in his arbitrary way, sent the objectors back to England.

Investigated by the Ecclesiastical Commission of 1607, the Scrooby Separatists moved first to Holland, where there was no religious persecution. But there they were confronted by an alien language and culture, and they could not establish themselves in a foreign land without losing their English identity, which they did not wish to do. Some of their children seemed to have no objection to assimilation, but this did not increase the satisfaction of their parents; neither did the approaching expiration of the Hispano-Dutch truce in 1621, which reawakened fear of renewed religious conflict in the Lowlands.

Settlements in the New World were made under "charters," granted, for a consideration, to various individuals and groups, on the assumption of the rights conveyed by discovery and exploration. It was not until Roger Williams came along that anybody was to be radical enough to maintain that the land belonged to the Indians and that nobody in England had the right to give away something he did not own. The colonists did negotiate with the Indians upon many occasions, but justice was not notably served, for nobody—least of all the natives themselves—had any idea of the real value of what was being bartered. And even Williams had to face practical realities to the extent of going to England to negotiate a Parliamentary charter for Rhode Island in 1644.

In any case, charters did exist, and settlements were made under them, but carelessness and conflicting claims and English ignorance of North American geography created endless confusion. Sir Ferdinando Gorges was the leading contender in early New England land grants and attempted colonization. In the very year of the Jamestown settlement in Virginia (1607), he attempted to establish a colony in Maine at the mouth of the Kennebec; later he sent Captain John Smith, whom the Pilgrims might have had as a guide if they had not turned him down, to explore the coast and come back with such names as New England, the Charles River, and Cape Ann. Even this was not the beginning, however. There had been an attempt to plant a colony on the Magdalen Islands at the mouth of the St. Lawrence in 1597. In 1602 Bartholomew Gosnold came to Cape Cod, Martha's Vineyard, and the Elizabeth Islands, and the next year an English hunting and fishing expedition reached Plymouth itself. Many fishers and fur traders came, establishing stations at such places as Beacon Hill, Charlestown, Chelsea, and Quincy. In 1639 Gorges became Proprietor of Maine. His claims came into conflict with those of the Bay colony, and there was much friction between them. New England's story has generally been told by writers friendly to the Puritans, and they have not wasted much sympathy on Gorges. It at least seems in order to recognize that few men have devoted themselves more persistently to a large and heroic enterprise and reaped so little reward.

Having tried unsuccessfully to secure a grant from what was known as the Council for New England, the Pilgrims finally sailed with the idea of settling in the "Virginia" territory by authority of the London Company, under a kind of joint stock company plan, shares being bought by English "adventurers" who risked their money but not themselves, adventurer-planters who contributed both, and ordinary planters who brought only their own capacity for work. But it was Cape Cod that was sighted, after a difficult voyage of nearly two months, on November 9, 1620, and though some attempt was at first made to sail south, this was soon given up, and the *Mayflower* anchored at Provincetown while exploring expeditions were undertaken. The Plymouth territory was explored between December 11

English Puritans escaping to America. New York Public Library Picture Collection

The *Mayflower*. Mural by N. C. Wyeth in the Metropolitan Life Insurance Company building, New York. Courtesy of Metropolitan Life Insurance Company

and 21, and the first house laid, near the site of an old Indian village, on what the rest of the world knew as Christmas Day but which to Puritans was only a "popish" holiday. In June 1621 the settlers did secure a patent from the Council for New England, and this was all the authorization they had until the "Old Charter," which defined the boundaries of the colony and conferred or confirmed certain fishing and trading rights, was issued in 1630. Since Plymouth never did secure a royal charter, Charles M. Andrews, the leading authority on American colonization, calls it "a de facto corporate colony."

Before this, however, the London merchants who had "adventured" in Plymouth, not satisfied with the returns they were receiving on their investment, moved to withdraw from the venture in 1624, and in 1627 an arrangement was concluded to buy them out. When civil war came to England in the forties and the monarchy was abolished, and again in 1660, when the Stuarts were restored, the legality of all colonial charters and patents was up in the air, and there was much maneuvering all along the line both to clarify status and to achieve a workable modus operandi.

An earlier event was much more interesting than any of these technicalities. Americans who boast of having ancestors who came over on the *Mayflower* would do well to check the status of their forebears on that famous vessel. Besides the "saints" and the ship's officers and crew, she carried "strangers," hired men, and indentured servants. Among the hundred and one passengers only thirty-five came from the Scrooby-Leyden group of Pilgrims while sixty-six had been recruited in London and Southampton. It is interesting that neither John Alden nor Miles Standish (the red-headed "Captain Shrimp," as his enemy Thomas Morton called him), who, thanks to Longfellow, are now perhaps the best known of the emigrants, were members of the Separatist group, though Alden must finally have become one of them and Standish was certainly in their inner councils on all practical affairs and wholly loyal to them.

It was the "discontented" and "mutinous" strangers who in a way became responsible for the Mayflower Compact. When they found that they were landing out of the jurisdiction of the London Company, they threatened that "when they came ashore, they would use their own liberty, for none had power to command them." To give themselves a weapon against anarchy, the leaders of the settlement thereupon drew up and secured agreement to a kind of civil equivalent to a church covenant and elected John Carver governor.

Though we may discount the extravagant claims sometimes made for the Mayflower Compact by enthusiasts who would find the seeds of all democratic government in it, it was all the Pilgrims had to operate under in 1620. If we ask how "discontented" and "mutinous" persons could be controlled by a document which some of them had not even signed, the answer must be that they were not so controlled absolutely, but the colony did hold together, and on the whole the non-"saints" seem to have behaved rather better than might have been expected. The people were more homogeneous socially than religiously, with far more "Goodman" and "Goodwife" than "Master" and "Mistress" among them. There were only about twenty university men during the first forty years, but a number of these were clearly, in Chaucerian phraseology, men "of great auctoritee." The terrible hardships in the beginning may have served to create a bond as well as a strain: the first cargo shipped back to England was captured by a French privateer, and there was no really bountiful harvest until 1623. In 1635, too, Plymouth was switched by the tail of a tropical hurricane. Indeed human nature appears in the Pilgrim story in a wide range of aspects;

The Departure of the *Mayflower*. Mural by N. C. Wyeth in the Metropolitan Life Insurance Company building, New York. Courtesy of Metropolitan Life Insurance Company

The signing of the Mayflower Compact, on board the *Mayflower*, Nov. 11, 1620. Engraving by Gauthier 1859, after T. H. Matteson. Library of Congress

The First Landing Place of the Pilgrims Nov. 11 1620 O.S. The Map in Mourt's Relation Shows That Near This Spot The Pilgrims First Touched Foot on American Soil. Erected by the Research Club of Provincetown 1917

Monument commemorating the Pilgrim landing. FPG (Freelance Photographers Guild)

A Currier and Ives print fancifully depicting the landing of the Pilgrims. Library of Congress

Mayflower II, a present-day full-scale replica of the *Mayflower*, is berthed at State Pier in Plymouth. We have little technical information about the original *Mayflower*, but designer William A. Baker incorporated the few references to *Mayflower* from Governor Bradford's account of the voyage into his research to produce a ship representative of the period. *Mayflower II* draws 181 tons, is 104 feet long, with a beam of 25½ feet and a draft of 13 feet. She was built in England and crossed the Atlantic in 1957 in 53 days with a crew of 33 men commanded by Captain Alan Villiers. Courtesy of Plimoth Plantation, Plymouth, Mass.

there seem even to have been arsonists! There were tensions between the "Old Comers" (the *Mayflower* and the slightly later *Fortune* groups) and the subsequent arrivals, and it soon appeared that people would not labor upon land held in common with anything like the zeal they would show in cultivating their own possessions. One of the *Mayflower* "strangers," John Billington, was hanged for murder in 1630, and five years later, the "saint" Isaac Allerton, who had served about ten years as assistant governor, was exiled for "fleecing his brethren." Yet, though Plymouth grew slowly, it did grow and even established satellite towns at Duxbury, Scituate, Sandwich, Yarmouth, and Taunton.

Governor Carver died in 1621, and William Bradford served thirty yearly terms between 1621 and 1656. "There was nothing arbitrary or selfish in his attitude toward his office," says Andrews, "but he was the ruler of the colony and in important crises bent the people to his will." Bradford was competent in handling his own affairs also; he shared a trade monopoly with Allerton and Standish, and he died the richest man in Plymouth. Puritans were not hermits; they thought of the Kingdom of God in community terms, and wherever they went they laid out towns and devised schemes of government for them. Plymouth centered about Leyden Street, which climbed from the beach to Fort Hill, which Captain Standish fortified. First assignments along this street were by yearly lot, but from 1624 permanent allotments were made. In the beginning the adult males met once a year, with no religious qualification, to elect the governor, but in 1623 limitations were placed on latecomers because they were not

The Mayflower Society House, Plymouth. Built in 1754 by Edward Winslow, great-grandson of the Pilgrim governor. Headquarters of the General Society of Mayflower Descendants. Plymouth Area Chamber of Commerce

Memorial tablet in the Leyden, Netherlands, to the Pilgrim pastor, John Robinson, who never reached America. New York Public Library Picture Collection

Pilgrim Hall, Plymouth. Built in 1824, Pilgrim Hall was designed by Alexander Parris, architect of St. Paul's, Boston. It has been in continuous use from the time it was built, and is one of the oldest museum buildings in America. Maintained by the Pilgrim Society, the building has undergone several changes since it was built—fireproofing in 1880, addition of the library wing in 1904, and substitution of the granite portico for the original wooden one in 1922—but its essential appearance has not been altered. It is located at 75 Court Street in Plymouth. Memorabilia of early settlers are exhibited here. FPG

members of the company. A legal code known as the Great Fundamentals was acquired in 1636, and beginning in 1643 delegates from the satellite towns met each year with the governor.

Like other seventeenth-century Englishmen, Puritans had a way of wearing out their wives with childbearing; consequently many of them married two or three times. Samuel Sewall buried eleven out of fourteen children, Cotton Mather thirteen out of fifteen. The curious Plymouth custom of "binding out" stepchildren to learn a trade necessitated a high percentage of children growing up in homes not their own. Culturally Plymouth never came within hailing distance of the Bay Colony, but it was not quite a wilderness. Of seventy inventories of possessions examined by one scholar only twelve failed to mention books; even Miles Standish, who was hardly a bookish type, had fifty, including the *Iliad* and Caesar's *Commentaries*. Bradford, who in his old age took to writing verses, reading philosophy, and studying the learned languages, had eighty and William

Pilgrims going to church. Mural by N. C. Wyeth in the Metropolitan Life Insurance Company building, New York. Courtesy of Metropolitan Life Insurance Company

Pilgrims going to meeting. Painting by George H. Boughton. Library of Congress

Brewster, who had been a printer, nearly four hundred.

Plymouth, Weymouth, Salem, Dover, and other settlements all antedated the Bay establishment; the one which most concerned the Pilgrims was Captain Wollaston's at Merry Mount (Quincy), which was taken over by Thomas Morton and remained a thorn in the side of both Plymouth and Massachusetts Bay until finally it was suppressed by force. According to Bradford, Morton "abused" the Indian women "most filthily" and established "a school of atheism" where he and

his cronies conducted themselves "as if they had anew revived and celebrated the feasts of the Roman goddess Flora, or the beastly practices of the mad Bacchanalians." Morton gave back as good as he got and better in *The New England Canaan* (1637), the only humorous contemporary account of colonial history, and it is not always possible to be sure whether he or his enemies are telling the truth. The charge of atheism was probably exaggerated, but Morton did endanger the colonists by selling both firearms and firewater to the

NEW ENGLISH CANAAN
O R
NEW CANAAN.

Containing an Abftract of New England,

Compofed in three Bookes.

The firft Booke fetting forth the originall of the Natives, their
Manners and Cuftomes, together with their tractable Nature and·
Love towards the Englifh.

The fecond Booke fetting forth the naturall Indowments of the
Country , and what ftaple Commodities it
yealdeth.

The third Booke fetting forth , what people are planted there,
their profperity , what remarkable accidents have happened fince the firft
planting of it , together with their Tenents and practife
of their Church.

Written by Thomas Morton of Cliffords Inne gent, *upon tenne
yeares knowledge and experiment of the
Country.*

Printed at AMSTERDAM,
By J A C O B   F R E D E R I C K   S T A M.
In the Yeare 1 6 3 7:

Title page of Thomas Morton's famous and notorious book on New England. Library of Congress

Statue of Roger Conant, first settler of Salem, by Henry H. Kitson, 1911. Washington Square West and Brown Street, Salem. U.S. Bureau of Public Roads, National Archives

Indians, and the frolicking of both races about the eighty-four-foot Maypole which Miles Standish hewed down was probably no more innocent than earlier such festivities had been in England. He also cut into the Pilgrims' Indian trade. Morton's history is a splash of color in old colony times and as such has always held an appeal greater than its importance. Hawthorne wrote a story about it, "The Maypole of Merry Mount" *(Twice-Told Tales),* and the historian John Lothrop Motley made it the subject of one of his two novels, *Merry Mount.* More recently Howard Hanson's opera of the same title was produced at the Metropolitan Opera House in 1934 with a distinguished cast. Morton was clearly no saint, nor wise man either, and though the Puritans succeeded finally in breaking him, he is a weak candidate for the martyrs' honor roll; but he was not a barbarian, and he may well have been right when he said, "I have found the Massachusetts Indians more full of humanity than the Christians and have had much better quarter with them."

More important than Merry Mount, if less picturesque, was the attempt of the Dorchester Company,

later known first as the New England Company and then as the Massachusetts Bay Company, to organize a settlement at Gloucester in 1623. They were interested in the fishing trade; the Reverend John White, one of their leaders, wished to provide a mission station for those engaged in such activities. Plymouth chose to regard the enterprise as an infringement of its territorial rights, and the endeavor did not prosper. Finally Roger Conant, a merchant who had been sent over by the Dorchester Company to sweep up the pieces, moved the survivors to Naumkeag, which was soon to be renamed Salem. Thither in 1628 came John Endicott and a party of some forty souls. When the autocratic Endicott assumed more authority than had been nominated in his bond, Conant and the other "Old Planters" removed to what is now Beverly. All of which brings us to the verge of what has been called "The Great Migration."

II

Neatly combining the interests of this world with those of another, the Massachusetts Bay Company was organized to cultivate trade, convert the heathen, and provide a refuge for those whose position in England, under King Charles I and Archbishop Laud, was becoming more untenable. To quote Charles M. Andrews once more, this enterprise

saw the transfer across the Atlantic of an organized, officered company, possessed of power to command and execute; an incorporated body, free to govern practically as it pleased; a state in the making. . . . It was led by the largest and most important group of men that ever at any time came overseas to New England; men of wealth and education, of middle-class origin with a quantum of political training, hardheaded and dogmatic, and more stubborn in their adherence to a religious and political purpose than ever were Bradford, Brewster, or Winslow. They looked upon themselves as commissioned by God to create a purer church and a cleaner social order than those which prevailed at home and were mastered by the idea of "the saving remnant," whom God had elected to do his will—an idea that has played a prominent part in the history of all religious sectarianism.*

Yeomen and tenantry predominated, and the servants, similar in status and character to the same class at Plymouth, were to create much the same kind of problem. But the governor, John Winthrop, was a Suffolk country gentleman who had been a J.P. at eighteen, and many of the clergymen had Cambridge degrees and had held livings in the Church of England.

During the winter of 1629-30 a fleet of eleven vessels had been readied. Four, including the *Arbella*, which carried Governor Winthrop and the charter, without the possession of which he and his associates had not been willing to sail, left England on March 29, 1630; the others soon followed. The year 1630 alone brought about fifteen hundred people, and it has been estimated that there were fifteen thousand by 1642, when political conditions in England prevented any considerable further emigration. By 1647 more than twenty communities had been established, mostly near the coast, with Dedham the farthest inland. As time passed, prosperity came with trade in cod, furs, and lumber, supplemented by rum, distilled from West Indian molasses. This soon involved our pious ancestors in the African slave trade, which brought foreign sailors and foreign ways into New England ports and many problems along with them, but the Puritans comforted themselves with the thought that by selling heathen Africans into slavery they were giving them a chance for salvation. Samuel Sewall's *The Selling of Joseph* (1700) was one of the very earliest antislavery appeals. Sewall was also the only judge who (in Old South, in 1697) ever made public confession of error in the Salem witchcraft trials.

The Colonial Period of American History, 4 vols. (Yale University Press, 1934-38).

When the *Arbella* landed at Salem, however, after more than two months at sea, all this was far in the future. Winthrop and his followers first intended one compact settlement, but Salem "pleased them not," and they moved on, Medford, Watertown, Roxbury, Dorchester, and Lynn all being founded before winter began. Except for the inadequacy of water supplies, they might have made Charlestown their headquarters, but when invited by William Blaxton, survivor of a Gorges colony, living on what is now Beacon Hill, they moved on to Shawmut or Trimountain, whose name was changed to Boston. Between lack of fresh food, inadequate housing, and disease, the first winter was almost as bad as Plymouth's, especially after intense cold set in on Christmas Eve. When the *Lion* arrived with provisions, the worst agony was relieved, but many went back with her, and some left their bones in King's Chapel burying ground, where they still lie.

Towns were constructed about a common, dominated by the church with the homes of the settlers around it and the fields beyond. Sometimes land was divided equally, sometimes not; sometimes to achieve equality or the appearance thereof lots were consulted. The Massachusetts Bay Colony has been called everything from a theocracy to a democracy; it was neither, though it had tendencies in both directions. The Puritans used biblical authority to bolster basically English conceptions of government; theoretically they had no more sympathy with democracy than with religious toleration, yet Edward Winslow told Governor Winthrop in 1645 that toleration would have carried in Plymouth if the governor had not prevented it from coming to a vote.

It is unfair to criticize the Puritans because they failed to allow others the freedom they themselves had striven for in England; the criticism is based upon a complete misunderstanding of what they were trying to achieve. At home they had been obliged to estrange themselves from the crown because the crown would have none of them, but they had never been rebels without a cause, and what had been rebellion in the Old World became authority in the New. They could not admit that because you have fought for what is right you are under an obligation to tolerate what is wrong. They came to America to set up the Kingdom of God there according to God's own precepts and under His authority, and they had no intention of tolerating those who set themselves against Him, whether they would lead the people back into the old bondage from which the men of the Massachusetts had escaped or, like Roger Williams, Anne Hutchinson, and the Quakers, forward into a new religious anarchy. "There is a vast difference," said John Cotton, "between men's inventions and God's institutions; we fled from men's inventions, to which we else should have been compelled; we

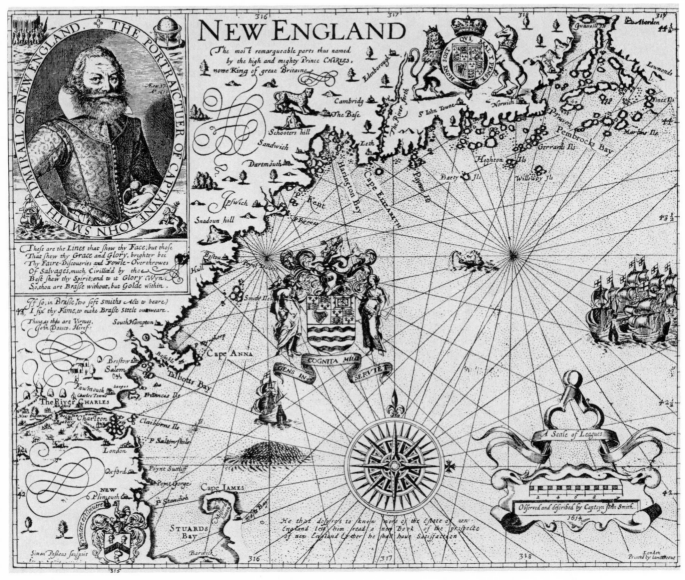

Map of New England, by Captain John Smith, 1614. Engraved by Simon van de Passe, c. 1616. New York Public Library Picture Collection

The Burial Hill, Plymouth. From Bartlett, *The Pilgrim Fathers*, 1853. Library of Congress

The arrival of the *Arbella*, June 12, 1630, mural by Charles Hoffbauer. This reproduction is used through the courtesy of The New England Mutual Life Insurance Company. Copyright 1943.

Burial Hill in Plymouth, where the dust
of the Pilgrims lies. FPG

compel none to men's inventions." Intolerant the Puritans were, like all who *know* they are right, but they were not inconsistent.

As for democracy, Winthrop called it "the meanest and worst of all forms of government," for he believed that "the best part is always the least, and of that best part the wisest part is always the lesser." Since democracy was not authorized in the Bible, it would have been impious to allow it in New England. Nevertheless profound democratic tendencies were inherent in Puritanism, and James Russell Lowell had a point when he declared that it "laid, without knowing it, the egg of democracy." If you make people directly responsible to God for their soul's welfare (instead of merely to the church), there is always danger that they may carry the same attitude over into the political field or even that they might in the end rebel against all churches and the state and reason itself. Puritan town meetings dealt with both civil and ecclesiastical affairs. God had instituted government to repair the ravages of the Fall, and Puritans assumed the unity of religious and political affairs. If you are going to use the basic idea of the covenant of the "gathered" church as an instrument of government, you are already well within hailing distance of the social contract theory; the control of rulers, declared Thomas Hooker, "belongs unto the people by God's own allowance." In Massachusetts nobody became a church member without going through the somewhat harrowing ordeal of convincing his fellow Christians that he had experiential knowledge

William Brewster. New York Public Library
Picture Collection

Old Brewster House (1690) in Kingston, Mass. U.S. Bureau of Public Roads, National Archives

of the saving grace of God. Thus voluntary submission and freedom through reconciliation to divinely constituted authority went hand in hand.

We should remember that Jamestown achieved representative government the year before Plymouth was settled, but in the long run the impulses and tendencies I have been describing may well have been more important than any specific, practical, mechanical arrangements, which did not always seem to be following a consistent line of development; the Bay Colony was virtually self-governing by 1634 and by 1652 she was a commonwealth. The Charter provided for the annual election of a governor, deputy governor, and eighteen assistants by a General Court consisting of all freemen or stockholders of the corporation, but in the beginning the officers exercised almost unrestricted power. In 1633 indeed John Cotton advocated that the magistrates should hold office permanently unless removed for just cause, but the freemen showed what they thought of that proposition by electing Thomas Dudley governor for the next year instead of the incumbent Winthrop. The restriction of the franchise to church members did not apply to local affairs after 1647, and town meetings apparently gave nonchurch members a chance to express opinions and make complaints.

America was a rebellious child toward the old country long before the emergence of the specific disputes which sparked the Revolution. In New England the movement toward independence may be said to have begun as far back as the transfer of the Massachusetts Bay Charter to this side of the ocean; thereafter the governing group resisted and, when possible, evaded almost every attempt to assert the authority of the home government. When Governor Endicott cut the Red Cross of St. George from the royal ensign, he was ostensibly protesting against "Popery," but the English regarded his action as directed against both the English church and state, and they were not far wrong. The act was sufficiently premature so that Endicott was censured and debarred from public office for a year, but one cannot but wonder as to the complete sincerity of the rebuke. In 1646 Robert Child declared that New Englanders were regarding England as a foreign country and viewing "this place" as "rather a free state, than a colony or corporation of England." Child and others prepared a Grand Remonstrance and Petition to the General Court in which they not only asked for the abolition of religious qualifications but complained of the absence of a "settled form of government according to the laws of England" and demanded a code to secure their liberties and ensure due process of law. He was fined, arrested, imprisoned, and prevented from sailing to England when a petition to Parliament was found among his papers, but the *Book of the General Laws and Liberties Concerning the Inhabitants of the Massachusetts* was achieved two years later. When in 1651 Parliament ordered Massachusetts to return the charter granted by Charles I, that it might be replaced

Brewster Gardens, in Plymouth, is the site of the Pilgrims' first gardens. After landing, Plymouth Colony was divided into 19 families or groups, and a plot of land along the Town Brook was assigned to each; the term "Pilgrim Meersteads" was used to describe these plots. On these plots the first houses were built (Leyden Street) and the land in the rear, sloping to the stream, was their gardens. Here herring were caught in April to fertilize the corn fields, and many springs supplied the households of the town. Elder Brewster's spring for years flowed freely and was piped up from brook level to a fountain in the center of Plymouth. Brewster Park follows the brook on both sides to its mouth. This area was unattended and all but forgotten, overgrown with weeds, etc., until plans began to take shape for the 300th (Tercentennial) celebration of 1920. Then a group of women in the local Plymouth Woman's Club, with many volunteers, undertook the task of cleaning it up and beautified the area. It was one of these women who suggested the name *Brewster Gardens*, undoubtedly because of the existence of Elder Brewster's original spring. Some of the first plantings for the area were given by Mrs. William H. Forbes, daughter of Ralph Waldo Emerson and his wife, Lydia Jackson of Plymouth. Nearby there is a tablet in memory of Mrs. Emerson and her brother, Dr. Charles T. Jackson, whose experimental work with ether as an anesthetic paved the way for its successful use. In 1923, the Daughters of the American Colonists gave a memorial bench in remembrance of those daughters of American Colonists who came to Plymouth in the ship, *Anne* in 1623. Here too is the bronze statue of the Pilgrim Maiden by H. H. Kitson, presented to the Town by the National Society of New England women. Courtesy the Dicksons, Plymouth, Mass. Plymouth Area Chamber of Commerce

Rationing food during hard times in Plymouth. New York Public Library Picture Collection

Miles Standish and his men raid the Weymouth Indians. New York Public Library Picture Collection

A nineteenth-century artist's notion of Miles Standish and his men on the march. Lithograph by Armstrong & Co., 1873. After J. E. Baker (artist). Library of Congress

The sword of Miles Standish. Fine Arts Commission, National Archives

by a Parliamentary charter, the colony made no reply whatever for a year and then sent a memorial in place of the charter. Coinage was begun without authorization in 1652, and when, after the Restoration, it seemed advisable to try to pacify Charles II in order to get a new charter from him, it is said he was told that the device on the colony's shilling was a token of loyalty because it represented the royal oak in which he had hidden after the Battle of Worcester!* But by the time Edward Randolph came over as a royal emissary, Governor Leverett told him bluntly that English laws did not apply in Massachusetts and that the colony would settle disputes in her own way.

Massachusetts was aggressive toward other colonies also, claiming possession of both Maine and New Hampshire and having territorial disputes with all her neighbors. In 1645, fearing pressure from both the Indians and the Dutch, Massachusetts, Plymouth, Connecticut, and New Haven formed what was known as the United Colonies of New England for their common defense (Rhode Island was not invited, not being considered stable enough). By weight of wealth and population, Massachusetts was dominant in all such attempts at cooperation, with a marked tendency to interpret obligations in the light of her own interests. In 1635, when Plymouth asked aid against a French force trying to claim the coast as far south as Pemaquid, Bradford complained that Massachusetts not only refused to help but actually sold supplies to the enemy. When Cromwell made war on Holland, both Connecticut and New Hampshire wished to attack the Dutch in America on the alleged ground that they were stirring up Indian attacks. Massachusetts refused on the ground that the war was not just (which it was not); the United Colonies, she now discovered, could wage only a defensive war. Seven out of the eight commissioners involved voted for war nevertheless, but Massachusetts refused to be bound by the decision, and the war was never prosecuted because peace came in Europe.

After long negotiations during which Massachusetts had conducted herself in the most difficult fashion possible, Charles II's government finally cancelled the charter in October 1684, and the colony became part of a royal province under Governor Edmund Andros, whose arbitrary rule ended with the fall of King James II in 1689. The new charter, issued in 1692 under William and Mary, gave the people the right to be taxed by

*Massachusetts made pine-tree, willow, and oak shillings, depending upon the die.

The statue of Miles Standish on the beach prior to being placed on monument at Duxbury, Mass. Sculptor unknown. Placed in position on monument in 1889. New York Public Library Picture Collection

William Bradford, the Pilgrim governor, as the sculptor Cyrus E. Dallin saw him. The plaster cast of this statue is housed in the Pilgrim Hall Museum at Plymouth—it was never cast in bronze. New York Public Library Picture Collection

a legislature of their own choosing, but the governor was now a royal appointee, and the laws passed were made subject to English approval. A property qualification for voters was substituted for the old religious qualification. Massachusetts was permitted to incorporate both Maine and the Plymouth colony, but New Hampshire was given a separate government. Both Connecticut and Rhode Island were allowed to continue under their old charters.

The other New England states, as we know them today, have slipped into this narrative without formal introduction, which is natural enough since most of the settlements came into being through either exile or voluntary departure from Massachusetts. The time has now come to consider them somewhat more systematically, though briefly, beginning with the most important—Connecticut.

Governor Bradford's Monument, Burial Hill, Plymouth. New York Public Library Picture Collection

III

Before 1632 only a few trappers, hunters, and explorers had viewed the forest wilderness that lay between Massachusetts and the Hudson River. Then Edward Winslow undertook to investigate the possibilities for settlement in the Connecticut Valley, and the next year Plymouth men established a trading post near Windsor and John Oldham undertook an exploring expedition from Massachusetts. After this, Thomas Hooker, Roger Ludlow, and John Haynes led a group from Dorchester, Watertown, and Newton to Hartford, Wethersfield, and Windsor; despite Hooker's comparative liberality, the basic motive for this emigration seems to have been not dissatisfaction with Massachusetts but a desire for fresh land and opportunity. John Ludlow pioneered in opening the coastal region to the west, leading to the settlement of Stratford, Fairfield, and Norwalk, and in 1647 settlers began to spread southward between Wethersfield and the mouth of the Connecticut River. In 1638 John Davenport, who had come to Massachusetts from England only the previous year, founded New Haven, where a "Plantation Covenant" was drawn up, and which soon expanded into Milford, Guilford, and Stamford.

If Hooker desired a more liberal state than had developed in Boston, Davenport wanted a stricter one. Religious tests were imposed in New Haven and allegiance was proclaimed to the "judicial laws of God as they were declared to Moses." There was no jury trial because it was not authorized in the Bible, death was prescribed for adultery, and there were severe penalties for Sabbath-breaking. If there was a Bible commonwealth in New England, it was New Haven, yet the English common law was the real basis of its code. The

title derived from Indian purchase, and the marginal references to Scripture in the code were added for authority after the document had been drawn up. The colony remained independent until 1662, when, for the first time, Connecticut secured a royal charter and New Haven was incorporated in it. Some of the diehards then moved to Newark, New Jersey, to try again to set up a colony based on their own ideas, and Davenport went to Boston, where, at age seventy, he became pastor of First Church, but his refusal to accept the Halfway Covenant (of which we shall hear later) split that congregation, his opponents laying the foundations of Boston's third church, the "Old South."

Both Thomas Hooker and John Winthrop, Jr., later governor of Connecticut, were sweet-spirited men. Winthrop was probably the most beloved New Englander of his time, and his removal from Massachusetts to Connecticut was regarded as a loss by the older colony. Nevertheless Connecticut's liberalism has often been exaggerated. It is ridiculous to call the Fundamental Orders of 1639 either "the first written constitution of modern democracy" or "the model for all constitu-

The oldest house in Provincetown. A typical Cape Cod cottage, built by Captain Seth Nickerson prior to 1800. U.S. Bureau of Public Roads, National Archives

tions that have since been adopted." Connecticut had no open religious qualification for voters, though she did have a property qualification. But she divided her people between "admitted inhabitants" and "freemen." Even the admitted inhabitants were required to take an oath: "So help me God in our Lord Jesus Christ," and as John M. Pomfret points out, this oath could only be taken by an orthodox Christian. Only freemen could serve as magistrates or vote for the higher officials, and freemen were selected from the admitted inhabitants by the magistrates or General Court. It does not seem likely that they can have chosen many "unsafe" persons.

Connecticut's population of about eight hundred in 1636 grew to two thousand in 1642, thirty-two hundred in 1654, and six thousand in 1665, after having absorbed New Haven. During the early years the economy remained largely agricultural and pastoral, with some traffic in furs. The country was wilder and more dangerous than Massachusetts, the settlements less concentrated, and communication between them more dif-

ficult, all of which contributed to a freer and more self-reliant way of life. Though some interest in schools was shown as early as 1641, educational achievements were long unimpressive; even meetinghouse facilities were sometimes inadequate. Yale University did not get under way until 1716, being warmly welcomed by those already distressed by the liberalism of Harvard, in Cambridge, Massachusetts, whose seniority carried back to 1636. There were many disputes with neighboring colonies over territorial claims, and James Truslow Adams, generally the devil's advocate in all matters related to Puritan shortcomings, calls Connecticut "even more reckless in its career of land-grabbing than Massachusetts."

The Restoration caused special distress in Connecticut because the colony had never had a royal charter. John Winthrop, Jr., went to England to secure one, and in 1662 he was successful. Even aside from the union with New Haven, what emerged did not satisfy everybody, but it was generous under the existent circumstances. The Fundamental Orders had ignored the king;

Man at the Wheel, Fisherman's Memorial, facing the sea at Gloucester Harbor, by Leonard Craske. The unveiling was to have taken place in 1923 for the Tercentenary Celebration, but the sculpture was not completed and the unveiling did not take place until August 23, 1925. FPG

Bay Path marker, 1633. On line of the first road across Massachusetts from Boston to Springfield. U.S. Bureau of Public Roads, National Archives

his authority was now recognized and the colony's relationship to him defined, but the existing system of government was sanctioned, and there were no reservations requiring either royal or parliamentary approval of the actions of the General Court. In 1687 Governor Andros tried to seize the charter. According to a picturesque, oft-told story, when the lights were extinguished in the room where the discussion was being held, the document was removed and concealed in a great tree ever afterwards known as the Charter Oak. Andros dissolved the government, but after his fall the charter was reinstated.

About Maine, New Hampshire, and Vermont much less needs to be said. The history of exploration and discovery in Maine goes back perhaps as far as A.D. 1000 and involves several nations. The grant which the

Blockhouse, Kittery, Maine. The blockhouse was the place where the families of each small pioneer community gathered for protection against the Indians. U.S. Office of War Information, National Archives

Council for New England made to Ferdinando Gorges and John Mason in 1622 embraced a good deal of what is now New Hampshire and Vermont. Small fishing, trading, and farming communities were set up at York, Saco, Cape Elizabeth, Falmouth (Portland), and elsewhere; in 1639 a royal charter gave Gorges feudal powers over his share, and this involved prolonged conflict with the holders of other real or assumed claims. A somewhat liberal government was set up by social compact around 1650. Most of the settlers were from western England, where Puritan influence was comparatively weak (Plymouth and Massachusetts had both drawn most heavily upon East Anglia, the most Puritan section of England), and·neither this fact nor the long-continued wilderness aspect of most of the country encouraged the development of religion, education, or culture. Between 1652 and 1658 Massachusetts expanded into Maine, and prolonged argument followed until, in 1677, she bought out the Gorges claim from one of his heirs under Charles II's nose. Thereafter she governed the territory as proprietor until the Charter of 1691 combined Maine and Massachusetts in one colony. Maine was a painfully exposed territory during both the French and Indian War and the Revolution, and she was not formally separated from Massachusetts until 1820, after many attempts and long negotiations.

The name New Hampshire was first applied to the territory between the Merrimack and the Piscataqua. There was a fishing and trading settlement by David Thomson at Little Harbor (Rye) as early as 1623, and in 1630 a company of colonists sent over from England

Route marker at Sandwich on Cape Cod, Mass. U.S. Bureau of Public Roads, National Archives

America's first printing press was brought from England in 1638 and is now owned by the Vermont Historical Society. In 1781 it was used to print Vermont's first newspaper which helped unite the colonies for independence. Culver Pictures

for fur trading occupied the same site and expanded into Strawbery Banke (Portsmouth). There was also a settlement at Dover. In 1638 there were Puritan settlements at both Exeter and Hampton. Massachusetts, which was hostile to both the Antinomians at Exeter and the Anglicans at Strawbery Banke, entered claims of jurisdiction which remained a bone of contention until 1679, when New Hampshire was made a separate province. After the fall of Governor Andros there was an abortive attempt at the establishment of a provincial government, then a brief attempted union with Massachusetts, but in 1692 a royal government was set up. Boundary disputes continued, however, throughout the colonial period.

Vermont's colonial history is briefer. The country was explored by Champlain in 1609, and there was an English settlement at Fort Dummer (Brattleboro) in 1714, but no extensive English settlements were established until after the British had taken Canada from the French. Both New Hampshire and New York claimed to own Vermont, and there were the too familiar colonial controversies over land grants.

After the French and Indian War, several thousand persons from Massachusetts, Connecticut, and New Hampshire (then the "Hampshire grants") came into Vermont, and this led to conflict with New York, involving Ethan Allen and his Green Mountain Boys. No move toward independent status was made until 1777; New Connecticut was the first name proposed. In July

1777 a constitution was drafted at Windsor. Manhood suffrage was established and slavery was forbidden.

Rhode Island was born out of Roger Williams's desire to establish "a shelter for persons distressed for conscience." Williams, born in London, began his American career as pastor of the church at Salem. He may have been, as he has been called, "temperamentally excitable" and "often hasty in speech and indiscreet in his efforts to enforce his opinions, and . . . of intensely strong convictions which he reached quickly and maintained without compromise," for he carried his separatism to the length of separating from his own church. In 1639 he became a Baptist, but he soon renounced this and for the rest of his life remained merely a "Seeker." But he rode the wave of the future, perhaps like no other man in colonial history.

Williams championed liberty of conscience and religious freedom for all, including Catholics and Jews, defended what we know as civil rights and due process of law, and stood for complete separation between church and state. As he saw it, the origin of the state was human, not divine; God had no pact with Massachusetts. Since only "soul weapons" might legitimately be used in "soul matters," the state had no authority over religious offenses; a state church which enforced Christianity by "carnal" means was a contradiction in terms. Therefore the state might not collect taxes for religious purposes nor enforce attendance at public worship.

Simon Bradstreet (1603-1697), governor of Massachusetts and husband of Anne Bradstreet. Engraved by H. W. Smith from a painting in the Senate Chamber of the State House, Boston. New York Public Library Picture Collection

Eleazer Arnold House, in Lincoln, Rhode Island, 1687, restored in 1952. The huge fireplace was built to heat a large room, which served as kitchen and dining room. Rhode Island Department of Economic Development

Williams also denied the validity of charter grants on the ground that the land belonged to the Indians and could no more be partitioned by the King of England than they could carve up Warwickshire. He was not sentimental about the Indians; for one thing, their lack of physical cleanliness disgusted him, but he differed from most Christians in having christianized his nose along with the rest of his anatomy. By preventing a threatened alliance between the Pequots and the Narragansetts he may have saved the colonies from an Indian war; when, in 1636, he was ordered to England, he chose instead to winter with Massasoit and his tribe (John Winthrop the elder has been widely credited with having warned him), and in the spring he became the founder of Providence.

William Blackstone, who cultivated "yellow seedlings," lived in Rhode Island before Williams, and in 1638 another group of religious exiles from Massachusetts, including Anne Hutchinson, her husband William, and William Coddington established a religiously motivated community at Portsmouth on Aquidneck Island in Narragansett Bay. Through Williams's

aid, they received a deed from the Indians, but Coddington was soon ousted from his leadership by another religious radical, Samuel Gorton, who put William Hutchinson in his place, and Coddington and his followers withdrew to become the founders of Newport. The two towns were soon united for administrative purposes, however, and in 1639 Warwick was settled from Providence and Portsmouth.

In the beginning the Rhode Island settlements were independent commonwealths, basing their authority on Indian titles and common agreement. Until Parliament granted Williams a charter covering "Providence Plantations" there was no real colony. Williams's move was necessitated by the danger to Rhode Island from the New England Confederation and the territorial presumptions of both Massachusetts and Plymouth. There was always tension between the mainland and the more prosperous and sophisticated island settlements, and the name Providence Plantations did not please those living in other settlements. In 1647 a federal system had been drawn up which regarded itself as "democratical, that is to say, a government held by the free and volun-

William Shirley, Governor of Massachusetts, watches the departure of British troops and the New England militia, for the expedition against Louisburg, at the mouth of the St. Lawrence River, in April 1745. Mural by Charles Hoffbauer. This reproduction is used through the courtesy of The New England Mutual Life Insurance Company. Copyright 1943.

Roger Williams. Engraving by Halpern from painting for Beredlet's *History of the Baptists*, 1847. New York Public Library Picture Collection

tary consent of all, *or the greater part* of the free inhabitants" (italics mine), and which guaranteed religious liberty and separation of church and state. But disagreements, separations, and reunions followed until the granting of a new charter by Charles II in 1663. Rhode Island had anticipated all the other colonies in recognizing the new king, probably because she felt the need of protection from her neighbors. The charter specifically provided that "no person within the colony, at any time hereafter shall be in any wise molested, punished, disquieted or called in question for any difference of opinion in matters of religion," and in granting it, His Majesty's Government made the special point that, "by reason of the remote distances of those places," the toleration granted there need not disturb what was being done in the English nation itself. If Rhode Island's neighbors were not pleased, they had to content themselves by quipping that a man who had lost his religion might be sure of finding it somewhere in Rhode Island. Williams himself regarded Quakers as seriously in error and engaged in controversy with them, but it did not occur to him to persecute them on that account.

The boundary line between Rhode Island and Massachusetts was not finally determined until 1746 and the Connecticut boundary not till 1727. Rhode Island had no prisons before 1656. There were only two executions during Williams's lifetime, two trials for treason (both ending in acquittal), and no trial for witchcraft. Educationally the record is less brilliant, no town having public education before 1670. The eighteenth century brought improvement in this area. Benjamin Franklin's brother James began a publishing career in 1727, and the Redwood Library was organized three years later. Around 1760 the great English philosopher George Berkeley spent three years in Newport, he and his circle giving Rhode Island culture a considerable shot in the arm. In 1763 Moses Brown founded the original Rhode Island College, afterwards Brown University.

It was greed for gold which most deeply stained Rhode Island's 'scutcheon. By 1675 she was exporting lumber, horses, and dairy products, and before long she found herself up to her ears in the West Indian slave trade, which reached its height between 1739 and 1760. The act of emancipation passed in 1652, the first in the colonies, remained a dead letter, and eighteenth-century Newport had thousands of Negro slaves, owned by all the well-to-do families in their town houses and country houses, the scene of a rich, fashionable, comparatively cosmopolitan society. Smuggling flourished also, and during the last decade of the seventeenth century Narragansett Bay became a haven for pirates and privateers. The issuance of letters of marque and reprisal during King George's War (1743-48) did not help these matters. But the great Newport preacher-theologian, Samuel Hopkins, hero of Harriet Beecher Stowe's novel, *The Minister's Wooing*, boldly attacked slavery, the Rhode Island Yearly Meeting of Friends condemned it, and at last, in 1774, the General Assembly forbade further importation of slaves.

Roger Williams after his banishment from Massachusetts. New York Public Library Picture Collection

IV

Early New England culture was dominated by Puritanism. Modern writers who, if possible, know even less about theology than about history, sometimes identify Puritanism with Fundamentalism (which, properly speaking, is a twentieth-century formulation), but the seventeenth-century Puritans were never Fundamentalists in the sense of being anti-intellectual. They shared the heritage of the Middle Ages, the Renaissance, and the Reformation, and their sermons relied upon logical demonstration, not pulpit pounding;

fire-and-brimstone preaching was never in vogue before the eighteenth century, when historic Puritanism had begun to break down. Puritans mistrusted "enthusiasm," among other reasons, because it subordinated reason to passion; there has probably never been a society in which theological distinctions were so much a part of the staple of conversation. Puritans came closer to the Fundamentalist position, however, in regarding the Bible as the supreme unquestionable authority in all matters, temporal and spiritual, and in making no allowance for contradictions and historical development within the Bible or for the presence of a human as well as a divine element in its pages. James Truslow Adams called them more Jewish than Christian.

Their God was the God of the Old Testament. Their Sabbath was Jewish, not Christian [it began at sundown on Saturday]. In New England, in their religious persecutions and Indian wars, the sayings of Christ never prevailed to stay their hands or to save the blood of their victims.

From the Puritan point of view, Christmas was a "Popish festival." This is Howard Pyle's picture of a Puritan governor interrupting Christmas sports. New York Public Library Picture Collection

John Endicott cutting the Cross out of the King's flag, 1634. New York Public Library Picture Collection

Though there is something in this, it is only fair to add that Christ's teaching and example did not carry much weight with mediaeval Catholics in their wars either, nor, for that matter, with modern Americans, who, for the most part, are neither Catholics, Jews, nor Puritans. Moreover, the great prophets of the Old Testament would not have been any more pleased with the aspects of Puritan conduct which Adams condemned than Christ himself.

Theologically the Puritans were Calvinists, and the only thing most of us now know about Calvin is that he taught predestination and election. "Christ," said Samuel Willard, "died for a select company that was known to Him, by name, from eternity." It has often been asked how Calvinists managed to go on living, believing that the bulk of mankind was reserved for burning and that nothing the individual might do could have any effect upon God's unalterable decrees. So far as the New England Puritans are concerned, part of the answer is that theirs was a much modified Calvinism. John Cotton said he loved "to sweeten my mouth with a piece of Calvin, before I go to sleep," but Samuel Eliot Morison reports having "found Calvin less frequently quoted in their writings than English theologians like Ames, Perkins, and Whitaker" and specifically that Thomas Shepard, pastor of the church in Cambridge, quotes the Jesuit Robert Bellarmine more often than he quotes Calvin. Aquinas was not unknown to New England Puritans, and they junked Calvin's Aristotelianism to the extent of accepting his "corrector" Ramus (Pierre de la Ramée), who not only introduced Platonic elements into their thinking but encouraged them to believe in the fundamental rationality of the universe and of human nature and tone down the elements of caprice and arbitrary choice inherent in Calvinism as originally conceived. More significantly, however, New Englanders undercut orthodox Calvinism by their "Covenant" or "Federal" theology, according to which God was conceived of as voluntarily, and without abating His perfect sovereignty, having after the Fall entered into an agreement with man, on terms which the human mind could understand, to accept those who came to Him in faith and tried to do His will and give them "a fair assurance" of salvation. If this was not wholly logical, it did afford a workable basis for reconciling the idea of divine sovereignty (whatever remnants of his originally divine nature man might retain, these were not sufficient for salvation without a special imparting of God's grace) and a voluntaristic element in religion, enlisting and rewarding the cooperation of the human will.*

By 1645 there were twenty-three churches in the Bay Colony. In theory, each had a pastor, who preached, and a teacher, who instructed in doctrine, but the two functions were not always clearly differentiated. Sermons were very long. Samuel Torrey is said to have prayed for two hours and John Cotton to have repeated his two-hour sermon on Sunday night to his household, though they had heard it in church in the morning. Attendance was of course compulsory, and the church was supported by tax funds. Magistrates were regarded as the "nursing fathers of the churches," and church and state worked so closely together that their functions

*The standard, masterly exposition of "Covenant" theology is Perry Miller's "The Marrow of Puritan Divinity" in his *Errand into the Wilderness* (Belknap Press of Harvard University Press, 1956).

Increase Mather (1639-1723), distinguished Puritan divine, minister of North Church, president of Harvard, and father of Cotton Mather. From a line engraving in Mather, *The Blessed Hope,* Boston, 1701. New York Public Library Picture Collection

sometimes seemed indistinguishable. On the other hand, the clergy had no priestly nor intercessory power, were not set apart from other men, and no mystical atmosphere surrounded them. All schools were lay schools. Church discipline, which was severe, was in lay, not clerical, hands. Even the adjective "Reverend" was hardly used before 1700.

As life in the colonies became more complicated and as seventeenth-century fires were unavoidably banked, both new ideas and new implementation appeared in the churches. As early as 1647 the Cambridge Platform endorsed the Westminster Confession, defined New England Congregationalism, and provided for cooperation between the churches, and in 1680 a more formal confession of faith was adopted which remained standard in Congregationalism for nearly two centuries. The famous Saybrook Platform of 1708 introduced no doctrinal innovations but brought Congregational and Presbyterian usage closer together, especially in Connecticut.

Long before this, the so-called Half-Way Covenant of 1657 and 1663 had testified eloquently to the decline of the old settlers' rigidity. For the first time, unbaptized persons were allowed to present their children for baptism even though they themselves had not experienced the "saving grace" which was necessary to permit them to be admitted to the Lord's Table and to function as full-fledged members of the church. Though bitterly opposed by the conservatives, the Half-Way Covenant was carried even further when, in 1699, the Brattle Street Church in Boston offered communion to all who

The First Parish Church (Unitarian) in Dedham, Mass. First sills laid January 24, 1762; completed at the close of 1763. Architect unknown. A handsome example of New England meetinghouse architecture. FPG

The steeple of Trinity Church, built in 1726, rises high above the ancient seaport city of Newport, Rhode Island. George Washington worshipped here and Admiral de Ternay, commander of the French Naval forces which came to the aid of the colonists in 1780, is buried in the cemetery. An exquisite hand-crafted wine-glass pulpit and beautiful box pews can be seen by visitors. Rhode Island Development Council

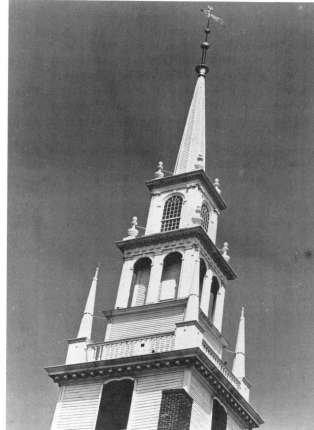

called themselves Christians and allowed them a voice in choosing their minister, and by Jonathan Edwards's grandfather, Solomon Stoddard, at Northampton, who gave communion to all who had been baptized.

Edwards himself (1703-1758) was another story: though he placed more emphasis upon conversion than election, he returned to a stricter Calvinism than that of the "Covenant" theology and insisted upon such strict requirements for church membership that he finally lost the pulpit he had inherited from his grandfather and was retired to the Indian mission station at Stockbridge. The Puritans were too intellectual ever to have placed much stress upon instantaneous conversion; for them the acquirement of grace was characteristically a laborious process, involving careful study and self-examination. This point of view is not easily conformable with revival preaching, and though Edwards did not originate the "Great Awakening" of religion which swept through the colonies between the 1740s and the 1760s, he had an important part in it. Though the revivalist preachers, of whom the most important was the gifted but not intellectual young Englishman George Whitefield, were conservative in theology, their emotionalism was best adapted to rousing the uncultivated, and they are often credited with some influence upon the burgeoning democracy of the time. But passion always carries the seeds of its own destruction, and as the revival spent its force, reaction came. Harvard, which had heard Whitefield gladly in 1740, spurned him four years later, and decorous, humanistic Anglicanism profited by accessions from those who felt that Puritanism and Congregationalism were selling out their birthright for an orgy.

Edwards's own association with such a movement was anomalous; he was the first important American philosopher and the possessor of probably the finest mind of the colonial period. It is a pity that he should now be best known by his horrendous sermon on "Sinners in the Hands of an Angry God." There is no denying that he preached this sermon, but to judge him by it alone would be a little like estimating Shakespeare's capacities by *Titus Andronicus*. During recent years such scholars as Perry Miller and Ola Elizabeth Winslow have given us a better understanding of him. Sensitive to virtually every aspect of human experience, Edwards had deep human feeling and was on fire with the love and the grandeur of God. His early death in 1758, following an unsuccessful smallpox inoculation, just after he had been called to the presidency of what is now Princeton University, was a very great loss.

Some Puritan punishments were cruel by modern standards, but there were fewer capital offenses in New England than across the water. Executions, though usually public, were comparatively infrequent, and many punishments for lesser offenses were remitted upon promise of atonement. The Puritans hanged (not burned) witches, but there were two cases of burning for arson and poisoning.

Though idleness was regarded as a deadly sin, partly because it wasted precious time but also because it provided an entering wedge for other temptations, children had dolls and toys, and outdoor sports were regarded as wholesome for young people. That horse-racing and even bear-baiting should have met with less opposition than the theater seems to posterity to reveal a curious standard. Nor were playing cards quite unknown.

Modern impuritans nowhere show their ignorance of the past more nakedly than in their curious notion that

The Reverend Jonathan Edwards (1703-1758), "the intellectual flower of New England Puritanism" and "the greatest American mind of the Colonial Period." Library of Congress

antiliquor and antitobacco sentiment (which is inspired by scientific and sociological considerations) derives from the Puritans. Cider and beer were the universal drinks, served with every meal including breakfast, even to the children, and alcohol flowed freely, sometimes to intoxication, even at ordination and funeral feasts. Tobacco was used by both men and women. Though John Eliot disapproved of it, he gave it to his Indians. Mary Rowlandson, the well-known Indian captive, a clergyman's wife, thought one might be better employed than "to lie sucking on a stinking tobacco-pipe," but she had been enough of an addict so that having taken two or three pipes, she would soon be ready for a fourth, and it seems to have been the waste of time involved rather than the stink that ultimately repelled her. Even in the twentieth century, the great stronghold of "dry" sentiment has been not New England but the Middle West.

Sexual standards were strict in the Puritan colonies. People did not usually marry any earlier than they do today, and we hear of men being punished for proposing to girls without first securing the consent of their parents and of whip and stocks being employed upon those who had been indiscreet enough to produce a child less than nine months after marriage. In 1646 there seems to have been an outbreak of venereal disease. No doubt many of these difficulties involved those who were not "saints," but this cannot always have been true; even John Winthrop, whose conversion was evidently a long and painful experience, confessed to

National Monument to the Forefathers, at Plymouth, designed by Hammatt Billings and now maintained by the Pilgrim Society. The cornerstone was laid August 2, 1859; the main pedestal was put in position in 1876. The Statue of Faith was erected in 1877. The dedication took place on August 1, 1889. The height from the ground to the top of the head is 81 feet; the length of the finger pointing heavenward is 2 feet 1 inch. Weight of the monument is 180 tons. On the main pedestal stands the figure of Faith: one foot rests upon Forefather's Rock; in her left hands she holds a Bible; the right hand, uplifted, points to heaven. On the four buttresses or wing pedestals are figures that are emblematic of the principles upon which the Pilgrims purposed to found their commonwealth. The first is Morality; the second, Law; the third, Education; and the fourth, Freedom. Below these seated figures are marble high-reliefs that represent scenes from the history of the Pilgrims. They are: the Departure from Delft Haven; the First Treaty with the Indians; the Signing of the Compact; and the Landing at Plymouth, shown here. FPG

having been "wild and dissolute" in his youth. How far Puritan youths were sexually stimulated by the curious custom of "bundling," which permitted them to lie together in cold weather, covered with blankets sewed down the middle between them, is speculative, but neither the public disciplining of sinners nor such pulpit denunciations of "natural works" as Thomas Shepard's statement that man's heart was "a foul sink of all atheism, sodomy, blasphemy, murder, whoredom, adultery, witchcraft, buggery" can have been calculated to keep people's minds off sex.

The Puritan emphasis on the importance of reading the Bible encouraged education, and the concentration of life about the common made it easier to administer. There was a schoolmaster in Boston in 1635, and Roxbury and Dorchester both built schools thereafter. In Massachusetts the law required the support of public education from 1647. Girls often stopped with reading or went on to writing under private instruction, yet by the eighteenth century many of them were learning French, music, art, etc. *The New England Primer, or Milk for Babes*, first published about 1683, had printed seven million copies by 1840. Boston's "Free Grammar School," or "Boston Latin," dates from 1635 and offered a strictly classical curriculum, and the famous Roxbury Latin School, which goes back to John Eliot, still ranks high. In 1636 the General Court gave £400 for a college at Newtown, and when John Harvard, dying in 1638, left his library and half his estate to the institution, it was named for him, and Newtown was rechristened Cambridge in honor of the university from which most of the Boston area's learned men had come. Though Henry Dunster is often called Harvard's first president, he was preceded briefly by one Nathaniel Eaton, whose misdemeanors caused him to be dismissed. Dunster made a good record, but he too lost his post after fourteen years of service because he had become a Baptist. In 1650 he obtained a charter from the General Court under which Harvard still operates. It was a mediaeval university in curriculum, but no religious test was ever imposed. The General Court passed one in 1699, but the royal governor vetoed it out of consideration for the Anglicans, and the resultant furore led to the resignation of Increase Mather as president.

The Puritans were not hostile to science as such. Since they believed in the absolute sovereignty of God, they could not permit nature to box Him in. Consequently they differentiated between "secondary causes" and the Primary Cause and always reserved God's right to intervene directly in the world that He had made. In Plymouth in 1623 eight or nine hours of community prayer for rain were credited with ending a dangerous drought. Sometimes Puritans were guilty of postulating shocking interventions and interpositions in their own behalf and to confound their enemies. "Yet

from the first," as Perry Miller and Thomas H. Johnson observed, they "were disposed to place more emphasis upon the rules than upon the exceptions." They were quite as alert as other intelligent men of their time to new developments in the sciences, and a philosophical society was formed in Boston in 1683.

If medicine was in a primitive state, the reason was not that New England was inhabited by Puritans but that they were living in the seventeenth century. As late as 1716 William Douglass of Boston was the only M.D. in the colonies; even the famous Zabdiel Boylston, who brought himself within danger of mob violence when he allowed Cotton Mather to persuade him to inoculate for smallpox during the terrible epidemic of 1721, did not have a degree.* Parturition was presided over by midwives, not physicians; children's diseases were rampant and often fatal; childbed fever and tuberculosis exacted a heavy toll. Herbs and simples were used freely, along with every kind of old wives' medicine, but some of the lay practitioners developed great skill. Edward Winslow served Plymouth Colony nobly when he won Indian friendship by curing the chief Massasoit of what had threatened to be a fatal illness, and John Winthrop, Jr., who had the best scientific library of his time and was interested in prospecting, iron-making, and many other kindred matters, had "patients" who ranged all the way from leaders of the colony to sick Indians.

If the Puritans were comparatively indifferent to beauty as ornament, they certainly appreciated beauty as form, and both their churches and many of the common articles used in their homes bear testimony to this. As biblical literalists, some of them regarded portraits as impious; the earliest New England portrait painting was done by sign painters while gravestones provided a medium for sculpture. Though some works of fiction do show up in colonial inventories and though there was a Boston edition of *The Pilgrim's Progress* in 1681, fiction was under suspicion because it was not "true" and the theater because it was associated with vice. A brave tavern keeper tried to put on a magic show in 1687, but Judge Sewall and others convinced him that this was not a good idea. At first only psalms were sung in the churches, the tune being "set" by a member of the congregation and the words "lined out" for the illiterate or those who lacked books. In 1640 Stephen Daye's press in Cambridge brought out *The Whole Book of Psalms*, or "Bay Psalm Book," edited by Richard Mather, father of Increase and grandfather of Cotton. As late as 1713 the liberal Brattle Street Church refused to accept an organ; it went instead to the Angli-

*Among Mather's many books was an immense medical treatise called *The Angel of Bethesda*. When Barre Publishers finally brought it out in 1973 with the cooperation of the American Philosophical Society, it was found to be of interest to believers in what we call psychosomatic medicine.

A colonial New England kitchen as depicted by an unknown nineteenth-century artist. U.S. Office of War Information, National Archives

cans, who, by this time, were established at King's Chapel. Yet we hear of a dancing master in Boston about 1720.

Log cabins were introduced into America by Swedes and Finns; there were none in New England before the eighteenth century. Wood was the favored building material, though there was some use of stone and brick, the latter especially in Boston. Houses were built of hewn and sawed timbers, constructed about a central chimney and covered with clapboards. Casements were leaded and roofs steep-pitched. Ceiling beams were left exposed, and the floors were of wide-hewn boards. When it became possible, the well-to-do went in for elegant, even luxurious interiors. Peter Harrison, a ship captain who settled in Newport, was not a professional architect, but he designed the Redwood Library and Touro Synagogue, Freeman's Hall, and Brick Market in Newport, Christ Church in Cambridge, and King's Chapel in Boston. John Smibert, who came over with Berkeley, opened an art store in Boston. There were gifted cabinetmakers and iron-workers, and John Hull and Robert Sanderson, who designed the first coins, inaugurated a line of craftsmen which included the two gifted silversmiths named Paul Revere whose work we still cherish. Samuel Eliot Morison, who has supplied

much information along this line, has remarked that Boston had a dozen goldsmiths before she had a single lawyer.

Governor Bradford's descendant, Gamaliel Bradford VI, the famous "psychographer" of the 1920s, once observed that "when the Pilgrims came to Plymouth in 1620, they brought with them the English conscience and intellect and energy, but, roughly speaking, it may be said that the English imagination stayed behind, with the children of Shakespeare." The settlements were a little early for Shakespeare's fame (the First Folio did not appear until 1623), but the Puritans were not indifferent to literature. Boston had a bookshop in 1645, and a library was set up in the Town House in 1657. Classical writers were highly regarded; so were Foxe's *Book of Martyrs*, More's *Utopia*, and Bacon's *Essays*. Louis B. Wright conjectures that George Herbert was the most widely read English poet. If "high style" fell into disrepute even in preaching almost from the beginning, this does not mean that dignity was ever neglected or slovenliness encouraged in either writing or speaking.

Utilitarian and theological works (the latter often highly intellectual) predominated among colonial writings, but they enjoyed no monopoly. If Governor Bradford's history of Plymouth was the most distinguished historical work, certainly Thomas Hutchinson's *History of the Colony of Massachusetts Bay* is important; so are John Winthrop's *Journal*, the *Diary* of Samuel Sewall, and Cotton Mather's amazing compilation of history and wonder, *Magnalia Christi Americana.* Schoolboys composed poems on classical models, involving elaborate rhetorical conventions popular at the time, and many divines used verse as a handmaid of divinity. And though not too much can be claimed for Michael Wigglesworth's *Day of Doom* (1662), probably the first American "best seller," which versified Puritan theology and Bible teaching and ran through at least ten editions, both Anne Bradstreet (*The Tenth Muse*, 1650, etc.) and the Westfield, Massachusetts pastor, Edward

Taylor, were in quite another class. Feminists should be proud that the first American poet worth talking about was a woman, though the fanatics among them may well regard it as "male chauvinism" that Taylor should be ranked ahead of her. His will prohibited the publication of his verses; his grandson Ezra Stiles, president of Yale, presented the manuscript to the Yale Library, and there it remained until Thomas H. Johnson discovered it in 1937 and published it two years later. Though Taylor may have profited by the popularity at the time his poems appeared of the metaphysical school to which in a general way he belonged, he was quite as good as he was then considered to be. He, not Bryant, as we so long believed, was the first American poet of real stature.

A colonial log schoolhouse. New York Public Library Picture Collection

Mid-nineteenth-century pictures of the old New England "dame schools." New York Public Library Picture Collection

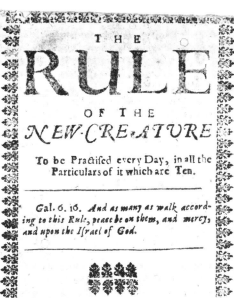

An early Boston title page. Rare Book Department, Free Library of Philadelphia

A page from *The New England Primer.* Library of Congress

Title page of *The Young Secretary's Guide* (Boston, 1708). New York Public Library Picture Collection

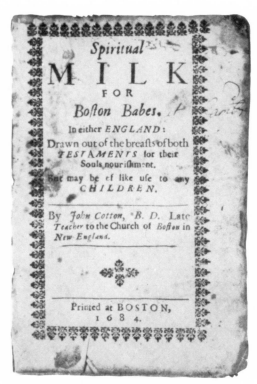

John Cotton's *Spiritual Milk for Boston Babes.*
New York Public Library Picture Collection

Roger Williams's *Key into the Language of America.*
New York Public Library Picture Collection

Title page of the *Bay Psalm Book*, printed at Cambridge, 1640, and the first book printed in what is now the United States. New York Public Library Picture Collection

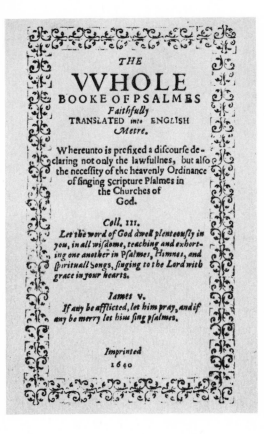

V

Puritan civilization faced what George Meredith might have called its "ordeals" or testings in connection with witchcraft and heresy. The former, though more publicized, was the less important.

The outbreak of witch-persecuting mania at Salem Village (now Danvers) in 1692, which involved adolescent girls and a West Indian hag, has fascinated the literary imagination from John Neal *(Rachel Dyer)* and Longfellow *(The New England Tragedies)* to Arthur Miller, who wrote *The Crucible* with one eye on the contemporary Joe McCarthy "witch-hunts." It cost twenty lives, and when sanity returned, there were 150 persons in prison and 250 more facing accusation. In minimizing its importance, I have no idea of pretending that it was not disgraceful, but there was nothing distinctively Puritan about it. In the seventeenth century belief in witchcraft was almost universal, and the agonies inflicted at Salem pale into insignificance compared with the chronic persecutions of Europe. Plymouth had an antiwitchcraft law but no execution; at Scituate a woman was tried but acquitted and the accuser of another was fined £5 and whipped.

Heretics were another story. Only Rhode Island welcomed Quakers, though Plymouth finally tolerated them in a restricted area, much as some holy churchyards have condescended to bury suicides along the fence. Branding, cropped ears, and bored tongues were among the agonies they suffered, though only Massachusetts went to the length of imposing death upon those who returned after banishment, and John Winthrop, Jr., declared that he would be willing to plead on his bare knees to save them.

Mary Dyer, whose statue now stands on a corner of the State House grounds in Boston, not far from the Common where her ghost is still reputed to walk, was first condemned to die with William Robinson and Marmaduke Stevenson in the autumn of 1659. At the last moment she was reprieved, removed from the gallows, and sent to Rhode Island in care of her son, but she returned the following spring and was hanged. Short of admitting that he had no right to take her life, Governor Endicott made every effort to save her; one gathers that he must have held it against her that she was so unreasonable as to force his hand. When King Philip's War broke out, there were fools who attributed it to God's displeasure over the laxity of Massachusetts toward the Quakers and newfangled methods of wearing the hair, and an Indian who helped one Quaker to escape to Rhode Island exclaimed, "What a God have these English who deal so with one another about the worship of their God!" At one point, the children of two banished Quakers were ordered sold into slavery to

Statue of Mary Dyer by Sylvia Shaw Judson, 1959, on the grounds of the State House in Boston. Courtesy Barre Publishers. Photo by Katharine Knowles

pay their fines for not attending church, but the plan failed because no ship's captain was enough of a scoundrel to be willing to take them. The worst ended in 1661 when the new king, Charles II, was told that "there was a vein of innocent blood opened in his dominions, which if it were not stopped would overrun all." He replied at once, "But I will stop that vein," and promptly sent Samuel Shattuck, himself a Quaker who had already been banished from Massachusetts, to carry "the King's Missive" to Endicott, ordering that all proceedings against Quakers be halted and that those under charges be sent to England. One may perhaps be pardoned for hoping that Shattuck may have enjoyed his confrontation with Endicott as much as an unregenerate man would have done.

This statue of Anne Hutchinson by Cyrus E. Dallin, erected in 1915, stands on the grounds of the State House in Boston. Courtesy Barre Publishers. Photo by Katharine Knowles

Anne Hutchinson was a harder nut to crack, for she was the Puritan's own, and she and her supporters, who included Governor Harry Vane (himself later martyred in Restoration England), her clerical brother-in-law John Wheelwright, who was banished to New Hampshire, and at first the distinguished John Cotton himself, split the Boston church. Mrs. Hutchinson was the great-grandmother of all Boston bluestockings, and in those days the meetings she held to analyze and evaluate the sermons of the clergy might well have been found shocking even if she had expressed no heretical ideas. Contemporary readers may find it difficult to understand how a whole community could be agitated over the difference between a "covenant of grace," which Mrs. Hutchinson championed, and a "covenant of works," which was all she would credit to the orthodox clergy. To her, however, the difference was both fundamental and important. Like the Quakers, she was rejecting religious formalism and institutionalism and insisting that religion was meaningless unless based

upon an "Inner Light," that is to say, a direct apprehension of God and the soul's own personal consciousness of its harmony with Him. If you had that, you had everything there was in religion, and if you did not have it, nothing else mattered.

There was very little hope for her after Vane had been defeated for reelection as governor and left the colonies in disgust, and if there had been, she would have squelched it when, in a moment of enthusiasm, she claimed, under fire, a direct revelation: "the mouth of the Lord hath spoken it." Catholics, Anglicans, and Puritans all agreed that revelation on matters of doctrine had closed with the last book of the Bible. Mrs. Hutchinson was banished in 1638 ("Say no more. The Court knows wherefore and is satisfied") and went with her husband to Rhode Island, as we have already seen. In 1642, after his death, she was killed by the Indians in what is now known as Pelham Bay Park in Westchester. Though she was an uncomfortable woman, it is hard to see how religion could retain vitality and admit progress without some such attitude of mind as she embodied. But it will not quite do to dismiss the objections of her opponents on the ground of their natural dislike of having all their functions as interpreters of God's will and defenders of the institutions which represented it in this world short-circuited. The Antinomian excesses which appeared in England under the Commonwealth, making every man his own judge in matters of religion and morals, showed what might easily happen to her doctrines in the hands of those who lacked her integrity; even in Massachusetts, one Captain John Underhill maintained that, being bound to Christ, he could do no wrong and need therefore pay no regard to laws and standards.

As for the Indians, in the 1920s a saying was current that when the English colonists came to this country,

> *They fell first upon their knees*
> *And next upon the aborigines.*

Any signs of awakening conscience toward Indians on the part of Americans are to be welcomed, but this is not quite what happened.

In the beginning, indeed, a desire to convert the Indians, whom some believed descended from the Ten Lost Tribes of Israel, was a minor motive in colonization. "Offend not the poor natives," John Cotton advised, "but as you partake in their land, so make them partakers of your precious faith." John Robinson also believed it "a thing more glorious in men's eyes than pleasing in God's, or convenient for Christians, to be a terror to poor barbarous people." Roger Williams, too, as we have seen, was always a friend to the Indians, but the language barrier made evangelization very difficult.

About 1643 the Mayhews started evangelizing the Indians on Nantucket and Martha's Vineyard, and in

Samoset bids the Pilgrims welcome to Plymouth, March 16, 1621. He returned shortly with Massasoit, Squanto, and others. Mural by Charles Hoffbauer. This reproduction is used through the courtesy of The New England Mutual Life Insurance Company. Copyright 1943.

1650 John Eliot, Roxbury pastor and Harvard overseer, began his miraculous work. Eliot's translation of the Bible into the Algonquin language was the first complete Bible printed in the colonies (1658), and we get some idea of the difficulties involved when we learn that the Algonquin language, which was highly inflected but not well adapted to the expression of abstract ideas, had never been written down.

Eliot preached before the local sagamore Waban in what is now Nonantum in 1646 and gave a demonstration of the accomplishments of his first converts at a church council in Cambridge the next year. Judging by some of the questions they asked him, they were not incapable of facing fundamental theological questions.

Why, they wished to know, did not God give all men good hearts and why, since He had the power to do so, did he not kill the Devil?

Eliot settled his "praying Indians" in towns of their own; the first and most important was set up at Natick in 1651. Here he spent a day every fortnight, making the long trip from Roxbury by horseback. Unhappily his great work was largely undone by King Philip's War, when his "praying Indians" were interned on Deer Island, a piece of cruelty and stupidity which suggests the treatment of Pacific Coast American Japanese during World War II.

When the colonists came over, they feared natives, serpents, and mosquitoes. The serpents never became

Statue of Massasoit, the Wampanoag chief, who befriended the Plymouth colonists. He was the father of Metacomet, better known as King Philip. Beyond the statue, the peristyle which shelters Plymouth Rock can be seen. Courtesy Plymouth Area Chamber of Commerce

much of a factor in New England; the trouble which developed with the Indians was largely the colonists' fault; with the mosquitoes their descendants still contend. The Pilgrims were fortunate in arriving at a time when the Indian population in the neighborhood had been decimated by disease. Toward the end of their first winter, they were visited by the friendly Samoset, who spoke English and who taught them much about how to live and raise crops in the new country, and introduced them to the Wampanoag sachem, Massasoit, with whom they concluded a treaty that was long faithfully kept on both sides. It was not all sweetness and light, however; even friendly Indians could be dirty and troublesome and had a way of inviting themselves to make prolonged visits and gorge themselves on the Pilgrims'

slender stock of provisions. Squanto and Hobomok virtually adopted the Pilgrims, but since Indians are no more perfect than white men, there was rivalry and apparently some intrigue between them; at one time, Massasoit was so enraged that he wanted Squanto's head and seems to have come close to getting it. When the Narragansetts sent an apparent challenge to Plymouth in the form of a bundle of arrows bound up in a snakeskin and the Pilgrims returned the skin stuffed with bullets, they were expressing more confidence than they really felt, but savagery was not quite outside the Pilgrim character, as they proved with their surprise attack on the Indians at Thomas Weston's rival trading station, from which they returned triumphantly with the head of Wituwamat to serve as a decoration above

Statue of the seventeenth-century Indian chief Ninigret, at Watch Hill, Rhode Island (1914); sculpted in Paris by Enid Yandell. Ninigret kept his tribe at peace through the seventeenth century and secured some tribal lands in the region for himself and his heirs. An Indian with Buffalo Bill's Wild West Show, in Paris at the time, served as the model. Rhode Island Development Council. FPG

their fort. John Fiske remarks rightly of the colonists' relations with the Indians that "there is nothing so pitiless as fear," but if this is an excuse, it applies to the natives quite as much as to the colonists themselves, and George Bancroft was right too when he remarked that "the fears of one class of men are not the measure of the rights of another."

In the most serious early conflict between the colonists and the Indians, the so-called Pequot War of 1637, a military expedition of Connecticut, Massachusetts, and Plymouth men made a surprise attack upon the Indians and slaughtered seven hundred persons in less than an hour. After this there was no more serious trouble until King Philip's War (1675-76) broke out under the son of Massasoit, whose Indian name

was Metacom. This horrible conflict brought terror to the whole frontier; more than a dozen towns were totally destroyed and a much larger number raided. It is said that one man of military age in every sixteen died in King Philip's War and that not one white man was left alive in Kennebec County. King Philip was apparently neither a wise nor a very effective leader, but the heaviest responsibility for the conflict would seem to rest not upon him but on the provocations offered by the whites. "The flinging of the child Astyanax over the walls of Troy," wrote Agnes Repplier, "was less barbarous than the selling of King Philip's little son into slavery. Hundreds of adult captives were sent at the same time to Barbados. It would have been more merciful, though less profitable, to have butchered them at

Hunter House, 1748, Newport, R.I. An early New England Georgian house with a balustraded gambrel roof, constructed for Deputy Gov. Jonathan Nichols, Jr. Rhode Island Department of Economic Development

Birthplace of Gilbert Stuart, Narragansett, Rhode Island. This building was the first snuff mill erected in this country, 1751. Rhode Island Department of Economic Development

home." One cannot but recall one John Bacon, who bequeathed a slave woman to his wife, with the proviso that if she outlived her mistress, she should be sold and the money realized used to purchase Bibles. The conscience of New England spoke through John Eliot: "To sell souls for money seemeth to me a dangerous merchandise." It was not to be the last time in American history that the voice of conscience would go unheard.

General Nathanael Greene homestead, Anthony, R.I. Rhode Island Department of Economic Development

The Boston Globe's Bicentennial edition of April 19, 1975, recording events of April 18 and 19, 1775, ninety-seven years before the first printing of *The Boston Globe*.

Chapter 2
Four Cities

I. BOSTON

BOSTON, THEY SAY, is not a place but a state of mind, and the saying is illustrated by the story of two nineteenth-century Transcendentalists whom a Millerite-Adventist informed one day, as they strolled down the street, that the world was about to come to an end. "That does not concern me," replied the first Transcendentalist; "I live in Boston." And the second added, "Let it end. We shall get on much better without it."

Stories about Boston's devotion to culture, her provincialism, and the snobbery of her "Brahmins" are legion, and many of them have bite and point. Edith Wharton used to say that in New York she was considered too intellectual to be fashionable while in Boston she was regarded as too fashionable to be intellectual. It was almost too much for Longfellow's equanimity when three Boston ladies, arriving late for Fanny Kemble's reading of *Macbeth*, trailed down the aisle to their front seats just as the actress was intoning:

> *What are these,*
> *So withered and so wild in their attire*
> *That look not like th' inhabitants of the earth,*
> *And yet are on't?*

As for the culture, it has been related of Henry James that he was startled when the policeman who was escorting him across Copley Square, during his last visit to America, inquired which of his novels he liked best, and that when he chose *The Golden Bowl*, the officer exclaimed, "Oh, thank you, sir; that is my favorite too!"

There is no denying that Boston snobbery is real, all the more so for its often serene unconsciousness and sometimes wonderful kindness to those who are willing to recognize and concede their inferiority. Yet it has its limits. When Oliver Wendell Holmes, the very type of the Beacon Street wit, was asked to write on "Medicine in Boston" for Justin Winsor's *Memorial History*, he objected that this would be like an oceanographer's dissertation on the tides of Boston Harbor. Boston, he said, "is a fraction of the civilized world, as its harbor is part of the ocean. In both we expect to find general laws and phenomena, modified more or less in their aspects by local influences." Certainly provincialism was never more scathingly, though unconsciously, rebuked than by the English lady delegate to a church conference who looked up Park Street to where the

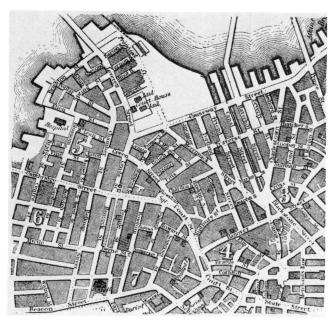

From the City Hall, State Street, to the City Jail, Leverett St. From Smith's Map of Boston, 1835. Library of Congress

Massachusetts State seal. Detail engraving by George Murray from the engraving "Declaration of Independence," published by John Binns, 1818. Library of Congress

Boston from the southeast, from an engraving by J. Carwitham (fl. 1730), for Bowles & Carver, No. 69 St. Paul's Church. London. FPG

Boston from the South Boston Bridge. Lithograph in *Itinéraire pittoresque de fleuve Hudson, et des parties latérales de l'Amérique du Nord 1828-1829*. Library of Congress

Boston seen from Dorchester Heights, from an aquatint by Robert Havell, 1841. Library of Congress

golden dome of the State House was shining gloriously in the morning sunshine and, in her most clipped British accents, jauntily inquired, "*What's* the building with the brass knob?"

In the beginning the Shawmut peninsula was connected with the mainland only by a narrow neck along what is now Washington Street, while the waters of the Back Bay reached to what is today the Public Garden.

The Trimountàin (Pemberton, Beacon, Mount Vernon) ran through the center of the peninsula. Beacon, the highest portion, was known as Sentry Hill, and a 1776 map, for obvious reasons, calls Mount Vernon "Mount Whoredom." Only Beacon Hill survives today, and that in a mutilated state, the rest of it having been cut down early in the nineteenth century to fill in the Mill Pond, thus sacrificing Bulfinch's handsome column, which

F. C. Yohn's conception of Old Boston Town House Square about 1657, from the Boston *Herald*, April 16, 1930. Library of Congress

had replaced the 1635 beacon and which is still pictured on the title pages of Little, Brown books. The Massachusetts Bay Colony settled between the Trimountain and the harbor, centering about the present location of the Old State House.

Boston territory has been enlarged both by filled-in land and by the annexing, sometimes under protest, of such neighboring towns as Roxbury, Dorchester, Charlestown, Brighton, and Hyde Park. The first bridge across the Charles, then reputed the longest in America, was built in 1786. The next was the still greater West Boston Bridge (1793), which opened up the West End, but the Harvard Bridge (Massachusetts Avenue) was not constructed until 1791. In 1821 a milldam was erected in the Back Bay to harness the tides for manufacturing purposes, but not much came of this, and the area became such an eyesore, stench, and health hazard that it was filled in not long after mid-century, thus making possible the development of a whole new area, including the Public Garden, adjoining the Common, and the spacious boulevard of Commonwealth Avenue. The home of schools, churches, museums, and libraries, this region of made land was destined, next after Beacon Hill, to become the most fashionable residence area in the city. In the 1850s the South End aspired to this eminence, but though many fine houses were built there, its distinction was brief; by 1885 it was turning into a lodging house area and by the end of the century it was something close to a slum. W. D. Howells's famous novel, *The Rise of Silas Lapham*, reflects the

The Old State House, as pictured in the *Massachusetts Magazine*, August 1791. Engraving by S. Hill. Library of Congress

The British Lion and Unicorn on the Old State House. FPG

Tower of the Old State House. FPG

Rear view of the State House, showing the replica of the Bulfinch pillar, formerly on the summit of Beacon Hill. Lithograph by J. H. Bufford, 1858, after a drawing by J. R. Smith. FPG

The State House in winter. Photograph by Samuel Chamberlain. U.S. Office of War Information, National Archives

The "New" State House, with its gold dome, overlooking Boston Common, the central portion of which was designed by Charles Bulfinch, 1798; headquarters of the governor and legislature of the Commonwealth. FPG

feelings of the period when the more prosperous and fashionable residents of the South End were beginning to remove themselves to the Back Bay. Population-wise, Boston was passed by both New York and Philadelphia about the middle of the eighteenth century, but the population increased steadily up to 1900 (561,000) and then tended to slow down, dropping 13 percent during the 1950s. The 1970 figure was 628,215.

John Adams, second President of the United States and the first from New England, from a lithograph by Pendleton, after a painting by Gilbert Stuart. Library of Congress

Grave of Samuel Adams, Old Granary Burying Ground, Boston. U.S. Bureau of Public Roads, National Archives

Though the first shots of the Revolutionary War were fired at Lexington and Concord, Boston did much to nurture the brooding rebellion. Samuel Adams had foreseen separation from England as early as 1768, and the Suffolk Resolve of 1774 came close to anticipating the Declaration of Independence. Nobody whose opinion matters now believes that England's colonial policy was wise or prudent, but the conflict between the colonists and the mother country was by no means the simple confrontation of right and wrong that we used to teach children in the history books. Sam Adams was a rabble-rouser who after the war even had his doubts about accepting the Constitution, and John Adams called John Hancock "an empty barrel." Hancock survives today in a handsome autograph and memories of a ceremonialism and dandyism worthy of Beau Brummell but ridiculous in a young republic; when Washington visited Boston in 1789, the New Englander even made a fruitless to-do about his feeling that the President should wait upon him as Governor of Massachusetts. "There have been but few men in history," wrote Henry Cabot Lodge, "who have achieved so much fame, and whose names are so familiar, who at the same time really did so little."

It was Sam Adams who, on December 16, 1773, spoke the words, at a protest meeting which had drawn seven thousand to the Old South Meeting House ("This meeting can do no more to save the country") which gave the "Mohawks" the signal to dump the tea into Boston Harbor, and it was those like-minded with him who made possible the intransigence which had triggered the street brawl (March 5, 1770) which the "patriots" dignified as the "Boston Massacre." But though the hotheads brought on a war, they did not wholly overthrow the community's sense of decorum. John Adams and Josiah Quincy defended the accused soldiers and succeeded in getting the captain and all but two of his men acquitted, and, for all its picturesqueness, there was almost a dull orderliness about the Boston Tea Party; the tea alone was quietly and systematically destroyed.

Washington took command of the Continental army in Cambridge, but the only battle actually fought in the Boston area was that at Bunker or Breed's Hill in Charlestown, on June 17, 1775. The British evacuated the town on March 17, 1776, after Washington had rendered it indefensible by mounting his cannons on Dorchester Heights, and when the Tories had left, a new "aristocracy" (Cabots, Lowells, Higginsons, Peabodys, etc.) moved in from Essex County and elsewhere to take over a leadership which, in many aspects, they still exercise. On July 17, the Declaration of Independence was read in Boston and the royal insignia burned, and in 1780 a new state government was formed.

Postwar economic depression increased Boston's dependence upon the sea and sent her ships to ever more

Granary Burying Ground, east of Park Street Congregational Church, on Tremont Street east of Park Street. Here are buried among others the victims of the Boston Massacre on March 5, 1770; Josiah Franklin and wife (parents of Benjamin Franklin), Peter Faneuil, Paul Revere, and John Phillips, first mayor of Boston. U.S. Bureau of Public Roads, National Archives

Paul Revere's engraving of the "Boston Massacre." FPG

The Boston Massacre Monument, by Robert Kraus, erected on Boston Common, 1888. FPG

Birthplace of John Quincy Adams, at Quincy, Mass. From *Gleason's Pictorial Drawing-Room Companion*, Boston, August 21, 1852. U.S. Bureau of Public Roads, National Archives

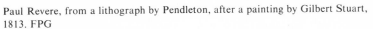

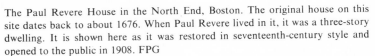

Paul Revere, from a lithograph by Pendleton, after a painting by Gilbert Stuart, 1813. FPG

The Paul Revere House in the North End, Boston. The original house on this site dates back to about 1676. When Paul Revere lived in it, it was a three-story dwelling. It is shown here as it was restored in seventeenth-century style and opened to the public in 1908. FPG

The Bunker Hill Monument, viewed from Monument Street in Charlestown, clearly visible from Boston. FPG

Paul Revere statue, by Cyrus E. Dallin, modeled in 1885, and installed in 1940 in the Paul Revere Mall between Hanover Street and Christ ("Old North") Church. FPG

distant ports. In 1787 five Boston merchants sent the *Columbia* and the *Washington* to the Pacific Northwest, from whence they carried furs to China. The *Columbia* returned in 1790, after having rounded the Cape of Good Hope. Though not a commercial success, this voyage opened up the way to an extensive trade which was to involve many Bostonians as sailors and investors and ultimately enlarge Boston's wealth.

The first news of the French Revolution aroused enthusiasm, but this was destroyed by the Terror and the rise of Napoleon, which strengthened Federalist (conservative or antidemocratic) tendencies and softened the old antagonism toward England. Jefferson's embargo brought hardship to all New England coast towns, and the end of the unpopular War of 1812, which involved action off the Massachusetts coast and stimulat-

The Battle of Bunker Hill. Engraved by Thomas Phillibrown after painting by Alonzo Chappel. FPG

ed efforts to fortify Boston, came just in time to squelch what might possibly have been a dangerous movement toward secession.

In 1822 Boston became a city, and the next year she had the good sense to choose Josiah Quincy (son of the Revolutionary patriot) as mayor. Quincy created the Public Garden and the Charles Street Mall, built Quincy Market (which involved altering the waterfront), improved sanitation, modernized and reorganized the police and fire departments, suppressed the vice district, and showed interest in education, penal administration, and a reasonable conduct of financial affairs.

Boston's feeling about the Mexican War for the extension of slavery was eloquently expressed by Lowell in the first series of *The Biglow Papers*, but Bostonians did not rush to become abolitionists. The tide began to turn after 1850, for though Daniel Webster supported the Fugitive Slave Law, many New Englanders gagged at it. In 1854 the fugitive Anthony Burns was defended by the author of *Two Years Before the Mast*, and Thomas Wentworth Higginson and other "gentlemen" led an attack on the Court House. Though Dana lost his case, it required the military of Suffolk County to

Statue of Daniel Webster, by Hiram Powers, erected in 1859, on the grounds of the State House, Boston. This was the second statue, as the first was shipped from Leghorn and lost at sea. Courtesy Barre Publishers. Photo by Katharine Knowles

get Burns to the Long Wharf through streets draped in mourning, and a group of ladies sent the Commissioner who had rendered the verdict thirty pieces of silver. Governor John A. Andrew ardently mobilized the state behind the Civil War, pleading from the beginning for the use of black troops. In 1863 the War Department agreed to the organization of the Fifty-fourth Massachusetts, under the gallant Robert Gould Shaw, but since he and half his soldiers were slaughtered within two months at Fort Wagner, it is hard to see that they achieved much more than to provide inspiration for the great Saint-Gaudens memorial at Beacon and Park streets. In Winsor's *Memorial History*, Francis W. Palfrey estimated that 26,175 Boston men had served in the war but wrung his hands over those who had paid bounties to keep out. There was even a draft riot in the city on July 14, 1863.

In 1898 William James, Charles Eliot Norton, Moorfield Storey, Gamaliel Bradford V, and others made Boston the center for protest against the imperialistic Spanish-American War. Sympathy with England made the two world wars more acceptable. Nearby Wellesley College dropped Emily Greene Balch, later winner of the Nobel Peace Prize during World War I, A. J. Muste lost his Newton pastorate, and Karl Muck was driven from his conductorship of the Boston Symphony Orchestra. Even here there were rays of light, however. When in 1914, it was reported that a Harvard benefactor proposed to deprive the university of a prospective $10,000,000 unless she dismissed the pro-German Professor Hugo Münsterberg. President Lowell immediately refused, and was praised by Theodore Roosevelt: "Harvard cannot afford to sell the right of free speech for ten million dollars or any other sum." Boston has not been altogether silent about either the Korean or the Vietnam War; in 1972 both the city and the state went for George McGovern, after which motor cars sported such bumper stickers as: "Don't Blame Me. I'm from Massachusetts."

Colonial Boston was predominantly English, but after the Irish Potato Famine the starving children of the Emerald Isle began arriving in droves and crowding into tenements in the North End, where it is estimated they had an average life expectancy of fourteen years.

←
Tombstone of John Phillips, first mayor of Boston in Granary Burying Ground east of the Park Street Congregational Church. U.S. Bureau of Public Roads, National Archives

→
A page from the *American Anti-Slavery Almanac* for 1840. Library of Congress

Illustrations of the American Anti-Slavery Almanac for 1840.

"*Our Peculiar Domestic Institutions.*"

Northern Hospitality—New-York nine months law. [The Slave steps out of the Slave State, and his chains fall. A Free State, with another chain, stands ready to re-enslave him.]

Burning of McIntosh at St. Louis, in April, 1836.

Showing how slavery improves the condition of the female sex.

The Negro Pew, or "Free" Seats for black Christians. | *Mayor of New-York refusing a Carman's license to a colored Man.*

Servility of the Northern States in arresting and returning fugitive Slaves.

Selling a Mother from her Child.

Hunting Slaves with dogs and guns. A Slave drowned by the dogs.

"*Poor things, 'they can't take care of themselves.'*"

Mothers with young Children at work in the field.

A Woman chained to a Girl, and a Man in irons at work in the field.

Branding Slaves.

Cutting up a Slave in Kentucky.

Paid.   *Unpaid.*

Hancock House. Building erected by Thomas Hancock in 1737 and given to his nephew the governor, by his aunt, Lydia Hancock. Engraving after artist A. J. Davis, circa 1820s. This was the noblest private mansion of the colonial period in Boston. U.S. Bureau of Public Roads, National Archives

Memorial to Colonel Robert Gould Shaw and the Fifty-fourth Massachusetts (Black) Regiment (opposite State House in Boston). Sculptor, Augustus Saint-Gaudens. Unveiling, May 31, 1897. Courtesy Barre Publishers. Photo by Katharine Knowles

Faneuil Hall, from W. H. Bartlett's *History of America*. Library of Congress

By 1855 there were fifty thousand of them, fifteen thousand of whom had come during the last five years, and in 1860 Boston's death rate was twice that of the rest of Massachusetts. By 1900 half Boston was Irish or of Irish stock and less than 11 percent of the old English stock. Later, crowded out of the North End by Italians, Russian and Polish Jews and others, the Irish made South Boston their stronghold ("Southie" claims to have produced more priests and nuns than any comparable area in America). Catholic services began in 1788, and the first bishop (1808) was a Frenchman, the greatly respected Jean Louis Anne Magdeleine Lefebvre de Cheverus, who built the first Cathedral of the Holy Cross. It took New Englanders a while to realize either that Irish Catholics were capable of assimilating New England culture or to learn to appropriate what they brought with them, and the destruction of the Ursuline Convent in Charlestown by a mob in 1834 may well

A kindergarten in the North End Industrial Home, 1881. Wood engraving in *Leslie's*, June 4, 1881. Library of Congress

James Michael Curley. Library of Congress

joyed four terms in Congress and one as governor. A great, flamboyant, extravagant builder, he vastly expanded services and construction in Boston but quintupled the city's tax rate. The secret of all these men was well stated by Boss Martin Lomasney: "From the standpoint of politics, the great mass of people are interested in only three things—food, clothing, and shelter. A politician in a district such as mine sees to it that his people get these things." He and the others did just that, at a time when nobody else seemed to care much about it.

Like other cities, Boston has had its spectacular, both pleasant and painful, events. The first hurricane after the settlement came in 1635; there was a "Great September Gale" in 1815; in our own time there was a very destructive hurricane in 1938, followed by others, fortunately less destructive, in 1944, 1954, and 1955. The century between 1750 and 1850 was called the "Little Ice Age" and 1816 the "Year Without a Summer." Destructive fires have raged since almost the first settlements; the Great Fire of 1872 is said to have burned 767 buildings over 67 acres and cost $75,000,000. But there were great fires in Chelsea in 1908 and 1973, and the Cocoanut Grove night club fire of 1942 killed 492 people in twelve minutes and inspired

have been the most disgraceful act in Massachusetts history. The nuns had been conducting a girls' school which was of excellent repute and attended by, among others, Protestant girls of good family. Crazy rumors had been circulated about the alleged mistreatment of both nuns and pupils; a committee of selectmen had investigated and reported that there was no foundation for them, but this did not prevent the attack. Afterwards there was a protest meeting in Faneuil Hall, but though the idea of compensation was raised in the legislature for many years, nothing was ever accomplished. A hundred persons were arrested, but only thirteen were indicted and one convicted, and even he was pardoned.

The old names still predominate in Boston finance and in many areas of business and culture, but the Irish long ago took over City Hall. Hugh O'Brien, the first Irish mayor, and a good one, was elected in 1885; Patrick Collins too was greatly respected. But both John F. ("Honey Fitz") Fitzgerald and James Michael Curley (hero of Edwin O'Connor's novel, *The Last Hurrah*) knew every trick of the machine politician and how to run a circus besides. Except for the period when he carried on the affairs of the city from a jail cell, Curley spent sixteen years in City Hall and en-

The Province House, made familiar to modern readers by Hawthorne's "Legends of the Province House" in *Twice-Told Tales*. Library of Congress

The Great Boston Fire, 1872, as depicted by Currier and Ives. Library of Congress

new safety regulations in Boston and elsewhere. In 1919 the Boston police strike elevated Governor Calvin Coolidge to national eminence because he spoke some eloquent words ("there is no right to strike against the public safety by anybody, anywhere, anytime") after having first attempted to sit out the strike while Boston lay at the mercy of the mob. There was a sensational murder in 1849, when John White Webster, the only Harvard professor ever hanged, killed Dr. George Parkman and burned his body at the Medical School, and in the early 1960s the "Boston Strangler" was sending the thoughts of the historically minded back to London's Jack the Ripper and causing parents who sent their girls to school in Boston to make them promise not to go out alone at night.

Boston put on festival attire to welcome Lafayette in 1784, Washington in 1789, and King Edward VII (as Prince of Wales) in 1860. Charles Dickens's two visits, in 1842 and 1867 (the second as a public reader), attracted so much attention that a whole book* has been

South Station. FPG. Photo by Paul Thompson, N.Y.

*Edward F. Payne, *Dickens Days in Boston* (Houghton Mifflin, 1927).

Summer Street. FPG. Photo by Paul Thompson, N.Y.

devoted to the subject. The novelist liked Boston better than almost anything else he saw in America. Annual festival occasions include the great St. Patrick's Day parade and, since 1907, Christmas Eve caroling on Beacon Hill.

Many Boston events have centered about the Common, which has been used for pasturing, drill, celebrations, agitations, and, in the early days, even execution and burial. One of the happiest events was the celebration of October 25, 1848, when Lake Cochituate water, brought in for Boston's water supply, shot up eighty feet above the Frog Pond. One of the saddest was the 1927 demonstration, involving Edna St. Vincent Millay and other distinguished persons, in defense of Sacco and Vanzetti, two radicals whom Massachusetts put to death for a 1920 killing of which thousands of people across the world refused to believe them guilty. As editor of *The Atlantic Monthly*, Ellery Sedgwick outraged conservative opinion by printing Felix Frankfurter's searching analysis of the evidence, perhaps the longest article the magazine ever published. Hope had been aroused when President Lowell of Harvard, President Stratton of M.I.T., and Judge Robert Grant were appointed by the governor to review the trial, and their decision against the defendants awakened great indignation. After the execution, *The Nation* appeared with MASSACHUSETTS THE MURDERER splashed across its cover, and John Dos Passos, not yet a conser-

vative, wrote an open letter to President Lowell in which he declared himself ashamed of his Harvard degree. In 1926, too, H. L. Mencken was arrested at "Brimstone Corner," before the Park Street Church, just off the Common, at the instance of the Watch and Ward Society for selling a copy of *The American Mercury* which contained an allegedly obscene story (the complaint was dismissed). This group had long made "Banned in Boston" both a mark of distinction and a laughingstock, while theater censorship had been bringing about such absurdities as the necessity of having Eugene O'Neill's *Strange Interlude* performed in Quincy. Today one cannot walk by the pornographic book and picture shops without gagging over much of what is displayed in the windows, nor, it is said, attend the theater without running the risk of being solicited. Evidently there is more than one way of being intolerable in Boston.

It is said that by 1832, ninety-three stage lines were operating out of Boston. The Boston and Worcester

→

State Street, Boston about the turn of the century. FPG

The swan boats in the Public Garden, with the Ritz-Carlton Hotel in the background. FPG

Above right

Norman cartoon of Sacco-Vanzetti trial. Road laborer Chisholm's description of the fleeing bandits. Cartoon by Norman Dedham. Boston *Post*, 1921. Courtesy of the Boston Public Library, Print Department

Nicola Sacco and Bartolomeo Vanzetti guarded by deputy sheriffs, entering the Norfolk County Court House at Dedham, Mass., October 31, 1921. The Bettmann Archive

Cleopatra's Barge, the Great Boston Sleigh, passing the Norfolk House, Roxbury, 1856. Wood engraving in *Ballou's*, March 11, 1856. Library of Congress

Cutting down Beacon Hill (note the Bulfinch column), from a lithograph by J. H. Bufford, after a drawing by J. R. Smith, 1811-12. Library of Congress

Christmas card announcement from Louis Prang, a German immigrant who established a great chromolithograph business in Boston in the 1860s which endured for many years and exercised a great influence upon American taste. Library of Congress

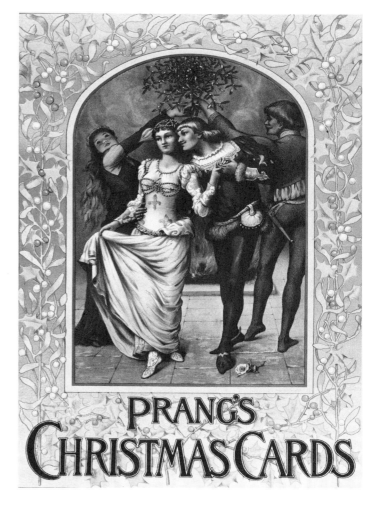

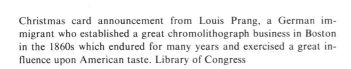

Cutting down Beacon Hill. Lithograph by J. H. Bufford, 1858. Library of Congress

was the first railroad, and there were eight different stations before 1850. In 1835 Harriet Martineau had traveled by railroad and steamboat between Boston and New York in twenty hours, which she thought very fast. During the sixties and seventies many engines were built at Taunton. Railroading encouraged the trek to the suburbs which Boston has shared with all large cities; when, about the middle of the twentieth century, the railroads did their best to kill their own business, many suburbanites were left with no means of transportation into the cities except private cars, which created smog and horrible traffic jams and began burying the countryside under ugly concrete. Horsecars had appeared on Boston streets in the 1850s; electric cars began in the late eighties. Boston's subway (1898) was the first in America. Local transportation is now controlled by the Massachusetts Bay Transportation Authority, which makes eloquent gestures in the direction of providing adequate transportation for all but still has a long way to go. Transportation of course stimulates and requires hostelries. The United States Hotel (1826), the Tremont House (1829), and the Revere House (1847) have long since vanished, but the Parker House (1854), home of the "Parker House roll" and the

Interior view of L. S. Driggs' lace and bonnet shop, Boston. Wood engraving in *Gleason's*, October 16, 1852. Library of Congress

"American Plan," still flourishes, and there are seasoned travelers who call the Ritz-Carlton the finest hotel in America.

Churches, schools, and the press have been valued in Boston from Puritan times, though little variety in belief or practice was tolerated in the beginning. Baptists and Quakers worshipped unmolested from the end of the 1670s. Governor Andros fostered Anglican (Episcopal) services, and the first Anglican church, King's Chapel, was erected in 1689 (the present building dates from 1750). From 1869 until his death in 1893 the great Phillips Brooks of Trinity Church was an institution. It is interesting that King's Chapel should have turned Unitarian as early as 1787, though Unitarianism as a denomination was not organized until later. Orthodox objection to the appointment of the liberal Henry Ware as Hollis Professor of Divinity at Harvard in 1805 stimulated the controversy, and William Ellery Channing's "Baltimore sermon" of 1819 furnished "liberal Christians" with a rallying point. In 1825 the American

Women voting at municipal election in Boston, December 11, 1888. Library of Congress →

Shipbuilding at East Boston. Note Bunker Hill Monument at right. Library of Congress

Fetridge & Co.'s Periodical Arcade, Washington and State streets. Library of Congress

King's Chapel, the second (and present) building, 1749. (Peter Harrison, architect) at Tremont and School streets. FPG

Park Street Church, built 1809. Architect, Peter Banner. Massachusetts Historical Society

Unitarian Association was organized. Unitarianism captured most of the Boston intelligentsia, and Harvard College too, taking over both the First and Second Churches, though the Third (Old South) remained orthodox; between 1884 and 1929 (now in a magnificent new building in Copley Square), their minister was George A. Gordon, whom many considered the greatest preacher of his time. When the liberals gained the ascendancy in a congregation, the orthodox generally withdrew, leaving the property, under protest, to the rebels, and this produced bad feeling and court action, which the conservatives lost. Andover Theological Seminary (1807) was established to take care of the orthodox young theologues who could no longer go to Harvard, and Park Street Church (1809) became the center of orthodoxy it has ever since remained. Even today it goes it alone as a "Congregational church," unaffiliated with the United Church of Christ, which has swallowed up most of the rest of the old Congregational denomination, a dynamic center of Fundamentalist theology and intense missionary endeavor. In time, to be sure, the Unitarians themselves produced such heretics as the Concord Transcendentalists and Theodore

King's Chapel—interior. The pulpit is the oldest in the United States. The Bible was given in 1768 by Mrs. Elizabeth Rogers. FPG

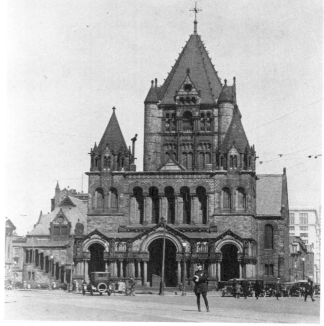

Trinity Church, 1874, in Copley Square, designed by Henry Hobson Richardson, assisted by Charles Follen McKim and Stanford White. FPG

The spire of Old South Meetinghouse, 1729, at Washington and Milk streets. FPG. Camera study by Arthur Griffin, Boston.

Old North Church—interior. FPG

The old and the new First Church of Christ, Scientist, the Christian
Science "Mother Church," in the Christian Science complex off
Huntington and Massachusetts avenues, 1894. The architect was
Franklin I. Welch; the new church, built in 1906, was designed by
Charles Brigham. I. M. Pei was the architect for the new church
complex, completed in 1973. FPG

Christ Church, Boston. Erected 1723. Lithograph by J. H. Bufford &
Co. Library of Congress

Parker, and Andrews Norton and others proved that "orthodox Unitarians" could be as inflexible toward dissenters as the Calvinists themselves had been.

Across the Charles in Cambridge, Harvard College began in colonial times, but in the early days education was for boys, and Boston did not acquire a high school for girls until after the middle of the nineteenth century. The Harvard Medical School began in 1782 (first in Cambridge, later in Boston); on October 16, 1846, anaesthetics were first used in surgery at Massachusetts General Hospital; today Boston has no superior on earth as a medical center. Harvard College was organized as a great university under Charles W. Eliot; A. Lawrence Lowell introduced the "house plan" and erected handsome buildings along the Charles. Both the

Old South Meetinghouse at Washington and Milk streets. Photo by H. C. White, Co., 1906. Library of Congress

Chauncy Hall School and First Congregational Church, 1857. School built 1873, razed 1908. A. C. Martin, architect. Church built 1808, Asher Benjamin, architect. Library of Congress

Mrs. Mary Baker G. Eddy, author of *Science and Health* and founder of Christian Science, from a painting by Alice Barbour. Library of Congress

Massachusetts Institute of Technology and Harvard's female affiliate, Radcliffe College, are in Cambridge. Tufts (Universalist, 1852) is in Medford and Brandeis (Jewish, 1948) in Waltham. Boston College (Roman Catholic, 1863) began in Boston but is now in Chestnut Hill. Within the city are Boston University (Methodist, 1869), Northeastern (1898), Simmons (1902), and now the rapidly growing Boston branch of the University of Massachusetts, to say nothing of many smaller schools.

Prominent among learned societies are the American Academy of Arts and Sciences, founded in 1780 by John Adams, which now publishes *Daedalus*; the Massachusetts Historical Society (1791), the oldest group in the United States concerned with colonial history; and the Colonial Society of Massachusetts, which supports *The New England Quarterly*. The Lowell Institute, founded on a bequest from John Lowell, Jr., in 1840, has ever since that date sponsored public lectures and, during recent years, college courses and television programs. The Boston Athenaeum (1807) was established by the Anthology Society, which sponsored *The Monthly Anthology* and *The North American Review*. The Boston Public Library, the first large, tax-supported free library in the United States, began in 1854; the Italian Renaissance palace it inhabits was designed by McKim, Mead, and White in 1887-95; an extensive addition was completed in 1972. It seems doubtful that any comparable area in the United States can match the library facilities of Greater Boston.

Boston Public Library, before 1916, photograph by Baldwin Coolidge. Courtesy of Boston Library, Print Department

Massachusetts Institute of Technology, Cambridge, as seen from Boston across the Charles River. MIT Historical Collections

The Great Coliseum. Location of the World's Peace Jubilee, held in Boston from June 17 to July 4, 1872.
Library of Congress

74

Copley Square, circa 1950, photograph. On the right is the Public Library. On the bottom left is Trinity Church; above Trinity Church is the Copley Plaza Hotel; and across the street, the S.S. Pierce building, now destroyed. Courtesy of the Boston Public Library, Print Department

Bird's Eye View of Projected Plan for Copley Square by McKim, Mead & White, c. 1900, photograph of etching. Courtesy of the Boston Public Library, Print Department

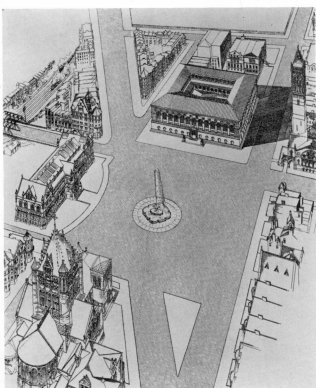

Plaque on site of home of John Singleton Copley, Boston. New York Public Library Picture Collection

The Boston *Advertiser*, founded in 1813, long enjoyed great influence and reputation; it now survives only as part of the name of a Sunday paper. For many years the highly literate and genteel *Evening Transcript* perfectly reflected both the virtues and the limitations of Boston Brahmins. It is gone now, and the *Post*, which spoke for Irish Boston, is gone too; the once powerful Republican *Herald* has been more or less swallowed up by the Hearst press and become the daily *Herald-American* and Sunday *Herald-Advertiser*; in modern Boston the liberal *Globe* reigns supreme. Boston publishing houses have always been highly respected: Houghton Mifflin Company; Little, Brown and Company (now controlled by Time-Life); and, especially during recent years, the Unitarian but not sectarian Beacon Press and, across the river, Harvard University Press.

Liberalism in any sense can hardly be called a factor, however, in the behavior responsible for the bad publicity Boston has been receiving during recent years in connection with the resistance shown in certain sections to court-ordered busing of schoolchildren in the interest of racial integration. One need not necessarily believe that busing is the inevitable answer to the problems that have arisen in this area, or even an acceptable one, neither need one fail to sympathize with the sense of community which has been preserved in certain areas after much of the rest of the city and America in general has lost it, to be disgusted and horrified by the sight on television screens of white mothers standing on street corners and shouting insults at Negro children. It must be added, I fear, that few intelligent people in the Boston area have any faith in the disinterestedness of the Boston School Committee or, for all the disclaimers of racial bias that have been made, can see any evidence that they have made any real effort to provide good schools in predominantly black districts.

Left

Benjamin West, an engraving by H. Meyer from the painting by T. Lawrence. Library of Congress

Right

Washington Allston. Johnson Fry & Co., after Chappel. Library of Congress

Literature is not the only art in which Boston has done well. Benjamin West, Washington Allston, Gilbert Stuart, John Singleton Copley, and others are among the early painters who, though they did not belong to Boston exclusively, still had important connections with the city. Charles Bulfinch (1763-1844) probably created more architectural beauty in the city than any other man, in addition to being a distinguished public servant. The central portion of the State House is today his most familiar monument, but he bankrupted himself over the ill-fated Tontine Crescent, comprising sixteen connected brick houses, suggesting London or

Gilbert Stuart: painting by Sarah Goodbridge. Library of Congress

Right

John Singer Sargent: a self-portrait painted in 1892. New York Public Library Picture Collection

Charles Bulfinch. Library of Congress

The Museum of Fine Arts at the present day: a rear view from the Fenway showing the Robert Dawson Evans Galleries for Painting, 1915. FPG

World War II Memorial in the Fenway. FPG

Bath, which was doomed by the expansion of the business district. The Museum of Fine Arts, especially distinguished for its Oriental and Egyptian collections, developed out of the Athenaeum, which in the beginning was an art gallery as well as a library, and was sponsored at its birth by that institution, Harvard, and the Massachusetts Institute of Technology. Its first independent home was a Gothic edifice in Copley Square; the oldest portion of its present vast building dates from 1907. Other distinguished museums are the Fogg at Harvard and the Isabella Stewart Gardner Museum (Fenway Court), which Mrs. Gardner, probably Bos-

Jenny Lind, "The Swedish Nightingale," lithograph, 1850, after the portrait by Edward Magnus. Library of Congress

William Morris Hunt: a self-portrait. Library of Congress

ton's greatest collector and perhaps its most picturesque personage, built at the beginning of the century to house her own collections and which was dedicated to the public after her death, with the proviso that nothing might be even slightly altered from the way she had arranged it.

Lowell Mason's presence in Lyman Beecher's Boston church brought that organization to the fore in the development of church music. The distinguished, still flourishing Handel and Haydn Society dates from

1815. Barnum brought Jenny Lind to Boston in 1850, where she had to sing in the Fitchburg Railroad Station. Tickets for her first concert were sold at auction, the top price paid being $625. In 1852 she was married in Louisburg Square to her accompanist, Otto Goldschmidt. The New England Conservatory of Music dates from 1867. It is the fashion to make fun of the great Peace Jubilees of 1869 and 1872 because they involved such an extravagance as the performance of the Anvil Chorus from *Il Trovatore* by a thousand instruments, one thousand voices, and a hundred firemen hammering on their anvils, to the accompaniment of organ, church bells, and discharge of cannon, but they did offer such distinguished artists as Ole Bull, Adelaide Phillips, Euphrosyne Parepa-Rosa, and Erminia Rudersdorff, mother of the actor Richard Mansfield, who came in 1872 and remained in Boston as a teacher of singing. In 1881 Major Henry Lee Higginson founded

Lowell Mason, one of the most important figures in early Boston musical life, from an engraving by G. E. Perine, 1873. Library of Congress

the Boston Symphony Orchestra, and at the beginning of the new century, McKim, Mead, and White built Symphony Hall to house it. Nowadays the BSO performs virtually all the year round. In the spring Symphony Hall turns itself into a beer garden for the "Pops" concerts; later there are outdoor performances on the Esplanade by the Charles and a whole summer season at Tanglewood in the Berkshires.

Though the most famous of all American prima donnas, Geraldine Farrar, came from Melrose, Boston has done much less well by opera than by symphony. The resident Boston Opera Company lasted only from 1909 to 1914, and after the fine Opera House which Eben D. Jordan had built was insanely torn down in 1957, the visiting Metropolitan company had to go first to a large movie theater and then to the barnlike War Memorial Auditorium at the Prudential Center. Of late years, Sarah Caldwell's Opera Company of Boston has mounted much-admired productions, but this group attempts only four such enterprises a year, and unfortunately lives from hand to mouth economically.

The Puritans had no sympathy with the drama. As late as 1791 a move to abolish the ban on playacting failed, and the actors who tried to present *Macbeth, The School for Scandal,* and *Venice Preserved* as "moral lectures" came to grief. In 1794 Bulfinch's Federal Theater was opened, but as late as 1841 the Boston Museum was attempting to achieve respectability by pretending that their plays were a kind of afterthought to the educational exhibitions. There William Warren and Mrs. Vincent were prime favorites for many years, and there, in 1849, Edwin Booth made his first appearance on any stage. In 1854 the Millerite Temple was rebuilt as the Howard Athenaeum, upon whose boards most of the great actors of the late nineteenth century appeared. Later it declined to vaudeville, still later to strip-tease burlesque, and finally to inactivity, until it burned just in time to avoid being torn down to make room for the new government buildings in what had become Scollay Square and its unsavory environs. A school was named for Charlotte Cushman, most famous of all Boston (and American) actresses, who began as a choir girl in Dr. Channing's church, and a hospital for Mrs. Vincent. The famous Lotta (Charlotte Crabtree), who began her career in California mining camp country, lived in her later years at Boston's Hotel Brunswick, which she owned, and died in 1924, leaving the largest theatrical fortune accumulated up to that time to charity. The Globe, the Copley, the Castle Square, and other famous Boston theaters are gone now, and today only three of the remaining "legitimate" playhouses are thus employed, principally for pre-Broadway engagements. Meanwhile semiprofessional, college, and café theaters attract some attention.

Some years ago, a delightful cartoon showed two dowagers en route to Boston, one presumably for the first time. "I must warn you," said the other in effect, "that most of Boston isn't there anymore. They've torn it down and replaced it with something else." Many a truth is spoken in jest. Except for the West Church and the Harrison Gray Otis house next door, which now accommodates the Society for the Preservation of New England Antiquities, the West End was virtually razed by bulldozers. Since then there has been legislation protecting some areas, and "urban renewal" has proceeded elsewhere in a more rational manner, with some persons even possessing themselves of fine old houses in the South End and attempting to rehabilitate that area as a residential neighborhood. Nobody can deny that the great new buildings in the financial district convey a sense of power, but I should hesitate to call them beautiful. When a highly ornamental subway station was built on the Common many years ago, it was bawdily objected that the Public Library had "pupped" there; there is far more justification today for the widely expressed fear that the new First National Bank Building, which bulges in the middle, might be getting ready to reproduce itself, which would be a horrible thing to contemplate. Even the builders of the new Christian Science complex have been criticized for dispossessing low-income families and erecting high-rental apartments, and it is hard to find any defense for a city which can tolerate the ruination of Frederick Law

Olmsted's beautiful Fenway by means of building an elevated highway over it. But the worst atrocities of all have been perpetrated in and just off Copley Square, where we now have a very ugly accumulation of concrete in the center and the whole area overwhelmed by the new John Hancock tower, which is not only hideous in itself but hopelessly out of harmony with all its surroundings. All in all, it seems a pity that the ban on skyscrapers was ever removed in Boston; she can never be more than a second-string New York, and it is sad to see her destroying her own distinctive character in such a bad cause.

II. HARTFORD

Charles Dickens thought Hartford "a lovely place," which he left with "no little regret" and expected never to "remember with indifference." He added that it was "beautifully situated in a basin of green hills" and that the soil was "rich, well-wooded, and carefully improved." It lies on the west bank of the Connecticut River, and in prerailroad days, its position near the head of river navigation and on the main coach road between Boston and New York was notably strategic for all purposes of trade.

The settlement of Hartford and other Connecticut towns in the mid-1630s has been treated in the first chapter of this book. The name dates from 1637. The city was organized in 1665 and incorporated in 1784. The "Fundamental Orders" were written there. The story of the state's charter having been hidden in the "Charter Oak" when Governor Andros tried to seize it may well be apocryphal, but when the great tree, conjecturally then about eight hundred years old, was blown down during a tempest, on August 21, 1856, its

Connecticut State seal. Detail engraving by George Murray from the engraving "Declaration of Independence" published by John Binns, 1818. Library of Congress

"The Charter Oak," painting by Charles DeWolf Brownell, in the Wadsworth Atheneum, Hartford. Courtesy Wadsworth Atheneum, Hartford

charter
Oak

Study

Thomas Hooker's House 1640.

Thomas Hooker's house, 1640. It was Hooker who led his congregation to Hartford from "Newtown" (Cambridge, Mass.). By Charles B. Woods. *The Hartford Times*

Above

"Montevideo," painting by Thomas Cole, in the Wadsworth Atheneum, Hartford. Courtesy Wadsworth Atheneum, Hartford

Below

"Hooker's Party Coming to Hartford," painting by Frederic Church, in the Wadsworth Atheneum, Hartford. Courtesy Wadsworth Atheneum, Hartford

loss was mourned like the death of a great man. Bells were tolled, leading citizens gathered around it, and Colt's Armory Band played the Dead March from *Saul*, "Home, Sweet Home" and "Hail, Columbia!"

Though Hartford sent forty-seven men to the Pequot War, she herself experienced no serious trouble with the Indians. Willis S. Twitchell's local patriotism attributes her freedom from massacres to her "honest treatment" of the red men, and though this may not completely cover the case, she certainly deserves credit for it, so far as it existed and as far as it goes.

In the early days, a watchman rang a bell through the streets an hour before daybreak (one person was required to be stirring in every dwelling within fifteen minutes), and church bells tolled good-night at 9 P.M. into the nineteenth century. Cruel punishments included branding, flogging, and cropping ears; theoretically a son could be put to death for striking or cursing a parent, but the extreme penalties were not often invoked. Forty years before the epidemic in Salem, however, nine persons were accused of witchcraft, of whom three were hanged. Early Hartfordians seem to have been greatly agitated over defamation. In 1646 one slanderer was sentenced to stand in the pillory, suffer whipping, pay a fine, and spend six months in jail, but

when one "goody" accused another of having blackened her name, the court decided that she had only told the truth! Sexual offenses may, as some believe, have been committed mainly by the servant class, but the zeal of the fathers to get everybody married and promptly remarried after a death (a girl of twenty-five was "an ancient maid," and at one time bachelors were taxed), though no doubt economically motivated in part, does not suggest that they had much faith in anybody's ability to live celibate.

When the repeal of the Stamp Act was celebrated in Hartford, there was an explosion of fireworks that destroyed the schoolhouse. In June 1774 the "First Hartford Convention" adopted resolutions condemning the importation of British goods. After the Battle of Lexington, four companies were raised; the Ticonderoga expedition was planned in Hartford, and a Hartford man was second in command. Though no battle was fought in or near the city, there was considerable wartime tension, and the inhabitants were always prepared for the worst. Troops marched through, and Washington and Rochambeau conferred. Prisoners, Tories, and some British officials were brought to Hartford, and several deserters were executed there. News of the peace achieved on January 20, 1783 was not received

The Hartford Convention: a contemporary cartoon. Library of Congress

until March 27. "As the express came solely to bring the news, and we had no doubt of its being true," reported the *Courant*, "the inhabitants of the town manifested their extreme joy by the firing of cannon, ringing of bells, and in the evening fireworks and illuminations."

We hear much of the degraded, irreligious character of society after the Revolution, but since children were still being required to stand when an elder entered the room and one young lady advertised that her father had given her permission to teach music, family discipline had obviously not wholly collapsed in Hartford. As a matter of fact, Sabbath traveling was prohibited or regulated up to the middle of the nineteenth century, and shops were required to close on Saturday night. Postwar economic conditions were bad, however, for the Revolution had cost much money, and Connecticut people were repaid in debased coin or not at all. In 1780 a phenomenally dark day brought fears of the Judgment, and an adjournment of the Council was only prevented by the protest of Abraham Davenport (worthily commemorated in Whittier's poem), who declared that if the Lord came, he wished to be found at his appointed task, and called for candles.

The depression in the shipping trade occasioned by the War of 1812 played an important part in turning Hartford's face toward manufactures. In December 1814 the Hartford Convention condemned the Madison policies, recommended that the states control defense, and proposed seven Constitutional amendments. This Convention has often been denounced as a move toward disunion, but however that may be, it should be remembered that the call was issued by Massachusetts and that among the seven Connecticut delegates only one was from Hartford.

In the 1820s the *Courant* was concerned about both lotteries and liquor, advocating total abstinence and (in 1832) refusing liquor advertisements. (A statewide prohibition law, passed in 1854, was not, however, effectively enforced.) The *Courant* was antislavery also, but opposed extremists on both sides, including Garrison, and advocated colonization of Negroes. Hartford was represented in the first Battle of Bull Run, and many Hartford men died at Antietam. Hartford banks lent the government a half million for military purposes, but Hartford and New Haven voted $200,000 each to assist those who wished to pay bounties to avoid the draft. Hartford was hard hit by the Panic of 1873, which came the same year it was finally decided that she should be the sole capital of Connecticut, an honor she had hitherto shared with New Haven. Richard Upjohn's capitol building was erected in 1879.

Hartford's prominence as an arms center brought her prosperity during both world wars, but after World War I, Attorney-General A. Mitchell Palmer's Gestapolike methods were nowhere more ruthlessly or illegally applied than there. Liberals of every stripe, especially those of·foreign extraction, were arrested and imprisoned without warrant or just because of suspicion as "anarchists" and "Bolshevists," including some who had only gone to the jails to visit the prisoners, and all this was shamefully supported by Connecticut newspapers and other local forces. In 1928 Alfred E. Smith received a frenzied welcome in Hartford. He

One of the first model 10s manufactured by the Royal Typewriter Company, Hartford. The model 10s were produced between 1906 and 1928. Smithsonian Institution Photo No. 32418-C

carried that city, New Haven, Bridgeport, and Waterbury, but though the Democrats polled a larger number of votes than ever before in Connecticut history, Hoover still won the state. In March 1936, when the Connecticut River rose thirty-five feet, the streets on Hartford's east side became canals and Bushnell Park a lake. Electric power was knocked out, and boats met arriving travelers. Over a thousand homes were evacuated, several lives were lost, and property damage ran to $25,000,000. On July 6, 1944, there was a heartbreaking accident, when the Ringling Brothers Circus tent burned during a performance and killed 168, many of them children.

Steamer service to New York began in the 1820s, and the railroads arrived early in the thirties. Hartford's position now seemed less impregnable than before, and the fear that Providence, Springfield, New Haven, and other communities might outstrip her encouraged industrialization. An almost encyclopedic list of products are or have been manufactured in the city, including bedsprings, candles, carriages, cotton goods, drop forgings, electrical equipment, engines and boilers, gold leaf, hats, hook-and-eye machines, leather goods, millwork, mirrors, paper, pewterware, plows, printing presses and ink, screws, sheet iron, shoes, soap, tinware, tools and dies, umbrellas, woolen goods, and other articles too numerous to mention. The state also claims an astonishing number of "firsts" in industrial processes and inventions, etc.; the list in the WPA "American Guide Series" runs to more than five pages of fine, closely printed type.

Before 1800 there were shipbuilding, clockmaking,

bellcasting, watchmaking, brickmaking, and furniture making (including the "Hartford—or Connecticut—Chest"). There was a fulling mill about 1700, and the silk industry began before 1750. Florence Crofut gives the Hart Woolen Company (1788) credit for the first commercial woolen mill in America, operated by water power; George Washington wore a suit made of their broadcloth on a public occasion, though he ungraciously stated that he did not think the material quite first rate. Rogers Brothers silverware goes back to 1847. In 1878 Colonel A. A. Pope built the first Columbia bicycle; by 1900 he was employing thirty-eight hundred people, and in 1907 he turned out the Columbia Electric Phaeton, of which one specimen was reported still on the road in 1938. In 1880 William Gray and others invented pay station telephone equipment. Pratt and Whitney developed standard length precision gauges and tools and in 1885 produced a standard measuring machine, accurate to the one hundred thousandth of an inch. During recent years they have taken on aircraft motors and established a great plant in East Hartford whose proximity has not proved an unmixed blessing to the city. From 1894 on, the Veeder-Root Company was busy developing cyclometers and various counting devices, including speedometers and counters on gas pumps. The Underwood Typewriter people arrived in 1889, to be joined by Royal in 1906, which was the same year that Alvin T. Fuller established, on $400, one of the most distinctive businesses of the twentieth century and began developing the "Fuller brush man" into what became almost a figure of latter-day American folklore.

Samuel Colt was born in 1814, the son of a Massachusetts manufacturer. At sixteen, while at sea, he constructed his first pistol model. Returning home, he first worked in his father's factory, then, at eighteen, made a lecture tour, demonstrating the uses of laughing gas. In 1836 he formed a company for manufacturing revolvers in Paterson, New Jersey, which soon failed, but the use of his pistols in the Seminole War marked the turning of the tide. He was granted a patent for revolving firearms, constructed a submarine battery, and laid a telegraph cable to Coney Island. Moving to Hartford, he established himself first on Pearl Street, then, around 1855, developed the great armory at South Meadow, whose elaborately organized factory embodied what were then very novel industrial plans and ideas. Colt's firm also manufactured Richard Gordon Gatling's "Gatling gun" and John M. Browning's automatic pistol, while the Sharps Company achieved a breech-loading rifle and later made Hotchkiss guns.

To the general public, Hartford is primarily "the insurance city." Though she does not monopolize the insurance business, she does have a very large share of it. It commands tremendous assets, and the enormous

Alfred C. Fuller and the first plant of the Fuller Brush Company in Hartford, 1906. New York Public Library Picture Collection

Sam Colt. New York Public Library Picture Collection

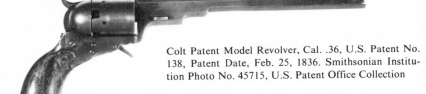

Colt Patent Model Revolver, Cal. .36, U.S. Patent No. 138, Patent Date, Feb. 25, 1836. Smithsonian Institution Photo No. 45715, U.S. Patent Office Collection

U.S. Semi-automatic Pistol (Browning's patent), Model 1902, Cal. .38. Manufactured by Colt's Patent Fire Arms Mfg. Co. Smithsonian Institution Photo No. 41982-C, Colt's Pt. Fire Arms Mfg. Co.

U.S. Sharps Breechloading Rifle, Model 1855, Cal. .53. Manufactured by Sharps Rifle Manufacturing Co., Hartford. Smithsonian Institution Photo No. 72075, Navy Department Collection

Armory of Colt's Patent Fire Arms Manufacturing Company. Lithograph in J. Deane Alden, "Proceedings of the Dedication of Charter Oak Hall . . . , 1860." Library of Congress

modernistic buildings in which it now houses have transformed the face of the city. The enterprise began with the need of merchants to be insured against the risk of sea voyages. The first known fire insurance policy was written in 1794, and Hartford's reputation was greatly boosted when, after a great fire in New York, in 1835, Hart's president went there and promised to pay all policies in full. The great Chicago Fire of 1871 involved seven Hartford companies, of whom Hart, Aetna, Phoenix, and Fairfield County paid all claims. In 1906 the San Francisco earthquake and fire cost Hartford firms $18,000,000.

Connecticut Mutual (1848) was the first life insurance company. Phoenix began in 1851 as the American Temperance Life Insurance Company, insuring only total abstainers, Travellers in 1863 with a policy costing two cents to insure a businessman's safety on his way home to dinner and back to his office. At first it insured only against travel risks, later becoming the first multiple-line company. In 1897 it issued its first automobile, in 1919 its first aircraft insurance policies. In 1913 it pioneered in group life insurance.

Disestablishment of Congregationalism as the state church in Connecticut was not fully achieved until

The Front and Market streets area before demolition to make way for the construction of Constitution Plaza. Greater Hartford Chamber of Commerce

Constitution Plaza. An outstanding urban renewal project with unique two-sided home office of Phoenix Life Insurance Company in the foreground. Greater Hartford Chamber of Commerce

Constitution Plaza at Christmastime. Greater Hartford Chamber of Commerce

The old and new homes of the Phoenix Mutual Life Insurance Company, an excellent example of how modern architects progressively achieve the uglification of American cities. Greater Hartford Chamber of Commerce

Lyman Beecher. Engraving by C. E. Wagstaff & J. Andrews from a daguerreotype. Library of Congress

Horace Bushnell. The Bettmann Archive

1818, though from 1791 dissenters had been excused from paying church taxes, provided they were supporting other religious establishments. When disestablishment came, Lyman Beecher first felt that religion had suffered a body blow, but he soon came to perceive that the power of the church had only been increased by being placed upon the only tenable, because purely spiritual, basis. Hartford Seminary Foundation was begun in the 1830s to save "the sound doctrines of New England Calvinism" for those who now found "New Haven Divinity" too liberal. Episcopalianism in Hartford dates back to 1761-62, Methodism to 1790, the Baptists to 1794, Universalism to 1821, Unitarianism to 1830, Presbyterianism to 1850. The local YWCA (1867) is called the second in the United States. The most famous Hartford clergyman of the nineteenth century was Horace Bushnell, pastor of North Church from 1833 to 1859. Joseph H. Twichell, first pastor (1865) of the fashionable Asylum Hill Church, in the Nook Farm district, who was a follower of Bushnell's, owes his fame among literary people to his close friendship with Mark Twain.

Mass was apparently first sung in Hartford by Rochambeau's chaplain in 1781. In 1813 Father Martignon, tarrying in Hartford over the Sabbath, is said to

Center Church. Hartford's first meetinghouse, 1636. This spot is at the southeast corner of present-day Meeting House Square. By Charles B. Woods. *The Hartford Times*

Center Church, fourth meetinghouse built 1807. Architect, Daniel Wadsworth, its minister. *The Hartford Times*

Center Church, third meetinghouse. Located at the southeast corner of Old Burying Ground, at virtually the same site as present Center Church, Main Street, corner of Gold Street. By Charles B. Woods. *The Hartford Times*

Center Church, second meetinghouse, 1670, same location as first meetinghouse. Artist, Charles B. Woods. *The Hartford Times*

South Church, Hartford, 1827. Congregational. The builder was Colonel William Hayden of Windsor and Hartford; there exists a recommendation of the Architectural Committee of 1824-25 to follow the plan of the North Church in New Haven. The Connecticut Historical Society

Reverend Thomas Gallaudet. Library of Congress

Lydia Huntley Sigourney, "The Sweet Singer of Hartford." Library of Congress

have preached from a Protestant pulpit, an amazing example of ecumenical tolerance for the period, but the first Catholic parish was not established before the 1820s. Congregation Beth Israel began in 1847; oddly enough, its first rabbi was also drama critic of the *Times*. Though Jews had entered Connecticut politics long before, there was no Jewish governor until Hartford's Abraham Ribicoff was elected in 1954.

Education in Hartford did not get off to a particularly brilliant start. In 1650 the state decreed the establishment of elementary schools in all townships containing fifty families or more and Latin grammar schools wherever one hundred might be counted, but no serious attempts were made to implement or finance this decree until toward the end of the century. Of course not all the early private schools can be traced. Lydia Huntley, later Mrs. Sigourney, opened a small school in 1815, and Catharine and Mary Beecher of Litchfield opened their school for girls in 1823. Four years later, Catharine, one of the important educators of her time, organized the Hartford Female Seminary. Noah Webster said that in his youth the Bible and Dilworth's spelling book were the texts the schools relied on. There was no geography text until 1789, nor a school history text. A system of public high schools was sponsored by Henry

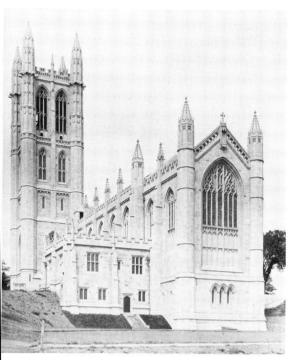

Trinity College Chapel. *The Hartford Times*

Barnard, whose influence began to make itself felt about 1838. Hartford set up its first public high school in 1847, following Middletown but antedating New Haven and New London. When Barnard wrote about education in J. Hammond Trumbull's *Memorial History of Hartford County* (1886), he chivalrously placed the ladies of Hartford "as high in intelligence, virtue, and accomplishment as those of any community," but was yet "obliged to confess [that] we have no certain evidence of the existence of any very good schools which they could have attended . . . till near the beginning of the present century." Three generations of the Gallaudet family were important pioneers in educating the deaf. In 1823 the Episcopalians established Washington College, after 1845 called Trinity College, whose Gothic chapel is one of the architectural glories of New England. The University of Hartford has now become an important part of the local educational scene.

Though a really vast amount of printing and publishing has been done at Hartford (including a hundred periodicals, it has been said, between 1764 and 1868), no Hartford firm has become a ranking American publisher. After the Civil War, however, the city became the center of the subscription book trade, whose agents

Trinity College, from an old print, when it was located where the state capitol now stands. *The Hartford Times*

View of Hartford from the river, with old-fashioned steamboat. Library of Congress

brought reading matter to vast numbers of Americans with no access to bookstores. But though the American Publishing Company gained fame as the publisher of Mark Twain's early books, most of their showy but not elegantly made volumes had little significance for literature. The *Courant* (1764), later united with the *Press*, claims to be the oldest American newspaper continuously published. In the early days it included much literary material. Charles Dudley Warner was once connected with it, and Gideon Welles was an editorial writer on the *Times* in the 1850s and returned to that paper after his service in Lincoln's and Johnson's cabinets.

Roger Wolcott's *Poetical Meditations* (1725) was the first book of verse published in Connecticut, and mention is made elsewhere of the "Hartford Wits." John G. C. Brainard (1796-1828), poet laureate of the Connecticut Valley, who exercised some influence upon Whittier, lived in Hartford toward the close of his life. Emma Willard (1787-1870), who published many textbooks and manuals of huge circulation, is now remembered only for "Rocked in the Cradle of the Deep." Hartford saw much of Noah Webster until about 1785, and he published his famous spelling book there, but Samuel G. Goodrich ("Peter Parley") achieved his most extensive publishing in Boston.

Henry Howard Brownell was an outstanding Civil War poet, and Henry C. Work, who wrote the temperance song, "Father, Dear Father, Come Home with Me Now," was the great man for war songs, including the notorious "Marching through Georgia." The stories and poems of Rose Terry Cooke were important in the New England local color movement.

Hartford's most important period as a literary center dates from the 1870s when Mark Twain, Harriet Beecher Stowe, and Charles Dudley Warner lived in close proximity and on easy terms of familiarity in the Nook Farm area. James Hammond Trumbull, first librarian of the Watkinson Library and a phenomenal linguist, contributed the learned and ponderous epigraphs to the Clemens-Warner novel, *The Gilded Age*, and Caroline Maria Hewins, for more than half a century at the Hartford Public Library, had great influence on children's libraries throughout America. John Fiske, historian and philosopher, and Edmund Clarence Stedman, poet, critic, and stockbroker, were born in Hartford, though their careers lay elsewhere. The most famous recent Hartford man of letters was Wallace Stevens, poet and insurance man. Odell Shepard, essayist, novelist, and scholar, was a professor at Trinity.

Among early nineteenth-century painters, neither William Gedney Bunce nor Dwight William Tryon re-

Charles Dudley Warner, 1897. Library of Congress

Samuel L. Clemens ("Mark Twain"). Library of Congress

Rose Terry Cooke. New York Public Library Picture Collection

Mark Twain's "English violet" house, at 351 Farmington Avenue, Hartford, designed by Edwin T. Potter, 1874, now restored and open to the public. Mark Twain Memorial, Hartford, Conn.

Harriet Beecher Stowe house, 1871, at 73 Forest Avenue. Open to the public. The Stowe-Day Foundation, Hartford, Conn.

Memorial to Spanish War Veterans, Bushnell Park. *Hartford Times* photo by Ted Kosinski

mained in Hartford. Later a good deal of activity centered around Charles Noel Flagg and the Connecticut League of Art Students. Frederick Edwin Church was the son of a Connecticut proprietor, and Frederick Law Olmsted, the great environmentalist and designer of landscapes, was born in Hartford in 1822. There is record of an orchestral concert as early as 1795. Jenny Lind's concert in 1851 was marred by rioting among those who, unable to gain admittance to Fourth Church, were trying to hear her from nearby roofs and fences; fortunately other visiting artists had better luck. Dudley Buck, important for American organ music, was born in Hartford in 1839, studied at Trinity, and was the North Church organist. There was a Philharmonic Orchestra between 1899 and 1924, and there have been many other musical organizations, to say nothing of the Hartford School of Music and kindred foundations.

In 1795 the *Courant* reviewed "a celebrated comedy entitled the *Dramatist* at 'the new theater.' " Opposition developed, however, and in 1800 there was a state law against "theatrical shows and exhibitions." A "Philo-Literary Society" tried it again in 1826, but its members were fined or imprisoned, and it was not until the middle of the century that jurisdiction in such matters was passed to the individual communities. In the meantime, of course, the drama had been trying to creep in under the guise of "moral lectures," etc., and

Bushnell Park. *Hartford Times*

there were many panoramas, dioramas, waxworks, circuses, exhibitions of wild animals, and freak sideshows like those presented later in amusement parks. Yet a clergyman recommended dancing as an elegant accomplishment as early as 1791 (the "Assembly" developed thereafter out of cotillion parties), and the prizefighter Heenan was allowed to give a boxing exhibition in 1860! Five years earlier, the *Courant*, though generally hostile to the theater, succumbed to *Uncle Tom's Cabin* and Cordelia Howard's Eva and urged citizens to see this "excellent moral drama." The actor-playwright William Gillette, the producer Charles B. Dillingham, and the stage and screen star Katharine Hepburn are Hartford's best-known theatrical celebrities, and The Hartford Stage is a respected modern professional company.

The 1970 census gave Hartford nearly 156,000 inhabitants. The city embraces one of the outstanding American Jewish communities, and there are numerous Italians, Slavs, and blacks. Mark Twain's beautiful "English violet house," now happily restored and open to the public, is the best known of all the fine and elaborate residences, in various imaginative and eclectic styles, which nineteenth-century architects produced in Hartford, not all of which, unfortunately, have survived. During the first two decades of the twentieth century, even the Bulfinch State House (1796) narrowly escaped razing; the Colonial Dames, the D.A.R., and

Governor's Mansion, Hartford. Greater Hartford Chamber of Commerce. Photo by *The Hartford Courant*

96

Present-day Hartford: The Travelers Insurance Co. is at the far left; the spire to its right is the Travelers (Insurance Co.) Tower. Phoenix Mutual Life Insurance Co. is at right center. The taller building at right center is One Financial Plaza; with the Travelers Insurance Co. directly in front of it. Next to the right is Hartford National Bank & Trust Co. The Old State House, designed by Charles Bulfinch in 1796, is visible in front of it. At the far right is the Connecticut Bank & Trust Co. Greater Hartford Chamber of Commerce

Present-day Hartford. Greater Hartford Chamber of Commerce

Senator Morgan G. Bulkeley all performed valiant service in blocking this commercially inspired barbarity. But Hartford has had a city planning commission since 1907, and 22 percent of her area is devoted to parks and squares, of which Bushnell Park, named for Horace Bushnell, the great theologian, in honor of the efforts he made to establish it, is the largest. There has always been some difference of opinion about Bushnell Memorial Hall (1930), which is an architectural hybrid, but whose auditorium Leopold Stokowski called the finest for music in the country. Probably no other city

Wadsworth Atheneum, exterior view. ➔
Courtesy Wadsworth Atheneum, Hartford

Hartford from the air. Greater Hartford Chamber of Commerce

can boast such a center as the Wadsworth Atheneum, designed in the early 1840s by Daniel Wadsworth to accommodate various intellectual and aesthetic interests. It now embraces the Public Library, the Avery Memorial Art Museum (with its valuable American and European paintings, the Wallace Nutting Collection of early American furniture, the Brainard Collection of Connecticut inn signs, and much besides), the Connecticut Historical Society, and the Morgan Memorial, given by J. P. Morgan, a Hartford native, in honor of his father.

Looking out from the Morgan Memorial. Courtesy Wadsworth Atheneum, Hartford

III. PROVIDENCE

In 1909 President W. H. P. Faunce of Brown University wrote of colonial Providence that "on the one hand it was a sacred ark, carrying within it a few great seers and prophets who discerned a principle which has since become fundamental in the Republic," while, on the other hand, "it was a cave of Adullam, where every eccentric and impossible spirit from all the other colonies made his way and claimed asylum." He added that "out of the most heterogeneous of all the thirteen colonies has come by natural reaction the state of all in the North most averse to complete social and political freedom, a state still true to the ideals of Washington rather than those of Lincoln."

Pictorial map of Rhode Island by Ernest Clegg. ⓒ Ernest Clegg. Reprinted from *Country Life*, September, 1925. New York Public Library Picture Collection

State seal of Rhode Island, detail engraving by George Murray from the engraving "Declaration of Independence," published by John Binns, 1818. Library of Congress

Old milestone marker, at Woonsocket, Rhode Island. U.S. Bureau of Public Roads, National Archives

Benefit Street, Providence. Many of the houses on this street were built during the early days of the Republic and have been restored during recent years. Rhode Island Department of Economic Development

Natural perhaps, yet on the surface paradoxical, nor is this the only paradox to be encountered. Individualism has never died in Providence. Benefit Street was laid out like a winding road to avoid "all the buildings and graves possible," and after a clergyman had declined to report the marriage ceremonies he had conducted on the ground that a citizen could not be compelled to labor for the city without compensation, the courts decided that twenty-five cents must be paid for every such report. Yet this individualism runs hand-in-hand with what most of the country regards as extreme conservatism. Rhode Island's whole system of government is antiquated, and in spite of the presence of a cosmopolitan population in which the Irish, the French, and the Italians are now the largest non-Anglo-Saxon groups, most of the wealth of the city is still held by a small minority who concern themselves comparatively little with the responsibilities of government.

Rhode Island is, of course, the smallest state in the Union, and there is none other in which the capital city and its environs take up so large a share of the total area. It is easy to understand, then, why city, county, and state functions should be more closely interwoven, and perhaps less logically differentiated, here than elsewhere. The Providence Chamber of Commerce claims that Rhode Island is not only the most heavily industrialized state in the Union but also the most thickly wooded. The 1970 census gave the city proper 187,000 inhabitants, yet it is said that no part of it is more than

Dorrance Street, Providence. FPG

The Joseph Brown House (1774), 50 South Main Street, long the home of the Providence National Bank, and now the counting house of Brown and Ives, is notable for its unusual curved façade. It is now owned by Brown University. Photograph by Douglas Armsden, Kittery Point, Maine

The John Brown House (1786), 52 Power Street, where Washington and many notable visitors were guests, is now occupied by the Rhode Island Historical Society. Photograph by Douglas Armsden, Kittery Point, Maine

fifteen minutes ride from the center. "There are plenty of beautiful old buildings in the East of the United States," wrote Christopher La Farge in 1952, "but there are none more lovely, or built with greater grace and sophistication than those in Providence," but he added that even on the fashionable East Side, you may walk in any direction "from the centre of its grace and charm" and quickly find it declining "architecturally into dreary wooden slums, or geographically into the open sewer of the Providence River."

It is not wonderful that the modern city should now boast of her new "towering skyline," the "bold, new urban-renewal projects" which are changing her counte-

nance, the "splendid new Civic Centre" on Weybosset Hill, the "new high-rise motor hotel, member of a national chain" next door, nor yet of the "well-organized, fully serviced industrial parks . . . along the great superhighways that form the area's transportation network." It would indeed be far more wonderful if she were able to boast of the absence of such things. But she has preserved, and is preserving, many of her old architectural beauties, and she has a right to be proud of her free-standing homes (she was slower in taking to apartment dwelling than many large cities) and the continuity of family life that has been preserved in many of them. ("I see you have fifty feet of self-respect between

Aerial view of downtown Providence. Rhode Island Department of Economic Development

your houses and the street," observed James Russell Lowell when he visited there.) Providence has exceptionally good drinking water and an abundance of public parks, and for a reputedly conservative city, she has made some interesting experiments. If the shopping mall is something "modern" in most American cities, her Arcade (architecturally modeled on the Madeleine in Paris), which contains seventy-eight shops, and whose pillars are supposed to be the largest in America outside the Cathedral of St. John the Divine, dates back to 1828. During recent years both the city itself and her industrial establishments have shown themselves mindful of environmental problems. India Point has been transformed from a junk heap to a recreational area on the northern reaches of Narragansett Bay, and the Fox Hurricane Barrier Dam, the first of its kind in the world, has been designed to protect the city from the floods which have ravaged it in the past. There is probably no other American city in which great fortunes, even when questionably amassed, have been more generously devoted to culture, beauty, and the public welfare, and nobody can read such a book as Margaret Bingham Stilwell's *The Pageant of Benefit Street Down Through the Years* without being made

aware that the social life of Rhode Island's capital has known great elegance and charm.*

The familiar colonial history of Providence has been treated in the first chapter of this volume, but she has received surprisingly little credit, if that is the word to use, for her services in getting the Revolution started. The Rhode Island historian, Samuel Greene Arnold, declared in 1858 that she had struck "the first bold blow in all the colonies for freedom" and shed "the earliest blood" which flowed in the war for independence. His reference was to the *Gaspee* incident of June 9, 1772. The blood did not flow to the length of fatality, but even a nonfatal wound can please a patriot when nothing better is available. The British schooner *Gaspee*, engaged in enforcing the hated navigation acts, ran aground upon Namquit Point while chasing an American sloop. This was just what John Brown and other leading citizens of Providence had been waiting

*Published by the Akerman-Standard Press, Providence, 1945. See also George Leland Miner, *Angel's Lane: The History of a Little Street in Providence* (Akerman-Standard, 1948) and Florence Parker Simister, *Streets of the City, An Anecdotal History of Providence* (Providence, The Mowbray Company, 1948).

The Admiral Esek Hopkins House, 1756, home of the first commodore and commander-in-chief of the Continental Navy. Rhode Island Department of Economic Development

Home of Stephen Hopkins, who signed the Declaration of Independence and was governor of Rhode Island between 1755 and 1768. Built around 1707. Stephen was the brother of Esek. Rhode Island Department of Economic Development

for. A crier went through the town summoning volunteers to meet at Sabin's Tavern; at ten o'clock that night, they boarded the *Gaspee*, wounded Lieutenant Duddington, removed the crew, and burned the schooner to the water's edge. Nobody was ever apprehended, though the privateer captain Abraham Whipple, who had commanded the expedition, received a message from Admiral Wallace, threatening to hang him at the yardarm, to which he replied: "To Sir James Wallace: Sir, Always catch a man before you hang him." Less than three years later, on March 2, 1775, Providence had her own tea party, at which, instead of dumping tea into the harbor, as Boston was to do, she burned the "pernicious article" openly in the marketplace, and the *Gazette* reported the death of "Madam Souchong," who, having formerly lived in repute, had now become "a common prostitute among the lowest class of people." Then, on May 4, 1776, with great courage, little Rhode Island declared herself independent of England, two months to the day before the Philadelphia declaration. She was much less forward, however, in helping to establish the new nation. Jealous of the regulation of her trade from without, she sent no delegates to the Constitutional Convention, and she did not ratify the Constitution until May 29, 1790, and then by a very close vote.

In 1815 the "Great Gale" caused floods in the lower town, driving vessels from the harbor up into the streets (the waters were to rise even higher during the hurricane tidal wave of 1938). But the most sensational event of the early nineteenth century in Providence was the Dorr Rebellion of 1842.

The state was still operating under the Charter of 1663, which restricted the suffrage and created gross inequalities in town representation in the General Assembly. Attempts at reform began as early as 1796, but since the legislature was controlled by the landholders, nothing was accomplished. Thomas Wilson Dorr, a lawyer, Harvard graduate, and son of a Providence manufacturer, emerged as leader of the reformers about 1834. In 1840 he founded the Rhode Island Suffrage Association; the next year his People's Party held

Old State House, Providence. Built in 1762, corner of North Court and Benefit Street. Here with the Rhode Island Declaration of Independence on May 4, 1771, was proclaimed the first free republic in the New World. Rhode Island Department of Economic Development

a convention and drew up a constitution providing for manhood suffrage. When it became obvious that the opposition was determined not to yield, the People's Party elected Dorr governor. Visiting New York on his way home from a fruitless mission to Washington, he found allies, encouragement, and vain promises of support. On May 17, 1842, his forces moved against the Providence Armory. The attempt failed; martial law was proclaimed in Providence; one clergyman assailed Dorr as "a William Lloyd Garrison propagating errors of the worst character, assailing all government, the Holy Sabbath, and the Christian Ministry." In 1843 he was given a life term of solitary confinement and hard labor. In January 1845 he was offered his freedom if he would pledge allegiance to the existing government. He refused, and in June he was freed unconditionally.

Thomas W. Dorr, mezzotint, 1845, by W. Warner after daguerreotype. Library of Congress

Meanwhile a new constitution had given suffrage to adult males with $134 worth of real property or who paid an annual tax of one dollar or more.

The Providence Yearly Meeting of Friends condemned slavery in 1770, and in 1774 the importation of slaves into Rhode Island was prohibited, but the involvement of Rhode Islanders in the West Indian slave trade was not interfered with until 1787. Rhode Island freed her own slaves three years before that, however. Moses Brown anticipated the state's action in his own household by eleven years, and his brother John also made some antislavery gestures. Yet as late as 1799 John wished to be informed why Americans should "see Great Britain getting all the slave trade to themselves." In 1833 an antislavery meeting was held in Providence.

In Civil War activity both the state and the city were more forward, and more than a thousand men left Providence, under Ambrose E. Burnside, only a few days after Lincoln called for volunteers. Burnside, manufacturer of a breech-loading rifle, and famous for his casualties, was Rhode Island's leading military figure during the conflict. After the war, he was business tycoon, Governor of Rhode Island, and United States senator. Before 1900 Newport, Kingston, South Kingston, Bristol, East Greenwich, and Providence had all served as capitals of Rhode Island on a rotating basis; in that year Providence became the only capital, operating from a magnificent new building by McKim, Mead, and White, with a dome only less impressive than that of the National Capitol in Washington. During the early years of the twentieth century, Rhode Island's Senator Nelson W. Aldrich was one of the Republican stalwarts who dominated Senate legislation and seldom erred on the side of radicalism.

Rhode Island's somewhat confused political situation is of course her inheritance from a past with which she has never made a really clean break.

At a very early date in the history of the plantation [wrote Gertrude Selwyn Kimball], it became necessary for the "distressed of conscience" to satisfy the good people of Providence that he was able and willing to provide for his own maintenance before he was permitted to taste of the "sweet cup of liberty" in their fellowship. He might safely be trusted to work out his own salvation, but he must furnish a practical guaranty of his ability to provide bed and board for himself and family.

The constitution adopted after the Dorr Rebellion gave overwhelming power to the legislature, and though this has been modified by subsequent amendments, every attempt to write a completely new constitution has been frustrated. What has emerged has been a kind of working compromise between popular and geographic representation, an arrangement which at one time gave Providence forty-two state senators.

When it came to economic considerations, however,

Rhode Island state capitol, 1902, designed by McKim, Mead, and White. Rhode Island Department of Economic Development

geography inevitably proved determinative. The soil of Rhode Island is rocky, and her agricultural economy achieved its first triumphs in the production of white corn meal (for Rhode Island johnnycake), greening apples (for pie), and Rhode Island reds. But the Providence area has seventy-six miles of coastline facing the Atlantic and much more on inland waters. Whaling and slave trading began early, but Newport retained the maritime lead until about the middle of the eighteenth century; as late as 1704, Providence decreed that no more "warehouse lots by the salt water side" should be assigned, since the space was needed for cattle. After the Revolution, however, shipping brought great wealth to the city, and the merchant princes lived in handsome, luxuriously furnished houses. The Halsey mansion even had a ghost which played the piano and a bloodstain which could not be removed but which manifested only to those sympathetically inclined and disdained the merely curious or scientifically minded, and the home of Sullivan Dorr was modeled on Pope's villa at Twickenham and had murals of Italian landscapes by Michael Corné. Perhaps the most important Providence family was that of the Browns, whose foundations ran back to colonial times, but whose great days came with Nicholas, Joseph, John, and Moses, the four sons of James Brown, who died in 1739. The Browns engaged

Gorham silver. The Gorham Manufacturing Company, now one of the largest producers of sterling silver and hollow ware in the world, was founded in 1818 by Jabez Gorham, when he opened a modest shop in Providence, specializing in silver spoons. Rhode Island Department of Economic Development

Samuel Slater: engraving after a painting by Thomas Cole. Library of Congress

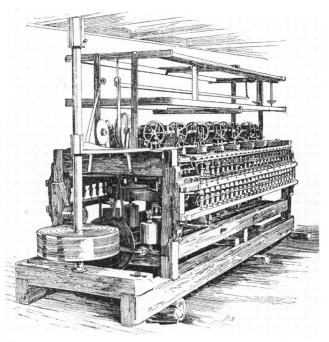

Slater spinning frame, 1890. From *Harper's Weekly.* Smithsonian Institution Photo No. 34789

in so many shipbuilding and trading ventures that at one time they were employing eighty-four vessels. After the Revolution John became the first Rhode Island merchant in oriental trade. After he had made his fortune, Joseph retired from business and became a scientist and an architect, a trustee of the Rhode Island College which later became Brown University, and Professor of Natural Philosophy there. It was he who designed for John the magnificent house on Power Street which John Quincy Adams thought the finest mansion in America and which now shelters the Rhode Island Historical Society.

But geography did not wholly favor Providence as a trading center. Her harbor is shallow for modern vessels, and as railroading developed, her communications with the interior fell behind those of Boston and New York. Samuel Slater set up his cotton mill in adjoining

An old view of Providence Harbor. Lithograph by Endicott & Co. after painting by J. B. Bachelder. Library of Congress

Providence Harbor. FPG

Pawtucket in 1790, and when the Browns backed him, their transition and that of their city from a trading to a manufacturing center had begun. Steam power came into the factories about 1812; by about 1850 the Corliss Company was building engines; by 1890 Providence was close to Philadelphia in wool manufactures. By this time too she had taken first place in the jewelry trade, which dated back to 1794, when Nehemiah Dodge began developing processes which, for the first time, brought jewelry within the range of middle-class people. Rubber goods, web and winding equipment, automotive filters, chemicals, electrical and electronic products, and precision tools are among other things that have been important to Providence economy. Gorham silver, Rumford Baking Powder, Speidel watchbands, Brown and Sharpe tools, and "U.S. Rubber" (now Uniroyal, Inc.) are familiar names everywhere in America.

The persons "distressed for conscience" for whose benefit Roger Williams founded Providence were Baptists as much as they were anything. They trace their

Statue of Roger Williams, in Roger Williams Park. Rhode Island Department of Economic Development

First Baptist Meetinghouse, Providence (1775), probably designed by Joseph Brown. The spire rises 185 feet from the ground. Rhode Island Department of Economic Development

beginnings back to 1639, and the present First Baptist Meeting House (1775) is one of our prized examples of colonial architecture. It still bears a plaque: "This church was founded by Roger Williams, its first pastor and the first asserter of liberty of conscience. It was the first Church in Rhode Island and the first Baptist Church in America." (Since the funds to build it were raised by a lottery, there were evidently some areas in which conscience was not oversensitive.) Pardon Tillinghast, who built the city's first wharf in 1680, received no pay for his services, as in his time salaried pastors were frowned upon; James Manning, late in the eighteenth century, was the Baptists' first "hireling shepherd." The Quakers were next in the field, about 1660, with George Fox himself visiting in 1672, and a meetinghouse built in 1723. The early 1720s also brought Congregationalists and Episcopalians. The former were split by the enthusiasm of the "New Lights" after the Whitefield campaign, and in 1743 the discontented faction withdrew, ultimately building the

Brown University campus. Rhode Island Department of Economic Development

renowned Beneficent or "Round-Top" Church. Methodism dates from about 1816. The 1820s brought Unitarians and Universalists and the thirties Roman Catholics and Swedenborgians, but there was no Presbyterian church until the seventies. The Calvinists called the First Universalist Church "Satan's Insurance Office," and one clergyman gave public thanks to God when it burned. The printed announcement of the installation of a two-hundred-pipe organ (1771-72) at the Episcopal King's Church sought to disarm the pious by quoting the Psalter: "Praise him with Organs"! Comparatively strict Sabbath laws survived in Providence late into the twentieth century.

The first Providence schoolmaster began his work in 1684, and the first schoolhouse was built in 1735. A high school building was erected in 1843. Rhode Island College, chartered in 1764, moved to Providence in 1770 and changed its name to Brown in 1804 when Nicholas Brown donated five thousand dollars. From the beginning it was provided that there must be no religious tests for students. The president must be a Baptist, but other offices were open to all Protestants. Religious controversies might be studied, but no sectarian views were to be taught, and the sciences must be "respected." Brown's Women's College became Pembroke in 1928. The Moses Brown School, now a Quaker preparatory school for boys, began at Portsmouth in 1784 and moved to Providence in 1819. Modern Providence has a considerable variety of schools on every level—general and specialized, secular and church-sponsored, including the modern thriving Rhode Island College, formerly Rhode Island College of Education and before that Rhode Island Normal School. For a city her size, she is rich too in libraries, embracing, besides a Public Library with a zealous, sometimes informal, outreach program, the Providence Athenaeum, the Rhode Island Historical Society, the John Carter Brown Library, with its outstanding collection of early books about the Western Hemisphere, and the Annmary Brown Memorial, with its impressive collection of printed books, 1450-1500.

The first newspaper was the Providence *Gazette and Country Journal* (1762). Today Providence gets local news from the morning and Sunday *Journal* and the *Evening Bulletin*, both published by the same company. D. B. Updike, who established the Merrymount Press in Boston and was considered the dean of American printers in his time, grew up on Benefit Street. Here too lived Sarah Helen Whitman, poet and, briefly, the love of Edgar Allan Poe. George William Curtis, author and orator, was born in Providence. Twentieth-century writers include Oliver and Christopher La Farge, Winfield Townley Scott, Brown's S. Foster Damon, and the master of "weird" tales, H. P. Lovecraft, influenced by Poe and Arthur Machen, who was published in the pulp magazines during his lifetime but who, due largely to the efforts of August Derleth, has become something of a cult since his death in 1937.

The earliest aesthetic expression in Providence took the form of furniture making and silversmithing, and

Brick School House, on Meeting Street, 1768, built by town and proprietors, one floor used for a school, and the other for town meetings, now an open-air school for handicapped children. Photograph by Douglas Armsden, Kittery Point, Maine

Market Building or the Market House, 1773, on Market Square, for many years the public market of the town, and the City Hall of Providence. It was given by the city to the Rhode Island School of Design, the present occupants. Photograph by Douglas Armsden, Kittery Point, Maine

some of the things that were produced are still prized. John Smibert was in Providence for a time. Gilbert Stuart's Rhode Island connections were largely with Newport, as were Edward Malbone's. Nineteenth-century landscape painting was strongly affected by the Barbizon School. Post-Impressionism began to thrive after the 1920s. Augustus Hoppin, magazine and book illustrator, was one of a family devoted to art and art criticism. The Providence Art Club and the Rhode Island School of Design are both important; the latter's museum has valuable French, oriental, and American holdings.

Providence has claimed "more musical organizations than any [other] city of its size in the United States." She has at any rate had a good many, and though visiting artists have sometimes called her audiences cold, they have certainly appeared there many times. The earliest concert on record was held in 1768. Jenny Lind sang in 1851, and it was a feather in the city's cap that its auction sale of her tickets should have realized a loftier "high" than Boston's. John Philip Sousa, the "March King," called David Wallis Reeves of Providence his master. Victor's leading "stock" soprano of the early days, Lucy Isabelle Marsh, lived in Providence part of her life and died in the city, and Nelson Eddy was born in Providence and sang in church choirs there before he became famous. The Rhode Island Philharmonic is today the leading orchestra.

The earliest attempt to present plays was made in 1762 by David Douglass, who called the place of performance a "Histrionic Academy." Though there was no law against playacting at the time, "great uneasiness was felt," because "so expensive amusements and idle diversions cannot be of any good tendency among us,

especially at this time, when this colony as well as others is laboring under the grievous calamity of an uncommon drought and a very great scarcity of hay and provisions." The exhibition was outlawed, therefore, but the sheriff attended the last performance, after which he rose in his place and read the order. In 1764 there was an exhibition of "many curious experiments, naturally representing the various phenomena of thunderstorms," which were shown in a manner "not inconsistent with any of the principles of natural or revealed religion." Four years later "a Person" who had "read and sung in most of the great towns in America" gave a reading or recital of *The Beggar's Opera*, impersonating all the characters and entering "into the different humors or passions, as they change from one to another." A postscript to the announcement indicated that the "Person" was willing to teach "young gentlemen and ladies" how "to read with propriety any author in the English language."

A theater was built at last in 1795; the legend on the curtain read: "Pleasure the means; the end virtue." In 1812 George Frederick Cooke created a sensation as Shylock and helped prepare the way for other great nineteenth-century actors, though Providence never came to be considered an outstanding theater town. The last "regular" stock company disbanded in 1931, about the time stock companies were folding all over America, but the Trinity Square Playhouse is considered one of the best regional repertory companies in the country, and the Henry A. Barker Playhouse is the home of a respected and long-lived amateur group. There is a street named after George M. Cohan, who was born in Providence, and the dramatist A. E. Thomas came out of a little theater group, the Talma Club.

Nelson Eddy (1901-1967), baritone, was a native of Providence. Library of Congress

IV. PORTLAND

Though the state of Maine is about the size of all the rest of New England together, it is still sparsely populated, and the 1970 census gave its largest city, Portland, a population of only a little over sixty-five thousand. "Greater Portland," on the other hand, which embraces Portland, South Portland, Westbrook, Scarborough, Falmouth, Cape Elizabeth, Cumberland, Freeport, Gorham, Gray, Yarmouth, North Yarmouth, and Windham, counts 157,000 souls.

Like Boston, Portland is built on a peninsula. The city is almost surrounded by Casco Bay, Back Cove, and the Fore River, and even today it can be entered without passing over water only from the northwest. The Eastern Promenade overlooks Casco Bay; from the Western one can see clear to the White Mountains in New Hampshire. The magnificent harbor, protected by a breakwater, is one hundred sixteen miles closer to Europe than any other American deepwater port and proved large enough to shelter the North Atlantic Fleet during World War II. Casco Bay contains so many islands that the actual number has always been argued about. In the old days, smugglers, wreckers, and pirates flourished here; today the islands are inhabited largely by fishermen, descendants of the early English settlers, traditional "men of Maine" in speech and ways of thought; who preserve much oral tradition relating to the sea and the supernatural.

The city of Portland occupies the central portion of the peninsula on which it rests. The Indian name of this region was Machegonne; later it was known as The Elbow, Casco Neck, or Old Casco. The name Portland dates from 1786, when what is now the city proper was separated from what until then had been called Falmouth and which included the present Portland, South Portland, Falmouth, Cape Elizabeth, and Westbrook. Like Boston again, Portland has made land, filling in both the waterfront and the back of the peninsula.

Christopher Levett, an Englishman, lived on Hog or

Portland Harbor. Engraving by Wellstood & Peters, nineteenth century. Culver Pictures

Portland Head Light. Photograph by Douglas Armsden, Kittery Point, Maine

House Island in Casco Bay through the winter of 1623-24, but returned to England in the spring, leaving a small company behind him. There is no record covering either his return or the fate of the company. In 1628 Walter Bagnall, who had been connected with Thomas Morton of Merry Mount, and who seems to have been a rascal, whatever Morton may have been, established a trading post on Richmond Island, where he was killed by the Indians three years later. Indian fighting was common during the second half of the seventeenth century; at one time there was a bounty of £100 on the scalp of any male Indian over twelve, and even Parson Smith received his share of "scalp money." There was considerable dissatisfaction too about the overlordship which Massachusetts claimed over Maine, and John Neal cuttingly calls the former Maine's mother-in-law.

What is now Portland was partly destroyed by Indians in 1657 and much more thoroughly by the French and Indians together in 1690, after which the site lay desolate for many years.

The English navigation and stamp laws aroused the same resentment in Portland as in Boston, and defiance and disobedience of the regulations was quite as bold. On October 18, 1775, Portland was shelled and burned by Captain Henry Mowatt of H.M.S. sloop, *Canceau*, who had previously been seized by the colonials for spying and released. Four hundred and fourteen buildings were burned and nearly two thousand persons left homeless. After the bombardment, the only building available until 1787 for sessions of the county court was the Widow Grele's tavern. Portland was a privateering center throughout the Revolution, and in 1779 shared

McLellan-Sweat House, 11 High Street, is the greatest existing example of Federal architecture in the state. One of the four Registered National Historic Landmarks in Portland. Photograph by Douglas Armsden, Kittery Point, Maine

Tate House, 1270 Westbrook Street, was built in 1755 by George Tate. National Historic Landmark. Photograph by Douglas Armsden, Kittery Point, Maine

in the expedition against Castine, but the war entailed terrible economic hardship, and though the scarcity of men sent wages soaring, a barrel of flour cost more than Parson Smith's annual salary.

In 1803 the fire-eating Commodore Edward Preble, commanding the *Constitution* ("Old Ironsides"), defeated the Barbary pirates off Tripoli and saved Ameri-

can ships and sailors from their depredations. His residence on Congress Street, next to the Wadsworth-Longfellow House, later became the Preble House, for many years a leading Portland hostelry. During the War of 1812, the smoke of the sea battle between the American *Enterprise* and the British *Boxer* could be seen from Portland. The *Boxer* was defeated and towed

City Hall and Market Square. *Gleason's Pictorial Drawing-Room Companion.* Culver Pictures

into Portland Harbor, but both commanders were killed and buried with honors in the Eastern Cemetery. Longfellow was literally truthful when he wrote in "My Lost Youth":

> *I remember the black wharves and the slips,*
> *And the sea-tides tossing free;*
> *And Spanish sailors with bearded lips,*
> *And the beauty and mystery of the ships,*
> *And the magic of the sea.*

But since he was not born until 1807, he probably availed himself of poetic license when he wrote:

> *I remember the sea-fight far away*
> *How it thundered o'er the tide!*
> *And the dead captains, as they lay*
> *In their graves, o'erlooking the tranquil bay*
> *Where they in battle died.*

In January 1815 the brilliantly privateering *Dash*, with many triumphs to her credit, sailed out upon one more adventure, unaware that peace had been signed, was overtaken by a terrific snowstorm, and was never heard from again.

The separation of Portland from the rest of the peninsula in 1786 was followed at last, in 1819, by the separation of the "State of Maine" from Massachusetts, and the next year she came into the Union as a free state, balancing the slave state Missouri, according to the terms of Clay's compromise. Portland was the capital of Maine until 1832; in that year she achieved her city charter and lost the capital to Augusta. In 1923 she adopted the council form of government.

In the middle of the nineteenth century both antislavery and temperance agitations were working to break down old party lines in Maine. Abolitionists met with the same opposition in Portland as in Boston, and for the same economic reasons. Elijah Kellogg and Samuel Fessenden were important antislavery workers, and Harriet Beecher Stowe wrote *Uncle Tom's Cabin* while living in Brunswick. Maine's outstanding temperance reformer was Neal Dow (1804-1897), who became mayor of Portland, and whose autobiography describes the disgusting drunkenness which disgraced public occasions during the early days. A total abstinence society was formed in Portland in 1834, and in 1846 the state achieved its first prohibition law.

Maine claims to have sent more men to the Civil War, in proportion to its population, than any other state, including five thousand from Portland alone, of whom more than four hundred did not return. For the city the most sensational event of the war occurred on June 26, 1863, when Confederate Lieutenant Charles W. Read, with twenty seamen, on a captured fishing vessel, seized the revenue cutter *Caleb Cushing* in Portland Harbor and took her out to sea. Pursued by the *Chesapeake* and the *Forest City*, Read and his associates blew up their prize but were themselves captured and taken into Portland as prisoners of war. At the Fourth of July celebration the year after the war ended, a great fire began which destroyed eighteen hundred buildings at a loss of $6,000,000 and left ten thousand families homeless. Government, business, and financial buildings and the homes of both rich and poor were swept away with fine impartiality; the sight afterwards reminded the literary and historically minded Longfellow of the ruins of Pompeii. But the ultimate results were not altogether unhappy. Streets were widened and redesigned, business relocated, and many fine brick buildings erected, largely within an incredible two years.

As with all coast cities, Portland has found her economic well-being importantly dependent upon the sea. She turned to shipbuilding early, and by 1727 she was supplying great pines from Maine's forests for the masts of the British Navy. Her first commercial boom was interrupted by Jefferson's Embargo, which brought

Neal Dow. Daguerreotype. Library of Congress

Victoria House (Victoria Mansion and Museum), at the corner of Park and Danford streets, built in 1859, is the work of Henry Austin, a distinguished eclectic architect of the Victorian period. Photograph by Douglas Armsden, Kittery Point, Maine

great distress to the city during the fourteen months it lasted. In 1852 she rebuilt her waterfront and created Commercial Street. In 1860 her fisheries were the second in the nation. She has often served as Canada's sea outlet. The first transatlantic steamer came in 1828, and at one time seven transatlantic lines were operating out of her port, to say nothing of coastal vessels. In our own time, South Portland has become the land terminus of the Portland-Montreal pipeline, and in 1968 it was estimated that tankers brought 263 million tons of oil into the port. When the railroads came in the 1840s, Portland businessmen were at first not enthusiastic about direct connections with Boston, fearing that this might attract business away from themselves, but they were zealous to have access to Canada and the American interior by both rail and canalboat. The Portland-Portsmouth railroad connection came first, and the great railroad builder John A. Poor made Portland the railroad center of northern New England. Today she has no passenger rail service and uses a ferry to the Casco Bay islands and Nova Scotia.

West Indian molasses was brought in for both sweetening and the making of rum; at one time Portland had nine distilleries. John Bundy Brown learned how to make granulated sugar from molasses, from which he developed a great business and the Bramhall residential area. Other important industries were canning and food processing and the manufacture of paper and pulp, furniture, matches, hand brushes, clothing, marine hardware, and industrial machinery. "Portland Glass" became famous, and the Lincolns ordered it for the White House. The chewing gum industry began in 1850 when John B. Davis commenced making spruce gum. The direct impact of the summer resort boom after 1900 was felt at such places as Bar Harbor and Poland Spring, but Portland shared in the commercial benefits and her harbor islands became summer resorts.

Though modern Portland has Italians, Poles, Syrians, Greeks, and others, with picturesque Old World customs still observed in some sections, its population is still "largely of English-Scotch-Irish extraction, with a generous admixture of Canadians and French-Canadians." All the building styles which have been in vogue during its history are represented along its tree-lined streets. Red brick and granite are much in evidence, and building has been less standardized than in many cities.

One of Portland's great benefactors was James P. Baxter, of the Portland Packing Company, who was mayor six times beginning in 1893 and served as president of the Maine Historical Society and the Portland Society of Art. Baxter gave the city her public library building, started the Associated Charities, and helped create a fine park system. Lincoln Park was laid out after the Fire of 1866 as a safety measure, and part of Deering was acquired at the end of the seventies ("And Deering's Woods are fresh and fair"), but this park as modern Portlanders know it was not completed until the 1930s. Baxter's Woods, a thirty-acre bird sanctuary, was acquired in 1935.

Portland enjoyed great prosperity during both world wars, which stimulated maritime pursuits and set off a real estate and commercial boom, but she suffered great hardship during the bitterly cold, rationed, flu-

Congress Square today. Photograph by Douglas Armsden, Kittery Point, Maine

ridden winter of 1917-18, and she was as hard hit by the Depression of 1929 as any American city; three of her banks failed, and for her F.D.R.'s "Bank Holiday" lasted three weeks. Like other American cities, she has been subjected to ordeal by "renovation" and "master plans," and the contemporary Maineway Plaza is about what such things are everywhere else. Early in the 1960s Greater Portland Landmarks was formed to restrain the destruction of early architecture, and in 1972 Walter Muir Whitehill could still feel that the city had "a distinctive character of its own," being "blessedly free of the monotony of Manhattan Island or of cities set in a boundless prairie" and creating an impression "not so much of isolated buildings of superlative quality, but of harmonious neighborhoods and streetscapes that have preserved enough of their original character to warrant respect."

In early New England religion was the only aspect of human culture whose respectability was beyond question, but Maine was never religious in the early Massachusetts sense. Opposition to tax-supported churches encouraged toleration for dissenters, and when the state constitution was adopted, it provided that no state funds might be used for denominational purposes. When the famous Thomas Smith, who served as both pastor and physician, began his ministry about the end of the first quarter of the eighteenth century, he reported the presence in his parish of approximately forty families, "some of which were respectable." The meetinghouse, however, was not, for at the outset it had neither pulpit, seats, nor glass in the windows. A new church, the famous "Old Jerusalem," was built in 1740 and housed many important gatherings until it was destroyed in the 1775 bombardment; a second parish was established under Elijah Kellogg. In 1809 Edward Payson, Kellogg's assistant, challenged the orthodoxy of Ichabod Nichols at his ordination as assistant minister of First Church, which thereafter moved toward Unitarianism and in 1825 joined the American Unitarian Association. Second Church remained faithful to Calvinism to such an extent that in 1923 it became Presbyterian. Portland Congregationalism began to exert its greatest influence upon the religious life of the nation, however, in 1881, when Francis E. Clark founded the young people's society of Christian Endeavor at the Williston Street Church.

Quakers appeared in Portland by 1743 but did not build their first meetinghouse until 1796. They created a sensation by heating their meetinghouses, which some of the orthodox viewed as a demand to be carried to heaven on a featherbed. Methodists organized in 1784 and built the Chestnut Street Church in 1812. The First Baptist Society dates from 1801. Lutherans built a church in 1877, but their early congregations were made up of Germans and Scandinavians.

Roman Catholic missionaries labored in the Portland area as early as 1698, but there was no local parish before the 1820s, and the first church was not erected until 1830. In 1853 the Diocese of Portland was established, embracing Maine and New Hampshire. While the Cathedral was in course of erection, it was partly burned in the Fire of 1866; after its rebuilding, the steeple was blown down on the day the building was consecrated. These unparalleled misfortunes must have been relished by Protestant bigots, for the establishment of the see had been keenly resented by the members of the Know-Nothing Party and others of similar mentality. There was rioting in the course of which two Maine (not Portland) churches were burned and one priest tarred and feathered. The Jews built a synagogue in Portland early in the twentieth century, but there was no Greek Orthodox church until 1924.

Among fringe religious groups, Shakers appeared late in the eighteenth century. The Swedenborgian Church of the New Jerusalem was organized in 1836 under the respectable auspices of a leading citizen, Dr. Timothy Little, who had become a convert. The First Adventist Church dates from 1850 and the Spiritualist Society from 1860. Christian Science appeared in the 1890s, but there was no church edifice until 1915. Portland has also had more than its share of fringe groups much further from center than any of these, and sometimes their activities have brought them into conflict with the law.

If early Portland was not notably pious, she was not inordinately devoted to learning either. The first school

Portland Gazette for September 9, 1799. Library of Congress

(for boys only) was not established until 1733, under pressure from Massachusetts. (From 1745 to 1760 the schoolmaster was Longfellow's great-grandfather.) The Portland Academy for Boys began in 1803 under Edward Payson and the Latin School in 1821. There was no high school for girls until 1850, but Westbrook Seminary (Universalist, 1831) pioneered in coeducation; it is now Westbrook Junior College. Modern Portland has, among many other institutions of learning, the Peabody Law School and a branch of the University of Maine (at Gorham), and Maine Medical Center is affiliated with the Tufts School of Medicine.

Portland's (and Maine's) first newspaper, the Falmouth *Gazette*, began in 1785. In 1860 the city had eleven newspapers, mostly weeklies; in 1972 she had two daily papers and one Sunday. John Neal's *Yankee* (1828) was the only Portland periodical that ever attracted much attention. The first book published in Portland is said to have been *The Universal Spelling Book* (1786). The "Bibelot" series of Thomas Bird Mosher (1852-1923), reprints of classics, on vellum and handmade papers in distinctive style, won considerable praise, and the late Fred W. Anthoensen, of the Southworth-Anthoensen Press, was one of the ranking printers of America and of the world.

Longfellow was unquestionably the most illustrious writer to whom Portland ever established a claim. Though he spent the years of his fame in Cambridge, Massachusetts, he was born and reared in Portland, and his first wife was a Portland girl.

Birthplace of Henry Wadsworth Longfellow, Portland. Library of Congress

Among many other Portland writers perhaps the best remembered today is the wildly undisciplined but in some aspects prescient John Neal (1793-1876). The names at least of the humorists Artemus Ward (Charles Farrar Browne) and Bill (Edgar Wilson) Nye survive, but though both were born in Maine, they wandered far afield and can hardly be considered Portland writers. Much more of the city were two other humorists, Nathaniel Deering, who also wrote plays, and Seba Smith, author of the once famous "Jack Downing Letters" and husband of Elizabeth Oakes Smith, who was also a writer. Madame Sally Wood, who is called Maine's first writer of fiction, though now forgotten, retains an historical importance for her pioneering use of Maine materials, and Ann S. Stephen was at least very prolific. Elizabeth Akers, wife of the sculptor, lives through one poem, "Rock Me to Sleep, Mother," which, though of no great intrinsic merit, deserves its immortality as an expression of one of the universal, vain hopes of mankind:

> *Backward, turn backward, O Time, in your flight,*
> *Make me a child again, just for to-night!*

Set to music by Ernest Leslie, it was sung by Christy's Minstrels, remained a favorite in army and prison camps into the twentieth century, and was recorded by Schumann-Heink.

The great Winslow Homer was born in Boston of Maine parents and later lived at Prout's Neck, ten miles south of Portland. A number of nineteenth- and early twentieth-century painters of some celebrity were connected with the city, including Charles Codman, Charles O. Cole, Charles Frederick Kimball, Charles Lewis Fox, and Walter Griffin, and, among sculptors, Benjamin Paul Akers, whose "Dead Pearl Diver" figures in Hawthorne's *Marble Faun*, and Franklin Simmons, who created both the statue of Longfellow in Longfellow Square and the Civil War memorial, "The Republic." There is an important collection of his work in the L.D.M. Sweat Memorial Art Museum (1908),

The Wadsworth-Longfellow House, on Congress Street, built by Longfellow's grandfather, General Peleg Wadsworth, in 1784-86. It was the first house built in the city whose all four walls were brick. The brick was brought in from Philadelphia, and there was enough of it to make the walls sixteen inches thick. The parlor, largest in the city, had the first piano in town. Here the poet spent his childhood and youth. Fine Arts Commission, National Archives

John Neal. Library of Congress

Orchestra) a great organ in Kotschmar's memory. Three distinguished American prima donnas—Annie Louise Cary, Lillian Nordica, and Emma Eames—came from Maine, though Nordica had little to do with Portland beyond singing there, as at the famous Maine Music Festival, which was held annually between 1897 and 1926. Perhaps the most distinguished Portland composer was John Knowles Paine (1839-1906), who produced *The Oratorio of St. Peter, Oedipus Tyrannus*, and a *Centennial Hymn* for the Philadelphia exposition of 1876. But Paine became Professor of Music at Harvard and died in Cambridge.

The theater had the same trouble getting started in Portland as elsewhere in New England and attempted some of the same subterfuges. The earliest record of play performance dates from 1794. In 1796 Elizabeth Arnold, mother-to-be of Edgar Allan Poe, appeared in Portland at the age of nine, and Shakespeare is said to have made his first appearance in Maine as an acted dramatist with *Romeo and Juliet* in 1799. But acting was not legal before 1820, and the first theater was not erected until 1829. We hear of Italian opera being sung after the Fire of 1866 and of the city being surfeited with *H.M.S. Pinafore*, but we also hear of business being so bad that such desperate expedients as "perfumed matinees" were resorted to, at which patrons were sprayed with sweet waters as they entered the auditorium. Nearly all great actors of the time appeared at the Jefferson Theater, which opened in 1897 and continued until 1933. Bartley McCullum pioneered in what is now called "summer stock" about 1891 and managed the Keith Stock Company in Portland, 1908 ff. During the early years of the century, open-air theaters flourished in what were known as "trolley-car parks" in the suburbs. Since the thirties, Portland, like most American cities, has been largely dependent for its "legitimate" theater on school, college, and "little theater" groups.

conducted by the Portland Society of Art, which itself dates back to 1882.

Portland has had a great wealth of musical organizations, reaching clear back to Beethoven Society of 1819. In 1837, while Haydn's *Creation* was being performed by the Sacred Music Society at Second Church, a startling manifestation of the aurora borealis appeared in the heavens, certainly one of the most timely astronomical manifestations on record. For many years, Herman Kotschmar, organist and leader of the Haydn Association Choirs, was a dominating musical influence in the city; in 1912 the publisher Cyrus H. K. Curtis, a native of Portland, gave the auditorium in the new City Hall (the home of the Portland Symphony

Chapter 3

Five Towns

I. PORTSMOUTH

AT THE HEIGHT OF HER ANCIENT GLORY, during the late seventeenth and early eighteenth centuries, Portsmouth, New Hampshire, is said to have had more liveried servants and everything that goes with them than any other place in New England. Her population, says Ralph Nading Hill, "was rather like that of a modern duchy, with a benign, if rich, hierarchy superimposed, like gold leaf over pine, on a population of merchants, shopkeepers, and artisans." Thomas Bailey Aldrich, one of her most distinguished sons, who, even after he had become editor of *The Atlantic Monthly*, insisted that he was not genuine Boston but only "Boston-plated," loved to resurrect, in his imagination, a picture of the "portly merchants" of his "Old Town by the Sea," as he called her, standing at the windows of their "musty countingrooms," dressed in "knee-breeches and

New Hampshire State seal, detail engraving by George Murray from the engraving "Declaration of Independence," published by John Binns, 1818. Library of Congress

Strawbery Banke: The Captain John Clark House as seen through the leaded glass window of the Sherburne House, Strawbery Banke's oldest building, dating from the seventeenth century.

Strawbery Banke: Boat Shop. Photo by Robert Swift

silver shoe-buckles and plum-colored coats with ruffles at the wrist, waiting for their ships to come up the Narrows." Though Aldrich also says that "the old town . . . has managed, from the earliest moment of its existence, to burn itself up periodically" (the Fire of 1813 was particularly devastating), America today thinks of her first of all as the proud possessor of one of the finest arrays of colonial mansions existing anywhere in America (fifty-five three-story edifices were counted in 1964), with their woods shaped to forms of beauty by ships' carvers before there were any professional architects in town.

Fire, to be sure, has not been the only destroyer. The Storer-Cutter mansion was torn down to make room for a bowling alley constructed of cement blocks, but though it seems a shame that capital punishment could

Strawbery Banke: Joshua Jones House (c. 1750) is part of a ten-acre historic preservation project embracing some thirty buildings. Photo by Robert Swift

Portsmouth, from the Navy Yard, Kittery, Maine, 1854. Lithograph by C. Parsons. Library of Congress

not have been inflicted for such a crime, the city knows better now, and the concerned citizens who formed Strawbery Banke, Inc. headed off the bulldozers to create a restoration of early Portsmouth. The junkyards and substandard dwellings were moved out, but twenty-seven fine houses were preserved and marked for restoration, and others moved in to occupy the open spaces that had been created.

To herself, however, modern Portsmouth is something more than a museum city; her Chamber of Commerce calls her the "major city in the second-fastest growing county in the United States." The Navy Yard, located on Fernald's and Seavey's Islands, and now devoted largely to nuclear-powered submarines, is actually in Kittery, Maine, but the Pease Air Force Base is in Portsmouth itself, and CE Avery, Booth Fisheries, Liberty Mutual Life Insurance Company, and Sylvania Electric Products are also important economically. Other elements in a diversified economy include building materials, shoes, food processing, and metal fabricating. After the Army Corps of Engineers finished their work in 1965, Portsmouth had a 35-foot deep, 400-foot wide ship channel, clear up the Piscataqua to Dover, and the Portsmouth Terminal of the New Hampshire Port Authority was completed four years later.

New Hampshire's only seaport, Portsmouth (to quote Aldrich again), lies "about two miles from the sea, as the crow flies—three miles following the serpentine course of the river." Aldrich relished "the rich red rust on the gables and roofs of ancient buildings," "the fitful saline flavor in the air," and the "dense white fog," which comes "rolling in, like a line of phantom breakers." Boston is fifty-two miles south, Portland forty-three miles north, and Concord, New Hampshire (the state capital), forty-five miles west. Nine miles off the shore to the southeast lie the Isles of Shoals, made famous by Celia Thaxter. Only the Piscataqua River and the harbor separate Portsmouth from Maine, with which she is now connected by three bridges. Ocean currents exercise a moderating influence upon both summer and winter weather, and tidal currents in the river help to keep the harbor free of ice. The geological structure is glacial moraine, and the countryside is flat to rolling, with both freshwater and saltwater marshes. The land, not well adapted to farming, is heavily wooded, which determined the early development of shipping and the lumber trade. Hawthorne says there was "a gray-headed shipmaster, in each generation, retiring from the quarter-deck to the homestead, while a boy of fourteen took the hereditary place before the mast, confronting the salt spray and the gale, which had blasted against his sire and grandsire." Resentment against England was generated, however, as soon as the Crown claimed all the finest and tallest pines to make masts for His Majesty's Navy.

The first recorded English visitor was Martin Pring, like Sir Francis Drake a Devonshire man, in 1603. Pring was looking for sassafras, which was believed to have medicinal value, and for navigable streams. He sighted the Isles of Shoals, explored the Saco, Kennebunk, and York rivers, none of which seemed hopeful, and then sailed about twenty miles upstream on the Piscataqua. He mapped the coast, touched at what is now Plymouth, and then returned to England; the log of his journey was published by Hakluyt. In 1614 came Captain John Smith, who recognized the mouth of the Piscataqua from Pring's description and named the Isles of Shoals "Smith's Isles." Though he seems not to have entered the harbor, he saw the hunting and fishing possibilities of the area, and, as Miss Winslow remarks, he "made his famous map of the shoreline that is printed somewhere in the early pages of every American history book to the present day."

The pioneer settler was a Scot, interested in fishing, trapping, and Indian trading, David Thomson (1623), who had secured a grant of six thousand acres, plus an island of his choice. With his few associates, Thomson cleared the top of a hill and built a fortlike house of pine logs with a stone chimney, called Piscataqua House, or sometimes Pannaway, after the point of the harbor at which they had landed. This was described by Samuel Maverick, who married Thomson's widow, as

Aerial view of Portsmouth. Photograph by Douglas Armsden, Kittery Point, Maine

Aquatint of old Portsmouth, ca. 1750. Library of Congress

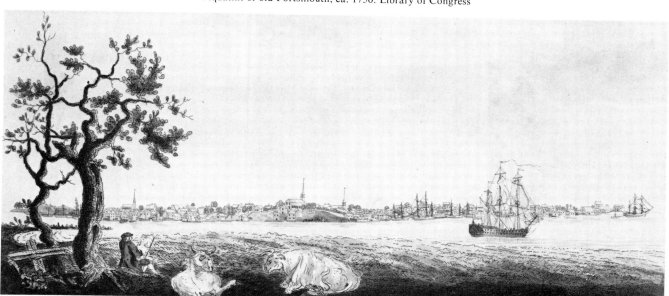

"a strange and large house," in "a large, high palizado," with "mounted guns, and a terror to the Indians."

The early history of the area is complicated, involved as it is with the loosely defined Gorges and Mason claims, and not now of great interest except to specialists. Other settlements besides Thomson's were made, and Portsmouth, Dover, Exeter, and Hampton came to be spoken of as "the four towns." In 1630 Walter Neale headed a group sent out by Mason and Gorges and interested mainly in fur trading and prospecting for gold. They built a "Great House" at the top of a hill covered with wild strawberries, and in time all the lower Piscataqua settlements, including Newcastle, Rye, Greenland, and part of Newington came to be called collectively by the name of the largest unit, Strawbery Banke. The Strawbery Banke settlement officially changed its name to Portsmouth in 1653, but "the Banke" remained a familiar appellation well into the eighteenth century.

John Mason died in 1635, just before he had expected to come out and take charge of the settlement, and public and private misfortunes removed Mrs. Mason from active participation in American affairs. The settlers proved equal to the crisis which followed; like the *Mayflower* Pilgrims, they made a "Combination" or Compact, and elected their own officers. The forcible annexation of the area to Massachusetts in 1652 meant Massachusetts taxes and New Hampshire representatives in the Massachusetts General Court as well as the coming of the Congregational clergy (the first settlers had been Anglicans), and these and other circumstances caused dissatisfaction. King Charles II sent commissioners to hear the arguments of the anti-Massachusetts faction not long after his accession, and Mason's grandson reentered his family's claims. The matter was not settled until 1679, when nobody got just what he had been asking for; the land grant was confirmed to the Mason heirs, but New Hampshire was made a royal province. Portsmouth was the seat of the provincial government from 1679 to 1808, when Concord became the capital, and in 1849 Portsmouth was incorporated as a city.

Portsmouth people had no serious trouble with Indians until late in the 1600s, and even then the town itself was not directly attacked. Early in the eighteenth century there was a bounty on Indian scalps. This is not the only item from the early days that has a touch of horror about it, though others are touched with humor and charm. From 1656 on there were accusations of witchcraft. Cotton Mather described poltergeist manifestations on the part of the Stone-Throwing Devils of Newcastle, and the case of Goody Walford involved "a clap of fire on the back" of her victim and the disappearance of the witch in the form of a cat, but there seem to have been no convictions, and Goody Walford even sued for and collected damages. Two picturesque items

date from 1662: a cage was somewhat tentatively ordered for "such as sleep or take tobacco on the Lord's Day out of the meeting in the time of public service," and a £5 bounty was placed on the head of every wolf killed within the town and nailed upon the meeting house! There were slaves too in the early days; later slavery just withered away in New Hampshire without being legally abolished. What is picturesque about this is not the fact but the special government, aristocracy, and courts which developed among the slaves, involving annual election of king and counselors, the determination of the slave's rank in the black hierarchy by reference to the standing of his master, and elaborate costumes and appurtenances. Robert Rogers, prominent at the time of the French and Indian War, was not a native of Portsmouth, but Portsmouth boys and men served with his "Rangers"; he married the daughter of the rector of St. John's and was regarded as a hero in the town. Having learned woodcraft from the Indians, Rogers became a surveyor and explorer. At twenty-four he brought a company of New Hampshire men to drive the French from the Bay of Fundy. He carried on guerrilla warfare around Ticonderoga and Lake George

John Paul Jones House, 1758. Gambrel roof dwelling at corner of Middle and State streets, owned by Portsmouth Historical Society. Captain Jones stayed here when outfitting the *Ranger* in 1777 and the *America* in 1782. Photograph by Douglas Armsden, Kittery Point, Maine

Coach house and stable of the Rundlett-May House, showing the same restrained classic detail as the main house. Photo by Samuel Chamberlain. U.S. Office of War Information, National Archives

Rundlett-May House, built in 1806. Photo by Samuel Chamberlain. U.S. Office of War Information, National Archives

Warner House at Chapel and Daniels streets (1718-23). Built by Captain Archibald Macphaedris, a rich Scottish iron merchant and member of the King's Council, this is the oldest brick house in Portsmouth. Photograph by Douglas Armsden, Kittery Point, Maine

The Moffatt-Ladd House at 146 Market Street. Built in 1763 it was the home of General William Whipple, signer of the Declaration of Independence. The mansion overlooks the wharves; a captain's walk is on the roof, and the shipping office of the original owner, Captain John Moffatt, adjoins the house. A colonial garden surrounds the house. Photograph by Douglas Armsden, Kittery Point, Maine

North Mill Pond, wash drawing by E. Whitefield, ca. 1852. The railroad roundhouse (the building with the flag) was built around 1850. Library of Congress

and in 1756 cut the French line of communication between Canada and Crown Point. A much pleasanter tale is that of the King Cophetua and the Beggar Maid kind of romance between the Royal Governor Benning Wentworth and the low-born Martha Hilton, whom he scandalized the town by taking as his bride, a story made famous by Longfellow in *Tales of a Wayside Inn*. She is said to have conducted herself like a great lady after their marriage and later to have made an unfortunate second match.

When the Stamp Act took effect, November 1, 1765, Portsmouth's George Meserve, who was in England at the time, was appointed to distribute the stamps in New Hampshire. As soon as he learned of his appointment, he resigned, but Portsmouth, unaware of this, celebrated the day of his expected arrival home by exhibiting, dishonoring, and burning images of him and of Lord Bute, the head of the British ministry, along with one of the devil. On October 31, *The New Hampshire Gazette* had published what it considered its final, black-bordered issue, the last which could appear without a stamp, and in the afternoon a funeral procession was held for "LIBERTY, aged 145 years," which would place her birth in the year the Pilgrims came to Plymouth. But as the coffin was being lowered, signs of life were discerned, the box was opened, and a living woman representing Liberty delivered, the proclama-

tion of the Stamp Act being buried in her place. Bells, cannons, flags, and bonfires shared in the subsequent jubilation, such being the weird manifestations of the histrionic impulse among people with whom it does not find its normal outlet in the theater!

Nine years later, on December 13, 1774, it almost seemed for a moment as if the American Revolution was about to begin at Portsmouth, for Paul Revere came riding, riding to warn that British soldiers were on their way to seize the gunpowder stored at Fort William and Mary in Portsmouth Harbor. The Sons of Liberty secured the surrender of the fort, bound Captain Corcoran and his four men, and carried ninety-nine kegs of powder through icy water to their boats from whence they were stored in secret places and used in the war. Portsmouth's Thomas Pickering became a war celebrity, and the most famous naval hero, John Paul Jones, had Portsmouth connections. Jones was at once a somewhat sleazy and a brilliant figure. The son of a Scottish gardener and the lover of a natural daughter of King Louis XV, he had himself been a slave trader, yet he chose to fight for "liberty" and "the rights of man" rather than for England. Though essentially an adventurer, he was a man of complicated personality and many graces, and certainly far from being wholly insincere. In 1777 he came to Portsmouth to take charge of the *Ranger*, whose flag had been made from portions of

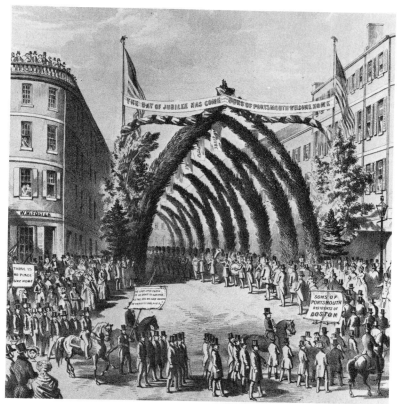

Grand procession of Sons of Portsmouth, July 4, 1853, in Market Street. Library of Congress

the silk dresses of the girls of Portsmouth, and on February 14, 1778, at Quiberon Bay, he secured from the French the first salute ever accorded the Stars and Stripes by a foreign power. Jones's most famous exploit was of course the victory of the *Bonhomme Richard* over the *Serapis*, but his American naval career ended upon a sour note. In 1781 he came to Portsmouth again to take command of the *America*, the largest ship that had yet been built for the American navy, and after excruciating delays, Congress decided to give it to France, as a token of gratitude for wartime aid, after *Le Magnifique* had been severely damaged trying to enter Boston Harbor.

By this time Portsmouth was an old hand at shipbuilding and everything that goes with it. The town built her first ship for the Royal Navy as early as 1690. Shipbuilding necessitated sawmills, required rope and sailcloth as well as lumber, and enlisted gunsmiths, blacksmiths, coopers, painters, coppersmiths, tinsmiths, and many others. Moreover it created wealth which gave occasion for carriage building and the activities of goldsmiths, silversmiths, clockmakers, and jewelers. After about 1730 wealth increased notably, and most of the great houses which still glorify Portsmouth were built between 1741 and 1820. Many had hip roofs and were built close to the streets with gardens behind and were surmounted by a "captain's walk" from which the

merchant could watch the harbor for returning sails. In 1761 a Boston stage began operating. It seems odd that Washington, who paid Portsmouth a four-day state visit in 1789, should have failed to appreciate the houses, thinking they ought to have been built of brick, a peculiar opinion indeed coming from the lord of Mount Vernon. Aldrich compared a Portsmouth man without a family portrait by Copley to a Bostonian who had no ancestor in the Old Granary Burying Ground!

Troubled conditions in Europe threw the oceanic carrying trade to American vessels between 1795 and 1812, when the War of 1812 cut it off, until revival came about 1824, when Portsmouth again got her share. In 1800 a great pier was built, 340 feet long, supporting a three-story building containing fourteen shops; nearby was the New Hampshire Hotel. In the days of sail, Portsmouth was two days nearer Europe than Boston. The great clippers began building about 1845 and ruled the seas in their beauty until the coming of steam around 1870. (Samuel Hanscom's *Nightingale* had Jenny Lind on both stern and bowsprit.) Trade reached as far as Scandinavia and Russia, while home industries included brewing, resort hotels, and much besides.

According to the 1970 census, Portsmouth proper now contains something over twenty-five thousand inhabitants, but there are more than one hundred and seventy thousand within a twenty-mile radius from city center. Portsmouth's affairs are administered by the City Manager Plan. The City Manager is the administrative head. The City Council, which numbers nine, determines policy, and the member polling the highest number of votes becomes mayor.

North Church (Congregational), built in 1854, and St. John's (Episcopal) occupy dominating sites in Portsmouth. St. John's was built in 1807, on the site of the old Queen's Chapel, to which Queen Caroline presented the communion silver in 1742. It also owns a copy of the extremely rare "Vinegar Bible" of 1717, in which the Parable of the Vineyard is misprinted as the Parable of the Vinegar. Today there are twenty-five churches in Portsmouth, including Roman Catholic, Greek Orthodox, and Jewish.

There was no regularly constituted school until 1696. The University of New Hampshire is not far away, at Durham, but the city contents itself, so far as higher education is concerned, with evening classes conducted in the Portsmouth High School building by the Portsmouth Center of New Hampshire College and with the New Hampshire Vocational-Technical College. The Portsmouth Public Library has since 1896 occupied a building, traditionally attributed to Bulfinch, which was built for the old Portsmouth Academy in 1809, while the private library, known as the Athenaeum, is housed in a much admired 1803 Federal building in the Adam tradition.

The Portsmouth Chamber of Commerce boasts "more than fifty cultural organizations within a 15-mile radius," but many of these are centered outside the city, and though Strawbery Banke conducts a summer musical festival in the Olde South Meeting House, on the whole the area seems richer in recreational than

St. John's Episcopal Church, Chapel Street, built in 1807. The church possesses many historic relics, such as a bell taken from the French at Louisbourg in 1745 and recast by Paul Revere in 1807. Photograph by Douglas Armsden, Kittery Point, Maine

Market Square, Congress Street. Photograph by Douglas Armsden, Kittery Point, Maine

aesthetic facilities. Daniel Webster practiced law in Portsmouth and began his political career while residing there. Aldrich and Celia Thaxter are the shining literary lights, and James T. Fields, the great Boston publisher, was born in Portsmouth, as was the humorist Benjamin P. Shillaber ("Mrs. Partington"). Portsmouth has figured in Sarah Orne Jewett's novel, *The Country Doctor*, in Aldrich's *The Story of a Bad Boy*, and, more recently, in *Northwest Passage*, by Kenneth Roberts.

The Navy built a prison at Portsmouth in 1891, and during the Spanish-American War, Spanish prisoners were held there. But the happiest event in the history of modern Portsmouth as touching international affairs, occurred in 1905, when President Theodore Roosevelt met representatives of the Russian and Japanese governments to help negotiate the Treaty of Portsmouth (September 5, 1905), ending the Russo-Japanese War, a shining example of United States intervention, not for war but for peace.

II. SALEM

Edward Ward, an English visitor to Salem in 1699, wrote, with superb malice, of her inhabitants that "there were formerly amongst them (as they themselves report) abundance of witches, and indeed I know not but there be as many now for the men still look as if they were hag-ridden." It seems ironical that the most disgraceful episode in Salem's history should have become both an important part of her legend and a tourist attraction. Fortunately she can also remember her past maritime glories and many distinguished sons.

The most distinguished of all, Nathaniel Hawthorne, whose desk as surveyor of her port may still be seen in the old Custom House, she lost to Concord, and William Wetmore Story removed himself to Italy when he decided to abandon his father's profession, the law, in which he himself had already gained distinction, for

Desk of Nathaniel Hawthorne, exhibited in the room in the Custom House where Hawthorne was employed. Courtesy, Essex Institute, Salem, Mass.

Portrait of Samuel McIntire by Benjamin Blyth ca. 1786.

South Church on Chestnut Street, 1805. Designed by Samuel McIntire; burned December 19, 1903. Culver Pictures

Custom House built in 1819. The Customs Bureau was responsible for collecting import taxes, which helped support the federal government of the new nation. Restored customs offices and shipping exhibits are open for tour. Salem Maritime National Historic Site, National Park Service →

Detail of Custom House. Salem Maritime National Historic Site, National Park Service

sculpture. But she never lost the self-taught carpenter's son, Samuel McIntire (1757-1811), whose beautifully designed buildings and magnificent woodcarvings still constitute one of her unimpeachable glories.

Until 1790 she was the sixth largest town on the Atlantic seaboard. More than $20,000,000 in duties are said to have been paid into her Custom House (there are records of single cargoes yielding almost $150,000). This was before the days of the great clippers; since her harbor was not deep enough to accommodate them, their vogue became a factor in her decline. The nine-acre Salem Maritime National Historic Site, established in 1938, and administered by the National Park Service, preserves a group of historic buildings and two wharves, and the varied materials in the Peabody Museum, whose collections date back to the

The Peabody Museum, established in 1799 by Salem sea captains, displays collections relating to maritime, natural, and ethnological history gathered from around the world. Courtesy of Peabody Museum of Salem

founding of the East India Marine Society in 1799, and whose building was erected in 1824 as their hall, illustrate the past vividly.

The witch-hunt began early in 1692 and was all over early in the new year. Two modern scholars have recently sought a sociological explanation for the aberration on the basis of the anomalous relations which existed between Salem Village and the Town and the bad feelings which had developed between families and social groups.* However this may be, what is to the credit of the community is the celerity with which she came to her senses afterwards and the frankness with which some of the persons involved avowed their guilt and tried to atone for it.

Salem's Chestnut Street has often been called the finest residential street in America, architecturally speaking, and this is not an unreasonable judgment.

*Paul Boyer and Stephen Nissenbaum, *Salem Possessed: The Social Origins of Witchcraft* (Harvard University Press, 1974).

The Witch No. 1, an imaginative picture of Salem witchcraft, from a lithograph by George H. Walker & Co., 1892. Library of Congress

Gallows Hill. By A. F. Bellows. Culver Pictures

Gallows or Witch Hill, located in the southwest part of Salem. Courtesy, Essex Institute, Salem, Mass.

Arresting a witch, 1650, illustration by Howard Pyle, from *Harper's New Monthly Magazine*, June-Nov. 1883. U.S. Bureau of Public Roads, National Archives

Imaginative painting of a witch stealing away children on a broom, "Salem, 1690." Copied from an old Essex Institute postcard. Courtesy, Essex Institute, Salem, Mass.

The Witch House, on Essex Street, built ca. 1642. "The reasons for calling the dwelling the Witch House are lost in the past, but tradition says that the magistrates, John Hathorne and Jonathan Corwin, held preliminary examinations of witnesses there in 1692." FPG

Confession of Salem Jurors. Library of Congress

CONFESSION OF SALEM JURORS, &c.

From Calef's "Salem Witchcraft." Page 294.

" Some that had been of several Juries, have given forth a paper, signed with their own hands, in these words:

" WE whose names are under written, being in the year 1692, called to serve as jurors in court at *Salem* on trial of many ; who were by some suspected guilty of doing acts of witchcraft upon the bodies of sundry persons.

" We confess that we ourselves were not capable to understand, nor able to withstand the mysterious delusions of the powers of darkness, and prince of the air ; but were, for want of knowledge in ourselves, and better information from others, prevailed with to take up with such evidence against the accused, as on further consideration, and better information, we justly fear, was insufficient for the touching the lives of any : Deut. xvii. 6., whereby we fear we have been instrumental with others, though ignorantly and unwittingly, to bring upon ourselves and this people of the Lord, the guilt of innocent blood ; which sin the Lord saith in scripture, he would not pardon : 2 Kings xxiv. 4 ; that is, we suppose in regard of his temporal judgment. We do therefore hereby signify to all in general (and to the surviving sufferers in special) our deep sense of, and sorrow for our errors, in acting on such evidence to the condemning of any person.

" And do hereby declare that we justly fear that we were sadly deluded and mistaken, for which we are much disquieted and distressed in our minds ; and do therefore humbly beg forgiveness, first of God for Christ's sake for this our error ; and pray that God would not impute the guilt of it to ourselves nor others ; and we also pray that we may be considered candidly, and aright by the living sufferers as being then under the power of a strong and general delusion, utterly unacquainted with, and not experienced in matters of that nature.

" We do heartily ask forgiveness of you all, whom we have justly offended, and do declare according to our present minds, we would none of us do such things again on such grounds for the whole world ; praying you to accept of this in way of satisfaction for our offence ; and that you would bless the inheritance of the Lord, that he may be entreated for the land.

" Foreman, THOMAS FISK,   THOMAS PERLY, Sen.,
      WILLIAM FISK,   JOHN PEBODY,
      JOHN BACHELER,   THOMAS PERKINS,
      THOMAS FISK, Jun.,   SAMUEL SAYER,
      JOHN DANE,   ANDREW ELLIOTT,
      JOSEPH EVELITH.   HENRY HERRICK, Sen."
[Not dated.]

Chestnut Street, Salem. Number 12, shown here, was designed by Samuel McIntire. Courtesy, Essex Institute, Salem, Mass.

The Peirce-Nichols house, at 80 Federal Street, was one of Samuel McIntire's first designs, 1782. Courtesy, Essex Institute, Salem, Mass.

But it is a short street which was not laid out until nearly the beginning of the nineteenth century, and only one of its residences (No. 12) was designed by McIntire, though he also did Hamilton Hall, known as "the social heart of the North Shore," where Lafayette was entertained in 1824 and generations of debutantes have since "come out." McIntire's South Church, which stood across the street from the Hall, burned in 1903. The mansion he designed in his twenties for Jerathmeal Peirce (now known as the Peirce-Nichols House), and famous for the woodcarvings which extend even to the urns on the fence posts, stands on Federal Street, and the brick Pingree House, perhaps his masterpiece, is on Essex Street, next to the Essex Institute. When he died at fifty-four, he was praised with equal warmth and sincerity as an artist and a Christian gentleman. Few men have done so much to bring beauty to the corner of earth that held them.

Old Salem has furnished the background for novels such as *Java Head* and *The Running of the Tide*; more factually it has been described by such writers as Mary Harrod Northend, Marianne C. D. Silsbee, and (per-

Interior of the Peirce-Nichols House. Samuel McIntire made fashionable architectural changes to this first floor east front parlor in 1801. Courtesy, Essex Institute, Salem, Mass.

The Gardner-Pingree house, at 128 Essex Street, was designed by Samuel McIntire in 1804-05. The "Federal" style of the architect became very popular in the post-Revolution period. Courtesy, Essex Institute, Salem, Mass.

Essex Institute, 132-134 Essex Street, displays collections of dwellings, furniture and furnishings, and books and manuscripts from the seventeenth through nineteenth centuries. Shown here are the main building and Plummer Hall on the left. Courtesy, Essex Institute, Salem, Mass.

House of the Seven Gables, photograph. The house, built in 1668 by John Turner, a Salem sea captain, is located at the foot of Turner Street. Hawthorne's second cousin, Susan Ingersoll, lived here. The house is now open to the public. FPG

haps most delightfully of all), Eleanor Putnam.* The atmosphere was not all luxury and splendor; the town was quite as distinctive in more humble matters. Hawthorne did not "make up" the cent shop remembered by every reader of *The House of the Seven Gables*; this institution, sometimes tucked inconspicuously under the eaves at the side of its owner's residence, was an established feature of the town. Salem even had her own characteristic confections—Blackjacks and Gibraltars—sometimes carried by her children into foreign lands and the flavor of home with them. To quote Eleanor Putnam, a Black-jack is

a generous stick of a dark and saccharine compound which combines a variety of flavors. In tasting a Black-jack you imagine that you detect a hint of maple syrup, a trace of butter, a trifle of brown sugar and molasses, and a tiny fancy of the whole mixture having been burnt on to the kettle,

and a Gibraltar

a white and delicate candy, flavored with lemon or peppermint, soft as cream at one stage of its existence, but capable of hardening into a consistency so stony and so unutterably

*Joseph Hergesheimer, *Java Head* (Alfred A. Knopf, 1919); Esther Forbes, *The Running of the Tide* (Houghton Mifflin, 1948); Mary Harrod Northend, *Memories of Old Salem, Drawn from the Letters of a Great-Grandmother* (Moffat, Yard, 1917); M. C. D. Silsbee, *A Half Century in Salem*, Fourth Edition, Enlarged (Houghton Mifflin, 1888); Eleanor Putnam, *Old Salem* (Houghton Mifflin, 1886).

flinty-hearted that it becomes almost a libel upon the rock whose name it bears.

Roger Conant, Salem's first settler, came to Cape Ann in 1623, under the auspices of the Dorchester Company (later superseded by the Massachusetts Bay Company), but he found this area inhospitable and in 1626 removed to what was then known as Naumkeag. When the Dorchester Company sent over a larger group under John Endicott two years later, Conant found himself superseded, and friction not unnaturally developed between the "old" settlers and the "new." The change of name from Naumkeag to Salem was supposed to indicate that peace had been achieved, but it may not have been so easy as that. Endicott himself was demoted when John Winthrop and his group arrived on the *Arbella* in 1630, with the charter of the Massachusetts Bay Company, but, as we have seen elsewhere, the Winthrop party moved on to Charlestown and ultimately Boston. After Winthrop's death in 1649, Endicott succeeded him as governor of the colony, which, except for three years, he remained until 1664, but even after he had removed to Boston, he continued to hold interests in Salem.

The first settlers found such an abundance of seafood that lobsters were fed to the pigs and herring was used for fertilizer, but an economy of plenty reigned in no other area. The first winter under Endicott was very hard; Dr. Samuel Fuller came from Plymouth to tend the sick, and indentured servants were dismissed for lack of provisions to feed them. Yet by the late thirties Salem had nine hundred inhabitants and was a high rate-payer compared to surrounding towns. In the beginning she had no fixed boundaries and expanded into what are now Marblehead, Danvers, Beverly, Manchester-by-the-Sea, etc., all of which were gradually separated from her. Deputies were chosen to represent her in the General Court, and in 1636 control of local affairs was vested in the towns. In 1643 Salem became the shire-town of Essex County.

Francis Higginson and Samuel Skelton, serving jointly, were the first Salem ministers; the church was gathered in 1629 and a building erected in 1635. But Higginson died in 1630, the year after his arrival, and Skelton four years later, leaving his more forceful assistant, Roger Williams, who had arrived in 1633, in a position of considerable influence until he was expelled from the colony in 1636. In 1635 came Hugh Peters, who proved liberal-minded and conciliatory, a power in town as well as church affairs and interested in fisheries and shipbuilding. He returned to England in 1641, became a leader under Cromwell, and was hanged after the Restoration.

Salem was never attacked by Indians, but Salem men were involved in both the Pequot War and King Philip's War, which the General Court thought God had sent to punish Massachusetts for, among other things, tolerating Quakers and permitting long hair on men and "netting, curling, and immodest laying out" their hair among the women. Old Indian scalps still hung on the walls of the Town House after the Revolution.

In 1744 raids by the governor of Louisburg on seacoast fishing towns led to the organization of an expedition against the fortress there under the command of William Pepperrell of Kittery. Days of prayer were appointed in the churches; George Whitefield contributed a motto: *Nil desperandum, Christo duce*; Parson Moody of York, who went along, is said to have carried a hatchet to destroy the images in the church. The amazing success of this foolhardy enterprise against seemingly impossible odds put a brake upon the French menace to New England fisheries, and the restoration of Louisburg to the French at the Peace of Aix-la-Chappelle pleased neither Salem nor the rest of New England. During the French and Indian War, there was another triumph in the attack on Port Royal, led by Sir William Phips, in 1690, but the expedition against Quebec, which followed, was a failure and brought wounded men and their families to be cared for in Salem. In 1697 Captain John Higginson wrote his brother that out of sixty-odd fishing ketches only about half a dozen were left.

During the events leading up to the Revolution, Salem was, if anything, more intransigent than New England as a whole. Most of the prominent Tories seem to have left the town as war drew nearer, though some returned after it was over. One group who had signed a document in support of Governor Hutchinson were tarred and feathered; St. Peter's Church had its windows broken; tea sellers were denounced, and it was ordered that their names should be read out in town meeting for seven years. The removal of the capital to Salem, under General Gage, after the Boston Port Bill had closed that city's harbor, pleased only the Loyalists and was short-lived. The Provincial Congress held its first meetings in Salem, after Gage had tried unsuccessfully to block the moves which led to its organization.

In February 1775, Gage sent Colonel Leslie to confiscate the war materials which had been stored at Salem. They landed at Marblehead on the Sabbath; when they reached the North Bridge, which they had orders to cross, the patriots—Richard Derby, Thomas Pickering, John Felt, and others—who had been warned, were waiting for them. Fortunately both sides displayed a forbearance and common sense which was wonderful under the circumstances and which did not reappear at another North Bridge elsewhere in April. After much parleying, it was agreed that Colonel Leslie should be allowed to carry out his orders by crossing the bridge, on condition that he would then turn his men about and march them back again, and this promise was faithfully kept. Nevertheless, Danvers lost more men than any other town except Lexington in the Lexington-Concord aftermath. During the war, Salem blocked her harbor channel and contributed to the recruitment of ten companies of fifty men each to defend the seacoast, and Salem men were prominent in the expedition to relieve Newport in 1778. Between those in the army and those at sea, there was a manpower shortage during the war; prices were high, and food, especially bread, was scarce.

Coastwise traffic with southern ports and the West Indies began early and consisted largely of small vessels —brigs, ketches, and sloops. Codfish and lumber were carried out, sugar and molasses in. New England needed wheat and salt (for her fisheries); the sugar and molasses she used for trade as well as home consumption; by 1791 Salem had seven distilleries turning molasses into rum. In 1790 there were about 50,000 feet of wharf in Salem, but by 1800 there were 250,000. After the English colonial navigation restrictions no longer applied, travel was extended to many distant places. Traders sometimes stopped in the Pacific Northwest for furs and the Sandwich Islands, to dry the furs and pick up sandalwood, then went to China to sell the sea otter and sandalwood for Chinese luxuries, and came home round the Cape of Good Hope; we hear of some ships turning over their cargo a dozen times and making a profit on each transaction.

The products and the places involved have an aura about them even today; how they must have stimulated the imagination in their own time it is hard for us even to imagine. Eleanor Putnam speaks of wine and prunes; nutmegs, mace, and cinnamon; raisins and almonds;

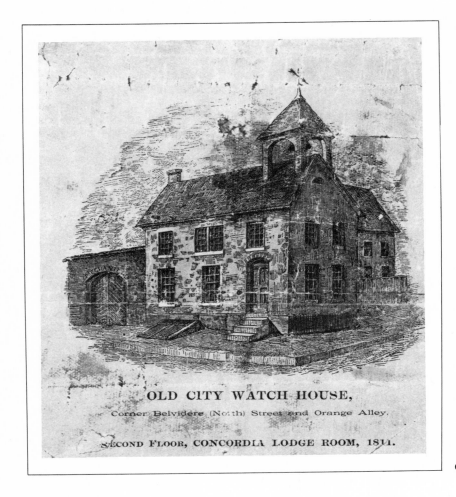

Old City Watch House. Library of Congress

Andrew Safford House, at 13 Washington Square. Built in 1818 for John Andrew, a Salem merchant engaged in the fur trade with Russia. FPG

Minerva, watercolor by J. Williams. Courtesy of Peabody Museum of Salem

palm oil, gum copal, and ivory; sugar and indigo; and "the drolly incongruous mixture, 'gin, cheese and steel,' brought by the brig *Minerva* from Amsterdam.'' There were furniture, mirrors, toilet articles, ivory carvings, lacquer trays, and tea caddies; paintings, books, and engravings; Indian textiles and bandanna handkerchiefs, which Salem men wore as neckties and women long used as tote bags; and blue Canton china in such quantities that it became standard everyday ware in Salem. Jonathan Peele brought in a cargo of pepper from Sumatra on which he is said to have cleared a profit of 700 percent, and at the end of the eighteenth century there were fresh treasures from Japan. Luxuries came from places like Batavia and Senegal which had not even been names to Americans before, and when the Chinese developed a passion for sea cucumbers from the Fiji Islands, New England sailors obligingly began bringing them in for a consideration of about $30,000 a year. Mariners accepted commissions from and made purchases for friends and even strangers, and

many homekeeping folks realized comfortable small profits on such ventures.*

The most picturesque thing about the ships was their figureheads; one, made for Elias Haskett Derby, was actually finished in gold leaf. Washington became a figurehead; there were also a "Salem Witch" and a number of Indian chiefs and princesses. George Crowninshield built a "floating palace" which he called *Cleopatra's Barge*, with which he is said to have hoped to rescue the fallen Napoleon and bring him to New England, but he died instead, and the vessel was sold to the King of the Sandwich Islands.

According to James Duncan Phillips, Salem and Beverly together had over two hundred privateers out

*James Duncan Phillips, *Pepper and Pirates: Adventures in the Sumatra Pepper Trade of Salem* (Houghton Mifflin, 1949) gives a fascinating account of this romantic traffic, which ran into many millions of dollars.

Naumkeag Cotton Mills, view from Derby Wharf. Photo taken about 1895. Courtesy, Essex Institute, Salem, Mass.

during the Revolution. More than one-third were captured or destroyed, but the ratio of captures to losses was six or seven to one. Pirates had always been a danger, and after 1785 the Dey of Algiers practiced international blackmail on a grand scale, holding more than one hundred Americans for ransom. In 1805 he demanded and received $800,000, plus a frigate worth $100,000 and the promise of an annual tribute of $25,000, which the United States continued to pay until 1815, when the Algerine War put an end to it. The position of the flag on homecoming vessels showed at a glance whether anybody had been lost during the voyage. As early as 1766, the Salem Marine Society was founded by eighteen Salem shipmasters to succor those in need of relief and their families.

During French-British hostilities in the Revolutionary-Napoleonic period, American ships were menaced by both nations. President Jefferson postponed war by imposing the Embargo, but after its repeal, England resumed harassment, and in 1812 the break came. Salem furnished forty vessels for the Navy, and on June 1, 1813, the town watched the bloody fight be-

tween the American *Chesapeake* and the British *Shannon* off the coast; the *Chesapeake* was sunk, and the public funeral Salem gave Captain Lawrence and Lieutenant Ludlow became something of an emotional orgy.

The war temporarily wrecked the maritime industry, but new outlets were soon found in Africa, Australia, and South America. When gold was discovered in California, Salem shipped goods and men around the Horn to San Francisco. What really ended her glory was the shallowness of her port, plus the fact that, as the country developed, she also found herself off the main trade routes to the interior.

The town contributed more than three thousand men to the Union armies during the Civil War, of whom some two hundred never returned. She had had from the beginning the trades and industries associated with shipbuilding, and she early became a market center; later a more varied economy was necessarily developed. Banking and fire insurance got started in the 1790s. The Naumkeag Steam Cotton Mills began in 1848 and were followed by tanneries and paint and shoe factories. After World War II textile plants began moving south. Today the manufacture of electronic equipment is important.

The support of the ministry in Salem was covered by a tax from 1645. By 1750 there were four Congregational churches. In the beginning, John and Samuel Browne were sent home to England for removing themselves from the church and organizing their own worship according to the Book of Common Prayer, but in 1733 an Episcopal church was built. George Whitefield preached to seven thousand in 1740, but the Great Awakening took little hold in either Salem or Marblehead.

In 1637 two visiting Quakers were kindly received by Lawrence Southwick and his wife, but were soon arrested and sent to Boston along with their protectors. A period of persecution and cruel punishment followed, but gradually toleration was won. Apparently last seriously interfered with in 1676, the Quakers were allowed a burying ground in 1678, and ten years later, Thomas Maule, an outspoken Friend who had become a successful brickmaker and trader, built a small Quaker meetinghouse. Thus the Quakers seem to have been the first religious society in Salem outside the establishment.

The most epoch-marking event in the religious history of Salem was the ordination in 1812 of Adoniram Judson, a native of Malden, and four friends at the Tabernacle Church, for this marked the beginning of the American Board of Commissioners for Foreign Missions and of the American missionary enterprise in the Orient. There was a touching incident during the Salem ministry (1783-1819) of the famous Dr. William Bentley. When he learned that a poor old Frenchwoman was dying in Salem with no priest to comfort her, Bentley, who was proficient in French, went to her, heard her confession, and gave her absolution. Then he wrote a report to Bishop Cheverus in Boston, who approved without reservation and thanked him for his courtesy and kindness.

"Young Mr. Norris" was chosen to teach school in 1639, and in 1644 provision was made for teaching poor children at the town's expense. The first school committee dates from 1712, when there was no attempt made to distinguish between elementary and more advanced education. There was a feeling that those who could afford it should take care of their children in private schools, of which there were many, especially for the girls. We hear much of the old-fashioned, picturesque "dame schools," often in private homes, which were short on scholarship but long on manners, and in some cases as rich in snob appeal and as choosy about their clientele as the more prestigious secondary schools of later days.

There was a bookshop in 1755, and the *Essex Gazette* was established in 1768. The Social Library, beginning in 1760, was the ancestor of the Athenaeum. Essex Institute, founded in 1848, now functions bril-

Salem's first Quaker Meeting House, frame erected ca. 1690 by Thomas Maule. Today, known as the Doll House, located on the grounds of the Essex Institute, it houses the Elizabeth R. Vaughan collection of dolls and toys. Courtesy, Essex Institute, Salem, Mass.

Left

Portrait of Adoniram Judson, the first American missionary to Burma, painting by Henry Cheever Pratt, ca. 1845. Courtesy, Essex Institute, Salem, Mass.

Right

Reverend William Bentley, copy made in 1828 by Charles Osgood of an oil painting by James Frothingham 1818-19. Courtesy, Essex Institute, Salem, Mass.

Alexander Graham Bell's public demonstration of his invention of the telephone, 1877, Salem, Mass. (From *The Story of New England* by Monroe Stevens.) Courtesy, Essex Institute, Salem, Mass.

liantly as art gallery, museum, research library, and publisher, besides acting as custodian of priceless historic buildings.

Salem has had many distinguished men besides those already mentioned. Timothy Pickering was important in Washington's administration, and the *New American Practical Navigator* (1802) of Nathaniel Bowditch (1773-1838), who left school at ten and studied navigation under an old British sailor, is still a standard work. The historian William Hickling Prescott was born in Salem, and the poet Jones Very "lived and died at 154 Federal Street." Alexander Graham Bell lived in Salem while teaching little George Sanders to speak and demonstrated his telephone at Lyceum Hall on February 12, 1877. The first music society that counts dates from 1814. Except for her builders, Salem has been more impressive for collecting than for creating in the realm of the arts, but Frank W. Benson won distinction as a painter and etcher of wild life. The theater tried it, unimpressively, as early as the 1790s, but there seems to have been more interest in such things as horse shows and exhibitions of wild animals; once, at least, we even hear of cockfighting. But a dancing master was tolerated in 1739, and dances were once held at the Sun Tavern even while church services had been suspended for fear of spreading smallpox!

Salem was incorporated as a town in 1630 and became a city in 1836. In the early days the principal intermixture in her English stock came from French Huguenots, with slight modifications from Irish, Germans, Swedes, and Danes. In modern times the Poles have become important. In 1970 the population was 40,556.

Modern Salem lives in the present as well as the past. Essex Street has lost many seventeenth- and eighteenth-century houses, but others, there and elsewhere, have happily survived; fortunately the great Fire of 1914, the most disastrous in Salem's history, did not take much of historic significance. Washington Square (named in 1802) is the site of the Salem Common, originally set aside "as a place in which persons may shoot at a mark forever." It has also served as a grazing area and training field and is surrounded by historic buildings. Pioneer Village, at Forest River Park, has attempted a reconstruction of the original settlement. Urban renewal enterprises, on the other hand, involve the development of a pedestrian mall shopping area, highlighted by East India Square; "a touch of old Salem" around Derby Square; the Old Market District; and Town Pump Square.

Aerial view of the results of the Salem fire, 1914. Courtesy, Essex Institute, Salem, Mass.

Pioneer Village, built for the Massachusetts Bay Tercentenary, depicts Salem living conditions as they were from 1626 to 1636. Photo by Mark W. Sexton

Pioneer Village: dugout or palisaded log hut. Photo by Mark W. Sexton

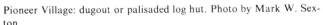

III. CONCORD, MASS.

The six square miles which make up Concord, Massachusetts, lie about seventeen miles northwest of Boston, where the Sudbury and the Assabet join to form the Concord River. It is an area of hills and ponds formed by glacial erosion, with rich meadow beds and small streams, though the early settlers were dismayed to find quicksands and poison plants setting traps for their cattle. The first inland settlement in Massachusetts removed from both seacoast and tidal river, Concord became the literary center of New England during the so-called "Golden Age." Hot in summer and cold in winter, it seems brooded over by peace as much as any spot on earth, but in the popular imagination the day when the Revolutionary War began there and at neighboring Lexington still dwarfs all other days in its long history; even Henry James spoke of the battle as "the hinge on which the large revolving future was to turn." Only Hawthorne seems to have been unmoved by such considerations. When he lived at the Old Manse, he had no interest in the battleground outside his windows; "nor would the placid margin of the river have lost any charm for me," he wrote, "had men never fought and died there."

Today Concord attracts tourists by the thousands, with the authors' homes open to the public, their graves the goal of pious pilgrimages on the ridge in Sleepy Hollow Cemetery, and the region around the battleground in charge of the National Park Service. Anniversaries of the battle have been celebrated on every possible occasion, never more notably than in 1875, when a Concord resident, young Daniel Chester French, his great potential still unknown, created his fine statue of the Minute Man (later the symbol on United States bonds and savings stamps), modeled from his own body reflected in a mirror, no professional being available.* On its base, where it stands before the North Bridge, is the first stanza of Emerson's "Concord Hymn," which had been written at the time the "Battle Monument" was erected in 1837:

*The celebration itself was a horror, partly because of cold, miserable weather, but also because Concord necessarily lacked the means to provide adequately for her 35,000 to 50,000 visitors. See David B. Little, *America's First Centennial Celebration: The Nineteenth of April 1875 at Lexington and Concord, Massachusetts*, Second Edition (Houghton Mifflin, 1974). Oddly enough, the Bicentennial celebration, though looked forward to with horror, passed off with comparative decorum.

North Bridge. "Here once the embattled farmers stood, And fired the shot heard round the world." Photograph by Keith Martin, Concord

Daniel Chester French's statue of the Minute Man (1874) at the North Bridge. The first stanza of Emerson's poem is inscribed on the base. Photograph by Keith Martin, Concord

Account of battle of Concord and Lexington from contemporary newspaper. Essex Institute, Salem, Mass. →

By the rude bridge that arched the flood,
Their flag to April's breeze unfurled,
Here once the embattled farmers stood,
And fired the shot heard round the world.

But fine as these lines are, there are visitors today who are more moved by the quotation from Lowell on the grave of the British soldiers nearby:

They came three thousand miles, and died,
To keep the Past upon its throne;
Unheard, beyond the ocean tide,
Their English mother made her moan.

It was in 1635 that the General Court authorized the settlement at Musketaquid, changing the name to Concord. The leading spirits were Simon Willard, merchant, fur trader, and a leader of the community in both civil and military affairs, and two clergymen, John Jones and Emerson's forebear, Peter Bulkeley. Both had been deprived of their English charges for Puritan leanings, but Bulkeley, who had money and aristocratic connections, had been handled rather gingerly. They were installed as ministers of the new town, and those

The Elisha Jones House, one of the oldest in Concord, Mass., showing the bullet-hole (in a small frame between door and window) made by a British soldier, as he fired in response to Jones's taunts during the retreat after the battle at the bridge. Photograph by Keith Martin, Concord

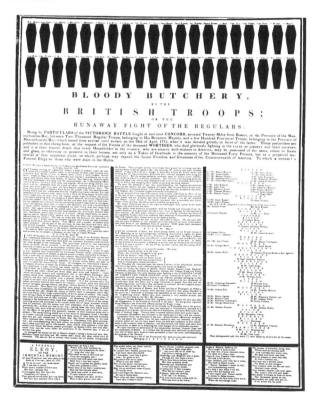

who wished to become settlers signed the church covenant. About twelve families were involved, but they did not all take up residence at once, and the first settlers seem to have dug out caves in the hillside and roofed them with sod above the door. Jones's incumbency did not last long; after a disagreement in 1644 he led an exodus to Fairfield, Connecticut. By this time there were about a hundred families in Concord, mostly of the yeoman class. More land had been granted and surveyed, and Concord Village (now Acton) had been acquired.

The settlement was made around what is still called

the Milldam, and which was then literally that, formed by the damming of a brook. Though the Algonquin Indians in the vicinity had been much weakened by disease before the coming of the English, the latter tried to ensure their future by "purchasing" the land from them, with the Indians retaining hunting rights.

Hardships during the second winter were particularly severe, and economic conditions were bad for a generation after 1644, when civil war and other turmoil in England cut off emigration. Trade declined, prices fell, and education languished. Concord itself was not attacked during King Philip's War, but Concord men were involved in expeditions to relieve other towns. When John Eliot's "Praying Indians" at Natick, Nashoba, and Wamesit were interned on Deer Island in Boston Harbor, though there was no evidence that they had aided the war against the whites, some were brought into Concord and placed in charge of John Hoar, who lived at what is now known as Orchard House. Later these persons were seized without legal warrant by Captain Samuel Moseley and ultimately enslaved. To his lasting honor, Hoar defended them to the limits of his power. A Boston court hanged two Concord men, Stephen and Daniel Goble, for killing three Indian women and three children, because justice demanded that both Indians and whites who committed atrocities must be treated alike. All in all, Concord lost about one-sixth of its men in Indian fighting, and there was more trouble after 1700, when the French used Indians as allies.

The Reverend Peter Bulkeley died in 1689 and was succeeded by his son Edward, of whose preaching we hear much, very little of which is favorable. He was followed by Joseph Estabrook, who died in 1711, after which the church in Concord sailed into troubled waters. John Whiting became a drunkard and had to be removed (which was not the end of the trouble since he persisted in claiming clerical prerogatives afterwards), and Daniel Bliss, an admirer of Whitefield, who preached in Concord during his pastorate, delivered hellfire sermons of which many of his parishioners did not approve. About a third of them withdrew and founded the West, or Black Horse, Church, so called because its meetings were held for a while in the Black Horse Tavern; of all people, this church called John Whiting, now apparently reformed, as its pastor. Bliss's daughter, Phebe, married Emerson's grandfather, William Emerson, the builder of the Old Manse, and after he died, on the way home from the expedition against Ticonderoga, where he had had a miserable experience trying to serve as chaplain, she married his successor, Ezra Ripley, who was ten years her junior. Ripley, who came to Concord in 1780 and became one of her most distinguished citizens, lived and served there until he died sixty years later, but his gravitation and that of his church toward Unitarianism led to the secession of dissatisfied Trinitarians in 1828.

Peter Bulkeley II, Edward's son, born in 1641, was very prominent in Concord affairs of the mid-seventeenth century. After the Restoration he represented Massachusetts in Charter negotiations in England. He stayed three years, and upon his return his fellow-Concordians found him unpleasantly fashionable and Britannic. He lost caste when he served on Governor Andros's Council and died in 1688, a disappointed man.

In the early eighteenth century, Concord became a trading center between Boston and the towns to the west, but a good deal of business was still done by barter, and taxes were often paid partly in goods and services. There were slaughterhouses, mills, and a tannery, but though William Munroe is credited with having made the first lead pencils in America, manufacturing became important only in West Concord, where the presence of the grim Concord Reformatory also strikes a somewhat discordant note.

One of Concord's most distinguished sons, Thoreau, bears witness to the presence of some Scottish and French infiltration in Concord. After war was declared between England and France in 1755, French subjects in Massachusetts were interned at Concord, and after the Acadian outrage which inspired Longfellow's *Evangeline*, some Acadians came there also. There were a few free Negroes very early, but there were not many Irish until they came to build the railroad, which reached Concord in 1844. Some of them stayed, and with Concord boys going west and farmers' daughters working in the mills, they were employed by Concordians, at first with many grimaces, as laborers and "hired girls." Both Emerson and Thoreau welcomed them, and the Alcotts paid a heavy price when they nursed an Irish family through scarlet fever and Elizabeth caught it, failed to recover properly, and went into consumption and died. In later years, Concord's John W. Brooks and Reuben N. Rice were to become important Western railroad magnates.

This, of course, was long after independence. Concord's town meeting debated the Stamp Act as early as 1765; later it sternly condemned tea drinkers. In October 1774 the Committee of Safety coined a famous phrase by voting "that . . . one or more companies be raised in this town by enlistment . . . to hold themselves in readiness at a minute's warning in case of alarm." By the end of January a hundred men were drilling on the Common. Both the first and the second Provincial Congresses held some of their sessions in Concord, and it was the decision of these bodies to store war materials there which led to the British expedition of April 18-19, 1775, and gave the region the chance to call itself "the cradle of American liberty." In the Concord engagement and its aftermath, when the "patriots" fired upon the "regulars," Indian-fashion, from behind walls and trees, the British lost 73 killed, 147 wounded, and 26 missing, the Colonials 49, 41, and 5. Concord lost three men at Bunker Hill, and Concord

Home of Peter Bulkeley, Esq., grandson of the Reverend Peter Bulkeley, Lexington Road. Concord Free Public Library

The First Church. Built 1712, enlarged 1792, remodeled 1841, destroyed by fire April 12, 1900, rebuilt in 1901. The Provincial Congress met before the Revolution in the original building. Concord Free Public Library

Statue of Emerson by Daniel Chester French, 1914, in Concord Free Public Library. Photograph by Keith Martin, Concord. Concord Free Public Library

men were taken prisoner during Benedict Arnold's expedition to Quebec. During the war, Concord became a center for army supplies, and Tories and prisoners of war created intolerable conditions by overcrowding her jails. A Boston town meeting was held in Concord in 1775, and Harvard College moved there for the duration, holding its classes in schools and churches. Concord was an old hand at recruiting its teachers from among Harvard students, but that was a different matter from boarding the lot of them.

Concord's town meeting has the honor of having been the first public body to urge that the Constitution should be drawn up not by existing legislatures but by a special constitutional convention called for this purpose. Post-Revolutionary conditions were far from comfortable and paper money became nearly worthless. We hear of the town paying $30 for a pair of shoes for a pauper. Shops closed down; food and clothes became scarce; soon there were more prisoners in jail for debt than for all other causes together. In 1786 Daniel Shays and (closer to Concord) Job Shattuck of Groton sought to prevent the courts from opening, thus halting action for debt. On September 12, two hundred men with sprigs of hemlock in their hats converged upon Concord for this purpose. Concord's forbearance and good sense prevented calamity (there was considerable open or covert hostility there to Boston-centered financial and mercantile interests). Later Shattuck was captured, wounded, tried, and condemned to death, but finally pardoned through the efforts of his Concord attorney. In 1787 the town meeting recommended a number of reforms, and gradually, nobody was quite sure why or how, conditions improved.

In the early days, Concordians sympathized with Jefferson against Hamilton's Federalists, whom they regarded as the party of the great Boston merchants, but in 1828 only four Concordians voted for Andrew Jackson. Though the Corinthian Lodge of Masons had functioned peacefully in Concord from 1787, the Anti-Masons carried a local election, achieving an overturn, in 1834, and the Know Nothing campaign of 1854 also roused great interest. The anti-Catholic fanatics who burned the Ursuline convent were tried in Concord (though only one was convicted); so was the Harvard killer, Professor John Webster, who was hanged in Boston. On July 4, 1840, there was a picturesque demonstration for "Tippecanoe and Tyler too." Nathaniel Hawthorne, who "right-thinking" people thought should know better, gave offense to many by supporting his old college friend, Franklin Pierce, for president. Hawthorne wrote Pierce's campaign life, and after he had been elected, the President rewarded him by sending him as consul to Liverpool.

In 1844 Concord's Samuel Hoar, who later presided at the Boston meeting which called for a state convention to organize the Republican Party, went to Charleston as an emissary from the Governor of Massachusetts to discuss South Carolina's habit of seizing every Negro who came into port on a Massachusetts ship. Though he found nobody willing to talk, Hoar found plenty eager to mob him and was reluctantly compelled to retreat in order to avoid an incident; the experience must have gone far to convince Concordians that the South was not going to be sweetly reasonable about slavery. Later Concord was much involved in underground railroad activities. Thoreau remarked slyly that the cabin near Walden Pond in which he conducted a scientific experiment to determine just how far a man could go in cutting down on the necessities of life in order to leave himself free for its luxuries, offered "advantages which it may not be good policy to disclose."

The high priest of Concord abolitionism was Franklin B. Sanborn, teacher and agent of the Emigrant Aid Society, who afterwards wrote much about Concord writers. It was he who hosted John Brown of Kansas in Concord, and he may even have been privy to his plans. When, after Harper's Ferry, Sanborn was summoned to appear before a Senate committee, he resisted. What followed involved a good part of the community and was exciting enough for a "movie," but the judge freed the intended prisoner. Concord was about as "subversive" over John Brown as she ever became. When the news of the raid arrived, Thoreau called a public meeting on his own responsibility. There was a memorial meeting the day Brown was hanged, and the next day Thoreau drove one of the raiders, Francis Meriam, to the train for Canada, in a carriage which had been borrowed from Emerson. Even that great man went off the deep end to the extent of saying something about Brown, in his dying, making the gallows as holy as the cross, to which Hawthorne bluntly replied that no man ever deserved hanging more.

The town sent off her first Civil War volunteers with a five-dollar goldpiece each and the promise to take care of their families. Concord Artillery became G Company, Fifth Massachusetts Regiment, United States Infantry, and promptly ran into discomfort, filth, mismanagement, and disease. At Bull Run they were routed, though they had not been placed where they could perform any useful service. Fortunately the five men reported missing were all later accounted for. Later Concord men were involved at Antietam, Fredericksburg, Gettysburg, and elsewhere. Louisa May Alcott ruined her health as an army nurse, and at home the Soldiers' Aid Society functioned nobly.

Concord went through later calamities along with the rest of America and in much the same spirit. It is disappointing to find Emerson's son sending young men off to eat "embalmed beef" in the Spanish-American War under the quaint delusion that they were serving humanity and the cause of liberty. Another distinguished Concordian, United States Senator George Frisbie Hoar, knew better, and everything he foretold by way of consequence from the imperialism to which

The Old Manse was built by Emerson's grandfather, the Reverend William Emerson, in 1769. Ralph Waldo Emerson lived there briefly as a child and again in the early 1830s. In it Hawthorne passed the first three years of his married life and his *Mosses from an Old Manse* (1846) made it famous. The house is now open to the public. Photograph by Keith Martin, Concord

Grist Mill, Barrett's Mill Road. Concord Free Public Library

Concord center circa 1840, by John Warner Barber, 1798-1885. Concord Free Public Library

Pencil sketch of Thoreau by Daniel Ricketson. Concord
Free Public Library

Thoreau's home. Concord Free Public Library

America then committed herself has since been abundantly realized. The official World War I Honor Roll
in Concord contains five hundred names, of which
twenty-five are in gold letters, a much smaller number
than were carried off by the influenza epidemic of 1918.
In 1932 Hoover carried Concord (as Taft had carried it
in 1912), but the town had already set up its Unemployment Commission. After F.D.R. had quoted Thoreau
(without credit) in his Inaugural Address ("the only
thing we have to fear is fear itself"), the town fell into
line, becoming one of the first 100 percent NRA towns
in Massachusetts and sharing and cooperating in many
relief and renewal projects.* According to Townsend

*F.D.R. never carried Concord, however. In 1964 the town found
Goldwater too much to swallow and went for Johnson by more than
1,800. In 1972, to her shame, she chose Nixon over the state's choice,
McGovern, but by only 236 votes. There was considerable opposition
to the Vietnam War in the form of meetings, marches, sermons, etc.,
but no town vote was taken.

Walden Pond. The site of Thoreau's cabin is across the water at the right. Photograph by Keith Martin, Concord

Replica of Thoreau's hut, situated on the grounds of the Thoreau Lyceum. Photograph by Keith Martin, Concord

Scudder, one-seventh of its population returned from World War II.

The continuing life of a community in its day-by-day activities is harder to write about than the great historic events, but in the long run it is much more important. Concord's great writers are not alone among her citizens in having permanently enriched mankind; it would be hard to overestimate our debt to Ephraim Bull, who

Concord, south side of mill dam, circa 1865. Concord Free Public Library

developed the Concord grape, and whose Grapevine
Cottage can still be seen near the Wayside. Poor Bull
had no business acumen to match his horticultural genius; he died in poverty: No man ever better deserved
the epitaph, "Where he sowed, others reaped."

In Concord, as in other Massachusetts communities,
the Calvinist-Puritan churches at first had things all
their own way. The Catholics had no church building
before 1863, and it took more than a decade after that
to get a Catholic on the School Committee. Before
long, however, there was a Catholic church in the
square, and the town seemed to bear up bravely.

In the early days, there was a central school in the
town and district schools in the "quarters," with a two-
to-three-months winter session, plus ten weeks in the
summer under a woman teacher who could be had at a
lower figure. Girls attended only the lower grades. In
1838 Thoreau and his brother John began teaching a
limited number of pupils in a private school which had
junked the idea that the best way to make a pupil learn
was to flog the information into him, and in 1859 the
"impractical" Bronson Alcott became Concord's progressive superintendent of schools at $100 a year. Just

Ephraim Wales Bull, developer of the Concord grape, bust by Anna
M. Holand, nineteenth century. Concord Free Public Library

Emerson House, on Cambridge Road, built in 1828. Ralph Waldo Emerson lived here from 1835 until his death in 1882. Photograph by Keith Martin, Concord

The Wayside, on Lexington Road. The original seventeenth-century house of Nathaniel Ball was enlarged by its later owners, the Alcotts in 1842, Nathaniel Hawthorne in 1860, and Margaret Sidney in the 1880s. Photograph by Keith Martin, Concord

after the Civil War, work began on a high school, and after 1891 elementary education was centered in the town, and what we now call "busing" began. For a decade beginning in 1879. Alcott's Concord School of Philosophy, meeting in the little wooden chapel to the left and the rear of Orchard House, presented distinguished speakers each summer and aired many lofty ideas. In our own time, the respected Concord Academy, founded in 1919 and now coeducational, attracted fresh attention when Caroline Kennedy became a pupil there, but the Xavier and Rose Hawthorne Catholic schools have been victims of that community's educational retrenchment.

Town books seem to have been loaned out as early as 1672, but the real Town Library did not begin until 1851; by 1873 there were ten thousand volumes and a new building. The Concord Lyceum was founded in 1829. During its first fifty years, it sponsored 784 lectures (301, including Emerson's 98, by Concord residents), 105 debates, and 74 concerts. Holmes, Lowell, Agassiz, Horace Greeley, Theodore Parker, Orestes A. Brownson, Henry Ward Beecher, and Edward Everett Hale were among those who appeared. During one season Thoreau booked 25 lectures on a budget of $109.20 and had $9.20 left over. But the town's parsimony in educational matters distressed even this distinguished "economist." It strikes a discordant note in the idyllic picture many of us have of Concord in the "Golden Age"; so too does the omnipresent drunkenness, though we may hope that Townsend Scudder exaggerates when he says that "there was scarcely a household not cursed with a drunkard." The heroic Dr. Josiah Bartlett, whose practice gave him good reason to understand what alcohol can do, became president of the Total Abstinence Society, and was persecuted in every possible way by both the drinkers and those who enriched themselves by them. When a vicious caricature of Dr. Bartlett was posted in the town, Emerson, who himself blew both hot and cold on alcohol, angrily beat it down with his cane. Organized charity began in 1814 with the Concord Female Charitable Society, and it is said that many controversial issues were threshed out in the Social Circle, founded in 1782, even before they reached the town meeting.

Concord has an Art Association, with both permanent and temporary exhibits by local artists and outlanders. The town has three of French's distinguished works: the Minute Man, the Melvin Memorial in Sleepy Hollow, and a fine seated statue of Emerson in the Public Library, which also has some of the paintings N. C. Wyeth made for Francis H. Allen's Thoreau anthology, *Men of Concord.*

The tourist influx, which began in the 1890s, has been an ever-increasing flood, especially in summer. Walden Pond has fought off the spoilers, though there was one narrow squeak, but it is better known today for girls in bikinis than as a refuge for solitaries. Thanks to

Little Women, Orchard House is the most popular Concord building open to the public, but the place of most varied interest is the extensive Concord Antiquarian Society, which contains period rooms and illustrates "the rambling growth of an old New England homestead." Its holdings began with the collections of Cummings E. Davis, before the value of such things was widely recognized, in the middle of the nineteenth century, and it has occupied its present building, across the street from the Emerson House, since 1930. Though Concord cherishes its antiquities, a plan to rebuild the Milldam in colonial style, somewhat after the fashion of the restorations at Williamsburg and elsewhere, was opposed in the twenties, for fear of giving its sponsor a monopoly of the business district, and received its coup de grace when the Great Depression began.

Orchard House. Home of the Alcotts from 1858 to 1877. Photograph by Keith Martin, Concord

IV. LITCHFIELD

Litchfield, the county seat of Litchfield County in northwestern Connecticut, lies on a hilltop east of the Housatonic Valley and just west of the Naugatuck. Hawthorne speaks of it as "occupying a high plain, without the least shelter from the winds, and with almost as wide an expanse of view as from a mountain top." Its exposed location has contributed importantly to the very severe weather which, in modern times, has joined with other considerations to cause it to be much more densely inhabited in summer than in winter. Hawthorne also says that "the streets are very wide, two to three hundred feet, at least, with wide, green

margins, and sometimes there is a wide green space between the two road tracks." In the beginning this was determined by the needs of the cattle driven over them rather than by aesthetic considerations, for the pride that Litchfield takes in her appearance is a modern development. As late as the 1870s, according to Arthur E. Bostwick, "it is a fact that the old colonial buildings were covertly sneered at or regarded with amused tolerance." The now prized 1828-29 building of the Congregational Church was actually moved away in 1873 to make room for a shingled Gothic structure, while it served as armory, dance hall, and cinema, until in 1930

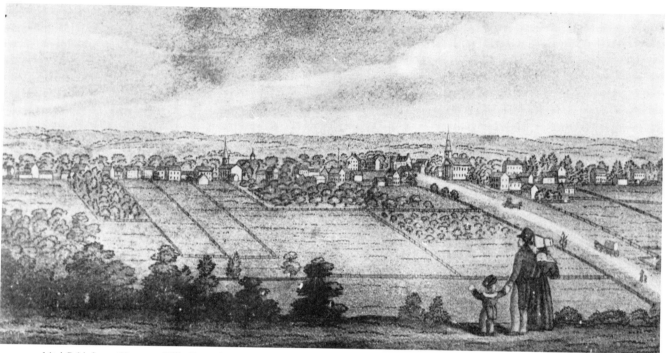

Litchfield from Chestnut Hill. From Barber's Historical Collections, 1836; photo from A. White's *History of Litchfield*. Courtesy of the Litchfield Historical Society

it was moved back and restored.

Litchfield may or may not be the most beautiful town in Connecticut, but surely none has cared more faithfully for her trees and her parks, and none has been more praised. At the end of the eighteenth century, the Reverend Dan Hutchinson spoke of it as "a delightful village, on a fruitful hill, richly endowed with schools both professional and scientific, with its venerable governors and judges, with its learned lawyers and senators, and representatives both in the national and state departments, and with a population enlightened and respectable. . . ." Later, Harriet Beecher Stowe, who, like her brother Henry Ward, was born during her father Lyman's pastorate there, thought of its beauties as having "impressed and formed my mind long before I had words to give names to my emotions, or could analyze my mental processes." Among these beauties were Mount Tom, "rearing its round blue head against the sky," the Great and Little Ponds, gleaming out "amid a steel-blue sea of distant pine groves," the wonderful sunsets, burning themselves out over Prospect Hill, "amid voluminous wreathings, or castellated turrets of clouds," and Chestnut Hill, "whose sides were wooded with a rich growth of forest-trees; whose changes of tint and verdure, from the first misty tints of spring green, through the deepening hues of summer, into the rainbow glories of autumn, [were] subjects of constant remark and of pensive contemplation to us children."

More recent writers have been no less enthusiastic. The great photographer Samuel Chamberlain, who credited Litchfield's preservation of its ancient beauties to its having escaped the industrial boom which followed upon the coming of the railroads, called it "an inland citadel of fine domestic architecture with few equals in this country. Litchfield has the air of a patrician community, well scrubbed and carefully groomed by multiple lawn mowers, but it is not forbidding." And when Richard Pratt visited the town in preparation for the architectural studies which appeared first in *The Ladies' Home Journal* and were then collected in *A Treasury of Early American Homes* (McGraw-Hill, 1949), his walks on North and South streets and around the Green made him think

of a room where all the choice old family pieces have been miraculously protected from the wear and tear of daily living, for time on end. But a parlor is a place you think of as set apart with doors closed and curtains drawn for special occasions, whereas Litchfield gets lived in every day, and looks it—but lived in by people who appreciate the heirloom houses, the Aubusson greenswards, the priceless canopy of the elms. I suppose it is the most unspoiled community of anything like its age in the country.

Unfortunately, the great elms and chestnuts he saw are gone now, and much of the historic furniture has been sold out of town.

The Indians called the Litchfield area Bantam; the

pioneers thought of it by such names as the New Plantation, Greenwoods, the Western Lands, and sometimes the Western Wilderness. They bought it for £15 from the Indians, who reserved hunting rights on Mount Tom, and named it Litchfield for Lichfield in Staffordshire. The settlements were made in 1720-21, and the settlers came from Hartford, Wethersfield, Windsor, Lebanon, and Farmington. Fearing Indian attacks, which never materialized, they built four forts and a palisade and stationed sentries at the edge of the village. The early nineteenth-century Litchfield historian, George C. Woodruff, says that "the first inhabitants were peculiarly careful that none but persons of good

Mount Tom. W. H. Sanford, photographer. Courtesy of the Litchfield Historical Society

Corner of South and West streets, Litchfield, by A. D. Benedict, ca. 1870. *Left to right:* Mansion House, Bishop & Sedgwick's Store, W. R. Coe Meat Market; the *Enquirer* newspaper (upstairs), F. D. McNeill (groceries, dry goods, etc.), the Court House. Courtesy of the Litchfield Historical Society

Beecher House, on North Street in Litchfield, was built in 1775 by Elijah Wadsworth. Home of Lyman Beecher and family. Shown here, front room ca. 1890. Courtesy of the Litchfield Historical Society

character should be permitted to settle among them. If a stranger made a purchase in the plantation, a proviso was sometimes inserted in the deed, that the inhabitants should accept the purchaser, and that he should run the risk of trouble from the Grand Committee."

Litchfield was a frontier community. She had no regular public conveyance to other towns for nearly seventy years after the settlement, and she had become a county seat before she had either mail service or a newspaper. In a memorial address delivered in 1851, Horace Bushnell stated that Litchfield people had worn homespun until recent years and went on to describe some of the implications of this:

Thus, if the clothing is to be manufactured in the house, then flax will be grown in the plowed land, and sheep will be raised in the pasture, and the measure of the flax ground, and the number of the flock, will correspond with the measure of the home market, the number of the sons and daughters to be clothed, so that the agriculture out of doors will map the family in doors. Then as there is no thought of obtaining the articles of clothing, or dress, by exchange; as there is little passing of money, and the habit of exchange is feebly developed, the family will be fed on home grown products, buckwheat, indian rye, or whatever the soil will yield. And as carriages are a luxury introduced only with exchanges, the lads will be going back and forth to the mill on horseback astride the fresh grists, to keep the mouths in supply. The meat market will be equally domestic, a kind of quarter-master slaughter and supply, laid up in the cellar, at fit times of the year. The daughters that, in factory days, would go abroad to join the female conscription in the cotton mill, will be kept in the home factory, or in that of some other family, and so in the retreats of domestic life. And so it will be seen, that a form of life which includes almost every point of economy, centers

round the article of homespun dress, and is by that determined.

Such circumstances do more than condition the economy, however. They make for a close-knit community in which even one's pleasures are created in association with one's neighbors or else simply do not exist, and therefore cause the character and the congeniality of those neighbors to be more immediately important than they are in the conditions under which most of us live today.

In another sense, however, Litchfield was not isolated. Speaking of the year 1792 at the bicentennial celebration in 1920, Mrs. George M. Minor declared that

Litchfield society . . . was renowned for its education and culture. The town was on the highroad of travel between New York and Albany by way of Danbury and Poughkeepsie, and between New York and Boston by way of Hartford, Danbury and West Point. Great, red four-horse coaches, we read, rushed daily through the town in all directions making more stir with horns and whips and clattering hoofs than their modern successor, the automobile, open cut-outs and all.

The last sentence may perhaps be a little highly colored, as befits a bicentennial celebration, but it did seem, at the end of the eighteenth century, as though Litchfield was going to be something very different from what it ultimately turned out to be.

We hear, among other things, of cotton mills, cabinet shops, and iron forges; of carriage building, tanning, shoemaking, bookbinding, dyeing; of the manufacture

The Litchfield Green: August 2, 1920, bicentennial celebration of the town's founding in 1719. Courtesy of the Litchfield Historical Society

Congregational Church, Milton, Conn., ca. 1967. Founded 1798. Courtesy of the Litchfield Historical Society

of a variety of hats; even of goldsmiths and silversmiths. Julius Deming, Colonel Benjamin Tallmadge (of Revolutionary War celebrity), and Oliver Wolcott even formed a China trading company, whose vessel, the *Trident*, sailed out of New Haven, and whose cargoes were carried by oxteam to Litchfield for distribution there to the inland merchants. In 1810 Litchfield was the fourth largest town in Connecticut; a century later she was the sixty-fourth. The basic reasons for the change were that Litchfield, on her hilltop, lacked adequate waterpower and that the routing of the railroads diverted industry to the river towns.

This, of course, was long after the settlement. Much of it was even after the Revolution, in which 504 Litchfield men are said to have served. On April 27, 1777, the fourteen men (some very old and some very young) who went to the relief of Danbury were said to be the last able-bodied men left in town. Ethan Allen had Litchfield connections, and the town shared the glory of his capture of Ticonderoga. During the war, the town served as headquarters for relief and inspection committees, and provisions and military supplies were stored there, including those taken at the capture of General Burgoyne. Important prisoners of war were kept at Litchfield also, including the royal governor of

The Gould Law School Building on North Street, a continuation of Reeve's Law School. From *White's History of Litchfield*, ca. 1820. Courtesy of the Litchfield Historical Society

St. Anthony's of Padua Church on South Street. Built in 1947; steeple raised on September 6, 1961. Courtesy of the Litchfield Historical Society

New Jersey and the mayor of New York. After the British had taken New York, New England-Pennsylvania travel was routed through the town. Washington, Lafayette, and Rochambeau all visited there, and, after Arnold's treason, Major André was placed in the custody of Colonel Tallmadge, who became greatly attached to him and was terribly moved by his execution.

When the news of the capture of St. Johns was announced, and received with rapture, during morning service at Litchfield, together with an appeal for clothing for the troops, the women of the town desecrated the Sabbath by addressing themselves to their looms and spinning wheels, instead of returning to church for the afternoon service, and were justified by their pastor on the ground that mercy was more important than sacrifice. But the most picturesque local incident of the Revolution occurred when the statue of King George III, removed from its pedestal at Bowling Green, New York City, was brought to Litchfield by oxcart and

melted and made into bullets in the apple orchard behind the Oliver Wolcott house.

Under the early Republic, Litchfield was strongly Federalist, and Jefferson proved a hard pill to swallow. When he was elected John Adams's Vice-President, the Reverend Judah Champion, prayed to God in behalf of "Thy servant, the President of the United States," and then added, "O Lord, wilt Thou bestow on the Vice-President a double portion of Thy grace, for Thou knowest he needs it." In 1806, when a Democratic (or, as he would have been called in those days, a Republican) editor, Selleck Osborn, was imprisoned after a libel suit, his became a *cause célèbre* of which the Democrats made good use, and in 1817, when "Toleration" and the disestablishment of the Congregational Church in Connecticut was the issue, the Federalist Oliver Wolcott, Jr., agreed to run for Governor on the Democratic ticket and was elected.

Litchfield men had their share in the Civil and in subsequent wars also. In the Spanish-American War, Litchfield had her own particular hero (welcomed home with fanfare in 1899), in the person of Lieutenant-Commander (later Admiral) George P. Colvocoresses, executive officer of the *Concord* under Dewey at the Battle of Manila Bay. Florence Elizabeth Ennis proved herself a gifted unconscious humorist when she wrote gravely of World War I that "Litchfield's daughters believed in 'preparedness' as well as her young men, and a number of them joined the Rifle Club, becoming so proficient that they were regarded as a real bulwark against the Huns, should Litchfield ever be invaded"! The great Shakespearean actors, E. H. Sothern and his wife Julia Marlowe, were summer residents of Litchfield during this period and took part in public ceremonies there.

Litchfield's first settled minister came in 1723. In 1762 a new meetinghouse was erected on the center of the green, and this was the edifice that seemed to the "childish eye" of Harriet Beecher Stowe to have been "fashioned very nearly on the model of Noah's Ark and Solomon's Temple."

How magnificent, to my eye, seemed the turnip-like canopy that hung over the minister's head, hooked by a long iron rod to the wall above! and how apprehensively did I consider the question what would become of him if it should fall! How did I wonder at the panels on either side of the pulpit, in each of which was carved and painted a flaming red tulip, with its leaves projecting out at right angles, and then at the grapevine, in bas-relief, on the front, with exactly triangular branches of grapes alternating at exact intervals with exactly triangular leaves. . . . But the glory of our meeting-house was its singers' seat, that empyrean of those who rejoiced in the mysterious art of fa-so-la-ing. There they sat in the gallery that lined three sides of the house, treble, counter, tenor and bass, each with its appropriate leader and supporters. There were generally seated the bloom of our young people, sparkling, modest and blushing girls on one side, with their ribbons and finery, making the place as blooming and lively as a flower-garden, and fiery, forward, confident young men on the other.

Lyman Beecher was the fourth pastor of the Litchfield church, serving there from 1810 to 1826, when he departed for the Hanover Street Church in Boston. It was during his last year in Litchfield that he delivered the famous sermons that have been called the beginning of the American Temperance movement, but Litchfield had had a Temperance Association as early as 1789. Ten years before that the Stove War had occurred, on the question of whether churches should be heated, except by foot-warmers furnished by the individual worshipper, a moral issue in those days. When the stove was introduced at the Litchfield church, one pro-stover warmed his hands over it and basked in its genial warmth, while a lady belonging to the opposite faction was so overcome by the heat that she was driven out of God's house. Only one person seems to have had the presence of mind to test these reactions by placing his hand on the stove and establishing that there was no fire in it.

Not all incidents in Litchfield religious history were as amusing as this. The establishment of an Episcopal society as early as 1745 was probably sparked by what

The Litchfield Female Academy, drawing by Dr. Z. S. Webb, nineteenth century. Courtesy of the Litchfield Historical Society

Litchfield Female Academy. Advertisement from early nineteenth-century newspaper. Courtesy of the Litchfield Historical Society

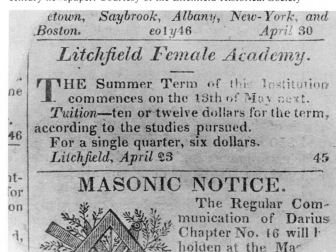

The Jail (*at left*, built in 1812) and The First National Bank of Litchfield (*right*), ca. 1967. The bank, a branch of the Phoenix Bank of Hartford, was founded in 1856. Courtesy of the Litchfield Historical Society

may have been well-founded dissatisfaction with the first Congregational pastor, Timothy Collins, but there can be no excuse for those who expressed their patriotism during the Revolution by breaking the windows in St. Michael's Church. (For two years, 1858-60, this church was served by the Shakespeare editor, Henry N. Hudson.) The indignities to which the Methodists were subjected in early Litchfield were even more disgraceful, and there were those who considered Christmas decorations in the Congregational church "papistical" even as late as 1859. The first Catholics in Litchfield had been Acadian refugees (one of whom married a Litchfield man in 1764), but there was no Catholic church building until 1868.

The first schoolhouse in Litchfield was erected in 1732; at one time there were twenty-eight school districts, each with its own small school, and many private schools besides. But the glories of Litchfield, educationally speaking, were the Law School, established and largely conducted by Judge Tapping Reeve and his associate, Judge James Gould, between 1784 and 1833 (Reeve died in 1823), and Miss Sally Pierce's school for girls, later the Litchfield Female Academy, which flourished during the same period.

The Reeve school, beginning in what looked like a little village schoolhouse, was the first law school in America, and Miss Pierce was one of the real pioneers in providing a respectworthy education for girls. The Law School trained one vice-president and an astonishing number of Cabinet members, senators and congressmen, Supreme Court justices, governors, college presidents, and others in distinguished positions, and Reeve pioneered in championing the legal rights of women. Miss Pierce's curriculum, modest at first, grew more comprehensive and innovative as time passed; her nephew and assistant, John Pierce Brace, estimated that three thousand girls passed through her hands. Like Judge Reeve's students, they came from far and wide and boarded all over the village, sometimes in the same house with the law students, thus showing that the twentieth century did not invent coeducational dormitories after all! This does not mean that the students were not carefully supervised. They were, but the supervision was not fanatical. Dancing and other forms of socializing were encouraged under carefully prescribed conditions, and though we hear of no "strolling players" in Litchfield before 1789, when a play by Shakespeare was acted in "Mr. Buel's Ball Room," the appearance of Miss Pierce's girls in such plays of her own composing as *Ruth* and *Jephthah's Daughter* were a very exciting part of the school year. Neither did she discourage dramatic composition by her pupils, as one of them, Catharine Beecher, herself later a distinguished educator, makes clear.

No more in Litchfield than in other towns has all the culture been monopolized by the schools. The *Enquirer*, which has called itself "the oldest weekly newspaper" in the state, began in 1825, but Thomas Collier had a printing office in 1784 and published the *Monitor and American Advertiser* until 1808 under frequent changes of name. According to Dr. Bostwick, "in the 70s no one's education was considered complete in Litchfield unless he or she had studied French," and since "the schools taught no languages but the dead ones," it was studied privately under Frenchmen and Frenchwomen in town who formed "an unbroken succession of character studies." There was an attempt to establish a public library as early as 1798, and not long thereafter there was a Lyceum. In its original form, what is now the Litchfield Historical Society dates back to 1856. Today, the town, considerably more cosmopolitan than of old, counts its population in excess of seven thousand. The Borough of Litchfield, which is its center, has fortunately been set aside as an Historic District.

V.   BENNINGTON

On a marker in a green plot near the Bennington Battle Monument there is an inscription which comes close to summing up the history and significance of the town.

FOR GOD AND FOR COUNTRY

The first Protestant church within the present limits of Vermont was organized here December 3, 1762. The settlers having arrived June 18, 1761. On this site was erected 1763-65 the first Meeting House in the New Hampshire Grants; a plain building of unpainted wood, fifty feet by forty. Replaced in 1806 by the present church edifice.

Here preached Jedediah Dewey, the first Minister of the Church, the trusted councillor of the Colonists. Here the forefathers met in prayer for assistance against the oppressive measures of New York and the overwhelming power of King George. Hither the settlers returned from the capture of Ticonderoga, the Battle of Bennington, the surrender of Burgoyne, to offer up their thanksgiving; here were brought the 700 prisoners captured on August 16, 1777.

For forty years the center of the religious life of the community, the Meeting House was also connected with the political life of the state. Vermont was an independent republic from January 17, 1777 to its admission into the Union March 4, 1791. The first legislature met at Windsor in 1778 and adjourned to Bennington for its June session held on this site. The laws for carrying on the government of this sovereign state were enacted at the session of the legislature which assembled in the Meeting House February 11, 1779.

Here met the convention consisting of one delegate from each town which on January 10, 1791, ratified the constitution of the United States by the signatures of 105 out of 109 delegates, thereby preparing the way for the admission of Vermont into the Union, as the first state after the original thirteen.

Let us see, then, what can be done to fill in this outline.

Bennington, Vermont, today includes the former Bennington Village (now merged with the town), North

The Battle Monument at Bennington Center stands 306 feet high and has 412 steps to the look-out floor. The battle of Bennington was fought here on August 16, 1777.

Bennington flag. Courtesy of Bennington Museum, Inc. Bennington, Vermont

Bennington, and Old Bennington. The country round about is less hilly than much of Vermont, but with Mount Anthony to the southwest and the Green Mountains toward the east. Old Bennington has handsome, harmonious modern residences standing among its cherished and carefully preserved eighteenth-century houses, all being grouped around Monument Avenue and dominated by the 306-foot granite shaft of the Battle Monument itself. Not many years ago, it was basically a summer town, with only a few year-round inhabitants, but this is no longer true. Bennington Village, on the Walloomsac River, is a manufacturing town of more than eight thousand which harbors textile plants and paper mills and serves as an important trading center. North Bennington, which centers on a plateau above the factories in the river bottom, has a little less than 1,500 inhabitants, engaged predominantly in woodworking and the manufacture of reproductions of colonial furniture.

Bennington was the first town chartered west of the Connecticut River in what was then known as the Wilderness or the New Hampshire Grants. The charter, issued by Governor Benning Wentworth of New Hampshire, for whom the town was named, covered six square miles and dates from 1749, though no settlement was made at this time. According to the traditional account, Captain Samuel Robinson, of Hardwick, Mas-

sachusetts, probably a descendant of the Pilgrim pastor, John Robinson, returning home from the Battle of Lake George, accidentally followed the Walloomsac instead of the Hoosac and was so captivated by the country around Bennington that he desired to settle there. After he and his associates had sought out the original proprietors and purchased their rights, Robinson led half a dozen families to settle at Bennington in June 1761; some thirty more families followed before Christmas, and on January 2, 1762, the first child, Benjamin Harwood, was born.

The land was divided into shares, with proper reservations for religious, educational, and other legitimate purposes, and the proprietors held business meetings to conduct the affairs of the settlement even before the town was organized; we have the minutes of the meeting held on February 11, 1762. A gristmill and a sawmill seem to have been set up in the same year. The first meetinghouse, begun in 1763, had a porch twenty foot square but no steeple; the second story was used as a schoolroom. The 1806 building was designed by Lavius Fillmore, who worked under the influence of Asher Benjamin; it and Fillmore's church in Middlebury are generally considered the finest in Vermont. It has fine Palladian windows and an open belfry, but the oval "windows" in the "lantern" above the belfry are actually designs in black paint.

Battle of Bennington, painting by Alonzo Chappel, ca. 1868-70.
Courtesy of Bennington Museum, Inc. Bennington, Vermont

Elijah Dewey of Bennington, prominent townsman and captain at
Battle of Bennington. Painting by Ralph Earl. Courtesy of Bennington Museum, Inc. Bennington, Vermont

Old First Church, Old Bennington. Built in 1805, it is considered one of the finest church buildings in America. The burial ground is the first and oldest in the state. The church and cemetery have been declared "Vermont's Colonial Shrine."

Bottom right

Old First Church cemetery: headstone of Jedidiah Dewey. Photo by Anita Duncan

Old First Church cemetery. Robert Frost is buried here. Photo by Anita Duncan

Interior of Old First Church.

Silk Road Bridge, one of Bennington's four covered bridges.
Photo by Anita Duncan

Samuel Robinson, "the first person appointed to a judicial office within the limits of the State," was the leading man in the early settlement, but unfortunately he did not live long. In 1766 he went to London to oppose the New York claims to the western lands, where he obtained an order from King George III in council, commanding the Governor of New York, "upon pain of his Majesty's highest displeasure, to make no grant whatever of any part of the lands in dispute, until his Majesty's pleasure should be further known," but was unfortunately stricken with smallpox as he was preparing to return home and died in October 1767. He was not, however, the only remarkable member of his family. His wife, a student and "a superior sort," wept that she must live in "the Wilderness," but when wolves attacked her cabin door while she was alone inside with her children, she emerged shouting to scare them away with firebrands, and her son, Jonathan, who became a noted trial lawyer, was an honest, highly emotional man, as much concerned with justice for his Indian clients as he was for his own kind.

In his spread-eagle way, George Bancroft describes the condition of Bennington around 1765:

Men of New England of a superior sort . . . had formed already a community of sixty-seven families, in as many houses, with an ordained minister; had elected their own municipal officers; formed several public schools; set their meeting-house among their primeval forests of beech and maple; and, in a word, enjoyed the flourishing state which springs from rural industry, intelligence, and unaffected piety.

The fly in the ointment was the controversy over land titles with New York (supplemented, at a later stage, by the aspirations of the Vermonters toward indepen-

dent statehood, apart from New Hampshire). Land grants conflicted so hopelessly in colonial America, and were set up in such cavalier disregard of American geography, that it is not necessary to try to find a villain in the controversy or to divide the adversaries into "good guys" and "bad guys" in order to understand how the people of Bennington and their neighbors felt when New York entered claims of retrospective and prospective jurisdiction, sent out surveyors, set up trials, and issued writs of ejectment, or cavalierly proposed that settlers should buy over again what they already considered themselves to own. Said Ethan Allen:

If we do not oppose the sheriff and his posse he will take immediate possession of our houses and farms; if we do we are immediately indicted as rioters; and when others oppose officers in taking such, their friends so indicted, they are also indicted, and so on, there being no end of indictments against us so long as we act the bold and manly part, and stand by our liberty.

Ideational as well as property considerations were involved, for the New Yorkers were aristocratic and the men in the Grants "fierce republicans." As the careful Bennington historian, the Reverend Isaac Jennings, puts it, "Had the New York jurisdiction, and the policy which the New York provincial government seemed determined to indissolubly wed with it, not been resisted, they would have established their lordly manors here, and become patroons of the Walloomsac and the Battenkill."

The struggle continued in one form or another for many years, but the hottest phase began about 1770 and involved Ethan Allen and his "Green Mountain Boys," so called because their opponents had threatened to drive them "into the Green Mountains." Allen, as colonel, commanded all the companies of this extraofficial group; Seth Warner was the captain of the Bennington company. Both were Bennington men, but it is Warner's statue which stands near the Battle Monument; one wonders if he was not considered safer, perhaps even more respectable, than the more flamboyant Allen, who was surely one of the most picturesque characters in American history. When the attorney general of New York advised him and his friends to yield because they must certainly be defeated, he replied that "the gods of the valleys were not the gods of the hills," and the Revolution was just getting under way when he was to demand and obtain the surrender of Fort Ticonderoga "in the name of the great Jehovah and the Continental Congress." Every schoolboy has thrilled to these utterances (or did, back in the days when schoolboys were still thrillable), and if Allen did not really voice them, it makes no great difference, for he was one of those persons whose legends always triumph over their lives.

The Green Mountain Boys met and made their plans at Stephen Fay's Green Mountain Tavern, where a stuffed catamount, snarling toward the New York border, expressed their feelings for them. The tavern, which later took to itself the name of the cat, burned in 1871, but the animal is still commemorated in bronze upon its site. The first skirmish occurred at Breakenridge Farm, which Sheriff Ten Eyck and a three-hundred-man posse had tried to seize; they were forced to fall back. Remember Baker was captured by the Yorkers but retaken before they could get him over the border. Allen's best biographer, Charles A. Jellison, declares soberly that it is "very probable that without him Vermont would never have come into being, or, once under way, could not have survived its early years of crisis." Jellison even hazards, perhaps more problematically, that "by capturing Fort Ticonderoga and securing control over the Champlain waterways during the early days of the Revolution," Allen may have "saved the new nation from being stillborn."*

Unfortunately, Fort Ticonderoga, captured in May 1775, did not stay captured, but was retaken by the British on July 6, 1777 (Allen himself had meanwhile been made prisoner before Montreal). With the American expedition against Quebec a failure, and with General Burgoyne victorious around Lake Champlain, there were public fasts in New England and New York, and Stockbridge, Massachusetts, was "greatly burdened with people who had fled from the New Hampshire Grants." The murder of Jane McCrea, daughter of a Presbyterian clergyman of New Jersey, by Burgoyne's Indian allies (unpunished, against the general's will, for fear of losing Indian support), while under escort to join her betrothed husband within the British lines, awakened widespread horror and indignation and was commemorated in literature and art.

On July 30 Burgoyne established his headquarters at Fort Edward, hoping to move to join General Howe at Albany, thus cutting his opposition in two and hopefully putting an end to the rebellion. Being short of supplies, he sent Colonel Friedrich Baum on what he thought of as a routine assignment to take possession of the stores he knew had been collected at Bennington: "Mount your dragoons; send me thirteen hundred horses; seize Bennington; cross the mountains to Rockingham and Brattleborough; try the affections of the country; take hostages; meet me, a fortnight hence, in Albany." But it did not work out quite that way.

General John Stark had been playing Achilles on his New Hampshire farm, but he consented to command the forces raised by the legislature, on condition that he should be allowed to fight under his own auspices and not as a part of, or under the command of, the main army. On August 9 he encamped at Bennington.

The fighting began with skirmishes on the fourteenth.

On the fifteenth it poured rain. Stark attacked at three o'clock on the afternoon of the sixteenth, having first uttered another great, perhaps legendary, word: "There are the redcoats, and they are ours, or this night Molly Stark sleeps a widow." He said the action lasted two hours; others make briefer estimates. Many fled from the British ranks, but the Hessian mercenaries, heavily armed and in full battle dress on a hot day, fought with stupid, dogged determination until Baum was fatally wounded. The fighting was ending in disorder when Colonel Heinrich von Breymann arrived with reinforcements, when it began again and continued, with wavering fortunes, until sunset, before the British gave up. According to Stark, the enemy lost over two hundred men killed, including a large number of officers, with seven hundred prisoners and considerable arms; Stark himself counted thirty American dead and forty wounded. Among the former, unhappily, were four of Bennington's "most respected citizens . . . all in the prime of life and all heads of families." Colonel Baum was buried in an unmarked grave on the riverbank, and the prisoners were marched into the village, where the women, who had been praying for victory, found ropes to tie them up.

Washington called the battle a "great stroke." Bancroft calls it "one of the most brilliant and eventful" victories of the war, and General Burgoyne is said to have been convinced by it that England must lose. It prepared the way for the more decisive victory at Saratoga and was all the more remarkable because it had been won by untrained troops against regulars. The sixteenth of August became a great holiday in Bennington. The cornerstone of the Battle Monument was laid in 1887, and in 1891 President Harrison dedicated it on the centenary of Vermont's admission to the Union. Today Bennington College is located on a hilltop a few miles to the north.

The First Church was the only church in town for sixty-four years. Samuel Robinson is said to have questioned all prospective settlers as to their religious convictions; if they were Congregationalists, they were invited to settle on the Hill, but if they had other preferences, they were directed to different parts of the township. Even today Vermont is said to have more Congregationalists in proportion to its population than any other state. Nevertheless Baptist and Methodist churches were organized in 1827, Episcopal and Presbyterian in 1834, Universalist in 1836, and Roman Catholic about 1855.

The First Church soon drew in persons from surrounding communities (settlements had been made as far northward as Danby by 1765), some of whom were definitely separatist in their convictions. Revivals were frequent, those in 1801 and 1831 being especially notable. The Reverend David Avery, who served from 1780 to 1783, kept a slave woman; it is good to read that one member withdrew from the church and suffered excom-

Ethan Allen, Frontier Rebel (Syracuse University Press, 1969).

Easter Dawn Mass: St. Francis de Sales Church, 1852. Painting by Vermont artist Leroy Williams (signed Roy Williams). Courtesy of Bennington Museum, Inc. Bennington, Vermont

munication rather than "commune with a brother who might have a slave." But the pastor of whom we hear most is the very first, the somewhat fire-eating Jedediah Dewey, forebear of the hero of Manila Bay, and builder of the oldest house in town (1763), which has been reputed the oldest frame house in the state. On Dewey's tombstone are these lines from *King Richard II*, chosen by himself:

> *Let's talk of graves, of worms, and epitaphs;*
> *Make dust our paper, and with rainy eyes*
> *Write sorrow on the bosom of the earth.*

It is said that tourists have been much struck by this as an expression of the "original ideas of the early settlers."

The most famous stories about Dewey, however, concern two encounters with Ethan Allen. In the first he comes off victorious, but in the second Allen is given the last word. Displeased with one of Dewey's sermons, Allen is reported to have declared, "It's not so," and started to leave the church, whereupon Dewey brought him to time with "Sit down, thou bold blasphemer, and listen to the Word of God." In the other anecdote, we find Dewey thanking God for the capture of Ticonderoga but making no mention of Ethan Allen. "Parson Dewey," cried that worthy, "please mention to the Lord about my being there!"*

*Allen's mind was as active as his body; see his *Reason the Only Oracle of Man* (1785). He was a Deist, not, as his enemies called him, an atheist. Like Mark Twain, Robert Ingersoll, H. L. Mencken, and many other skeptics, he tripped himself up by attempting to destroy propositions which he did not have sufficient scholarship even to state fairly, but if anything could provide justification for him, it would be the savage and unchristian comments which learned and pious men made concerning his book.

The Vermont Gazette (1783) was the first newspaper published in Vermont; in 1849 it became *The Bennington Banner*. The earliest attempt to establish a library was made in 1793; the Old Academy Library building on Monument Avenue was designed in 1821 as "the finest building in the state." The lower floor was formerly used as a district school, and the First Church used the upper floor at one time as a prayer room. We are told that dramatic entertainments, beginning at six o'clock, were held in the Court House as early as 1787, and we know that the Hutchinson Family and others gave concerts there, but in 1822 a week of horse-racing and theatrical entertainment outraged the pious to such an extent as to lead to prohibitory legislation which remained in force for many years. Perhaps it was not the idea of theater but the circumstances surrounding it which awakened indignation on this occasion; certainly there was plenty of dialogue and elocution in the "exhibitions" given regularly on the last day of school. The settlers had shown their concern for education from the very beginning. Among the early schools above the elementary level, Clio Hall (1780) is probably the best remembered. In our own time, Bennington College, a progressive and somewhat experimental girls' college, has carried the fame of the town to many who have not even heard of the Battle Monument.

Chapter 4

The Golden Age of New England Letters

I

AMERICAN LITERATURE may be said to have begun its coming of age and to appeal beyond its own borders with the publication of *The Sketch Book* of Washington Irving in 1819-20, followed by both William Cullen Bryant's first collection of *Poems* and *The Spy* by James Fenimore Cooper in 1821. New England cannot claim either Irving or Cooper, but Bryant is a borderline case. From 1829 until his death in 1878 he was the bold, outspoken, liberal editor of the New York *Evening Post* through one of the great formative and critical periods of American history. But he was born in Cummington, Massachusetts, in 1794, the grandson of the Calvinist, Federalist squire of the town, and, like Longfellow, he was related to John Alden and Priscilla Mullins. His first poem worth noting, "The Embargo," published in a Boston paper when the poet was fourteen, represents the New England Federalist hatred of President Jefferson that followed his sponsorship of the Embargo which ruined New England coast towns. He also bitterly opposed the War of 1812 and at that time took up a secessionist position for Massachusetts.

Bryant's first collection was published in Cambridge the same year he had read his Phi Beta Kappa poem at Harvard. There were only eight pieces in the volume. Perhaps "To a Waterfowl" was the most nearly perfect, but much the most ambitious was the "Thanatopsis," in which eighteenth-century influence was still strong and which, despite the writer's personal Christianity, is essentially pagan or classical in its attitude toward death. In its original form, it went back to Bryant's sixteenth year, but it was not printed until 1817. Bryant's father sent it to *The North American Review*, whose editor hesitated to accept it because he could not believe it original work. "Phillips," said Richard Henry Dana, "you have been imposed upon. No one on this side of the Atlantic is capable of writing such verses." This judgment was not unreasonable; nobody ever had.

Though Bryant was not exclusively a nature poet, it is said that 60 out of his 190 poems deal with nature. He had an affinity of spirit with his friend Thomas Cole and the Hudson River painters, but nature as he first knew it was New England nature, and the rather sombre cast of his mind attracted him especially to the New England landscape in winter. He would seem to have discovered nature for himself in his native environment, but his reading of Wordsworth certainly helped to interpret his experience to him, and in such poems as "Oh Fairest of the Rural Maids" he wrote of the Berkshires and his own family in what seem distinctly Wordsworthian terms.

For Bryant poetry was an art of suggestion, not, like

painting and sculpture, of imitation. He was as sure as Poe that poetry must excite the imagination, but he refused to believe that this was its sole function. He granted that teaching was not poetical in the ordinary sense of the term, but he did believe that those "truths which the mind instinctively acknowledges" were suited to poetical expression. Sincerity and a worthy theme were necessary to the production of poetry, but neither would suffice without the resources of craftsmanship.

> *Then summon back the original glow, and mend*
> *The strain with rapture that with fire was penned.*

Like T. S. Eliot he was interested in the relationship between tradition and the individual talent. Between too much imitation and "an excessive ambition of originality," carried to the length of failure to communicate, he was all for the former, but he was far from believing "that a narrative poem should be written on the model of the ancient epic." Though he had no sympathy with the anti-American prejudices of many critics in his time, poetry for him was poetry; he applied the same standards of evaluation to works produced on both sides of the water. Above all, he refused to grant, in any measure, that poetry had no place in an age of science and reason, for he believed that its ultimate sources were in the human mind and that these were the same for Americans as for other peoples. Indeed the very absence in America of myth "which accounted for everything" might turn out to be an advantage because it necessitated the concentration of the poet on the age and the people among whom he lived.

Before Bryant the heroic quatrain had been the favorite verse form for American poets, but he began to use other forms even in his youth. He turned out blank verse (in his translations of the *Iliad* and *Odyssey*), sonnets, and Spenserian stanzas, but his favorite verse form was the quatrain, which he varied with great skill. His most interesting point as a prosodist is the allowance he makes for the admission of occasional trisyllabic feet in iambic measures; this was so far from being accepted in Bryant's time that many readers did not know how they were expected to read such lines. All in all, if one wishes to consider Bryant the pioneer New England poet, he did not start either poetry or poetic theory out badly.

Only, of course, he was not really that. We have already glanced at Mrs. Bradstreet and Edward Taylor in the colonial period. But we never knew we had Taylor until almost 1940, nor did Mrs. Bradstreet mean anything to what Van Wyck Brooks called the "flowering" of New England. There were other, more "modern" poets, however, preceding Bryant and during his lifetime, who, though they do not loom large now, ought at least to be mentioned in passing.

Longfellow, distinguishing between the "actual" and

William Cullen Bryant, painting by Samuel F. B. Morse, 1825. New York Public Library Picture Collection

Bryant as editor of the New York *Evening Post*, as *Harper's Weekly* saw him at the time of his death in 1878. New York Public Library Picture Collection

the "ideal" in poetry, cites Goethe, Wordsworth, and Bryant as representative of the first "school" and Byron, Schiller, and Percival for the latter. The one unfamiliar name which we are obviously intended to know quite as well as the others gives the modern reader a shock, but during the 1820s James Gates Percival (1795-1856) was often called the leading American poet. He was the foremost representative on this side of the water of what might be called the *Werther* school of romanticism, even to the extent of attempting suicide in his youth, but he had a hard life, for his economic failure as a poet was complete, and he did not do much better in a number of endeavors in science. Nevertheless he must have had more stamina than he is sometimes credited with, for he ultimately achieved some distinction as a geologist, and he waited for the natural end, which came in Wisconsin while he was engaged in geological labors there.

Older than Percival were "the Connecticut Wits"—John Trumbull (1750-1831), Timothy Dwight (1752-1817), Joel Barlow (1754-1812), and others, who wrote in the neoclassic manner. Such fame as they still command today belongs largely to Barlow. If *The Vision of Columbus*, revised and enlarged as *The Columbiad*, in which the discoverer foresees the future greatness of America, has few readers today, it was a great book in its time (and an early example of de luxe American publishing), and *The Hasty Pudding*, a mock-heroic piece which praises other aspects of New England besides the dish indicated in its title, still counts its admirers.

"The Sweet Singer of Hartford," Lydia Huntley Sigourney (1791-1865) published sixty-seven volumes which enjoyed popularity and respect in their time, but though some of her verses are not so bad as they have been reputed, her sentimentalism brought upon her the sad fate of surviving mainly as a joke. On the other hand, the interest in black literature which has developed in our time has redirected attention to the Boston African slave girl, Phillis Wheatley (1754?-1784), whose poems, some of them occasional, were based on eighteenth-century models. She seems to have been a charming person who enjoyed both amazing good fortune and bitter disappointment during her short life, and she herself was probably more interesting than any-thing she wrote, remarkable as her work was for one in her circumstances.

The elder Richard Henry Dana (1787-1879) was much more important. He lost his place as an editor of *The North American Review* because his Romantic sympathies were considered too radical, but he clung to Federalism and Trinitarianism after most of his friends had abandoned both, thus managing to be out of step all along the line. Though his literary career as a whole ended in disappointment, he published essays as well as poems and a fairly well-known novel, *Paul Felton*. He was the father of the Richard Henry Dana (1815-1882) who wrote *Two Years Before the Mast*, in its own way a prose classic worthy of comparison with *Robinson Crusoe*. Based upon personal experience, it was the fulfillment of Dana's vow that "if God ever gave me the means, I would do something to redress the grievances and relieve the sufferings of that class of beings with whom my lot . . . had been cast," but Dana did not stop with writing; as a distinguished lawyer, he remained the sailor's friend as long as he lived, an outstanding exemplar of the conscience and humanity of the Boston Brahmins.

Nathaniel Parker Willis (1806-1867) was younger and more "modern" than the elder Dana, and his later years belonged to New York, but he was born in Portland. His father was the founder of *The Youth's Companion* and a deacon of Boston's Park Street Church, and he was educated at Boston Latin, Andover, and Yale. Though he died at Cornwall-on-Hudson, he was buried at Mount Auburn in Cambridge, and Longfellow, Holmes, and Lowell were among his pallbearers.

Timothy Dwight. Library of Congress

Joel Barlow. From a painting by Chappel. New York Public Library Picture Collection

John Trumbull, painted by Waldo & Jewett, engraved by A.B. Durand. Library of Congress

Phillis Wheatley. Library of Congress

Richard Henry Dana (1787-1879). Lithograph, *New York Graphic*, November 22, 1877, from a photo by Warren. New York Public Library Picture Collection

Richard Henry Dana (1815-1882), author of *Two Years Before the Mast*, in 1840. New York Public Library Picture Collection

Two Years Before the Mast

A Personal Narrative

By

RICHARD HENRY DANA, Jr.

BOSTON AND NEW YORK

HOUGHTON MIFFLIN COMPANY

The Riverside Press Cambridge

N. P. Willis, after the portrait by Lawrence. New York Public Library Picture Collection

Title page of *Two Years Before the Mast*—this is not the original edition but a more modern one. New York Public Library Picture Collection

Willis is an outstanding example of how completely posterity may choose to forget a man who has occupied a prominent place during his lifetime; we are told that there was a Boston gentleman who had never heard of Goethe but who, upon being made aware of his existence, inquired whether he was the N. P. Willis of Germany. Though Willis's first popularity was won with the scriptural paraphrases which were in tune with the taste of his time, his natural affinity was with a much lighter kind of verse and especially with the facile travel sketches, imitated by many writers, which he threw off in rapid succession, beginning with *Pencillings by the Way* in 1835. But he tried almost everything. *Tortesa the Usurer* is an important early nineteenth-century play, and he produced many short stories. Though he was not profound, he may well deserve more respect, both as a writer and as a man, than is often accorded him now that belles lettres is out of fashion.

II

The poets who really represented the Golden Age were Ralph Waldo Emerson, Henry Wadsworth Longfellow, John Greenleaf Whittier, Oliver Wendell Holmes, and James Russell Lowell. Collectively their lives extended from the birth of Emerson in 1803 to the death of Holmes in 1894. Both Longfellow and Whittier were born in 1807; Longfellow died in 1882, about a month before Emerson, but Whittier lived ten years longer. Holmes came along in 1809, Lowell not until 1819, but he had a somewhat shorter life, dying the year before Whittier. Emily Dickinson, whom many readers of today would grant parity with the "great" poets, was not born until 1830, but she died in 1886, when all the others except Emerson and Longfellow were still alive.

Emerson wrote much more prose than verse, and the high poetic claims often made for him are sometimes questioned both by those who think of him as a Yankee moralist or religionist and those who are troubled by his limitations as a poetic craftsman. Nobody who is at all sensitive to poetic quality can fail to feel the majesty and beauty of such verses as

Music pours on mortals his beautiful disdain

or

O tenderly the haughty day
Fills his blue urn with fire,

nor the perfection of such short poems as "Days" and the "Concord Hymn," but Emerson's high poetic quality is rarely sustained; all the passages which have inflamed the imagination are very brief, sometimes even single lines. He resembled Poe, whom he despised and called "the jingle man," both in the roughness and ineptitude of which he was sometimes inexplicably capable in his verses and in the narrowness of his emotional range. His poetic sensibilities were not stimulated by the flush and clash of everyday passions which inspire many poets, and he often seems indifferent to conventional smooth beauties; in "Merlin" indeed he urges the poet not to encumber his brain "with the coil of rhythm and number" but rather to "mount to paradise/By the stairway of surprise." His conception of art was organic, and he was much more given to symbolical and implicational methods of presentation than many of his contemporaries. None of these considerations seem quite to cover his case, however, for some of his very best poems are fairly regular, his own tastes in poetry were fairly conservative, and he often criticizes others severely for the same faults of which he himself is guilty.

The essential point is that Emerson had the *mind* of a poet—perceptive, intuitive, not logical nor systematic—and this may be seen in his essays quite as clearly as in his poems. He never argues or persuades. He does not reason out truth but perceives it and proclaims it; his affinity is with the prophets of the Old Testament and with gnomic or oracular utterances of all kinds, in which it hardly seems necessary to add that he was in harmony with the tenets of the transcendentalism of which he is generally considered the outstanding representative. Whether transcendentalism really was a "movement" might well be questioned, but it *was* a way of looking at life. What the transcendentalists transcended, or tried to, was man's imprisonment in the five senses, aspiring toward a direct, intuitive apprehension of spiritual realities by virtue of a spiritual sensitiveness which they, like Kant, believed to be inherent in human beings. Minor, didactic poets begin with the moral and apply poetic ornamentation to it like a veneer; Emerson

Ralph Waldo Emerson. Library of Congress

never does this. Man, even poetic man, may think, even pray, as well as vibrate; with Emerson the idea, or truth, and the poetic inspiration coincide. His poetry would not be either better or worse without the moral and spiritual meaning which inheres in it; it would simply not exist at all.

None of the "right-thinking" persons of his own time were ever in danger of thinking of Emerson as a conventional moralist. Unable to perceive that the self-reliance he advocated was essentially a reliance upon the God within us, or man's share of divinity, some thought he was merely encouraging selfish people to exercise their natural tendencies toward aggrandizement. Once, when it was suggested to him that the inspiration he professed to follow might come from below rather than above, he replied calmly that though this did not seem to him to be so, if he were the devil's child he must live for the devil.

He began his career as a Unitarian minister in Boston, but the year after the death of his beautiful, gifted young wife in 1831, he resigned his pulpit, ostensibly because he could no longer conscientiously administer the sacrament of the Lord's Supper but actually because the spontaneity which for him was the heart of the spiritual life had come to seem increasingly impossible under the prescribed conditions of ecclesiasticism. After his second marriage in 1835 he made his home in Concord and earned his living as a lecturer, for his books never sold well enough to pay his way.

He was a man in whom what are often considered disparate qualities existed in harmonious balance, combining strength and great gentleness to an extraordinary degree; if he was incapable of discourtesy, he was equally incapable of being swerved one inch from his chosen course. Nor did his heavy reliance upon intuition ever lead him in the direction of anti-intellectualism. He read prodigiously in a wide variety of writers and thinkers, many of whom were little known in his America. He was steeped in the Bible, in Plato and the neo-Platonists, Catholic mystics, seventeenth-century religious writers, and, most remarkably, especially in later life, Hindu and Persian literature, but what he found in all of these was more like consanguinity of spirit than authority. Emerson had the gift of finding what he needed in his reading, or that which interpreted him to himself. There is a delightful story about a little girl who, being required by her teacher to commit to memory an Emerson poem of her own choice, astonished everybody by choosing the difficult "Brahma." When she was asked why she had thus chosen, she replied that some of the other poems she had considered were hard to understand but that this one was easy because it simply affirmed that God was everywhere. She was a truly Emersonian child, and who shall deny that she understood him better than some who have tried to write learned books about him?

Emerson was not, nor did he ever claim to be, in the

technical sense, a philosopher, but, as Charles Eliot Norton well observed at the Concord centenary celebration in 1903, he held to "the Unity of Being in God and Man . . . the creation of the visible, material world by mind . . . and . . . the identity and universality of moral law in the spiritual and material universe." His emphasis upon self-expression, his harmony with the nonmaterialistic aspects of modern scientific thinking, his organicism, and his stress upon the psychological aspects of aesthetic experience all give him an affinity with moderns, but perhaps we need him most of all for his faith in and exemplification of goodness in perfect freedom. He praised ecstasy; he even understood those who have conceived holiness in orgiastic terms, but his own balance, common sense, and excellent taste always saved him from being seduced by such vagaries. If free men cannot live virtuous, sensitive, and socially useful lives, it is difficult to see how democracy can survive, for this would throw us back upon a choice between tyrannical regimentation and anarchic dissipation and waste. Perhaps Emerson's survival as a force in the modern world is in no small measure due to the inspiration of his example in this aspect.

It was Longfellow, however, who was the archetypical poet of New England in the Golden Age and of America too and beyond it, both in time and in space, for in England he was described as the foremost poet of the English-speaking world in the very year of *In Memoriam*. Five thousand copies of *The Courtship of Miles Standish* were sold in Boston on publication day; the New York *Ledger* spent $4,000 on "The Hanging of the Crane"; *Harper's Magazine* postponed its publication date in order to be able to include "Morituri Salutamus" after he had read it at his fiftieth Bowdoin College class reunion. Today many moderns see Whitman as the embodiment of the teeming, burgeoning America of his time, but his contemporaries refused to read Whitman, whose oddities and rebellions formed a much higher barrier for them to get over than Longfellow's gentilities. Longfellow attempted bigger things than most of his contemporaries; whole generations learned what poetry was from him and had their conception of it determined by him. His lyrics expressed their hopes and their aspirations; they were entranced by his undeniable storytelling skill in the ballads and *Tales of a Wayside Inn*; of his more ambitious enterprises—*Evangeline* (the first enduring long poem in American literature), *The Song of Hiawatha*, *The Golden Legend* (afterwards taken up into the *Christus*), and *The Courtship of Miles Standish*—only the *Legend* failed of resounding success. The only gifted sonneteer among the "Schoolroom Poets," he used the Italian, not the simpler Shakespearean, form; even his greatest detractors have not been able to denigrate his accomplishment here nor in the sophisticated lyrics of his last years. Whatever else may be said of him, he certainly had the widest range and the greatest technical skill of any of his contemporaries.

His beautiful house in Cambridge (once Washington's headquarters) is now a National Historic Shrine, and he still has his admirers among both critics and general readers, but there is no denying that he has lost more than many of his contemporaries (if only because he had more to lose), and it will not do to ascribe this wholly to the rising tide of barbarism in a world which has made gentility a dirty word and bawdy (which was once unprintable) a term of praise and which finds it as difficult to distinguish between sentiment and sentimentality as between *like* and *as* or *shall* and *will*. A professional scholar, an accomplished linguist, and a learned man, Longfellow valued simplicity and clarity both in art and in life while his descendants cherish obscurity and complexity. There was a certain blandness in both his art and his temperament which, in times like these, one can hardly fail to be conscious of. At his worst, he *is* sentimental, and anthologists have done him a disservice by continually reprinting such a poor poem as "A Psalm of Life," which has now lost the inspirational power it possessed in its own time as an expression of independence and the pioneer spirit, when (though it is now hard to believe it) it was admired and imitated by (of all people) Baudelaire.

We cannot admire a poet because we think we ought to if he does not speak to us directly, but we can fail to

Henry Wadsworth Longfellow, photograph by Julia Margaret Cameron. He raised the beard after the burns he sustained in attempting to help his wife when she was burned to death in 1861 made shaving difficult or inadvisable. New York Public Library Picture Collection

This beautiful house at 105 Brattle Street, Cambridge, Mass., was built by Henry Vassall in 1759 and used by George Washington during the Revolution. Formerly known as the Craigie House, it was for many years the home of the poet Henry Wadsworth Longfellow and is now the Longfellow National Historic Site, administered by the National Park Service. FPG

Longfellow, from a pastel by Francis Alexander, 1852. New York Public Library Picture Collection

Longfellow as a student at Göttingen, 1829, a self-portrait. New York Public Library Picture Collection

hear what he is saying if we are deaf or have been deafened, and much of the reaction against Longfellow has been occasioned by misapprehensions concerning him. We tend to think of him as conventional and imitative, yet much of what seems to us his conventionality was established by him; he had no exaggerated reverence for tradition. Though he was ultimately a fairly wealthy man, he was a comparatively poor boy, but when it came to earning a living, he turned not to the law, as his father intended, but to the then novel teaching of the modern languages, which he helped to establish as a part of American education, and when he began to write he was a "new poet" whom many readers found obscure and not sufficiently uplifting. "The Skeleton in Armor" was severely criticized on this score, and as late as *Hiawatha*, a Boston paper objected to his use of "the silly legends of the savage aborigines" and failure to "teach a single truth." Longfellow could write like the imagists when he wanted to, as in "Daylight and Moonlight" and *Kéramos*, but mere impressionism did not seem to him the poet's whole function. If he wished "to charm, to strengthen, and to teach," this was less because he was fond of moralizing than because he was interested not only in the surface of life but also in its meaning. He thought, and thought clearly, about what we call the psychology of the poetic inspiration (like Keats he believed that if poetry does not come as naturally as leaves to a tree, it had better not come at all), and for him the purpose of the imagination was not "to devise what has no existence, but rather to perceive what really exists . . . not creation but insight." He was a Christian humanist and his subject was human life; for the most part, he avoids the sentimental nature pantheism that was so widespread in his time. Above everything else, his characteristic note is that of a sensitive, cultivated man, brooding over and assimilating a great cultural inheritance.

In his moral and literary ideals alike, Longfellow generally strikes us as very American or Anglo-Saxon; actually he was one of the pioneer American cosmopolitans. His knowledge of European languages and literatures, painfully acquired through extended European residence and study, was surpassed by few contemporaries; through his own poems and translations and his great anthology, *The Poets and Poetry of Europe*, he introduced many Americans to European writing and became one of the outstanding interpreters of Continental civilization in the United States, and if this be

Longfellow in 1850, from a daguerreotype made in Boston.

Fanny Appleton, later Mrs. Henry Wadsworth Longfellow, from the painting by G. P. A. Healy, in the Longfellow House, Cambridge.

The Courtship of Miles Standish, the title page and the first page of the text. Library of Congress

taken to indicate his inferiority to, say, Whitman or any of his successors, Whitman himself comes to his rescue when he declares that

America and the world may well be reverently thankful—can never be thankful enough—for any such singing-bird vouchsafed out of centuries; without asking that the notes be different from those of other songsters; adding what I have heard Longfellow himself say, that ere the new world can be worthily original, and announce herself and her own heroes, she must be well saturated with the originality of others, and respectfully consider the heroes who lived before Agamemnon.

Yet, though Longfellow had no intention of cutting Americans off from their cultural tradition, he always used an American, not a European, stick of measurement, and if some of the things he said about Europe were quoted out of context, the general reader might be more inclined to attribute them to Mark Twain than to him. His essay on "The Defence of Poetry," published in *The North American Review* in 1832, anticipated much of what Emerson was to say five years later in the Harvard Phi Beta Kappa oration which has been widely hailed as signalizing an intellectual declaration of independence. "Paul Revere's Ride" is only one among many examples which might be cited to show the free, often bold use which Longfellow made of American and New England materials among his shorter poems,

and of the longer efforts only *The Golden Legend* is European. His interest in Indians, emerging almost at the beginning in "Burial of the Minnisink" and flowering in *The Song of Hiawatha*, though it revealed no intimate knowledge, did show considerable sympathetic interest. For a writer whom the popular imagination identifies primarily with the domestic affections, Longfellow had a remarkable interest in primitivism; if "The Saga of King Olaf" has obviously been fed by literary influences, its presence in his canon still indicates a wider range of interests than he is always given credit for.

John Greenleaf Whittier, the "barefoot boy" of Haverhill, a Quaker abstemious beyond his peers, the only bachelor among them and the only one who never went to Europe nor to college nor learned a foreign language, was a less accomplished technician than Longfellow, but he often fares better with modern critics because of his stronger indigenous quality. He was born on a farm his family had owned since 1647 and in a house they had built in 1688, and he was certainly closer to the New England soil than any other major poet before Robert Frost. No more than the Burns he admired and in some ways resembled was Whittier ever that fabled animal, an "untutored genius," but the tutoring he received was largely self-directed. He read widely, and he did much better with exotic materials than most untraveled persons have done; both Scandinavia and the Orient interested him as sources of lit-

Mr. and Mrs. Henry Ford and Miss Martha Hopkins (teacher) with pupils before Red Stone School (of "Mary Had a Little Lamb" fame), which was removed from Sterling, Mass., to the Wayside Inn property at Sudbury, Mass. FPG

An old photograph of the Wayside Inn, Sudbury, Mass., which furnished the setting for Longfellow's *Tales of a Wayside Inn*. Clay Allen photo

John Greenleaf Whittier, bust by William Ordway Partridge. New York Public Library Picture Collection

Whittier's birthplace, near Haverhill, Mass.
Massachusetts Historical Society

Whittier in later life. From a lithograph
by Armstrong & Co., 1887. Library of
Congress

erary material, and his Italian pieces have reminded more than one critic of Browning. He attempted few long flights; *Snow-Bound*, the supreme "Yankee pastoral" whose absence from American literature he had lamented, exemplifying the "poetry of human life and simple nature, of the hearth and the farm field," and "The Pennsylvania Pilgrim" are his most sustained longer pieces, for *The Tent on the Beach*, which started out to be a kind of *Tales of a Wayside Inn*, has never been accounted one of his great successes. He tied himself to temporalities by writing abolitionist verse, much of which has now mainly an historical value, though there are pieces like his attack on Daniel Webster for his capitulation to the slave power, "Ichabod," which transcend their occasion, making it merely a point of departure for an expression of love, compassion, or indignation which still moves. The religious lyrics, on the other hand, are as timeless as the antislavery poems are timely; the work of a writer whose own religious society made no use of music, they have broken through denominational barriers and become a part of public worship in all Protestant churches. But though the general atmosphere of Whittier's religious poems is quietist, there is nothing soft about them, and both "Our Master" and "The Eternal Goodness" involve controversial aspects generally unapprehended by those who fail to see them in their historical context. "The Eternal Goodness" is a gentle but quite uncompromising attack upon Calvinism and what seemed to Whittier its savage conception of the character of God, and "Our Master" specifically rejects not only sacramentalism and millenarianism but also biblical literalism and authoritarianism, along with every aspect of creedalism and institutionalism which erected barriers between the individual worshipper and the spirit of God operating directly through mystical insight upon his own soul.

Whittier was far from giving all his time to poetry. His success as a poet came late in life; after having starved so far as authorship was concerned through many years, he suddenly and unexpectedly came into great prosperity and popularity with *Snow-Bound* and died leaving a surprisingly considerable estate. It is often said that he devoted his early years to journalism and reform activities (he edited a number of abolitionist papers and knew what it meant to face a mob) and his later years to authorship, but this is not quite accurate. His poetical ambitions went back to his boyhood, and he published a considerable quantity (though not quality) of verse during his early years. A passionate man who seems at one time to have cherished political ambitions, he generally chose to exercise his political influence by working on hopeful candidates behind the scenes, and he was very skillful at such work. He en-

"Oak Knoll," the home of Whittier's relatives, Mrs. Woodman and the Misses Johnson, at Danvers, Mass., where the poet spent much time in his later years. The Bettmann Archive

The kitchen in the birthplace of Whittier, Haverhill, Mass. Note his boots in front of the fireplace. The Bettmann Archive

couraged, then, being disappointed in him, helped abort the political career of Caleb Cushing, and he was an important influence on Charles Sumner, whom he helped steer into politics. Certainly Whittier himself never placed ambition ahead of duty but paid, and paid gladly, the price of a clear conscience. He was "a man, and not a mere verse-maker"; when he published his antislavery manifesto, *Justice and Expediency*, he burned many bridges behind him and took his place with the outcasts. Afterwards he said he was more proud of having done that than of seeing his name on the title page of any book, and he had a right to be. Perhaps it was because he knew so little of Europe that he thought more consistently in American terms than many Easterners in his time, but it is surely to his credit that, for all his saturation in New England, he was never in danger of identifying it with America. The prospect of building a railroad from Chicago to the mouth of the Columbia thrilled him, and after the Civil War he was far more interested in labor problems,

woman suffrage, and other causes than many old abolitionists who, having won their particular fight, were now tempted to rest upon their oars and await the millennium.

Though Whittier is always thought of as a poet, his journalistic activities necessitated the writing of more prose than verse, and nothing that has been written in our time concerning the iniquities of the Vietnam adventure and other crimes has more fire in it than what he wrote about the Mexican War in 1843. Few of the editorials have been reprinted, but three out of the seven "collected" volumes are devoted to prose, though only one item, the novel *Leaves from Margaret Smith's Journal*, ranks with his finest work. This is one of the neglected minor classics of American literature; aside from Harriet Beecher Stowe's *Oldtown Folks*, I know nothing worthy of comparison with it in kind. It is written in the form of a journal kept by an English girl during a visit to Massachusetts in 1678-79. The Massachusetts countryside is triumphantly alive in it; it embodies rural customs and local superstitions; it touches all the "concerns" with which the Quaker conscience was involved. *Margaret Smith's Journal* is indeed as authentically New England as *Snow-Bound* and it adds up to a fascinating synthesis of Whittier's interests as a man and his talents as an artist.

Though it is his only novel, it is not otherwise anomalous among his works. His first book, *Legends of New England*, which contains both prose and verse, was published in 1831, only nineteen years after the first collection by the Brothers Grimm, before the word "folklore" had been coined, and nearly half a century before the establishment of the English Folklore Society. In 1843 came his first wholly poetical work, *Lays of My Home and Other Poems*, and in 1847 his prose study of *The Supernaturalism of New England*, some of which had already been serialized. Thereafter New England was most visibly present in such pieces as "Cassandra Southwick," "The Double-Headed Snake of Newberry," which harked back to Cotton Mather, the splendid "Telling the Bees," and others. It was just as well that legendary and historical materials should be placed in the same division of the collected poems. Whittier treated both the same way; like Longfellow he knew that in literature aesthetic and imaginative considerations must prevail, and "Skipper Ireson's Ride" is even more inaccurate historically than "Paul Revere's Ride." Perhaps the most unusual piece is the amazing "Prelude" to "Among the Hills," which gives as realistic a picture of New England farm life as *Snow-Bound* was idyllic—

> *Shrill, querulous women, sour and sullen men*
> *Untidy, loveless, old before their time,*
> *With scarce a human interest save their own*
> *Monotonous round of small economies,*
> *Or the poor scandal of the neighborhood*

and actually throws the mind forward to what Hamlin Garland was so much later to do for the Middle West in *Main-Travelled Roads*; in its very different way, this piece is as remarkable and as characteristic of New England as Lowell's radiant "Sunthin' in the Pastoral Line" in the second series of *The Biglow Papers*. This kind of thing is not necessarily the best work among Whittier's poems but it is certainly the most distinctive. All in all, the proportion of quite first-rate poetry is probably comparatively small in all areas of his work, but the best of it is surely indispensable for New England literature and civilization. As somebody has said of God, if there were no Whittier, it would have been necessary to invent him.

Considerably younger than Longfellow, James Russell Lowell seems closer in spirit to him than Holmes, who, though born in "a gambrel-roofed house on the edge of the Harvard Yard," lived in Boston and came to be thought of, along with Mrs. Longfellow's brother, Thomas G. Appleton, as the typical Beacon Street wit.

James Russell Lowell, a lithograph by Armstrong & Co., 1878. Library of Congress

Longfellow, though he adopted Cambridge, was born in Portland, and though one of the most eminent among Cantabrigians, he wore this, like all other honors, lightly. Lowell was born into what has always been a distinguished New England family, at "Elmwood," the very house in which he died, and he took it all very seriously indeed.

Lowell was a many-sided man and he had a far more varied career than any of the others. Even as a writer it remains an open question whether he was more important as a poet or as a critic, and there have always been those who have been convinced that he would have plowed deeper and accomplished more if he had not scattered his shot. He inherited the Smith Professorship at Harvard when Longfellow gave it up and became a great Dantean and a distinguished philologist. As the first editor of *The Atlantic Monthly*, when it was established in 1857, he published all his friends; later he was joint editor with Charles Eliot Norton of *The North American Review*. Still later he served as American ambassador to both Spain and England.

During his early years Lowell was a very enthusiastic and intensely reform-minded young man; though he never served the abolitionist cause with Whittier's single-minded zeal, his antislavery writings still fill two volumes. He was right when he found himself "very curiously compounded of two utterly distinct characters," one half being "clear mystic and enthusiast, and the other humorist." He added that he thought he had the capacity to become either a Saint Francis or a "Pantagruelist." His modern readers seem to relish his poetry most for its humor; *A Fable for Critics*, later imitated by his kinswoman Amy Lowell, in her *Critical Fable*, is still amusing and often penetrating in its evaluation of his contemporaries, and not even the almost fanatical modern disinclination to read dialect has quite killed *The Biglow Papers*. The First Series, published in 1848—Lowell's *annus mirabilis* which also ushered in the *Fable, The Vision of Sir Launfal*, and an important

Lowell. Photo by Brady

"Elmwood," Cambridge, Mass., built by Thomas Oliver, on what was once known as "Tory Row," about 1767. James Russell Lowell was born and died in this house. It is now the property of Harvard College. FPG

collection of *Poems*—is pacifist propaganda directed against the Mexican War:

> *Ez fer war, I call it murder,—*
> *There you hev it plain an' flat;*
> *I don't want to go no furder*
> *Than my Testyment fer that.*

The Puritan insistence upon individual responsibility for conduct has never been more uncompromisingly expressed:

> *Ef you take a sword an' dror it,*
> *An' go stick a feller thru,*
> *Guv'ment ain't to answer for it,*
> *God'll send the bill to you.*

When the Civil War came, however, Lowell's pacifism collapsed, and the tone of the Second Series is different.

The romantic and religious *Launfal*, whose "What is so rare as a day in June?" was once on every schoolboy's tongue, does not seem to have manifested comparable survival value, possibly in part because of its glaring structural deficiencies, though its social sensitiveness is still in harmony with the modern temper. The "Ode Recited at the Harvard Commemoration" after the Civil War is famous primarily for its remarkable tribute to Lincoln, which, oddly enough, was an afterthought, not read at the ceremony. And unfortunately far too few readers have ever discovered "The Cathedral," which, with all its rambling, is still one of the most important religious poems of the nineteenth century, a thoughtful consideration of faith and doubt in the modern world and an odd anticipation of Henry Adams's *Mont-Saint-Michel and Chartres*.

Lowell's essays include his vindication of Puritan character in "New England Two Centuries Ago" ("the history of New England is written imperishably on the face of a continent, and in characters as beneficent as they are enduring"), "A Good Word for Winter," "My Garden Acquaintance" (which is about birds), and the hard-hitting "A Certain Condescension in Foreigners," which, many years later, when the situation had changed, inspired an equally trenchant piece by Agnes Repplier, "On a Certain Condescension in Americans." But Lowell's most important prose comprises the extended critical essays about great writers, mostly British, which he collected in *My Study Windows* and the two series of *Among My Books*, titles chosen by the publishers but disliked by the author, who thought them egotistical. Like Henry James, Lowell was comparatively indifferent to antiquity; unlike him, he had no use for the realistic movement in his own time; he called *Leaves of Grass* "a solemn humbug," disliked Ibsen and the French naturalists, and refused even to read the Russian novelists of whom English readers were just becoming aware. For him "the true ideal" was "not opposed to the real . . . but lies *in* it, and blessed are the eyes [like Shakespeare's] that find it." But though he knew what he believed, Lowell never attempted an elaborate formulation of critical principles, nor are his essays rich in what Van Wyck Brooks called "general ideas"; rather they represent the response of one sensitive, gifted man to the literary expression of another individual, as set forth in a rich, allusive,

Oliver Wendell Holmes, from an engraving by Timothy Cole after a drawing by Wyatt Eaton. New York Public Library Picture Collection

often tapestried style, sometimes as highly figurative as that of Lowell's poems. From the point of view of scientific criticism (if there is such a thing) or critical method, Lowell's essays may leave much to be desired (though he was an early president of the Modern Language Association, one shudders to think of what he might have said about some of its latter-day publications), but he had great knowledge and sensibility, massive common sense, and enormous gusto. A "bookman" who never forgot that literature was created for delight and that if it does not succeed in pleasing, it will not succeed in other aspects but will simply be dead, he did as much to foster the development of literary appreciation in America as any man who has ever lived. If his readers have now shrunken to that "fit audience though few" which Milton hoped for, those who are capable of caring for him at all may still be counted on to care for him deeply.

Oliver Wendell Holmes was different first of all because he alone among these men was a scientist, a professor and one-time dean at the Harvard Medical School. He devised the terms anaesthetic and anaesthesia after the use of anaesthetics in surgery had been demonstrated at the Massachusetts General Hospital, and he declared himself thankful that he had lived, "though nothing else good should ever come out of my life," for having been able to publish, in the face of ridicule from ignorant, insensitive, and prejudiced colleagues, the essay on puerperal fever which saved so many new mothers' lives. Holmes's medical knowledge strongly affected both his poetry and his prose. His novel, *Elsie Venner*, a pioneer piece of what we now call science fiction, was a doctor's plea for a more humane criminology, and he even favored the tetrameter

line in verse because he thought it accommodated itself best to the normal rate of breathing.

It is not quite accurate to think of Holmes as essentially an occasional poet or writer of *vers de société*, though during his lifetime it could almost be taken for granted that he would appear, verses in hand, at any festival occasion in the Boston area; one could be almost as sure that Dr. Holmes would do that as that Professor Longfellow wouldn't! He did write "Old Ironsides," which saved the *Constitution* when she was threatened with destruction; he did explore New England history in such poems as "Grandmother's Story of Bunker Hill Battle"; and the sequence called "Wind-Clouds and Star-Drifts" is a thoughtful commentary on science and faith. Essentially, however, Holmes *was* a humorist—a bustling, birdlike little man, both snobbish and loving—and his reputation now rests more securely upon his four "breakfast table" books than on his verse.

The first of these, *The Autocrat of the Breakfast Table*, began its serial course in the first number of *The Atlantic Monthly* and was credited by the editor Lowell with having kept the magazine alive.* It was certainly one of the great immediate successes of American literature, and its sale, when it appeared in book form, would be sensational for a book of its kind even today. Moreover the three later breakfast table books were inferior only in the sense that since they presented "the mixture as before," they lacked the charm of novelty.

The boardinghouse background gave Holmes a chance to introduce as many American types as anything he might have devised, serving his purpose almost as well as the pilgrimage framework served Chaucer in the fourteenth century. It gave him the opportunity to introduce a slight dramatic quality into his work, developing embryonic characters who expressed divergent points of view, with some of the more eccentric among them giving utterance to ideas he might not have wished to express in his own person. But though there is a slight climax in each volume, Holmes never really permits himself to cross the line which separates essay from fiction, though he often seems on the verge of doing so.

*The importance of *The Atlantic Monthly* as providing a vehicle for New England literature can hardly be exaggerated. *The Dial*, which lived only two years, had printed some fine things but was handicapped both by its minute circulation and as the specialized organ of the transcendentalists, and the ponderous *North American Review*, important for scholarship and criticism, did not carry creative writing. Though the *Atlantic* was not started by the house which, after many realignments and changes of name, became known as Houghton Mifflin Company, it was soon acquired by them. With all due respect to Little, Brown and other publishers, this house became almost synonymous with New England writing, and its directors and editors, notably James T. Fields, wielded such fostering influence as few publishers have ever exercised.

Holmes was well versed in various fields of interest all the way from medicine to pugilism. He was charmingly opinionated and able to express himself without ponderousness; he was "intensely interested in my own personality," and he knew how to project this personality without offensive egotism. Famous for his conversation, he devised for his papers a form which allowed him to preserve the variety, the desultory, easy, graceful quality of good talk. As a stylist he was graceful and accomplished, and he manifested the qualities of a virtuoso in his capacity for quick changes of mood without destroying the impression of a fundamental underlying unity, which inhered not in the subject under consideration but in quality of mind and point of view. His broken continuity, suggestions of new ideas, and the hints of fresh developments that he was forever throwing out—all this (though perhaps influenced by Sterne) was very advanced literary technique for its time. Holmes was an inveterate punster; when a somewhat petty controversy developed as to which doctor should be credited as the pioneer anaesthetist, it was he who suggested that the monument in Boston's Public Garden should be dedicated to Ether (either), which was done, and so it remains to this day. But this was only a crude manifestation of an interest in words and a skill in using them which was often impressive; all the breakfast table books are virtual tissues of analogies. They attack Calvinism; they attack spiritualism and homeopathy (both of which were strong in Boston in Holmes's time); and they comment upon a wide variety of themes all the way from anti-Semitism to literary realism, always returning sooner or later to the relationship between faith and knowledge which was one of Holmes's abiding interests. It can hardly be necessary to add that he produced the most distinguished son of any New England poet, the namesake who became one of the most famous and respected of all Supreme Court justices.

Besides these outstanding figures, there were of course minor poets in the Golden Age, men like Ellery Channing (1818-1901), nephew of the father of Unitarianism and himself father of the historian Edward Channing, and Jones Very (1813-1880). Both were encouraged by Emerson, who had a gift for putting up with difficult people, and Very may have had a sprinkling of actual madness, but he has had modern admirers, notably Gamaliel Bradford. Besides these persons, there was the recluse of Amherst, Emily Dickinson, who was not a minor poet, though since she published only three or four poems during her lifetime, she was known to few literati besides Thomas Wentworth Higginson, apparently the only person she ever asked for advice, and Helen Hunt Jackson, herself then a famous poet but now remembered only as the author of *Ramona*, who perhaps understood her better than anybody else in her time, and it was not until 1955 that

Emily Dickinson. New York Public Library Picture Collection

Photograph of Emily Dickinson, taken when she was about seventeen. New York Public Library Picture Collection

we had a definitive edition of her work, edited, oddly enough, by the same man who brought Edward Taylor back to us, Thomas H. Johnson. Emily Dickinson's 1775 poems are all very brief and many of them extremely cryptic, but contrary to what many readers seem to suppose, she did not write free verse; instead she based her poems on the familiar measures of the hymnbook, freely varied and manipulated to avoid a singsong quality.

In her dependence upon intuition and inspiration, Emily Dickinson was the perfect transcendentalist, but she had no use for the elaborate intellectual scaffoldings of transcendentalism. These things are the products of the masculine, intellectual mind, and she was all feminine spontaneity. There was even something of feminine caprice and lawlessness about her cavalier infractions of the rules of prosody or her departures from them, for what Henry Adams felt about the Blessed Virgin as an element leavening the rigidity of mediaeval religion, as men had conceived it, may very well be applied to her in the aesthetic sphere. It has been reasonably suggested that some of her oddities were due to her following of Connecticut Valley provincial usage, natural to her though unfamiliar to us, but others must have been caused by a passion for extreme economy and condensation which led her to be as cruel to syntax as Shakespeare could be in his final phase. Her experience was pitifully limited, yet she handled all the great themes of lyric poetry—love, death, nature, God—with compelling authority; even more than the Brontës, she shows us that what a writer needs is less great experience than a great attitude toward experience.

She was one of the great religious poets of the world, but there is no other religious poet who is anything like her. She has been called less God's child than God's little rascal, much preoccupied with "the underside of his divinity," and she seems to have felt that she knew God well enough to take liberties with Him. Cynicism, even occasional cruelty, lay within her range, and conventionally-minded people may well be excused if they sometimes find her shocking or even blasphemous. Sometimes, however, her levity or irreverence merely evidences a deeper insight, gained through her secure possession of an individual slant which nobody else ever possessed, as when she wonders whether Christ did not laugh on the cross, since after all he had won, purchasing salvation for mankind. She can be equally startling in purely human matters, if there were any such for her, untouched with divinity, as when she wrote Higginson, off to the Civil War, "Should you, before this reaches you, experience immortality, who will inform me of the exchange? Could you, with honor, avoid death, I entreat you, sir. It would bereave your Gnome." It used to be said that seeing Kean act was like reading Shakespeare by flashes of lightning. That is the way Emily Dickinson must be read. The lightning which illumi-

Nathaniel Hawthorne in 1840, painting by Charles Osgood. Courtesy Essex Institute

nates the darkness is probably never quite the same for any two readers. But there may be more light in one flash than in pages and pages of perfectly chiseled verse.

III

New England fiction of the Golden Age has been less famous on the whole than its poetry. There were many writers, some widely read in their own time, none of whom can have more than cursory mention here while some must fail even of that. The two great exceptions are Hawthorne and Mrs. Stowe.

Nathaniel Hawthorne (1804-1864) was born in Salem, served as American consul at Liverpool, and finally settled in Concord. His American ancestry, which ran back to the beginnings of New England, included Quaker- and witch-persecutors, but his father was a sea captain. Henry James, who, on one side of his genius, was influenced by him, remarked that he made the best possible use of his New England heritage by transmuting it into the stuff of art and imagination. Though Hawthorne lost the theology of his Calvinistic forebears, he largely retained their attitude toward life, and

Hawthorne with his publishers, James T. Fields (*on the left*) and William D. Ticknor (*on the right*). New York Public Library Picture Collection

it is James himself who warns us away from what Perry Miller called the "sentimental or impressionistic gabble" of "the fanatical symbol-hunters and the irresponsible would-be psychoanalysts" among his modern admirers who would find Hawthorne's own traumas and complexes in his work by reminding us that "the duskiest flowers of his invention sprang straight from the soil of his happiest days." Though he was quite as good a man as his peers and as much the idealist, Hawthorne was less evasive and more unashamed than some of the others in his confrontation of life, both a Democrat and a democrat who generally has no difficulty in meeting modern liberals on their own ground. His indifference to theology never disturbed a settled faith in God and in immortality. He believed in the infinite value of every human soul and knew what even the horrors of technology have not yet taught many of us, that the unpardonable sin is to treat human beings as things.

He began using his New England heritage in his short pieces—*Twice-Told Tales* and *Mosses from an Old Manse*—some of which are parabolic, some fanciful, and the best, like "Young Goodman Brown," among the finest in our literature. His genius had more depth than breadth, and he only succeeded in producing four full-length novels—*The Scarlet Letter, The House of the Seven Gables, The Blithedale Romance*, and *The*

Marble Faun. It is interesting that the first three appeared in successive years, beginning in 1850, his one period of amazing fecundity, which also produced *A Wonder Book* and *Tanglewood Tales* and his campaign life of his friend Franklin Pierce; the last followed after his return from Europe in 1860. He himself preferred to call these works romances, since he was more interested in presenting the "soul" or essence of human character than in preserving what Hamlet calls the very age and body of the time, his form and pressure; though adhering to "the truth of the human heart," he desired to present it "under circumstances, to a great extent, of the writer's own choosing or creation."

The Scarlet Letter, an outgrowth of his own mulling over the past during his employment in the Salem Custom House, goes back to the early days of the Massachusetts Bay Colony. In the much less sombre *Seven Gables* he moves down toward the present, with much less of the devil in his inkpot, but the present is brooded over by the past,.with its heritage of evil. His most realistic book was *The Blithedale Romance*, which he based upon his own experience as the least "clubable" of men at the Transcendental community which George Ripley and others had established in 1841 at Brook Farm (now in West Roxbury), but even here he wished "merely to establish a theatre, a little removed from the highway of ordinary travel, where the creatures of his brain may play their phantasmagorical antics, without exposing them to too close a comparison with the actual events of real lives." Finally, *The Marble Faun* represents his fullest capitulation to romanticism, with Italy affording "a sort of poetic precinct, where actualities would not be so terribly insisted upon as they are, and must needs be, in America," a land "where there is no shadow, no antiquity, no mystery, no picturesque and gloomy wrong, nor anything but a commonplace prosperity, in broad and simple daylight."

The Scarlet Letter is the unquestioned masterpiece, one of the great American novels you can count on your fingers, perhaps even the fingers of one hand. Yet it is the least "modern" of the quartette—formal, distant, developed in terms of a series of tableaux, more like an opera than either a play or a novel, with a dialogue at times suggestive of the Elizabethans. One of the most austere of books, its subject is not adultery but the pangs of conscience, for the adultery is over and done with before the book begins. Hester Prynne, condemned to wear the scarlet letter on her bosom to proclaim her sin, gets her chance for salvation, but her partner, the Reverend Arthur Dimmesdale, is lost until the end, when he saves himself, as by fire, by acknowledging his sin upon the pillory and dying from the long ordeal of concealment. The author condemns nobody except the wronged husband, Roger Chillingworth,

Nathaniel Hawthorne, the so-called "Motley photograph," by Mayall. Courtesy Essex Institute

Statue of Nathaniel Hawthorne by Bela Lyon Pratt in front of the Hawthorne Hotel in Salem. Courtesy Essex Institute

who, alone suspecting the truth, destroys himself as a spiritual being by dedicating his life to revenge. Hawthorne did not believe that the sins of the soul can be punished either by the state or by other humans, but he also refused to accept Hester's view that "what we did had a consecration of its own." Like Shakespeare, Hawthorne never mixes his colors; with him right never looks like wrong nor wrong like right. At no point does the reader fail to sympathize with Hester, but her problem is not solved until her return to Boston in the last chapter, for not until then has she finally cut all the ties which had bound her to her past.

To stress the importance of this novel is not to belittle Hawthorne's other work; he would still be an important writer if he had never told Hester's story. One easily understands why William Dean Howells, the champion of realism, whose own novel, *The Undiscovered Country*, was probably influenced by it, should have been especially fond of *The Blithedale Romance*, and one should understand too why those who prefer moonlight to "the common light of day" should feel special affinity with both *Seven Gables* and the *Faun*. The more relaxed atmosphere of the *Seven Gables* has its own charm, and the richly textured *Faun* is in a sense the progenitor of all American novels about Italy and about art. Nobody has ever really understood or explained why Hawthorne was unable to finish a fifth novel; he certainly tried hard enough, struggling with such themes as the elixir of life, a bloody footstep, a missing heir, and (anticipating Mark Twain) an American claimant to a great English estate. What he left of these we have in *Doctor Grimshawe's Secret, Septimius Felton*, and "The Dolliver Romance," but he finished none of them, and they never achieved the form he intended. The illness from which he suffered at the end, and which killed him at sixty, was never diagnosed, and we do not know whether it was wholly physical or partly psychosomatic. But there are fine things in these last works; if he had been able to finish them, they surely would have caused him no shame. Nor, so far as what survives can indicate, does his attitude toward life seem to have changed.

Harriet Beecher Stowe (1811-1896) was a very different story. She was a member of one of America's great clerical families (Lyman Beecher was her father and Henry Ward Beecher the most illustrious of her brothers), and when she published *Uncle Tom's Cabin* in 1852, she reached, "at one step," as Longfellow observed, "the top of the stair-case up which the rest of us climb on our knees year after year." A careless, eccentric writer, even by nineteenth-century standards, hers

William Dean Howells in early life. New York Public Library Picture Collection

Harriet Beecher Stowe. Engraved by B. Young from an original portrait, 1853. Library of Congress

Harriet Beecher Stowe, from a photograph, 1884. Library of Congress

were freehand drawings compared to Hawthorne's etchings, but they had power in them suggestive of Daumier or Thomas Nast. Modeled on the storytelling technique of Sir Walter Scott, *Uncle Tom's Cabin* long outlasted the "peculiar institution" of slavery which it attacked and helped destroy (the dramatic version was never off the boards between 1853 and 1930), not only because of its masterly sketches of Topsy and other incomparably vivid characters but even more because of the author's sure grip upon the basic human emotions.

Yet though it made her fame and she was absolutely sincere in all she said in it ("God wrote it," she thought), in a sense it is no more typical of her than her Italian fling, *Agnes of Sorrento*, nor the modern society novels (*Pink and White Tyranny*, etc.) which she did toward the close of her career. Temperamentally Mrs. Stowe was far more a family woman, a devotee, and a romancer than a reformer, and New England, not the South, was what she really knew. The Beechers probably did more than any other family to finish off the old Calvinism, but Mrs. Stowe knew it and had had it and everything else that belonged to old-time Puritan New England and the New England way of life bred into her bones beyond any other writer of her ability who has ever lived. Her most distinguished treatment of these matters is in *The Minister's Wooing*, and *The Pearl of Orr's Island* is a charming idyll, but if one would really be steeped in the old New England village life (and to understand not only its "ways" but the spirit which informed them), one had best turn to the more sprawling *Oldtown Folks* and its lesser pendants, *Sam Lawson's Fireside Stories* and *Poganuc People*. Surely no writer who has left us three books each as important in its way as *Uncle Tom's Cabin, The Minister's Wooing*, and *Oldtown Folks* need fear to confront the future with some confidence.

Mrs. Stowe was neither the first New England regionalist nor the last, being preceded by Catharine M. Sedgwick (*A New England Tale*, 1822, etc.) and followed among others by Sarah Orne Jewett (*The Country of the Pointed Firs*, at least, is an unquestioned masterpiece), Mary E. Wilkins Freeman, and Alice Brown. But these writers take us out of the Golden Age into the New England afterglow. Louisa May Alcott, daughter of Concord and of Bronson Alcott in the days of Emerson and Hawthorne, though born many years after Mrs. Stowe, died before her. Miss Alcott did not get very far with her adult novels, but she achieved a phenomenal success with *Little Women* (1869), still a very important American fiction. Many years later, in 1903, Kate Douglas Wiggin produced its closest rival in *Rebecca of Sunnybrook Farm*, a slight story in comparison yet a book of great charm, without a single false note in it. And this time there can be no question about the afterglow, for as Fred Erisman has had no difficulty in showing, *Rebecca* represents the

Louisa May Alcott, 1888, from a wood engraving. Library of Congress

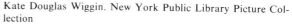

Kate Douglas Wiggin. New York Public Library Picture Collection

application of transcendental principles to juvenile literature.* Perhaps some day somebody will even connect the considerably less literary "Glad Book," Eleanor H. Porter's *Pollyanna* (1913) with a later development of New England idealism in Christian Science.

Both in the Golden Age and during the afterglow there were writers who hovered on the fringe of New England literature without belonging to it. Herman Melville, for example, started the *Moby-Dick* voyage out from New Bedford and was a friend and neighbor of Hawthorne's while the latter lived in the Berkshires, yet he is certainly much more a New York than a New England writer. Among the fictionists of the afterglow unmistakably New England, perhaps none was more representative than Whittier's friend, Elizabeth Stuart Phelps (1844-1911), of Andover and Newton, who won fame with *The Gates Ajar*, which is less a novel than a conversation piece, designed to comfort bereaved women after the Civil War, but went on to more significant work in such novels as *A Singular Life, The Silent Partner*, and *The Story of Avis*, which deal with religion, feminism, labor problems and other vital themes.

More strictly confined to our period were the clergyman William Ware, who wrote *Julian* (1841), a successful novel about the home life of Jesus, and the abolitionist and humanitarian, Lydia Maria Child, who went back to Plymouth with *Hobomok* (1824) and to classical Greece with *Philothea* (1836). The perfect transcendentalist novel was Sylvester Judd's *Margaret* (1845), and Maria Cummins, whose *The Lamplighter* (1854) still holds a quaint charm, may represent the "damned mob of scribbling women," not all New Englanders, whom Hawthorne complained of as swallowing up the reading public of his day. The disciple of Dickens, J. G. Holland (1819-1881), editor of the Springfield *Republican* and founder of *Scribner's Monthly*, was a figure of greater stature, and *Arthur Bonnicastle, Sevenoaks*, and *Nicholas Minturn* are good second-class novels, better than many that are being read avidly today.

*"Transcendentalism for American Youth: The Children's Books of Kate Douglas Wiggin." *New England Quarterly*, XLI (1968), 238-47.

Mary Pickford as Rebecca of Sunnybrook Farm, peering over a copy of the book by Kate Douglas Wiggin, a publicity shot for the 1917 film.

Eleanor H. Porter. New York Public Library Picture Collection

Herman Melville, photo ca. 1860. Library of Congress

Elizabeth Stuart Phelps. New York Public Library Picture Collection

Lydia Maria Child. New York Public Library Picture Collection

Henry David Thoreau in 1854, from a crayon portrait by Samuel Worcester Rowse. Library of Congress

IV

Nonfiction prose writing of the period took many forms, most of which must be passed over here. Some of the best of it came from the transcendentalists, and Emerson's prose has already been glanced at in connection with his poetry. Henry David Thoreau (1817-1862) wrote both prose and verse, but the interest in his poems which has been expressed during recent years seems largely confined to those who have already been attracted through his prose. Thoreau is the patron saint of those who would carry Protestant and Puritan individualism to its ultimate length and exercise it with reference to both sacred and secular matters; he was "difficult" even for Emerson. During his lifetime he published only two books, *A Week on the Concord and Merrimack Rivers* and *Walden*; in our own time he has come to be regarded as perhaps the most vital among all American writers. Young Russian revolutionists caught inspiration from him, and British Socialists carried *Walden* in their pockets. "Civil Disobedience" could hardly have been more important for American

Thoreau from an ambrotype by E. S. Dunshee, 1861. Copyright, 1924, by Eugene A. Perry.

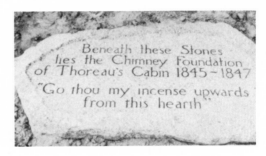

Thoreau's hut at Walden, by May Alcott from *Concord Scenes*, Thoreau Society of America, print by Charles Barker, 1975. Concord Free Public Library

The actual site of Thoreau's cabin, discovered on November 12, 1945, is about twelve rods beyond the cairn shown here, which was originally believed to be the hut site.
This stone (*right*) was laid in 1947 to mark the site. New York Public Library Collection

civil rights leaders of the sixties, and through Gandhi it probably exercised the largest influence of any American book upon world affairs.

Thoreau spent a night in jail rather than share the guilt of slavery and the Mexican War by paying the minute tax which had been assessed against him, but his period of solitary residence near Walden Pond was not motivated by any desire to establish a hermitage; he was conducting a controlled experiment to try to determine what were the minimum bare essentials of man's material life, so that a larger share of his energy might be set free for the things that have real value and significance. Though he never married, he saw no value in self-denial for denial's sake and never deprived himself of anything except in order to make it possible for him to acquire something better. Not essentially either a naturalist or a nature writer (though he had scientific achievements to his credit), he was "a mystic, a transcendentalist, and a natural philosopher to boot," who saw nature as the visible garment of spiritual reality and valued her on that account. "Man is all in all, Nature nothing, but as she draws him out and reflects

him." And again he says, "If it is possible to conceive of an event outside of humanity, it is not of the slightest significance, though it were the explosion of a planet." Though he is the most provincial of all great writers, his provincialism was not determined by any feeling that Concord was better than other places because he had happened to be born in it but rather to the conviction that every environment contains what is needed to support human life and feed the aspirations of the human spirit and that there is no use rushing off to a superficial view of other environments before you have thoroughly explored your own.

Though Thoreau remarked cruelly of Harvard that it taught all the branches of learning and none of the roots, he was a good classicist and reasonably well versed in modern languages. He read widely in Elizabethan and seventeenth-century literature and, like Emerson, relished the oriental scriptures in translation. He was one of the great masters of the English sentence (Henry Seidel Canby reasonably called the battle of the ants in *Walden* as fine as the best of Defoe). Like the metaphysicals, he used physical, even sexual, images to

A small granite stone, marked "Henry," marks Thoreau's grave in Concord's Sleepy Hollow Cemetery. The Thoreau family plot is opposite the Hawthorne plot and next to the Alcotts'. Emerson's grave is farther along the ridge. New York Public Library Picture Collection

A. Bronson Alcott, contemporary sketch. New York Public Library Picture Collection

describe what he believed about style. "It is in vain to write on chosen themes. We must wait until they have kindled a flame in our minds. There must be the copulating and generating force of love behind every effort destined to be successful." He tried to write sentences "concentrated and nutty," sentences "which are expensive, towards which so many volumes, so much life, went; which lie like boulders on the page, up and down or across; which contain other sentences, not mere repetition, but creation; which a man might sell his grounds and castles to build." If he waited long in Elysium for the readers who must come to him absolutely upon his own terms if they were to come at all, he probably did not mind, for he was as patient as he was stubborn.

Three other persons connected in one way or another with transcendentalism—A. Bronson Alcott (1799-1888), Orestes A. Brownson (1803-1876), and Margaret Fuller (1810-1850)—were not primarily writers. Brownson published a vast quantity of words but nobody has ever claimed that he possessed a great literary gift, and both Alcott and Margaret Fuller recognized frankly that their gifts were primarily oral. Margaret's "Conversations," at the end of the thirties, attracted the most brilliant women of the Boston area at a price far higher than what was generally paid for lectures at the time.

All three of these persons were in some measure eccentrics. Alcott, a perfect type-figure of the idealist, was successful from every point of view except that of earning a living; Emerson called him "the most extraordinary man and the highest genius of the time," and Thoreau said he was the sanest man he had ever known. Brownson, who was in order Universalist, Unitarian, proto-Marxist, and finally a devout Roman Catholic quite capable of attacking the Jesuits, Archbishop Hughes, and Cardinal Newman himself, had a habit of shifting his position with every new philosopher he read, so that his contemporaries declared it to be a waste of energy to refute his arguments on any subject, since sooner or later Brownson was sure to do the job himself. Yet, though he remained capable of fantastic judgments to the end, neither Brownson's courage nor his intellectual vigor ever failed, and few men have

Building, on Orchard House property, in which Bronson Alcott conducted the summer School of Philosophy to which celebrities came from near and far. U.S. Bureau of Public Roads, National Archives

Orchard House on Lexington Road in Concord, Mass. School of Philosophy building is on the left. Concord Free Public Library

grappled so boldly with so wide a range of intellectual, moral, and social problems.

But if Alcott was the most lovable of these persons, Margaret Fuller was certainly the most picturesque and her life by all means the most exciting. Her *Woman in the Nineteenth Century* was the first important American feminist document, and though she never achieved an attractive style, by the time she had finished her work for Horace Greeley's New York *Tribune*, she had established herself as a critic worthy to rank with Poe,

and certainly no less opinionated. In 1836 she sailed for Europe, where, in Italy, she established a liaison with an impoverished Italian nobleman whom she later married, was caught up in revolutionary activity, and rendered heroic hospital service during the siege of Rome. When the ship in which she was returning to America with her husband and child was wrecked on Fire Island, all three persons were drowned. Emerson, William Henry Channing, and James Freeman Clarke joined forces to produce a memoir.

A. Bronson Alcott on the steps of the School of Philosophy. Concord Free Public Library

Margaret Fuller, engraving by R. Babson and J. Andrews after Plumbe daguerreotype. Library of Congress

Jared Sparks, engraving by S. A. Schott after T. Sully. Library of Congress

American historical writing goes clear back to Governor Bradford, as we have seen. In our period, Jared Sparks (1789-1866), J. G. Palfrey (1796-1881), and George Ticknor (1791-1871) laid important foundations. Palfrey produced the first great *History of New England*, and Sparks edited the writings of Washington, Franklin, and other Revolutionary figures, and an immense *Library of American Biography*. Ticknor's *History of Spanish Literature* went farther afield, but his influence upon scholarly writing was very great. The undisputed king of the literati among Boston Brahmins, in his great and generously shared library on Park Street, Ticknor preceded Longfellow in advanced study in Europe and in teaching at Harvard; through the direction he gave him and others, he guided American scholarship for years to come.

Among his followers was George Bancroft (1800-1891), but when Bancroft returned from Europe with a Göttingen Ph.D., he had become Europeanized to such a degree, and had picked up so many new and radical

John Gorham Palfrey. Library of Congress

ideas about education that he and the university now wanted nothing to do with each other. He left Harvard accordingly and became co-founder of the Round Hill School for boys at Northampton, Massachusetts. When he turned Democrat, the situation worsened, for Democrats were not respectable in Bancroft's New England, and he found the doors of old friends closed against him. As Secretary of the Navy under Polk he helped establish the Naval Academy at Annapolis; later he became minister to Great Britain and Prussia and a friend of Bismarck's who was publicly excoriated by Victor Hugo at the time of the Franco-Prussian War.

Between 1834 and 1874 Bancroft published what started out to be a comprehensive *History of the United States from the Discovery of America to the Present Time*, based upon primary sources. But Volume X only saw him through the Revolution, and "*to the Present Time*" was dropped from the later volumes. In 1882 there was a two-volume *History of the Formation of the Constitution of the United States of America*.

Bancroft used his diplomatic and other connections to obtain access to materials, traveled and corresponded widely, and employed agents to ransack archives for him everywhere. He did an herculean job, toiling fourteen hours a day into his eighties. His interpretations, however, were less impartial than his researches. Bancroft accepted the nineteenth-century conception of "progress" and saw the culmination of human history in American democracy and nationalism, which was being used by the Divine Wisdom to work out His will in the world. He was a political historian who largely ignored social and economic factors and a highly rhetorical writer. But he did attempt to place the history of the United States in some relationship to the history of the world, and he greatly increased the store of resources upon which historians might draw.

More important as literature was the work of William Hickling Prescott (1796-1859), John Lothrop Motley (1814-1877), and Francis Parkman (1823-1893). The first two of these devoted themselves to foreign themes—Prescott to his *History of the Reign of Ferdinand and Isabella the Catholic*, *The Conquest of Mexico*, and *The Conquest of Peru* and Motley to *The Rise of the Dutch Republic* and *The History of the United Netherlands*. Edward Eggleston saw Prescott as belonging to the "drum and trumpet" school of history; one may of course accept the characterization without the scorn which informed it. He was attracted to a Spanish subject because of the interest in things Spanish which Ticknor and others had fostered and because the opening of the Spanish archives in 1780 had placed a great new storehouse of fresh materials at the disposal of historians. An artist-historian, influenced by Voltaire, Mably, and Barante, Prescott believed that historical writing should be organized like literature to achieve dramatic interest and make a point, and he called his theme in *The Conquest of Mexico* "the most poetic subject ever offered to the pen of the historian" and "superior to the *Iliad* in true epic proportion." Motley gained an advantage with American readers, however, by tying up his work with their own institutions and convictions, for he presented the Dutch struggle against Spain as a kind of prelude to the American Revolution, with his great hero William of Orange as a kind of Dutch Washington, and he painted his great "scenes" with a Carlylean or cinematic vividness and as sharply drawn a contrast between good and bad characters as even the cinema ever achieved. Parkman was more original in the sense of finding a brand-new subject in the "old French war," beginning with *Pioneers of France in the New World* and ending with *Montcalm and Wolfe*, seven distinct works, a whole shelf of books as redolent of the great American forest as the novels of Cooper himself.

That works requiring such extensive research as the writings of Prescott and Parkman should have been produced by men who were almost blind stands among the most impressive and inspiring testimonies we have to the strength of the human will. Sometimes Parkman could use his eyes for only five minutes at a time, and sometimes he had to alternate minutes of use with minutes of rest, but even when he could add only five or six lines a day to his manuscript, he never gave up. Pres-

William Hickling Prescott. Engraving after painting by Chappel. Library of Congress

Francis Parkman, detail of memorial by Daniel Chester French. Library of Congress

Francis Parkman. New York Public Library Picture Collection

Parkman's desk, showing his noctograph. New York Public Library Picture Collection

cott's trouble went back to a bit of college rowdyism, when a Harvard classmate threw a piece of bread in the dining hall and struck him in the eye. For his writing he used a device called a noctograph, with wires to guide his hand, and he trained his memory to such an extent that he could compose a chapter of sixty pages in his head and revise it mentally without setting down a word. Parkman, whose problem seems to have been partly psychosomatic, had many other ailments; there was an element of masochism in him; he called his writing instrument a gridiron; like Ernest Hemingway, he lived on a gridiron, testing himself in every way to prove that he could "take it." An agnostic, who mistrusted modern humanitarianism, including abolitionism, he presented a front which seems to have cracked only in his passionate love for cats and roses.

Prescott, who had a much more genial temperament, might have led an idle life if his sense of duty had not interfered. Fond of social gayeties, he would instruct his servant to pull the covers off his bed to force him to get up in the morning and make bets with himself to produce a certain amount of work by a certain time; if he failed he must pay a fine, which went to charity.

Motley was a handsome, perhaps rather showy, Boston aristocrat, who knew everybody and moved in the most exclusive circles. Lady Byron thought he looked more like the poet than any other man she had seen. He was trained at Round Hill under Bancroft and at Harvard; like Bancroft he studied in Europe and became a friend of Bismarck, and like him too he became an American diplomat. Neither Motley nor Prescott was sympathetic toward Catholicism, but since Prescott's Catholics were shown in conflict with pagans, not Protestants, his prejudices did not importantly affect his histories, which were well received in Spain, stimulating Spanish researches, and admired by Archbishop Hughes and other fair-minded Catholics. Motley's situation was different; with him judgment was always quite as important as record. Protestant liberty is always "noble" and "grand" and Catholic absolutism is "decadent" and "ruthless"; his William of Orange is semidivine, but his Duke of Alva "possessed no virtues" and his King Philip II was "capable of any crime."

When Parkman refrained from such judgments, it was not because he was more tolerant but because, as an artist, he preferred a more objective narrative, aimed at "resurrecting" the past and causing it to live again before the reader's eyes. He was neither pro-Indian nor pro-Jesuit, but being the kind of man he was, he could not resist recognizing the heroism in both Indians and Jesuits and responding to it sympathetically. In their own time, both Prescott and Motley sold more widely, in expensive editions, on both sides of the Atlantic; Parkman has manifested greater survival value.

John Lothrop Motley. Library of Congress

Scribners put his collected works into their standard "Library of Modern Authors," and not so long ago every schoolboy still read *The Oregon Trail*, which is not, of course, a part of the French War series but deals with a Western adventure of Parkman's own early years.

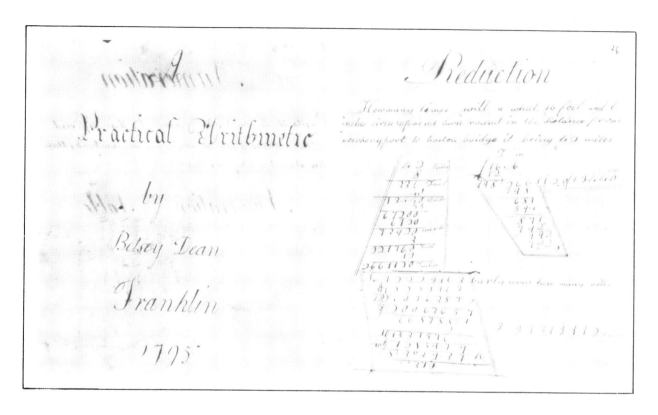

Pages from old school books. New York Public Library Picture
Collection

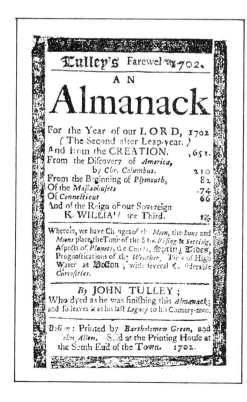

Q. Is pride commendable?
A. By no means. A modest, self-approving opinion of
our own good deeds is very right — it is natural — it is
agreeable, and a spur to good actions. But we should not
suffer our hearts to be blown up with pride; for pride
brings upon us the ill-will of mankind, and displeasure of
our Maker.

The Elementary Spelling-book, which appeared in
1829, had a frontispiece and seven pictures in the

FABLE II.—*The* COUNTRY MAID *and her*
MILK PAIL.

From a Webster's speller dated 1789.

text. There was also an illustrated edition containing the identical material that was in the other except
that every spelling page had a narrow cut added at
the top. The lists of words in the Elementary were
newly arranged and were more comprehensive than
in its predecessors, but the most noticeable change

Chapter 5

Toward a
New England
Portrait
Gallery

I. COTTON MATHER

For *Grace* and *Art* and an Illustrious *Fame*
Who would not look from such an Ominous Name?
Where *Two Great Names* their Sanctuary take,
And in a *Third* combined, a Greater make.

THUS, A CONTEMPORARY EULOGIST of Cotton Mather. The *"Two Great Names"* were those of his two grandfathers, John Cotton and Richard Mather; in general report he himself stands as the "Puritan priest" par excellence. But he lived from 1663 to 1728, when the glory of the Puritan morning was already fading, and his life was a struggle to preserve and recharacter its faith in a period affected by multitudinous new influences of which he, as a scholar and a sensitive man, strongly felt the influence. It was natural enough then that the man whom a contemporary had described as "pious but not affected, serious and grave, but neither morose nor austere; affected without meanness; and . . . 'facetious without levity,' " should sometimes have been seen by his posterity as "a subtle priest, self-seeking, vain, arrogant, inconsistent, mischievous in his eternal business . . . even if honest, dreadfully deluded

and grotesquely lacking in judgement." Barrett Wendell, who sums up these charges, and who pioneered in the modern reinterpretation of this controversial figure, though conceding that Mather possessed "a hot temper and a quick tongue," was also impressed by his "resolute abstinence from evil speaking." "It would be hard, I think, to find another diary so long and so free from scandal."

Cotton Mather's paternal grandfather, Richard Mather, born in Lancashire in 1595, was an English Puritan clergyman, suspended for nonconformity, who came to Boston in 1635 and became pastor at Dorchester, where he died in 1669. His son, Increase, born at Dorchester in 1639, was graduated from Harvard but took his M.A. at Trinity College, Dublin, and attempted to become an English clergyman; it was the Restoration that drove him back to Boston, where he became pastor of the Second (or North) Church in 1664, where he remained until his death in 1723. He was president of Harvard College from 1685 to 1701, and between 1688 and 1692 he represented Massachusetts in Charter negotiations in London.

Cotton Mather's two grandfathers, John Cotton and Richard Mather. New York Public Library Picture Collection

Cotton Mather's own life, spent entirely in New England, was not, in the usual sense, eventful, though he was involved in the downfall of Governor Andros and exerted, or attempted to exert, political influence during the administrations of both Sir William Phips and Joseph Dudley. By the time he was twelve, he had mastered Latin, read the New Testament in Greek, and commenced the study of Hebrew; ultimately he possessed at least seven languages. He received his bachelor's degree from Harvard at fifteen and his master's three years later. He corresponded with Addison, Defoe, and Sir Isaac Newton, and with theologians and other scholars throughout the Western world. He was elected a member of the Royal Society and received a D.D. from Glasgow University; few colonials were in such close touch with Western European culture. When his childhood stammering threatened to keep him out of the pulpit, he seriously considered medicine, but the Lord removing the impediment, he was ordained and joined his father at the North Church, where he continued for the rest of his life. He was married three times—to Abigail Phillips, Elizabeth Hubbard, and Lydia George, fathered fifteen children and buried all but two of them. His last years were darkened by many sorrows. His political influence declined. His father was forced out of Harvard College, of which he himself would have liked to be president, and he shifted his interest and support to the more orthodox Yale. His proudly named son Increase went so hopelessly to the bad that his death must have been a relief as well as a sorrow, and his last wife, who seems to have been something of a fribble at best, though he had judged her at the outset as "a very valuable fish," lost her mind and involved him in the affairs of her kin to such an extent as to bring him within hailing distance of the debt-

or's prison. At one time he even feared he might be obliged to sacrifice his library, the finest in New England and "darling of my little enjoyments." His own publications numbered between four and five hundred titles, embracing not only theology and religion but history and biography, criticism, public affairs, science, and belles-lettres. There were eighteen publications in 1700 and fifty between 1725 and 1728. His magnum opus is *Magnalia Christi Americana: or, The Ecclesiastical History of New England from its First Planting* (1702). *The Christian Philosopher* (1721) sought to reconcile science and religion. His compendium of medical lore, *The Angel of Bethesda*, was not published until 1972, and his most extensive work, *Biblia Americana*, an immense compilation of illustrations of Scripture, still remains in manuscript.

It may be difficult to make twentieth-century readers even understand what was at stake in many of the controversies which seemed matters of eternal life and death importance to the Puritans, but to attempt to dismiss or explain either Increase or Cotton Mather by labeling them "reactionary" or even "conservative" will not get us far. Of course they sympathized with the theocratic ideals of the days of the founders and tried to preserve the ancient values. But both, and Cotton in particular, were quiveringly aware that they must speak to the age in terms which the age could comprehend. When Increase went to England in 1688, he would have liked to secure a renewal of the old Massachusetts Charter, but when this proved impossible, he accepted a compromise, and the diehards never forgave him for it. Moreover both he and his son had the wit to perceive that the men of Massachusetts could not take advantage of William and Mary's Act of Toleration without

Engraving of Cotton Mather after mezzotint done in 1728 by Peter Pelham. The first mezzotint engraved in the colonies. New York Public Library Picture Collection

Title page, Cotton Mather's *Late Memorable Providences*, second printing, 1691. Library of Congress

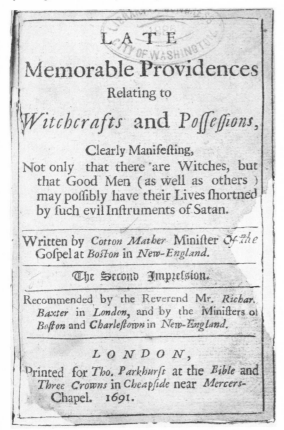

Through his own ecstatic experiences in prayer and meditation, he even came close to believing in direct revelation, which he had earlier repudiated when it was championed by Quakers and Antinomians. "There is no escaping church tyranny, but by asserting the right of private judgment for every man in the affairs of his own salvation." Moreover he realized that even the unregenerate were entitled to the rights of human beings and to protection against both church and state when these were infringed.

Cotton Mather's Massachusetts had lost more than her old Charter. She had also lost much of her old zeal. Without ever really giving up the idea that New England was the new Israel, Mather was therefore driven to distinguish between the inner and the outer, the physical and the spiritual Israel. Though he never abandoned the old Calvinism, we do find him chafing at its limitations. He believed that nothing in the Scriptures was against reason, though much was beyond it. He respected reason, but he would not have God bound by it, for God's Will must be free. He gave a larger place to emotion and insisted more strongly upon surrender than those who had formulated the Federal Theology. He urged men to "try" to believe, even though he knew that only God's Grace could enable them to succeed in this. Increase had already taught that inability to believe was willful, the believer excluding himself by attachment to his own sins and will, but he had also been willing to view conversion as a gradual process to such an extent that children growing up in Christian homes might very well not be able to tell when it had occurred. He had believed too that a man who had "hopes" of salvation should be encouraged to come to the Lord's Table in spite of his doubts. And Cotton inclined to feel that if a man really desired to love Christ, he might take this desire as a sign that Grace had been given and with it assurance of salvation. Within its limits, his social consciousness was keen. He gave himself in unwearying charity and patient ministry to the humble, and he opposed not only drunkenness, profanity, and lust but also the oppressions of rich merchants and budding capitalists. For all his emphasis upon "Doing Good," Cotton Mather did not believe that men could buy their salvation with good works, but he did find evidence of religious decline in social evil.

He inherited his interest in science from his father, who approached it with a view to studying out God's total design in creation. For Cotton there was no great gulf fixed between natural and supernatural. He found evidence of the character of both God and Christ in nature, and there was no human or animal experience in which he did not try to find a spiritual significance. What he is most honored for today is the courage he showed when he encouraged Zabdiel Boylston to inoculate for smallpox during the terrible epidemic of 1721, which killed 884 people out of a total population of 11,000. The orthodox considered inoculation an impious attempt to force the hand of God. Benjamin Frank-

also accepting the principle that "for every man to worship God according to his conviction is an essential right of human nature." Ultimately Cotton Mather wanted not only toleration but a kind of ecumenicism embracing all non-Arian Protestant groups. He welcomed Congregational-Presbyterian union and in 1718 preached at the ordination of a Baptist minister.

lin's brother thought it as great an outrage as the hanging of Quakers and witches, and one public-spirited citizen flung a bomb in at Mather's window (it failed to explode) with the message: "Cotton Mather, you Dog, Dam you! I'll enoculate you with this, with a pox to you." These objectors are not without their defenders among modern scholars. Mather and Boylston did not know enough to inoculate, we are told, and inoculation as they administered it was not safe; posterity has only praised them because they guessed right. But it is hard not to sympathize with Mather when he declares that he "would rather die for my conformity to the Blessed Jesus in essays to save the lives of men from the destroyer than for some truths, though precious ones, to which many martyrs testified formerly in the flames of Smithfield," and he made himself the patron saint of all pragmatists when he cried: "Experience! Experience! 'tis to thee that the matter must be referred after all; a few empirics here are worth all our dogmatists."

But if the inoculation controversy has fostered Cotton Mather's fame, the Salem witchcraft trials have clouded it, for they are primarily responsible for the notion of him as a witch persecutor which has persisted to this day. In the form in which this view is generally expressed it is nonsense. Cotton Mather took no part in the witch trials, and though Increase believed George Burroughs guilty, both the Mathers urged caution and the inadmissibility of "spectral evidence," that is, the testimony of the accusers that the accused had appeared to them in supernormal guise. ("It were better that ten suspected witches should escape than that one innocent person should be condemned.") Cotton Mather even knew that confession itself was not always conclusive evidence of guilt. What he did do, most unfortunately for his reputation, was to make the best defense he thought possible for the judges after the event, when he published *The Wonders of the Invisible World.* Not satisfied with blaming him for this, his enemies often berate him for not repudiating the witchcraft "superstition" altogether. Unfortunately hardly anybody did that in his time; even his bitterest enemy, Robert Calef, in his *More Wonders of the Invisible World,* contented himself with rejecting the Satanic compact on the ground that there is no warrant for it in Scripture. In his time, Cotton Mather tried his own hand at curing persons afflicted with evil spirits or hysteria (as the reader prefers), and in this endeavor he seems to have shown considerable patience and wisdom. He was certainly not a cruel man, for even with notorious sinners, he preferred charitable admonition to punishment. He was also a tender and indulgent father who did not try to force a religious profession even upon his own children, and this tenderness extended toward young people in general. Nor did he turn his back upon Uncle John Cotton when he disgraced his noble name and clerical profession by sexual sin.

In one respect at least, his right to be called "modern" is clear: he was "nervous," tense and excitable to a degree. His son Richard says that father expected to be great from the time he was five; certainly he was conscious of his heritage and aware that it entailed prestige as well as heavy obligations. In some measure, he therefore developed self-pity and self-righteousness; once he wished there was even one man in the world willing to do for him what he would do for any man. This does not mean that he undervalued Christian humility. He confesses envy, pride, doubt, spiritual "deadness," "vileness," even the temptation to despair, though he denies that he ever tried to revenge an injury. A strictly moral man, he still obviously understood sexual temptation. He seems to have been strongly attracted by the witty, intelligent, perhaps worldly Kate Maccarty, who audaciously wooed him after his first wife's death, and might have married her, had her reputation not been "blown upon"; since this would have saved him from the terrible Lydia George, it may be unfortunate that he did not. But the modern reader is likely to be more repelled by his self-conscious forbearances than his resentments. "In all my sad things I discover a conformity unto my Savior, who was a man of sorrows, and acquainted with griefs." From a pious desire to fill up the sufferings of Christ, it is only a step to the conviction that because you suffer, you must be Christlike yourself.

Cotton Mather's shortcomings cannot be fairly judged except against the background of the incredible strains under which he lived. Neither the Calvinistic foreordination and election nor Mather's own conviction that the Second Coming of Christ was imminent were calculated to foster ease in Zion. Though his conscience always troubled him because he could not manage to get up before eight o'clock, he worked something like a sixteen-hour day. As Kenneth Silverman says, "his staggering energy issued in specific acts of kindness: money for the poor, firewood for the sick, consolation for the grief-stricken, care for the orphaned, letters of recommendation or encouragement for the young, visits to the languishing, uplift for the degraded." Upon his grueling work schedule he superimposed six or seven daily periods of private devotions and all-night prayer vigils and fasts (he is said to have fasted some 450 times). Once he devoted himself to three days of prayer, beseeching God to deliver his wife's daughter from a worthless husband, "but above all, that it might be by his becoming a new creature, if that might be obtained"; instead the man died! He had visions of angels and devils and experienced supernatural assurances and denials. His self-examination was endless: when he had a toothache, he tortured himself trying to discover whether this was punishment for his having sinned with his teeth. And all this occurred while he was living in a seventeenth-eighteenth-century household in which fifteen births occurred and miscarriages besides, plus all the diseases to which children and maidservants were subject under the conditions which prevailed in those days. When the children had smallpox, they called him to pray with them, he says, ten to a dozen times a day, "besides what I do with my neighbors."

It is not strange that such a man should have been or become what we might call neurotic; the only wonder is that he lived or did not become a raving lunatic. As for his intellectual difficulties and contradictions, most of them seem to have stemmed from his position as a transitional figure. Accepting many new ideas, he tried also to preserve the old. But whatever mistakes he may have made in specific instances, a general condemnation of him on this score can only be entered by one who believes that all the virtues belong to innovation and none to tradition.

II. NOAH WEBSTER

"I finished writing my dictionary in January 1825, at my lodgings in Cambridge, England," wrote Noah Webster. "When I had come to the last word, I was seized with a trembling which made it somewhat difficult to hold my pen steady for writing. The cause seems to have been the thought that I might not then live to finish the work, or the thought that I was so near the end of my labors. But I summoned strength to finish the last word, and then walking about the room a few minutes I recovered."

It sounds more like an artist or a prophet than a scholar, to say nothing of the "harmless drudge" which Dr. Johnson (of all men!) envisaged as the maker of dictionaries. But Webster had never been in any danger of the scientific coolness and detachment which the modern world associates with scholarship. He grew up amid Revolutionary enthusiasms and shared in the birth of the American nation. Europe was "grown old in folly, corruption and tyranny"; laws were "perverted," manners "licentious," literature "declining," human nature "debased." Over here life had a chance for a fresh start, but this could never be realized unless America could become "as independent in *literature* as she is in politics—as famous for *arts* as for *arms*." Of course this involved a great deal more than linguistic reform. It meant correct moral and religious principles and a reasonable conduct of our national affairs, such as George Washington exemplified when he refused to become involved in the war between England and France. But the importance of sound linguistic principles could hardly be overestimated, for it was through words that men communicated with one another, and without national speech unity, we could hardly become one people.

Webster was born in West Hartford, Connecticut, on October 16, 1758. He traced his ancestry back to John Webster, who moved from Massachusetts to Connecticut with Thomas Hooker, and then later, after an ecclesiastical dispute, moved out of Connecticut jurisdiction with about forty other persons and settled at what became Hadley, Massachusetts. Noah Webster was

The best-known portrait of Webster. New York Public Library Picture Collection

Title page, Webster's *Compendious Dictionary of the English Language*, 1806. Library of Congress

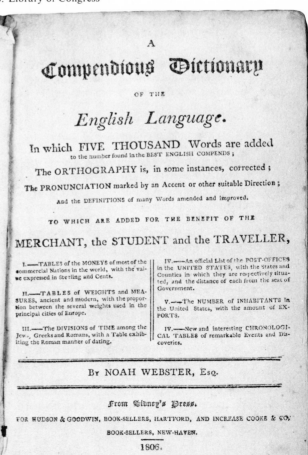

Noah Webster and his books, lithograph, Milton Bradley Co., 1891. Library of Congress

graduated from Yale in 1778. In 1775 he had played the flute for Yale students, drilling after Lexington, and "led the company with music" when Washington passed through New Haven on his way to take charge of the army at Cambridge.

He taught school at Hartford and elsewhere and studied law under Oliver Ellsworth. In 1781 he was admitted to the bar, but his law practice was never extensive. Yale gave him an M.A. in 1781 and an LL.D. in 1823. The first edition of his "Blue-Backed Speller," ultimately known as *The American Spelling Book*, appeared in 1783.

In 1785 he set out on an extensive tour in the interest of securing copyright laws to protect his own publications and those of others, lecturing all the way from Portsmouth to Richmond. In 1788 he became editor of *The American Magazine*, in 1793 of *The American Minerva* newspaper, both of New York and both Federalist organs. In 1789 he married Rebecca Greenleaf of Boston and set up housekeeping in Hartford. The *Prompter* essays were first published serially in the *Courant*; the book went through nearly a hundred editions.

In the course of his career Webster lived in Hartford, New Haven, Amherst, and New York; it was at New Haven that he achieved the greatest local recognition. He held many public offices and published more books than can be listed here. His great monument, *An American Dictionary of the English Language*, appeared in 1828. In 1831 he addressed Congress on copyright; the law passed that year crowned his long agitation. In 1832 came his *History of the United States*, in 1833 *The Holy Bible . . . with Amendments to the Language*. The Yale faculty approved his version, which became standard in Connecticut and anticipated later revisions. He died at New Haven on May 28, 1843.

Webster worked for twenty-six years on his dictionary and invested some $30,000 in it. Except for his Bible, it was his last work of consequence. It had been preceded by his smaller *Compendious Dictionary* and his *Dictionary of the English Language, Compiled for the Use of Common Schools*, but it was the speller that marked the real beginning of his career. This was Part I of his *Grammatical Institute of the English Language*, of which Part II was a grammar and Part III a reader. The speller was the great success. By 1814 it had appeared in one hundred editions, and by 1875 a million copies were being sold annually. The total sale is said to have approximated one hundred million. The Webster family lived on it for years at a royalty of less than a penny a copy, though it was often pirated and the author was often cheated even when it was not. It accepted "general custom" as standard, introduced changes in syllabification and pronunciation, and did much to establish language usage in the United States. It was carried into new communities in the West, and the South valued it so much that in some unauthorized editions Confederate sentiments were added to it in Civil War times. "We have a unity of language no other people possesses," said Jefferson Davis, "and we owe this unity, above all else, to Noah Webster's Yankee Spelling-Book."

Webster's activity as a publicist was prompted only

in part by his scholarly interests. It was because he realized from the beginning that there was no sense in publishing unless you could protect your work that he began his agitation for copyright laws. But he was interested in his country as well as himself, and he would have been the first to recognize that his books were worthless unless they served the common welfare. He supported the Constitution and President Washington's policies and opposed Jefferson's Embargo, and he was importantly involved in founding both the Union School in New Haven and Amherst College. *A Brief History of Epidemic Diseases* was inspired by the yellow fever epidemics that began in 1793, and after he joined the Congregational Church in 1808 (he had always been a religious man, but Calvinism had given him trouble), he came out with *Peculiar Doctrines of the Gospel, Explained and Defended.*

Webster saw an American dictionary as a necessity because of the changes that had come about in the use of language in the United States through the new conditions which had emerged in American life. Some words had died; others had been born, and still others, transmogrified, reborn. Moreover, he believed that "the people of America, in particular the English descendants, speak the most *pure English* now known in the world," and though he was ridiculed for this by Anglophiles, if Elizabethan and seventeenth-century English is to set the standard for purity, he was quite right, for this had been better preserved in America than in England. Harvard was cool toward the new dictionary and *The Monthly Anthology* actively hostile. One writer thought it should be called "Noah's Ark." But Webster had many qualifications which in the long run carried the day. By 1813 he had learned twenty languages, to which he later added others. He realized the importance of Sanskrit, and he perceived that English was a Germanic, not a Latin, language, a fact which made it absurd to treat English grammar as if it were Latin grammar, as many of his predecessors had done. He corrected many mistakes in etymology, and he was a gifted definer. In a way, even his idiosyncrasies increased the value of his work, for his tendency to drag his own principles and prejudices into everything he did created what we should now call "human interest." He wished to "offer moral and religious instruction" and "inculcate patriotic feelings" (in 1794 he even added a "Moral" and a "Federal Catechism" to his speller). There is a great deal of moral and religious teaching in the dictionary also, and under the word "property," he argued at some length in favor of copyright.

Perhaps it was a handicap that to Webster American pronunciation should have meant New England pronunciation; when he lectured outside of New England, some localisms were observed in his own speech. In the early days he wanted simplified spelling and a phonetic alphabet, and Jeremy Belknap referred scornfully to "the fugitiv Essays, ov No-ur Webster, eskwier junier,

critick and coxcomb general of the United States." Later the phonetic alphabet was quietly dropped and the simplified spelling limited at last to the dropping of the final "k" in words like "musick" and of the final "e" in words with a short vowel in the last syllable, the use of "s" instead of "c" in words like "defense," and of "er," not "re" in "theater," and the omission of "u" in "honor." But Webster continued to defend "ain't," "them horses," "Who did he see?" "I come home last night," and "aks" (for "asks"). Once he had got over his early Rousseauism, he profoundly mistrusted the common people in political matters, but he continued to respect their authority in language. Perhaps, after all, he might have been less shocked to find his name on the controversial Third Edition of the Merriam *New International* than many persons suppose!

The antagonism which Webster awakened in his contemporaries was not entirely their fault. He was an admirable human being but not in all respects a lovable one. He was a woodpeckerish, irritating man; when "Peter Parley" encountered him unexpectedly in Europe, he saw "a tall slender form, with a black coat, black small-clothes, black silk stockings, moving back and forth, with its hands behind it." He was just when he said of himself that "I have contributed in a small degree to the instruction of at least four million of the rising generation; and it is not unreasonable to expect that a few seeds of improvement, planted by my hand, may germinate and grow and ripen into valuable fruit, when my remains shall be mingled with the dust." But he was equally just when he described himself as "bold, vain, inexperienced." He liked to give criticism but not to receive it. An older scholar called him "a literary puppy," and a sincere admirer thought him intolerably affected upon the lecture platform. In his heart he remained a schoolmaster all his life, and he had all the faults, as well as all the virtues, of the breed. The label of *The Prompter* on his essays was only too apt: "The writer of this little book took it into his head to prompt the numerous actors upon the great theater of life." That idea was never dislodged from his head, and he was never greatly disposed to allow for the possibility that other heads might contain other ideas. He was a faithful husband and a loving father, but one of his grown daughters complained that they were all treated as if they were still children. He had little aesthetic sensitiveness. Though he cared for music, he was suspicious of both fiction and drama. In his eyes, a city "planned and constructed for the greatest possible convenience" was "completely beautiful." When he visited the gardens at Versailles, he presumed that "all the kinds of plants or nearly all are to be found in the large gardens in New York and Philadelphia." In his view, man had "but little time to spare for the gratification of the senses and the imagination." Even too much reading was dangerous; he did not want people educated "above their station." And his priceless comment on

Cambridge University is that "the colleges are mostly old stone buildings, which look very heavy, cold and gloomy to an American, accustomed to the new public buildings in our country."

In its more extreme aspects, Webster's Federalism is not likely to awaken admiration today either. He would have preferred being the subject of a limited monarch to being subjected to the caprices of an ignorant multitude. He questioned manhood suffrage on the ground that it deprived property owners of their just rights. "Our laws principally respect property, that is their great object; and it is very improper that it should be at the direction and disposal of those who have little or no interest in it." Once at least he suggested that no man should vote until he was forty-five or hold office before he was fifty. He also supported a state church on the ground that a moral and religious citizenry was required to protect the rights of all.

Webster's record as a whole is much better than this, however. Though his discovery of Sanskrit bolstered his faith in the historicity of the biblical Tower of Babel story, he rejected the Mosaic authorship of the Pentateuch and rebuked the Adventist William Miller on the ground that he could not frighten people into religion though he might be able to drive them to despair and insanity. His services to the copyright cause have already been spoken of. He appreciated the importance of preserving old documents before many Americans did and himself published John Winthrop's journal. He criticized President Jefferson bitterly for what we should now call his "spoils system" appointments. He perceived that American opposition to foreign intervention in America must logically carry the corollary of American nonintervention in Europe and Asia. He attempted to formulate rules governing the rights of neutrals at sea and proposed a maritime league with Great Britain which might well have prevented the War of 1812. He objected to the dispossession of the Cherokees, disliked the employment of girls in factories, understood the dangers of alcoholism, and wanted slaves raised gradually to the status of free tenants or independent farmers. He advocated city planning, unemployment insurance, and post office inspection. He urged forest conservation and prison reform. As a schoolmaster, he understood the importance of health and hygiene for education and deemphasized corporal punishment. All in all, there cannot be many men in whom the New England conscience functioned more faithfully or fruitfully, and both his range and his zeal are the more impressive because they coexisted with the execution of a great work of scholarship which must in itself have been sufficient totally to absorb the energies of most men. Surely it is an ungrateful posterity which would withhold him due meed of admiration simply because he "prompted" so much!

III.   WILLIAM LLOYD GARRISON

. . . I *will be* as harsh as truth, and as uncompromising as justice. On this subject I do not wish to think, or speak, or write, with moderation. No! no! Tell a man whose house is on fire, to give a moderate alarm; tell him to moderately rescue his wife from the hands of the ravisher; tell the mother to gradually extricate her babe from the fire into which it has fallen;—but urge me not to use moderation in a cause like the present. I am in earnest—I will not equivocate—I will not excuse—I will not retreat a single inch—AND I WILL BE HEARD.

Such was William Lloyd Garrison's challenge and manifesto in the first number of *The Liberator*, published in Boston on January 1, 1831, and both the strength of the man and his limitations appear in it.

Garrison was born at Newburyport, Massachusetts, on December 10 or 12, 1805. His father was a sailing master who fell upon evil times, became a drunkard, and deserted his family. His mother was a worthy but far from sensitive or loving woman. At nine, the boy was apprenticed to a shoemaker, later to a cabinetmaker, then, in 1818, more fortunately, to the publisher of the Newburyport *Herald*, where he began to find his way. His first appearance in print found him expressing antifeminist sentiments as "An Old Bachelor." His mother, who was sure authors starved to death, won-

Statue of William Lloyd Garrison by Olin Levi Warner on Commonwealth Avenue, Boston. New York Public Library Picture Collection

dered whether the capitals indicated Ass, Oaf, and Blockhead, surely one of the choicest examples of maternal encouragement on record.

In 1826 he acquired the Federalist *Essex Courant*, which he renamed the *Free Press*, as whose editor he discovered a young poet named John Greenleaf Whittier, and from which he proceeded to the *National Philanthropist* and, at Bennington, Vermont, the *Journal of the Times*. He identified himself with antislavery when he proceeded to Baltimore in 1829 to become coeditor with Benjamin Lundy of the *Genius of Universal Emancipation*, stopping on the way to deliver an important address at Boston's Park Street Church. In opposition to Lundy, he opposed colonization and advocated immediate emancipation. The paper soon came to an end, but not before Garrison had "libeled" a New England slaver and been jailed at Baltimore, an experience which he exploited skillfully in the interest of his cause. *The Liberator*, supported at the outset by the New York merchant and evangelical reformer, Arthur Tappan, achieved only a small circulation, largely among blacks, but was widely quoted, north and south, and stirred up immense controversy until Garrison suspended it at the end of 1865.

The year 1832 was an eventful one for Garrison. He founded the New England Anti-Slavery Society, at African Baptist Church in Boston, proclaiming that man cannot be "the property of man" and disclaiming all violence. In *Thoughts on African Colonization* he accused the American Colonization Society of regarding Negroes as property and being actuated by the selfish desire of getting them out of the way of the whites. There were two million slaves in America at this time and a half million free blacks. In ten years, at the cost of more than $100,000, the Society had succeeded in transporting fewer than two thousand; of the eighty-four transported in 1824, twenty-four had died. Garrison also made the first of his four trips to England, this time to raise funds for Negro education. Not successful in this aspect, the trip was a personal triumph and helped build an alliance between British and American abolitionists.

In 1833 Garrison went to Philadelphia to share in the founding of the American Anti-Slavery Society, and in 1834 he married Helen Benson, daughter of a veteran abolitionist, after a very hesitant and cautious courtship in which the lady had surely done her fair share. The couple settled first in Roxbury, Massachusetts. This was a happy marriage, which produced six children, but Garrison never allowed family obligations to interfere with his mission, and necessities, to say nothing of luxuries, were often in short supply. He could hardly have made out with a mate less completely devoted to him and to his cause.

In 1835 he was mobbed and nearly lynched on the occasion of a women's meeting in Anti-Slavery Hall in Boston, but was saved by the authorities and lodged for

The Grammar School and Garrison Birthplace, Newburyport, Mass., from photographs in *William Lloyd Garrison 1805-1879, The Story of His Life Told by His Children*, Vol. I, 1885. Library of Congress

safekeeping in the Leverett Street Jail, where he received his friends, wrote a poem on the wall of his cell, and recorded that he had been confined there "to save him from the violence of 'a respectable and influential' mob, who sought to destroy him for preaching the abominable and dangerous doctrine that all men are created equal." This was not the only mob Garrison ever faced but it was by all means the most dangerous. The incident became the occasion of winning Wendell Phillips to the abolitionist cause.

Garrison's remaining years were devoted to continued organizational and editorial work in behalf of abolition and other causes and were punctuated by bitter invective against his opponents and, at times, almost equally bitter criticism of his allies. In 1854, at a Fourth of July celebration at Framingham, Massachusetts, he burned, first, the Fugitive Slave Law and, then, the Constitution of the United States, as "a covenant with death and an agreement with hell" because it made provision for slavery. After *The Liberator* had been suspended, he became a frequent contributor to *The Independent*. His wife was an invalid from the end of 1863 to her death in 1876, and his own health was greatly impaired during his last years. He died in New York on May 24, 1879.

Though Garrison became the most famous of the American abolitionists, he was of course by no means the only one. His services to the cause were very great, and it is neither necessary nor possible here to weigh and evaluate them precisely with reference to those of others. Today he often repels potential admirers with his almost hysterical rhetoric and the violent and intemperate abuse he hurled at all who ventured to disagree with him. His path through life was strewn with broken friendships; he even broke with Whittier, a man with whom it was impossible to quarrel. When Samuel J. May urged him to moderate his indignation and bank his fires, he replied, "Brother May, I have need to be all on fire, for I have mountains of ice about me to melt." So he had, but it is doubtful that he melted them by turning *The Liberator* into what Emerson called a "scold." He himself boasted that the constitution he drew up for the New England Non-Resistant Society was one of the most " 'fanatical' and 'disorganizing' instruments penned by man" and that it "upturned almost every existing institution on earth." When a "deadly missile" was thrown at the British abolitionist George Thompson at Lowell, Garrison displayed it at the Anti-Slavery office, to show how "the Citizens of low(h)ell" had behaved. George Bancroft was "an ambitious, unprincipled, time-serving demagogue, who would sell his country as Judas sold his Lord." The great William Ellery Channing's book on slavery— "calumnious, contradictory, and unsound"—contained "a farrago of impertinence, contradiction, and defamation." At one time or another, Garrison seems to have denounced every religious denomination (the Methodist General Conference was "a cage of unclean birds and a synagogue of Satan"); he also attacked foreigners like Father Mathew and Louis Kossuth when they failed to take a stand on American slavery. Even Wendell Phillips was guilty of "egotistical assumption" and "swollen self-complacency" when he dared to disagree with Garrison as to what course abolitionists should pursue after emancipation.

This was not Garrison's only handicap as an antislavery leader, however. Others were his determination to marry antislavery to a host of other reforms quite unrelated to it, his cavalier disregard of ways and means and indifference to implementing even slavery reform, his increasing estrangement, as he grew older, from all the churches (though not from religion itself) and consequent alienation of many who ought to have been among his allies, and, above all, the opposition to government he developed, which caused him to outlaw all political avenues toward reform, including voting and holding office.

Pacifism, temperance, and women's rights (on which he began to split the antislavery movement as early as 1838, when the question of admitting women as delegates to an antislavery convention came up in Boston), were the most important of these causes. Of course it was a credit to Garrison's penetration that he should have perceived that abolition was not the whole gospel and that slavery had its roots in larger maladjustments and that he should therefore have sought "the emancipation of our whole race from the dominion of man, from the thralldom of self, from the government of brute force, from the bondage of sin." Influenced by the "Perfectionism" of John Humphrey Noyes and others, he came to see all government as belonging to Anti-Christ because tainted by its use of force, but even those who supported his other causes regretted his scattering his shot by attacking on all fronts simultaneously. When an abolitionist leader sponsors an Anti-Sabbath Convention in the midst of an antislavery fight on the ground that Sabbatarianism is a form unauthorized by the Gospel, and because *all* life should be holy, it is difficult to believe that he has much sense of proportion. Even on slavery itself Garrison had curious blind spots. His "liberalism" went the whole way, accepting even interracial marriages, but through all the years he advocated immediate emancipation, he seems to have given little thought to what must follow its achievement, and after the war he was cold to Negro suffrage (this was one of the issues on which he clashed seriously with Phillips). On the other hand, it was all to his honor that he should have become keenly interested in free trade during his later years and a champion of the rights of Indians and Orientals (he attacked James G. Blaine on American immigration policies). Only on the labor question was he consistently conservative. Nothing suggestive of socialism ever tempted him.

Garrison rejected both church and state because they were tied up with slavery, and the Constitution as a proslavery document and a bulwark of the slave system. He began advocating disunion about 1842; from 1844 he proclaimed "NO UNION WITH SLAVEHOLDERS." (Inconsistently, he did urge his readers to petition Congress to dissolve the Union.) In Garrison's mind all this was tied up with, and necessitated by, his nonresistance principles. But the man who wrote his inflammatory editorials can hardly be considered a pacifist by temperament, whatever he may have been by conviction.

Before the war, Garrison sympathized with, though he did not condone, David Walker's inflammatory *Appeal*, Nat Turner's insurrection, and John Brown's raid, and prayed for the success of the Mexicans against the United States. When Lovejoy was killed in 1837, he regretted that he had defended himself with "carnal" weapons. He did not bless the use of force in Texas, though he thought that if it ever could be justified, it would be there. When South Carolina seceded, he rejoiced in the annulment of the "covenant with death" but still looked for a peaceful separation. But from the Emancipation Proclamation on he was an ardent Lincoln man and a supporter of the war. He offered only a token opposition to the enlistment of his son George in the army, and he was a guest of the government when the Stars and Stripes went up at Fort Sumter again on April 14, 1865. Wartime editorials in *The Liberator* were about as consistent and disingenuous as such editorials are generally. Garrison now declared that he had never granted the South the right of secession and that abolitionists in general had never been disloyal to the Union or accepted nonresistance! Nor would he admit that there was any conflict between the principles he had proclaimed for many years and his support of the war.

Garrison has been attacked on the ground that he found as much self-expression and self-assertion in abolitionism as other men find in activities which claim no special moral value of significance. The criticism is curiously irrelevant. Every man must achieve self-asser-tion and self-expression; otherwise he must wither away and become a nonentity. The distinguishing mark of the good man is simply that he comes to himself in an activity which conduces to human welfare. Garrison was not always wise; neither did he wholly avoid the morasses of self-righteousness. After winning a great triumph in Scotland, he wrote his wife that he was happy "to be accounted worthy to assist in filling up the measure of the sufferings of Jesus!" But it is not fair to ask him for a different kind of accomplishment than his nature qualified him for. He was an ethical absolutist. "The question of expediency," he declared, "has nothing to do with that of right." His voice was a trumpet call to the conscience of his time, and this is all he was fit for. Probably no such man can ever complete a great reform, but probably it cannot get started without him either.

IV.   LUCY LARCOM

Lucy Larcom. New York Public Library Picture Collection

Lucy Larcom, poet, teacher, editor, friend of Whittier and Phillips Brooks, and author of the minor regional classic, *A New England Girlhood*, was a perfect product of the old-time New England faith in piety and hard work. She was born in Beverly, Massachusetts, on March 5, 1824, the second youngest in a family of ten children. Her father, a retired shipmaster turned shopkeeper, traced his American ancestry back to 1655 in Ipswich. In later life it seemed to her that if she had been born "elsewhere than in this northeastern corner of Massachusetts, elsewhere than on this green rocky strip of shore between Beverly Bridge and the Misery Islands," she would have been "somebody else and not myself." In 1867 she wrote:

The coast here is not remarkable. Just here there is a deep, sunny harbor, that sheltered the second company of the Pilgrim settlers from the Mother-Country, more than two centuries ago. A little river, which has leave to be such only at the return of the tide, half clasps the town in its crooked arm, and makes many an opening of beauty twice a day, among the fields and under the hills. The harbor is so shut in by islands, it has the effect of a lake; and the tide comes up over the wide, weedy flats, with a gentle and gradual flow.

Every third person one met in the streets was or had been "Shipman," "Skipper," or "Captain," and many had voyaged to Hong Kong or Gibraltar. The better-dressed women owned Canton crepe shawls or Smyrna silks or Turkish satins; some families had Mongolians, Africans, or natives of the South Seas as dependents, and green parrots, monkeys, and tropical songbirds for pets. Rich and poor were "book words" only, and a romantic child might be as eager to see a beggar as a king. But George Edward Woodberry, who was a Beverly boy, and whom, in his youth, she encouraged, was right to see more dread than love of the sea in Lucy's poems; she always felt safer with rivers and mountains. "Almost every house had its sea-tragedy. Somebody belonging to it had been shipwrecked, or had sailed away one day, and never returned." Lucy's own brother was more fortunate, for, though his ship was attacked, robbed, and set afire on the high seas by pirates, he and his fellow sailors got back home, and the pirates were captured, brought into Salem for trial, and hanged at

The Boott Cotton Mills at Lowell, Mass., as pictured in 1852. Library of Congress

Boston. Such poems as "Hannah Binding Shoes," "Skipper Ben," and "Hilary" show that the writer had an imaginative comprehension of all the sorrows involved in the seafaring life.

Poverty came close enough to the Larcoms when, after the death of the father in 1835, the mother moved her family to Lowell so that she might act as a kind of combined lodging house keeper and housemother in one of the "corporation houses" that had been set up there for the girls who worked in the cotton mills developed by the Lowell and Appleton interests. Here there were plenty of beggars too, quite unromantic and "always of Hibernian extraction," and Penobscot Indians, "men and women alike clad in loose gowns, stove-pipe hats, and mocassons; grotesque relics of aboriginal forest-life." At eleven, Lucy herself went to work in the mills, where she continued, with intervals, until, in 1846, she went with her sister and brother-in-law to Looking Glass Prairie, in St. Clair County, Illinois, where she taught in a number of elementary schools. In 1849 she entered Monticello Female Academy, at Alton, Illinois, where she was both student and student-teacher. In 1852 she was graduated, after which she returned to Beverly. From 1854 to 1862 she taught at Wheaton Seminary, Norton, Massachusetts; thereafter her teaching was irregular. For a number of years she was one of the editors of *Our Young Folks*.

Lucy Larcom's first book was *Similitudes from the Ocean and the Prairie* (1854). The next year she won the prize offered by the New England Emigrant Aid Society for the best Kansas song, which was widely distributed and sung. Her first collection of *Poems* appeared in 1868; in 1884 a greatly enlarged gathering emerged in Houghton Mifflin's "Household Edition." She edited *Child Life* and *Child Life in Prose* with

Whittier and other collections on her own. *A New England Girlhood* (1889) found wide acceptance; so did such late devotional books as *The Unseen Friend* and *As It Is in Heaven*. She died in Boston on April 17, 1893.

"Nature came very close to the mill-gates" in the days of Lucy's service there. The slope behind the mills was a green lawn, and she passed to her work "through a splendor of dahlias and hollyhocks." It was a strange chapter in American industry, marking an important step in the process of taking cloth-making out of the home and establishing it in factories. In its own time what was being done at Lowell was widely admired, by both Americans and foreign visitors, including Charles Dickens, who was greatly impressed by the contrast with factory conditions in England, and Lucy Larcom herself called the long blank verse poem she published about the mill life in 1875 *An Idyll of Work*. A twelve- to fourteen-hour day, at wages ranging from $1.80 to $6.00 a week, plus room and board, may not strike us as quite idyllic, yet it is a fact that the girls sent money home to their families, paid off mortgages, sent younger brothers to college to prepare for the ministry, or saved to put themselves through Mount Holyoke later on. In 1845 the Lowell savings banks held $100,000 that had been deposited by mill girls. Actually, they were not "mill girls" in the later sense of that term (when, later on, such came into the factories, both moral and intellectual conditions sharply declined), but the daughters of good New England families who had been brought up to respect both the dignity of labor and themselves. They were not ashamed that they needed to earn money, but they had no intention of becoming "wage slaves," a term which probably none of them had ever heard. By Massachusetts law, the children

Original model of cotton gin. Smithsonian Institution
Photo No. 73-11288

Progress of Cotton. Smithsonian Institution Photo Nos. 52557, 52557A,
B, D

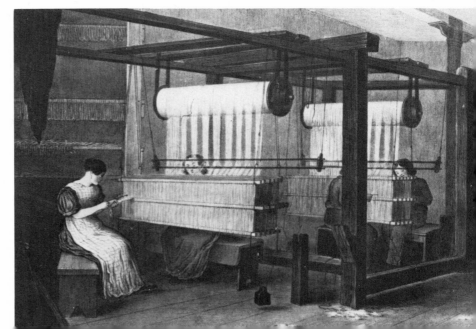

among them were required to spend at least three months of the year in school, and though the working day was cruelly long, conditions and surroundings in the mills were pleasant, and, in some departments at least, the work was light. Lucy's first job required her to change the bobbins on the spinning frames every forty-five minutes, the rest of the time being her own, and after she had become a "book-keeper" in the Lawrence mills, she had time during the day for both reading and writing. In the mills themselves, books were not allowed (one girl was rebuked for having smuggled in her Bible!), but apparently Lucy was never interfered with for pasting newspaper clippings of poems she admired around the window. Though unsympathetic moderns have sometimes inclined to the view that the millowners were more concerned for the girls' spiritual than their material welfare, but reversed this scale of values in looking after themselves, few of the employees seem to have needed supervision. They industriously attended not only church services but Lyceum lectures as well, hearing the foremost speakers of the day, one of whom reported that four-fifths of his audience were girls who were busily reading before he began his discourse and industriously taking notes afterwards, and they formed "Improvement Circles," in which they studied German, botany, ethics, and other subjects. More remarkably still, they not only read but wrote, publishing several magazines of their own, culminating in *The Lowell Offering*, which achieved a circulation of four thousand copies and became the subject of a lecture by Philarète Charles in Paris!

Lucy Larcom never resented the claim of the mills on her time except when it interfered with her studies. She had no more interest in machinery than in mathematics, the only one of her studies that frustrated her (she could feel the poetry, she declared, but she could not take the steps). It is amazing that a girl in her circumstances should have been able to read so widely, not only standard creative literature but learned philosophical writers as well. In later life she professed not to enjoy teaching nor think she did it well; she also expressed much the same kind of doubts about herself as a social being as those that plagued Emerson. Since Wheaton required her to teach "history, rhetoric, English literature, logic, intellectual philosophy, and composition," all in the course of a year, it is not surprising that her health finally broke under the strain, but though her methods were informal, somewhat unsystematic, and what we should now be tempted to call "progressive," she inspired devotion in her charges and established sustaining and enduring relations with many of them.

As time went on, Lucy Larcom became increasingly a devotional poet and writer, but nobody could have been less of a bigot. Though she was considered to have a cheerful temperament, she won no immunity from fear, doubt, and depression. "Doubt is not an unhealthy

symptom," she declared; "it argues the possibility of belief." She feared a breakdown in health long before it came; she also feared, apparently without cause, that her mind might give way; these considerations seem to have influenced her decision not to marry. At thirteen she joined the Congregational Church, a step she later regretted after she had come to reject all the essential points of Calvinism, and for many years she lived without a .church affiliation. She read Plato, Coleridge, Swedenborg, even, in later years, the Theosophists; but the religious writers who helped her most were Horace Bushnell, F. W. Robertson, and Frederick Denison Maurice. In 1879 she began attending Trinity Church in Boston to hear Phillips Brooks, and a new era in her religious life began. At first she feared what she considered the exclusivism of the Episcopalians ("the dissidence of dissent and the protestantism of the Protestant religion" which was her heritage was not lightly to be cast off), but Brooks was no more exclusivistic than she was; in 1887 she shared in open Communion at Trinity, and in 1890 she united with the church. Her religion was always, however, essentially mystical, and neither theological nor ecclesiastical: "the thought of a present God, who is a personal Friend to every Soul." This God she knew through Christ. "God exists as impersonal Spirit, but I know Him only as a person through Christ. The historical Christ is entirely true to me, as the only way in which God could humanly be known to us." Once she told a pupil, "I never knew there was any other way to live." The only criticism she ever made of Emerson was that he refused "to call his inspiration by its right name." In the intellectual scaffoldings of theology she had no interest whatever; when Solomon Solis-Cohen told her that "no professed Christian can exceed many Jews in love for the pure and lofty character of Jesus, and we can readily accept that character, as a manifestation of God in man, while we decline to accept the superstructure of the church," she stressed the Hebraic character of old New England Puritanism, deplored the cruel treatment of Jews by Christians, and affirmed her conviction "that Jew and Christian were really one, only they did not understand each other." As a poet she made some of these same points with considerable eloquence in "Our Christ" and "The Heart of God."

Lucy Larcom's first contacts with poetry were made through the hymnbook. Her sister promised to give her a book when she had memorized fifty and teach her to write when she had memorized a hundred. Since she had been reading her New Testament since she was two and a half, she had no difficulty in achieving all this before she was five. When she was seven, she began scribbling verses of her own. They "just grew," as if they were breathing or singing, she said; she "could not help writing them," though she dreamed many that she never did get written down. She soon learned that "poetry must have prose to root itself in; the homelier its earth-spot, the lovelier, by contrast, its heaven-breathing flowers." Her own poems deal with nature, with humble New England life, and with God. The hymns which attracted her most in the beginning were those which had nature in them. She is one of the great poetic authorities on New England flowers ("The weed, to him who loves it, is a flower"), and Oliver Wendell Holmes said she herself was as much a product of Essex County soil as the bayberry.

In her poem "A Thanksgiving," which Whittier greatly admired, she triumphantly fused nature, humanity, and the supernatural:

> The world we live in wholly is redeemed;
> Not man alone, but all that man holds dear:
> His orchards and his maize; forget-me-not
> And heart's-ease in his garden; and the wild
> Aerial blossoms of the untamed wood,
> That make its savagery so home-like; all

> Have felt Christ's sweet love watering their roots:
> His sacrifice has won both earth and heaven.

> Nature, in all its fulness, is the Lord's.
> There are no Gentile oaks; no Pagan pines;
> The grass beneath our feet is Christian grass;
> The wayside weed is sacred unto Him.

When "The Rose Enthroned" was published without signature, it was conjecturally, and not unreasonably, attributed to both Emerson and Lowell. "The Chamber Called Peace" is suggestive of Poe, and no American poet would need to be ashamed of "A White Sunday" or "Wild Roses of Cape Ann." If she was not a major poet, Lucy Larcom was nevertheless a genuinely gifted writer with a high degree of technical competence. She exemplifies the sensitive, cultivated, devoted womanhood which the New England civilization of her time could produce, and it does not suffer by reference to such an exemplar.

V.   CHARLES FRANCIS ADAMS, JR.

Henry Adams wrote two of the most brilliant books ever produced in this country—*Mont-Saint-Michel and Chartres*, "a Study of Thirteenth-Century Unity," and *The Education of Henry Adams*, "a Study of Twentieth-Century Multiplicity." The thesis of the latter is that he never was educated; one gets the impression of a man defying the universe, challenging it to educate him, and raising up all the defenses of ignorance against it. He himself admitted that ignorance was his "favorite protective pose," self-depreciation his "vice," and "morbid self-contempt" his moral weakness, all of which lends force to Robert Spiller's observation that, like Whitman, Adams assumed "a romantic pose . . . for dramatic intensification"; only where Whitman's was a pose of "vigor and success," his was one of "reticence and failure."

If all this was true of Henry Adams, it was no less true of his brother, Charles Francis Adams, Jr. (1835-1915), son of the Charles Francis Adams (1807-1886) who was Lincoln's ambassador to England, grandson of President John Quincy Adams, and great-grandson of President John Adams. The Adams temperament was well represented in him. James Russell Lowell said that "the Adamses have a genius for saying even a gracious thing in an ungracious way," and when the younger Charles found this statement in Lowell's published letters, he thought it so true that he was not insulted but delighted. But his life experience, as we shall see, departed sharply from the traditional lines.

Charles Francis Adams, Jr., was born on Hancock Avenue, almost in the shadow of Boston's State House, on May 27, 1835, and grew up there and at the Adams family home in Quincy. He went through the standard educational mill—Boston Latin and Harvard—and then studied law in the office of Richard Henry Dana, Jr., whose biographer he became, and his partner, Francis E. Parker, not because he wanted to, but because it seemed the thing for a young man in his position to do. He was admitted to the bar in 1858, through favoritism, he thought, for he believed he had no more qualifications than a child, but he never took any interest in practicing law nor had any success at it. The first

Charles Francis Adams, Jr. Library of Congress

Charles Francis Adams in camp during Civil War days, flanked by Lieut. G. H. Teague on his left and Capt. E. A. Flint on his right. New York Public Library Picture Collection

thing he did which interested him deeply seems to have been his article of "The Reign of King Cotton" which Lowell published in the *Atlantic* in April 1861.

When his father was elected to Congress, the son gravitated to Washington, and in 1860 he got his first view of what Bostonians called the "West" as Senator Seward's guest on a political junket. In December 1861 he received a commission in the First Massachusetts Cavalry, and served through the Civil War, except when absent on sick leave, until June 1865. In the fall of 1864 he was transferred to a colored regiment, the Fifth Massachusetts Cavalry, and he was mustered out a brigadier-general. In November 1865 he was married to Mary Ogden, and soon thereafter settled down to writing about railroad problems and regulation. This led to his appointment to the Massachusetts State Board of Railroad Commissioners, on which he served from 1869 to 1879.

He was president of the Union Pacific Railroad from 1884 to 1890. During the first five years he met with considerable success in reorganizing the road and straightening out its difficulties with the government, but in the final analysis his efforts failed, and the Union Pacific was turned over to his old enemy, Jay Gould. Adams had discovered his interest in historical research in 1874 when asked to deliver an address at the 250th anniversary celebration of the settlement of Weymouth, Massachusetts, and his later years were devoted to scholarship and public services. He lived in Quincy, in Boston's Back Bay, in Lincoln, and finally in Washington, where he died on March 20, 1915.

Adams saw his whole youth and education as "a skilfully arranged series of mistakes." He hated Boston. He hated Boston Latin. He hated First Church and pretty much all churches. If he did not hate his father, he certainly came pretty close to it, nor is there any indication that his mother meant very much to him. The house at 57 Mount Vernon Street, where the family lived after 1842, threw a shadow across his whole early life. He hated it when he first saw it at the age of seven, and when he locked the door and walked away from it forty-seven years later, he thanked God that he need never see it again. "Drunk or sober," he hated Boston society too, for there was nothing to it except Boston! And when the old Latin School building was torn down many years after he had left it, he still hated the institution so much that he rejoiced in the destruction.

He saw his grandfather, John Quincy Adams, as "a very old-looking gentleman, with a bald head and a white fringe of hair—writing, writing—with a perpetual inkstain on the fore-finger and thumb of the right hand." Though the old man was kind, he was not companionable, and there was nothing about him to interest a boy, but he did appeal to the imagination in a way that the boy's father, who "was built on more rigid and narrower lines," could not. Him Charles could never forgive for not having cultivated his interest in athletics or sending him to boarding school! All he gave his father credit for was that he had not sent him to "common school." "I believe in school life; and I believe in the equality of men before the law; but social equality, whether for man or child, is altogether another thing."

He thought it a mistake to tutor and enter Harvard as a sophomore, and about the only good the college did for him was that it enabled him to discover his aptitude for writing. With proper teaching and encouragement, he might have become a fair Greek scholar, but he found neither and consequently failed to develop. Even his aptitude for writing was not an "overpowering call"; it failed to "dominate" him, and so this too came to nothing. Later he supported President Eliot's effort to break the stranglehold of the classics but disbelieved in his elective system. As a Harvard overseer, he worked hard to reform the college, and when he was defeated, he decided that Harvard was, like Hamlet's Denmark, one of the worst of the "confines, wards and dungeons" in the world.

After all this, Adams's statement, "I am . . . naturally inclined to be otherwise-minded, and a bit iconoclastic" does not seem an exaggeration. He never ceased to analyze himself; as his biographer, Edward Chase Kirkland, says, "the world was always an arena in which Charles tested and appraised his own qualities." He might have been "a philosophical statesman" or "a literary politician"; he became neither. In his own view, he had no *savoir-faire*, no objectivity, tact, quick discernment, or ability to grasp an opportunity. He was weak of will and deficient in staying power. Even in Europe he was able to enjoy himself only after a fashion. "That I failed, and failed woefully, to avail myself of my opportunities, goes without saying; for it was I!" He scattered his energies and always kept too many irons in the fire. Such skill as he possessed took the form of a perverse ingenuity in avoiding his best opportunities. These self-judgments and others occur and recur wearisomely throughout his autobiography. Possibly he was not fair to himself; certainly his attitude cannot have been favorable to achievement.

Worse still, all this ruthless self-evaluation never conduced to a saving knowledge. It was his opinion that "the accumulation of wealth is not the loftiest end of human effort," and his judgment of moneyed men was devastating. Their gift for accumulation was not only detached from all other human capacities but completely unassociated with any of man's nobler aspects. Yet he devoted himself primarily to money-making for more than twenty years, investing and speculating in land, mines, railroads, manufacturing, and much besides. In Boston he and his brother John Quincy owned the land between Cottage Farm and the intersection of Commonwealth Avenue and Beacon Street now largely occupied by Boston University. But he also extended his operations into Texas, Utah, and the Pacific Northwest. He controlled stockyards in Kansas City (Kansas) and Denver. At one period he slept on the train more often than at home. Yet all the while he hated "that great, fat, uninteresting West," including Chicago. He achieved a very large income but ran up enormous debts and incurred terrific interest obligations, often extending himself unwisely and escaping destruction more by chance than wise management. Inevitably he also quite sacrificed peace of mind. In the Union Pacific chapter, he even came very close to the practices which, as a railroad reformer, he had condemned in others, though never for wholly selfish reasons.

Adams's cultivated perversity nowhere shows up more clearly than in his military experiences. He was far from being a militarist. At the beginning of the Civil War he stood with Seward and his father for conciliation, judging Charles Sumner, whom he had hitherto greatly admired, almost a madman in his intransigence. Later, when Seward hoped for war with England to heal American disunity, Adams turned resolutely away from him. He called Cleveland's truculent Venezuelan message "drunken rhodomontade." In the Spanish-American War crisis, he was a pronounced anti-imperialist—with a characteristically low opinion of his allies in the cause.

Yet he thought of his Civil War service, which he "succeeded in getting through without sustaining any lasting personal or physical injury, or any moral injury at all," the most valuable part of his education. Indeed it seems to have been almost as good as boarding school! He enjoyed military action rapturously. "It was a truly glorious existence," and the excitement of battle was "grand." But, for all that, he judged himself to have "staggered and blundered through the war," having no proper aptitude for soldiering and never encountering the superiors who might have given him the guidance he needed. Here again he had no magnetism, was not "quick, daring or ready-witted," and did not know how to act quickly in emergencies. Under proper supervision, he would have made a really good inspector-general for an army corps, but the only time such a post was offered to him, he lacked the wit to accept it. Both at Antietam and at Gettysburg, he did not fight but slept, at Antietam "in the height of the battle and between the contending armies," waiting for the orders to advance which never came. He relates the circumstances with such relish that one cannot but believe he felt a certain satisfaction in running true to form!

Nevertheless Charles Francis Adams, Jr. was still a man of ability who accomplished much. As anyone who will check through his cards in any large library may speedily discover, for a man who did so many other things, he turned out an astonishing amount of writing. *Three Episodes of Massachusetts History* is an important work. For his life of his father he did pioneering research both here and in England at a time when "method" in historical writing was less clearly understood than it is today. *A Chapter of Erie* was an original contribution to railroad history, and, as Mr. Kirkland says, "an exposé of the stock exchange and of corrupt government as much as it was of railroads." As president of the Massachusetts Historical Society, Adams was important in the 1912 publication of Bradford's *History of Plymouth Plantation* and much besides.

Indeed, Adams's literary and scholarly aptitude was such that one is sorely tempted to lament his other activities as a kind of whoring after strange gods. Yet whatever judgment may be passed upon him as a businessman, it would not be reasonable to ignore the value of his many public services. Without his pioneering work as a railroad reformer, or its equivalent, the Interstate Commerce Commission could hardly have come into being. It would be hard to find anywhere a more impressive record of community activity than he and his brother John chalked up in Quincy during the years Charles lived on President's Hill. They reorganized the town meeting, improved and extended the local government, freed the town from debt, created a public park, built and established a library, and set up a school system which became nationally famous. Later, in 1892, Charles became chairman of a commission appointed by the Massachusetts legislature to devise a system of parks and public reservations in the Boston area; among other things, this saved the Blue Hills and Middlesex Fells from the spoilers misnamed developers, established open spaces along the Charles River, and led to thè establishment of a Metropolitan Parks Commission. When Adams died, his brother Henry cried that "Charles was worth three of me!" However that may be, such services as these should keep his name in honored remembrance, despite all his flourishes and the ineptitudes with which he debited himself.

VI. ALICE FREEMAN PALMER

Alice Freeman Palmer was not the teacher who, upon being asked what she was teaching, replied, "Twenty girls," but she would have understood the answer. To all intents and purposes she became president of Wellesley College in 1881, when she was only twenty-six, though the full title did not come until the next year. At the end of 1887 she resigned to become the wife of Harvard's Professor George Herbert Palmer, philosopher and Greek scholar. During the brief years between she placed Wellesley upon a solid scholastic foundation and made one of the strongest and most lasting impressions of any American college administrator. When she died, her husband received more than two thousand letters from persons in all walks of life. Four college presidents joined to honor her at the memorial service in Harvard's Appleton Chapel, and countless girls have been inspired by her husband's account of her life.

Wellesley's founder, Henry F. Durant, was an intense evangelical who had been converted under the preaching of D. L. Moody, whom Alice Freeman, whose theology was very different, also greatly admired for his sincerity, largeness of sympathy, and freedom from cant. She was as anxious as Durant that Wellesley girls should be good Christians, but she had no sympathy with ignorance, sentimentalism, sectarianism, or unreality, and it was impossible for her to undertake an assault upon a personality even in the interest of religion. She was far from established at Wellesley when, one day, Durant commanded her to approach a girl at once and talk to her about her salvation. She flatly refused. She would make it her business to get acquainted with the girl and try to guide her, but she would not broach such a subject with a stranger; she even told Durant that he did not know anything about girls because he had never had a daughter, his wife was unlike any other woman who had ever lived, and he had never been a girl himself. As a man who had founded a school for girls, and was devoting his life to it, Durant found this hard to take, but he managed it; thereafter, when she disagreed with him, he would always say, "Well, I suppose I don't understand girls; I've never been a girl myself."

Alice Freeman's paternal grandfather had left Connecticut for pioneer New York, and she was born, on February 21, 1855, in Colesville, Broome County, and grew up in the Susquehanna Valley. Her father was first a farmer, then a country doctor. Her real education began at Windsor, and in 1872 she was graduated from the Academy there, having been trained mainly in Greek, Latin, French, and mathematics. Determined, under great difficulties, to secure a college degree, she then went to the University of Michigan (she always believed strongly in coeducation), where President James Rowland Angell was so strongly impressed by her that he admitted her, with conditions, despite the inadequacy of her preparation. At Michigan history became her principal academic interest; she received her B.A. in 1876, one of eleven girls in a class of seventy-five and a participant in the Commencement pro-

Alice Freeman Palmer as a child. Artist unknown. Library of Congress

gram. In 1875, however, conditions of financial stringency in her family had necessitated her withdrawing from college temporarily to teach in Ottawa High School, where she acted as interim principal (she was already establishing her habit of beginning at the top!), and this meant more conditions, increasing the load she had to carry through the rest of her college career and imposing an additional burden upon her never robust health.

After her graduation, she taught at Lake Geneva and at Saginaw High School; this was hard, ill-paid work, performed under difficult conditions and while carrying heavy family burdens, but her success with her pupils was distinguished. Wellesley's first offer to her was in mathematics, the second in Greek; she declined both. In 1879 she went there as professor and head of the Department of History, teaching fifteen hours a week, plus one public lecture and a daily Bible class, overseeing her assistant in history, "advising" the senior class, and having charge of a portion of the domestic work! She continued as president until 1887; then, when Palmer "called [her] to take the quiet name of wife," she moved to Cambridge.

When The University of Chicago was founded, President William Rainey Harper desperately wanted her as a professor of history and as dean of women, at the same time offering Palmer three times his Harvard salary as professor of philosophy. Neither offer was accepted, but between 1892 and 1895 Mrs. Palmer did accept a deanship which permitted her to be in residence in Chicago only twelve weeks (or one University of Chicago "quarter") out of each year. She led a very active "retirement" life; she was a frequent public speaker; her house was thronged with guests from far and near; she was forever being consulted on educational problems. A Wellesley trustee, she also had a share in laying the foundations of Radcliffe and was a member of the Massachusetts State Board of Education, the College Alumnae Association, and much besides. She planned the Massachusetts exhibit for the World's Columbian Exposition, and each year she was involved in the annual campaign, successful during her lifetime, to keep Cambridge "dry."

On December 6, 1902, she died in Paris, where she and her husband were spending his sabbatical, after a brief illness and an emergency operation. There was tuberculosis in her family, and she had brought a cough to college which clung to her through most of her life, but the end had nothing to do with such weaknesses. It was caused by intussusception of the intestine, a rare disease, of unknown cause, in her time at least, generally fatal. It left her philosopher-husband wondering whether the world must not be called irrational "if out of deference to a few particles of disordered matter it excludes so fair a spirit."

Alice Freeman's work at Wellesley was a pioneering enterprise. The institution was chartered as a "female

Two photographs of Alice Freeman Palmer. Library of Congress

seminary" in 1870, became a college in the mid-seventies, and graduated its first class in 1879. When its collegiate foundations were laid, Mary Lyon's Mount Holyoke was still a "seminary," and Vassar was the only established woman's college; the foundations of Smith were being laid contemporaneously. Modern readers must not be misled by Durant's piety; he had no intention of permitting it to become a substitute for scholarship. Opposing the tyranny of the textbook, he encouraged library and laboratory work, was liberal in the matter of electives, fostered art and music, and sponsored exercise though not competitive sports. Both Vassar and Smith had men presidents; Durant insisted upon an all-female staff; girls could not be expected to go into higher education unless the way was opened for them to make use of what they had learned.

Alice Freeman Palmer, Hall of Fame, medal by Thomas Lo Medico. New York Public Library Picture Collection

College life at Wellesley was very different from anything known today. Until 1885 students and faculty lived and worked together in one building, College Hall, and even in 1887 Miss Freeman was telling Palmer that six hundred people met her in close relations every day and that her time was largely at their disposal. In a sense it agreed with her. She had grown up in a poor family, caring for the younger children, and in college her classmates were already bringing their problems to her. But it was a strain nevertheless, and we must keep it in mind if we would judge fairly the almost national controversy precipitated by her desire to retire and marry. Even Dartmouth's President Tucker asked Palmer, "Will you tear Harvard to pieces or tear Wellesley?"

One of the great hurdles that the crusade for higher education for women had to surmount was the widespread conviction that there was no use investing in women because a woman would always leave everything else to get married. Now, having rendered such valiant service to the cause, was Alice Freeman to betray it by proving the skeptics right? These agonies tormented nobody else quite so much as the persons most directly involved. They debated the issues with each other and themselves almost ad infinitum, with Palmer even serving at times as devil's advocate. They toyed with the notion of making him president of Wellesley or of a joint presidency but soon came to see the absurdity of both proposals. Two considerations determined the final outcome. It became increasingly clear both that Alice Freeman's health could not stand many more years of the kind of strain under which she lived at Wellesley and that the most important part of her work there was done. One who knew her well said: "It would have been dangerous for one person to have so much power had not that person been Miss Freeman." If the institution was to survive, it must become self-sufficient and not dependent upon any single individual.

In his luminous biography of his wife, George Herbert Palmer described what she did at Wellesley in some detail. Yet the best part of it will not yield to description; one can only say that, like all great teachers, she gave herself, and she was one of those rare human beings who awaken the powers of those whose lives they touch and enable them to rise above themselves. Her photographs do not suggest a beautiful woman, though we are told they do not do her justice. Her charm was in her manner, her kindness, her everready response. She could not deal with any human being without establishing a personal relationship with him, and when she greeted or consulted with a student, she gave the impression of being more interested in the individual before her than in anything else in the world, not because she made an effort to do so, but simply because it was true.

For all her passion for education, she was no scholar; for all that great poetry meant to her (and there were few to whom it meant more), she was not even bookish. In her early days she planned graduate study toward the Ph.D., but practical difficulties always intervened, and it may be doubted that she could have found fulfillment along this line. After her death, her husband wrote a book on ethics because she had suggested it, but he was never able to interest her much in philosophy. "She was a woman of action, ideals, and practical adjustments." Like many artists, she had an intuitive understanding of a great many things about which she knew very little in a systematic or scholarly way; she drew more from life directly and less from life through books than the scholar does. She was not introspective nor much given to self-examination; about her own concerns and her inward being, she maintained almost as impenetrable a reserve as did Longfellow. As a public speaker, she always talked *to* her audiences; few of her eminence have come so close to being completely extemporaneous. Her husband even felt that her multitudinous letters were limited in reader interest because she concentrated so absolutely upon her correspondent.

Alice Freeman Palmer was very nearly an ideal woman, but she had none of the characteristics which so often make idealists a trial, and no doubt this was a large factor in the wide influence she commanded. A country girl, she combined high-mindedness with a frank acceptance of the facts of life and was never squeamish or affected. For all her practical, executive ability, she was never "orderly" in a systematic or mechanical kind of way, but was rather, as her husband says, "a careless gipsy." She had a temper and was capable of depression. She early discovered that she could not afford to be "sensitive," but she knew her rights and those of the college and was quite capable of insisting upon them uncompromisingly and immovably, when the need arose, against both men and women. As a disciplinarian she could be severe when severity was called for. She told one educator who had asked her for a teacher possessing all possible intellectual and moral virtues, with beauty thrown in to boot, for $600 a year

that Wellesley had no $600 angels in stock, and an Englishman who inquired whether four years in college would not spoil a girl's "chances" was told that they well might with some men but that the girl probably would not mind.

She knew how to work; she also knew how to withdraw and relax; even in the midst of problems, she could dismiss trouble and failure and sleep like a child. She loved bird-watching, sewing, preserving, and, in her later years, photography. She also loved bicycling, and it was a cruel irony that the only serious accident in which she was ever involved should have been caused by a boy who knocked her down with his bicycle. She was at home in her Father's world, and her spirituality was never incompatible with absorbing, ever-varying delight in all its lovely aspects. In his own incomparable way, her husband summed up the meaning of her life when, at the close of his biography, he wrote: "Strength continually went forth from her. She put on righteousness and it clothed her, and sound judgment was her daily crown. Each eye that saw her blessed her; each ear that heard her was made glad."

VII.   WILLIAM JAMES

The old bromide about the James brothers was that William could write philosophy as if it were fiction while Henry had to write fiction as if it were philosophy. The relations between the two were close, even when they had the Atlantic Ocean between them. The gentler Henry, William's junior by a year, worshipped his brother in his youth and never really got over it, and the more explosive William never quite outgrew his early sense of seniority either. The novelist greatly respected William's work, without ever really understanding it (he always intended to read *Principles of Psychology* but never got around to it), but William frankly detested the elaborate stylistic involutions of Henry's famous "later manner" and expressed his dislike so frankly that his brother finally told him he had better not try to read him unless he could get over the idea that the criterion of excellence in fiction was a minute fidelity to the outward trappings of everyday life in Cambridge, Massachusetts.

The Jameses were Irish, not English, and not of New England origin. William's grandfather, the rich William James, made his fortune in Albany, and the philosopher who fathered American "pragmatism" was born, on January 11, 1842, in New York's famous Astor House, before whose portals Horatio Alger, Jr. was to be fond of opening his stories about boys who made good. His father, Henry James, Sr., has been judged by some as great a man as either of his two famous sons. His two younger sons were failures, however, and the only daughter, Alice, though a remarkable person, was a nervous invalid. Indeed the whole James clan, including William himself, were neurotic, the principal exception

William James, a self-portrait of ca. 1866. New York Public Library Picture Collection

being the only great artist among them, the novelist, who escaped through inheriting the stable temperament of his mother, Mary Robertson Walsh.

Henry James, Sr., was an independent religious philosopher, a saint as mischievous as Emily Dickinson, who carried his fear of creedal and institutional domination to such fantastic lengths as to cut himself off from both wide influence and effective functioning. The children grew up accordingly, between frequent shift-

Henry James, with his brother William James, about 1901. New York Public Library Picture Collection

ings hither and yon, on both sides of the Atlantic, in a cosmopolitan atmosphere in which they benefited by frequent, stimulating contacts with distinguished men and women, while both their education and their religious training were haphazard and unsystematic (William's M.D. from the Harvard Medical School in 1864 was his only earned degree), and Henry, though settling in England, never, as his secretary, Theodora Bosanquet, once remarked, really became a native of anything except the James family. William, however, does definitely belong to the history of New England. From the time the family came to Newport in 1860 to permit him to study painting with William Morris Hunt, both he and his parents were New England- (mainly Cambridge-) based, though the restless William did tear off to Europe with rather strange frequency for a man who was not a comfortable traveler and who aggressively proclaimed to his more cosmopolitan brother that he preferred Cambridge to any other place in the world. When he gave up painting, he entered Harvard's Lawrence Scientific School, where Charles W. Eliot was his master, and from 1872 until 1907, he taught at Harvard (when he was not away on leave) in physiology, psychology, and philosophy. In 1910, more dead than alive from angina, he managed to drag himself back from his last visit to Europe, in time to die at his country place, at Chocorua, New Hampshire, on August 26.

He might well have lived longer had he been willing, during his later years, to follow such routine as is imperative for a man with a heart condition, but he found it impossible to do this. William James had been much slower in finding his way than Henry. Before entering medical school (he was never to practice medicine), he listed his options, in "ascending order," as Natural History, Medicine, Printing, and Beggary. He had no career until he began teaching physiology, on a one-year appointment, at the age of thirty, and he did not publish his first book until 1890, when his magnum opus, *Principles of Psychology*, which he had, twelve years before, contracted to deliver to Henry Holt in two

years, finally materialized. During his later years, however, he not only became an active lecturer and a prolific writer, producing, among other things, *The Will to Believe and Other Essays*, *Talks to Teachers*, *The Varieties of Religious Experience*, *Pragmatism*, and *A Pluralistic Universe*, but also experienced physical risks and exertions which might well have exhausted a man in his physical prime.

William James was a man of vivid personality and intense, quick sympathies, who responded spontaneously not only to every instance of want or deprivation which he encountered but to every form of life; once, having seen "four cuttle-fish" in an aquarium, he wrote his wife that he wished they had one of them for a child —"such flexible intensity of life in a form so inaccessible to our sympathy"! Inevitably he stimulated almost everybody with whom he came in contact. Logan Pearsall Smith called him the most charming man he ever knew, and even George Herbert Palmer thought his judgments of his students and others likely to be "corrupted by kindness." But a man of his health and tem-

William James in later life. New York Public Library Picture Collection

perament could not give so much of himself without feeling drained in consequence.

In his youth he was explosive, exaggerated, and self-assertive, even in his own family, and though he regarded his marriage, in 1873, to Alice Howe Gibbons as having "saved" him, it did not change his makeup. The William Jameses loved each other and their children deeply, but their marriage followed no placid path, and in some ways James seems to have been more en rapport with his mother-in-law than with either his wife or his own mother. Henry James had not been alone in finding his brother a complainer, and though Alice too had a temper, it is clear that she had need for considerable restraint and learned to exercise it. Even before angina struck him, James had ills enough—poor eyes, backaches, headaches, insomnia, and nervous indigestion—but the presence of the psychosomatic element is obvious, and his perpetual running off to Europe and elsewhere, as well as his addiction to "cures" whose inutility for him would seem already to have been abundantly demonstrated, bears further testimony to this.

All this is to be regretted for the suffering it caused him, yet it was a very important part of his equipment, for he developed his philosophy as a means of meeting his own and, by implication, all human need. Until 1870 James was a scientific determinist, unable to find moral meaning in life, a condition which drove him to the verge of despair and kept him on the brink of suicide. It is now known that "The Sick Soul" whose experiences he described under a disguise in *The Varieties of Religious Experience* was himself. Like his father before him, he experienced what Swedenborgians call a "vastation," a vision of supernatural evil and malevolence which not only reduced him to "a mass of quivering fear" but forced him either to achieve an affirmation of life by exercising a freedom of the will whose existence he could not logically demonstrate or else simply cave in and "*frankly* throw the moral business overboard."

He chose to believe, to act, and to live, and the thinker who helped him most to make this choice was Charles Renouvier, who, by defining free will as "the sustaining of a thought *because I choose to* when I might have other thoughts," inspired him to make believing in the freedom of the will the first act of his own free will. In later years, another Frenchman, Henri Bergson, profoundly reinforced Renouvier; among his younger contemporaries, James found most consanguinity in F. C. S. Schiller and John Dewey.

It was no accident that James should have moved from physiology through psychology to philosophy. He helped establish experimental psychology and the psychological laboratory, for he perceived that without such grounding psychology could never become a true science. But though he even experimented with mescal and other drugs before such experimentation became fashionable, he soon found that bodily functions disso-ciated from mental did not interest him deeply. Scornfully rejecting the popular notion that conclusions derived "from the twitching of frogs' legs—especially if the frogs are decapitated"—were scientific, while those attested by "the feelings of human beings—with heads on their shoulders—must be benighted and superstitious," he turned his back on automatism. He had good reason to know that the body conditions the mind, but he had also learned that a man's beliefs and his mental state affect the physical processes. It was completely in character, therefore, that he should have become one of the founders of the American Society for Psychical Research and that when, in 1884, the medical profession in Massachusetts, alarmed by the growth of Christian Science, sponsored a bill to outlaw all nonmedical healing, he should have incurred their lasting enmity by opposing and helping defeat this "fiercely partisan attitude of a powerful trade-union, demanding legislation against the competition of 'scabs.'" James was never completely convinced by the psychics, but he knew that phenomena did occur in the seance room—and out of it—and he insisted that to dismiss these without investigation was simply unscientific. He was not a Christian Scientist either, though he used Christian Science practitioners at times and believed himself to have derived some benefit from them, but he was not enough of a dogmatist to be willing to rule out beforehand any sincere attempt, by any means, to alleviate human misery.

James gave passion and will a place of comparable dignity beside reason, arguing that even those philosophers who considered themselves purely rationalistic were influenced by their temperaments. The mind makes its own inevitably personal selection out of "the fringe of consciousness," choosing, rejecting, and organizing. On this point he would surely have accepted the later statement of the novelist John Buchan (Lord Tweedsmuir):

Every man has a creed, but in his soul he knows that that creed has another side, possibly not less logical, which it does not suit him to produce. Our most honest convictions are not the children of pure reason, but of temperament, environment, necessity, and interest. Most of us take sides in life and forget the one we reject.

To refuse to make such a choice "until all the evidence is in" is, in effect, to choose negation or death, for all the evidence never can be in during our lifetimes or while we are in the flesh. It was upon this basis that James attended daily chapel services at Harvard and championed the "will" or the "right" to believe, for it is faith, not doubt, that creates, and, as Mary Austin once observed, the most important thing is not to believe a religion but to practice it. But, he would add, we must hold all our beliefs provisionally and stand ready to modify or abandon them should we receive more light.

In no sense does this mean that belief is an arbitrary thing. In the last analysis, a man believes as he loves, not so much what he wishes to believe as what he must believe and cannot live without believing. To argue that this is "wrong" because he does not "know" the "truth" would be another way of saying that it would be better for him to die or that philosophy is more important than life. It was James's glory that he never believed this. He made philosophy a part of life, with every phase of man's being involved in it, which respected the totality of human experience and served all human needs. Human will, mind, and emotion are a part of the cosmos; it is fitting therefore that they should have a share in molding the cosmos. Man's organizing intelligence belongs to nature and to experience; if he discovers truth, he also, in a measure, creates it.

All this sounds rather more like religion than like philosophy as it is ordinarily conceived, and though James calls himself "hopelessly nonevangelical" and commits himself to no doctrine, he yet frankly affirms that "religion is the great interest of my life." In the degree to which he emphasized the experiential element in philosophy and played down the exclusively intellectual element, he certainly helped to bring it closer to religion, for the New Testament also teaches that faith without works is dead and that devils believe and tremble. James himself funked nothing, but he found a kind of evangelistic fulfillment in the popularizations of his thought which he achieved in later years, and this could hardly have failed to be true of a man who tested even philosophy by its human utility. Though he claimed to have no capacity for mystical experience himself, he saw this as the ultimate basis of all religious belief and insisted that the undeniable existence of such experience "absolutely overthrows" the notion that all knowledge is received through the senses. For him the value of religious faith was found in the way it deepened and enlarged the significance of man's moral choices by tying them up with the universe itself. His God was more immanent than transcendent, but he refused to allow Him to be swallowed up by the world as the pantheist does, and he insisted that an impersonal God like Herbert Spencer's, who establishes no real contact with men, has no meaning for us and therefore is no God at all. At times, as when he says that "our lives are like islands in the sea, or like trees in the forest," he seems to come within hailing distance of Emerson's Oversoul. If he does not positively affirm immortality, he plainly desires it and insists that the dependence of the mind upon the body under all conceivable conditions has not been demonstrated. When his little son Herman died, he felt that the child must "be reserved for some still better chance" and that "we shall in some way come into his presence again," and, during her final illness, he wrote his sister Alice that "when that which is *you* passes out of the body, I am sure that there will be an explosion of liberated force and life till then eclipsed and kept down."

James was about as "good" a man as has ever lived, and he must have had about as little bad conduct as any man to be ashamed of. But he believed profoundly in the reality of evil and found much of life's meaning in man's ability and obligation to ally himself with God in combating it. Since war embraces all conceivable evils, his famous and influential paper on "The Moral Equivalent of War" was therefore completely characteristic of him. Here he develops the need of devising some means to release peacefully and constructively the heroic energies which war releases—and wastes—so destructively. President Kennedy's Peace Corps has been widely cited as an application of what he meant. Both William and Henry James opposed the Spanish-American War and the imperialism which followed it, and William had been almost equally agitated over Cleveland's sabre-rattling Venezuela message, which robbed him of sleep for a week and caused him to feel that the peace cause had been set back by a generation.

James's universe was neither wholly rational nor wholly irrational but a combination of the two. Like the Personalists, he relieved God of responsibility for evil by making Him finite, not infinite, yet trustworthy so far as the commitment of our lives and our cause to Him is concerned. This leaves room in the cosmos for chance, novelty, accident, without reasoned malevolence, and if a world which is still being created in necessarily imperfect, it has the advantage of challenging us to identify our wills with the will of God and ourselves assume a share in the Divine activity.

VIII. CHARLES W. ELIOT

That a man born with his whole right cheek nearly covered with an ugly "swollen, liver-colored welt," or nevus, so that all his life he had to be photographed in profile, should have become the leading American educator of his time, transforming a small New England college, with an outmoded, hidebound curriculum, into one of the great universities of the world, and that he should have crowned forty years of distinguished service there by an old age as "a man of influence, a leader in good works, a public figure, an eminent personage, and finally 'the first private citizen in the country,' " to whom two presidents offered the English ambassadorship, and whose advice and opinions the newspapers and magazines solicited and featured on every conceivable subject—this, surely, constitutes a testimonial to character and ability which it would be hard to surpass.

To be sure, Charles W. Eliot also had his advantages. He was born, on March 20, 1834, at 31 Beacon Street in Boston, the direct offspring of two distinguished families, the Eliots and the Lymans, and with connections with both the Ticknors and the Nortons. One grandfather, Samuel Eliot, had left a fortune of $1,200,000; the other, Theodore Lyman, had invested the money he made in the East India trade and the Pacific Northwest fur trade in the new textile companies. Both Charles Eliot's father and a Lyman uncle were elected mayor of Boston (the latter helped save Garrison from the mob), and the father also served in the state legislature and in Congress. The boy played (and battled boys from the North End) on the Boston Common, across the street from his house, went to school in the basement of the Park Street Church and at Boston Latin, where he enjoyed declamation but nothing else until he came to the Greek and Latin poets during his last two years, attended church with his family at King's Chapel, and spent his summers swimming, rowing, sailing, driving, and riding at Nahant. In 1853 he was graduated from Harvard, virtually at the head of his class. His father would have liked him to go into business, but in 1854 he wrote his mother a long letter, explaining logically and systematically why he had "chosen the profession of a student and teacher of science," and to this resolve he was faithful, even when financial considerations tempted him to abandon it, as in 1865, when he might have had a superintendency in the Merrimack mills at Lowell, at a much higher salary than he could ever have expected to earn as a teacher.

By this time money was an important matter, for in 1857 the family fortune had been lost, making Charles's parents and sisters dependent upon him and a legacy he had received from his Lyman grandfather. His path was not a smooth one, either personally or professionally. He began his teaching, which was in mathematics and chemistry, at Harvard, but when, in 1863, she denied him the Rumford Professorship, he left her, and when he returned to Boston, after two years in Europe, he became a professor of chemistry in the new and still experimental Massachusetts Institute of Technology. In 1858 he married Ellen Peabody, daughter of the minister of King's Chapel, who was to bear him four children, of whom only one survived him. Two died in babyhood, and another, his namesake, with terrible suddenness, at the age of thirty-seven, just after he had established himself as a landscape architect. Moreover, Ellen Eliot herself died, in the spring of 1869, just one day after her husband had told her that the Corporation had chosen him as the next president of Harvard College.

Charles W. Eliot. The Bettmann Archive

Charles W. Eliot, shortly before his ninety-first birthday. The Bettmann Archive

When Eliot became president, Harvard had only twenty-seven men on its faculty. The curriculum comprised Latin, Greek, and mathematics, with smatterings of history, science, and European literature. Declamation was heavily stressed. There was an elaborate set of disciplinary rules, whose infraction in any particular affected the student's academic standing (Eliot was to cut the rules book from forty pages to less than five). The range of elective courses was narrow. The few great scientists on hand, like Agassiz and Asa Gray, did most of their teaching in the Lawrence Scientific School, whose standards were considerably lower than those of the College, and had no voice in College policy. The modern languages, though taught on an elementary level, were not highly respected. Very little attention was paid to any English literature since Chaucer, and so great a scholar as Francis James Child spent most of his time on elementary composition. There were few advanced courses in any field; the classics themselves were taught as grammatical exercises, not living literature. Rote learning and memorization were stressed all along the way, and teachers were encouraged to be drillmasters and disciplinarians, whose function was not to stimulate the student's thinking but to give him the answers and then grade him on his ability to give them back to him.

The professional schools were worse off than the College. Since the A.B. was not required for admission, they were easy to get into, and examinations were informal and easy to pass. In the Law School, which *The American Law Review* once described as "a disgrace to Massachusetts," students "read law" for eighteen months much as Americans had long been reading it in lawyers' offices and then received their degrees much as a matter of course. Those who attended the Divinity School for the stipulated period and took the required courses were generally regarded as having been graduated. The Medical School, which had no endowment, lived on its fees; a student could fail his examinations in four subjects out of nine and still receive his degree.

Eliot's changes were introduced gradually and in the face of considerable opposition. Not until 1885 did he succeed in getting Greek dropped as an entrance requirement. It was not that nobody before him had ever been aware of the shortcomings of the old system. George Ticknor had tried to import ideas fom the German universities. F. H. Hedge had called Harvard "a more advanced school for boys" and its president "the chief of the college police." But Eliot was the leader of the revolution, and it was the revolution of a builder. Before his time the president had confined himself almost wholly to the College. Eliot presided over the meetings of all the faculties, making his weight felt everywhere, and nothing affecting the institution in any aspect was too petty to engage his attention. The calendar was revised. The physical plant was overhauled and the future planned for. Administrative changes were introduced. Men of the calibre of Henry Adams, John Fiske, William James, and Charles Eliot Norton were added to the faculty. Lectures replaced recitations. Laboratory work replaced the textbook in science courses. Undergraduates mingled in their classes with those enrolled in the new Graduate School. Best of all, students were offered a much wider range of choice in courses.

"The elective system" is what still comes first to mind in thinking of Eliot as an educator, but his conception of it is often misunderstood. If Harvard was to become a university of modern men, Eliot had no choice but to sponsor it; otherwise there could be no chance for modern studies to get more than a toe through the door. By 1878-79, accordingly, rhetoric, with the writing of themes and forensics, was the only prescribed exercise in the College after the freshman year. But the result was far indeed from planned chaos, for Eliot's elective system presupposed "a well-ordered series of consecutive courses in each large subject of instruction." Eliot was not interested in "classes" or in "Harvard men" as a type. "College life" meant nothing to him, and he was cold toward his successor A. Lawrence Lowell's tutorial system and the gathering of freshmen into a freshman dormitory. To him each boy was an individual, and no predesigned course could possibly meet his needs. The thing to do was to find out what kind of person he was and then help him develop what he had to its utmost limits.

In my opinion to direct a hundred boys upon the same course of study for four years in college is a careless, lazy, unintelligent, unconscientious method of dealing with them, and I will never again be responsible for the selection of a course of study intended for any such use in college. I am willing . . . to take any amount of trouble to advise and direct the individual boy; but I will not lay out any uniform course for boys by the hundred, or even by the score.

Electives enabled a serious student "to select his studies in accordance with his tastes and capacities," the assumption being that he would do better work and more of it in a field which enlisted his interest than in something which was only forced upon him. There is enough drudgery involved in even the work which interests us most, if we attempt to do it at all well, so that nobody need worry that the disciplinary values of education will be lost under such an arrangement. As Eliot saw it, there was enough pain in life as it is; it was not necessary to go out of the way to look for it because you thought it was good for somebody.

Eliot was hardly a scholar, even in his own field. His training in chemistry had been superficial, and when he went abroad after his break with Harvard in 1863, he showed more interest in public instruction and allied matters than in his own specialty. "The process of acquisition is delightful," he said. In the early days of his presidency, the classicists opposed him as a materialistically minded innovator, but there were also scientists who feared him as a mere technologist who threatened to turn Harvard into a trade school. If he fought a valiant battle to win for science the place it now enjoys in the college curriculum, it must not be forgotten that he also fought for history and the modern languages, for English literature and for art and music. In his belief in a scientific education, he was no such extremist as Thomas Henry Huxley. When he decided to become a teacher, he prayed that he might never "think that my profession is the world, or that my horizon bounds the universe." "This university," he declared in his inaugural address, "recognizes no real antagonism between literature and science, and consents to no such narrow alternatives as mathematics or classics, science or metaphysics. We would have them all, and at their best."

He had no great interest in research for its own sake, and during the early years at least, he had little or no money with which to subsidize it at Harvard (he always offended his more worldly subordinates by tending to think of scholars as a comparatively ascetic community). It was entirely fitting, therefore, that he should have given Johns Hopkins and its president, Daniel C. Gilman, the credit for having stimulated his interest in the development of the Graduate School, and whatever disadvantages the limitations of his zeal in this direction may have entailed, they did help him to keep values in reasonable relationship. He would have had no sympathy with the distinguished educator in the Boston area who announced some years ago that scientific research must continue, no matter where it led or what results it entailed. That, he would have said, was to emulate the physician who reported that the operation was a success but the patient died. For Eliot research, like everything else, was made for man, not man for research.

If he was not a scholar, Eliot was hardly a bookman either, though he was devoted to Scott and Dickens from his boyhood. Chaucer's Man of Law's Tale seemed to him quite worthless, and he was repelled by Romney's portraits of Lady Hamilton because he did not approve of the model! He once declared that for a college professor an evening at the theater was an evening wasted. He balked at including Rousseau in "The Harvard Classics," the "five-foot shelf" of books he prepared for Collier's in 1910 as a surrogate for a liberal education, though he finally agreed to include something from Émile, but he had to have all Milton's poems because he was "the great poet of civil and religious liberty" and all Burns's because he was "the great poet of democracy." But if critics sniff at the criterion implied, it is only fair to note that many of the great creators of literature would have accepted it, and in any case it testifies again to Eliot's determination to judge everything by its relationship to the comprehensive needs of life and thus preserve a sense of the whole.

For him these needs were basically moral and religious; whoever in the nineteenth century saw science as the enemy of religion, Eliot most certainly did not. For him the universe was "the temple built by God," and when he announced his choice of occupation to his mother, he said that " 'To do all to the glory of God' should be the ruling motive of a Christian's life." There was no cant in this. A Unitarian by inheritance and conviction, Eliot discarded both authority and supernaturalism from his religion, but he de-sectarianized the until-his-time Unitarian Harvard Divinity School. In 1887 he summed up what he believed to his son, who became a distinguished clergyman: "God is love, progress, and inspiration; man is capable of love, improvement, and eternal aspiration; Jesus was the best of ethical and religious teachers; Christians are people who pursue the Christian ideals as set forth in the Gospels." Many years later, in 1901, he wrote a renegade clergyman that "life would look intolerable to me if I lost faith in the God that Jesus describes in the first three Gospels, or in the Creator of a boundless universe of order and beauty." And, less than two years before the end, he made his testimony even more personal: "The teachings of Jesus Christ help me very much as I too wait for the leap in the dark."

Remarkable as Eliot was, one need not try to paint him larger than life. He had many of the prejudices of his class, and from time to time he expressed opinions which seem quite unacceptable today. Fifty years after his death, it does not seem necessary to cite them. He probably would not hold them today, and even in his own time they seem to have had little influence upon his conduct. Thus he had no sympathy with the Catholic Church, yet he rejoiced when the first Catholic was elected to the Harvard Corporation. His own inheritance was both "Brahmin" and "waspish," but his "John Gilley, Maine Farmer and Fisherman" is perhaps the most winning thing he ever wrote—"we cannot but believe that it is just for countless quiet lives like this that God made and upholds this earth"—and the Gilleys were of partly Jewish ancestry. Eliot could be brusque, and his honesty sometimes bordered on eccentricity. When he was compelled to bestow an honorary degree upon Henry Cabot Lodge, whom he did not admire, his salutation was chilly; when Prince Henry of Prussia came to Harvard, Eliot made the audience gasp by welcoming him not as the Kaiser's brother but as Queen Victoria's grandson! What all except his intimates called his coldness had been developed, at least in part, by his lifelong knowledge that a stranger's first impulse at the sight of his face was to shudder, and his frequent failure to greet people was due at least in part to vision so defective that he could not recognize a friend fifteen feet away. He did not speak to students when he passed them in the Yard, but when a boy came down with the smallpox, he moved out of the President's House so that the patient might be cared for there. Again and again he amazed both students and faculty members who had not supposed he knew or cared anything about them by showing, when the chips were down, that he possessed an intimate knowledge of all their habits and needs as well as a keen interest in them.

Eliot never had a headache in his life and never took more than ten minutes to get to sleep; generally, even after a stormy faculty meeting, sleep was instantaneous, and he could recruit his strength with ten-minute catnaps almost at will. His great gift was administration; he was a doer, a man of power and action, but he encouraged free discussion even against himself and went out of his way to assure his opponents that their attitude toward him could not possibly affect their promo-

tion. He listened as well as he spoke; he was never per-
turbed or resentful; and everybody knew that his word
could be relied upon absolutely. When he was on his
deathbed at Northeast Harbor, Maine, he told his son
that he was going to die on Saturday, and that this
would be best because the Sunday train to Boston
was more comfortable than the weekday train. He did
not quite make it, for he lived till Sunday (August 22,
1926), and this may well have been the closest he ever
came to breaking a promise. For the newspapers his
death was ill-timed, for Rudolph Valentino died next
day, and they gave him all the headlines.

IX. RICHARD, CARDINAL CUSHING

This chapter began with a sketch of "the Puritan
priest" of colonial Boston, Cotton Mather. In the middle of the twentieth century, the Cardinal Archbishop
Cushing was not only incomparably the most famous
Boston clergyman but by all means her best-known
private citizen. One could hardly ask a better testimonial to Boston's progress as an Irish Roman Catholic
city.

Richard James Cushing was born in South Boston,
August 23, 1895. His father, who was from County
Cork, worked a grueling, eleven-hour, seven-day week
as a blacksmith in the trolley car repair pits of the Boston Elevated Railway. His mother, from County Wa-
terford, had been a cook in the household of a Yankee
judge. There was no luxury in the Cushing household,
nor much learning, but there was plenty of piety, integrity, and affection.

After graduating from the Oliver Hazard Perry
School, Richard dropped out of South Boston High
School during his freshman year, but a perceptive priest
saw him enrolled in Boston College High, from which
he proceeded to Boston College itself and St. John's
Seminary. He was ordained in 1921.

Unsuccessful in his first appointments to parish
work, he appealed to Cardinal O'Connell for a foreign
missionary assignment, but was assigned instead to
"Proppy," the Office of the Propagation of the Faith,
where he soon manifested the incredible energy and
devotion that was to characterize him for the rest of his
days, expanding and developing the society, filling a
phenomenal number of preaching and speaking engagements, even buying shoes and candy for the children in
the South End. Six years later he became director of
the society.

In 1939 Pope Pius XII made him a domestic prelate
with the title Right Reverend Monsignor and, two
months later, over his protest (he protested almost all
his promotions) Auxiliary Bishop of Boston, in which
capacity he continued his work for "Proppy" and also
served as pastor of Sacred Heart parish in Newton
Centre. In 1944 he became Archbishop of the Boston
Diocese and in 1958 a Cardinal. In 1970 he retired "for
reasons of health and age," and on November 2 he
died.

Cardinal Cushing in 1960. New York Public Library Picture Collection

Archbishop Cushing with President Eisenhower in 1954. New York Public Library Picture Collection

Though Pius XII made Cushing a Papal Count in 1954, the red hat waited for John XXIII, who bestowed it within two months of his accession. It has generally been assumed that the rugged, earthy Boston prelate was not quite Pius's idea of a prince of the church. Cushing himself declared that he had a voice like a fish peddler, and anybody who ever heard him reciting the rosary over the radio will know what he meant. He did not believe he was qualified for the cardinalate "psychologically, intellectually, and by nature," and though he collected enough honorary degrees to paper a room, he did not believe he deserved these either. But John XXIII was clearly his man; it was his own opinion that John understood him better than he understood himself. "The Pope is a very kindly and humble man. I hope I'm not being irreverent but he is somewhat my type." It was no accident that his widest influence in the Church and his real emergence as a religious leader should have come during John's papacy. These considerations can easily be overstressed, however. Though he was probably well advised to give up the idea he had once entertained of becoming a Jesuit, Cushing's failure to become a scholar was due less to intellectual limitations than to the fact that he had more interest in other things. Though there was more than one crisis in his academic career, he won a reasonable share of honors and even tutored other boys in Latin and Greek while in college. He wrote decent English in a thoroughly responsible manner and was capable of clear and consecutive thinking.

His most spectacular success was as builder and administrator. As his best biographer, John Henry Cutler, put it, "No combination of twenty American bishops had ever raised as much money for domestic and foreign missions as had Cushing, and as a builder he has had no peer in ecclesiastical history." By 1967 he had achieved $300,000,000 worth of construction. He had established eighty-six new parishes and founded schools on every level; and his hospitals were serving three hundred thousand patients a year. The specialized enterprises he sponsored, like the Catholic Guilds for the Blind and Deaf (open to all) were too numerous even to be enumerated in anything short of a book-length study. He opened a seminary for older men who wished to become priests, pioneered in the use of radio and television, and built chapels in travel terminals and business districts. Besides the large amounts he raised from donors like the Kennedys and Governor Fuller, he brought in an unceasing flow of small contributions, every one of which was acknowledged within forty-eight hours by a personally signed note. Yet only half the money he raised was expended in his own diocese. He universalized the Church and her interests, widening the horizon of Boston Catholics to the width of the world. In twenty years he brought sixty religious orders into Boston. After the Bay of Pigs fiasco, he raised $1,000,000 in ransom money at the drop of a hat.

Cardinal Cushing carries a young polio victim from the plane, en route to Lourdes in 1961. New York Public Library Picture Collection

New York Public Library Picture Collection

His personality was as important an element in his success as his abilities. He was emphatically, in the Dickensian sense, a "character." The humor which bubbled out of him when he was in a good mood was often unabashedly "corny," and an admirer called him "the clown prince of compassion." He loved to be photographed and thought nothing of exchanging his biretta for a little girl's bonnet. He himself referred to his regalia as "haberdashery," "glad rags," and "Santa Claus costume," and rarely wore his pectoral cross: "I have crosses enough without carrying one adorned with jewels." "What do you think of this joint?" he would ask a visitor whom he was showing through the episcopal palace whose long marble hallways reminded him of bowling alleys. When he moved into it, he reduced Cardinal O'Connell's staff, disposed of his limousines, and sold the expensive furniture and art works for charity. He avoided having his ring kissed whenever possible, telling one girl not to kneel because she was too heavy to pull up and advising one group of fashionable ladies to save their knees for scrubbing.

Yet he was a formidable, unpredictable man. The nuns he took to Fenway Park to watch the Red Sox and the lonely old people for whom he gave a Thanksgiving dinner at Blinstrub's Village found him a gay, charming host, and he lavished limitless love and pity upon the retarded children whom he called "exceptional children," "forever children," and "little angels with broken wings," but it was better not to cross him when he was not in the mood. To be sure, this was partly because, toward the end, he was a very sick man. For years he lived on borrowed time, and he was still working an eighteen-hour day when he had no physical right to be alive. He suffered from asthma, emphysema, and bleeding ulcers, and slept in an oxygen tent. In 1953 he had two operations within about ten days, one to remove the prostate gland, the other a cancerous kidney. In 1956 he was told he had eight months to live; he lived for fourteen more years, and if he fainted during a public address, he continued it as soon as he had revived. But even if he had been a well man, he would still have been volatile, explosive, what opera singers and movie stars like to call "temperamental." He sometimes spoke without consideration and was much too honest and spontaneous to be tactful. Yet outgoing though he seemed, there was an impregnable wall of reserve in him which nobody ever breached, and though it was his lifelong aim always to take his priesthood seriously but never himself, he had no intimate friends and was well aware that "I go it pretty much alone."

Joseph Dever says that Cushing was a conservative into his mid-fifties and a liberal thereafter. Though it may not have been quite so simple as that, he certainly manifested an extraordinary capacity for growth and change at an age when it has become impossible for most men. To be sure, the record is not without its fluctuations. He disappointed many when, as late as 1966,

he took the hard line in a dispute which led to the expulsion of eight rebel students from St. John's Seminary. He defended Franco, admired J. Edgar Hoover, and had much to say about Communism, not all of which was wise. After he had endorsed the John Birch Society, withdrawn his endorsement, and then apologized for withdrawing it, Bostonians might well have been pardoned for wondering where he stood and whether he knew. To a lesser extent, he also blew hot and cold on the American Civil Liberties Union, despite his own belief in civil rights. He would rather have been a missionary in South America than anything else, and he believed that it was there that the real stand against Communism must be made. But he wanted to fight it with spiritual weapons alone, and he showed real insight in his understanding of the social and economic conditions that were working for the Communists there and real courage when he called upon his own Church to get rid of her landholdings in South America and detach herself completely from the iniquities of the social order there.

He spoke out against the Vietnam war and the agitation for universal military training. Though he disappointed some of his fellow members of the NAACP by opposing civil rights boycotts and failing to work up any enthusiasm for busing, he repudiated all notions of racial superiority, opposed segregation, and outlawed it in Catholic schools. As a member of the Boston Public Library board, he distinguished clearly between a public library and a parish library and exerted no influence toward censorship. He certainly had political influence, and it would not be correct to say that he never exercised it, but he was very cautious and restrained about it, even in behalf of John Kennedy, whom he called his dearest friend. He denounced the Supreme Court decision on prayer and Bible reading in school as a step toward paganizing America but took up a melioristic attitude on questions involving parochial schools. He proclaimed publicly that Catholics were bound by the authority of the Church only in faith and morals and advised them never to vote for anybody "because he or she is of a specific faith, nationality, or color." In 1948 he helped defeat a referendum on the question of permitting the dissemination of birth control information, but by 1968 he was among those disappointed by Pope Paul's encyclical, *Humanae Vitae*, which declined to liberalize the Church's stand on this issue.

Cardinal Cushing was an early advocate of the use of English in the Mass. He encouraged laymen to assume a larger role in the affairs of the Church, led in the movement to beatify Pope Pius X, took a moderate position in the controversy over priestly celibacy, and advocated the abolition of the *Index Expurgatorius* before Vatican II expunged it. He married Catholics to non-Catholics in the church edifice from the time he became Archbishop and opposed exacting a promise that the children of such unions must be reared as

Catholics as both an encouragement to hypocrisy and a violation of the rights of conscience. He was a great bridge-builder between Catholic and Protestant, between Christian and non-Christian. "How any one who believes in God could be anti-Semitic, or anti-Protestant, or anti-Catholic, I don't know." "If the world is to be saved, it is men of goodwill who will save it, all men of goodwill."

He acted effectively, though slowly at the outset, and not without prompting, when the "Christian Frontiers" fanatics were molesting Jews in South Boston and elsewhere in the forties, and in 1948 he became the first high-ranking Catholic prelate to address a Jewish body. In Rome he worked effectively for the Vatican Council declaration exonerating Jews of blame for the Crucifixion and for the declaration of religious freedom, which asserts that "if in his attempts to know the will of God, a man falls into erroneous interpretation of that will, no man and no power on earth has the right to induce him to act contrary to the dictate of his conscience."

In the early fifties the Boston Archdiocese was torn by a conflict with the director of St. Benedict Center, near Harvard Square, the Jesuit priest, Leonard Feeney, and his followers, who came to consider themselves the true Church on the salvation issue and the Archbishop, the Pope, and all the rest as heretics, and extended their hate campaign, which culminated in their excommunication, to disturbances and arrests as far west as Chicago. Under great provocation, Cushing showed the patience of a saint toward Feeney, but he held the line. "We are told there is no salvation outside the Church—nonsense! Nobody can tell me that Christ died on Calvary for any select group!" On March 31, 1963, he announced his availability for talks in Protestant churches.

Cardinal Cushing was thoroughly human, and he obviously had his limitations. He gave no indication of having ever heard of "tainted money." Racetrack operators and liquor dealers were among his heavy contributors; at one time he kept coin containers in Boston bars. When, early in the sixties, CBS exposed widespread gambling corruption in Boston, his devotion to the Boston police proved stronger than his indignation against evil and lawbreaking. "In my theology," he irrelevantly declared, "gambling itself is not a sin any more than to take a glass of beer or of hard liquor is a sin. It's the abuse that makes gambling or drinking in-

toxicating liquor a sin." He did not spell out the difference between use and abuse, and, all in all, this was probably the last thing the community needed to be told at the time. He seemed betrayed by his emotions again when Jacqueline Kennedy determined to marry Aristotle Onassis in defiance of the Catholic prohibition of marriage to a divorced person; for a little while, his impassionate defense of her against her critics seemed to be driving him into an anti-Church position and brought such an avalanche of hate mail upon him that he actually wondered whether he ought to resign.

But these things are spots on the sun. Cardinal Cushing's ultimate claim and appeal rest upon his almost superhuman services as a faithful shepherd. "A prince of the church," Harvard called him in giving him a degree, "ever mindful of the needs of the least of his flock." When he became a bishop he took as his ecclesiastical motto "Ut Cognoscant Te"—"That they may know Thee, as we also have known Thee, that there is no God beside Thee, O Lord" (Ecclesiasticus 36:5). He saw himself functioning in a time when intellectual skepticism and moral indifference were not so much attacking Christianity as ignoring it. Deploring "the breakdown of family piety and parental discipline," he deplored even more "the widespread worldliness of the clergy, which I would characterize as the great weakness of the Catholic church in modern times." As he saw it, a good priest must be "a living tool" or "slave" of Christ, working as though everything depended upon him and praying as though it all depended upon God. It is no exaggeration to say that Richard James Cushing worked himself to death serving "the least of the brethren," and never allowing large institutional plans to take the place of personal contacts. He collected and spent hundreds of millions and died without an estate. As Bishop he would appear without warning in the night to comfort sufferers in the Boston City Hospital. He reached out to German prisoners at Fort Devens during World War II and himself carried the sacrament and the hope of salvation to condemned murderers in their cells. A retarded child made an apron for him, and he wore it on television because he knew it would make her proud. Once he told a desperately sick person he had tried to comfort that "if the prayers of a fool like me can help you, you'll get better." But if Richard Cushing was a fool, he was that rare variety known as the Fool in Christ.

Chapter 6

A New Nation

I

ALTHOUGH THE REVOLUTIONARY WAR began in Massachusetts, the Battle of Bennington was the only conflict of importance fought on New England soil after Bunker Hill and the evacuation of Boston by the British. This does not mean, however, that New England escaped from the war lightly. The fighting there, largely in the form of coast raids, was without decisive effect upon the outcome of the struggle, but this did not make it less painful for the persons involved in it. As a matter of fact, New Hampshire was the only state never invaded.*

Perhaps what is now Maine was the area that suffered most. Falmouth was nearly destroyed in 1775, and after the British had taken the Castine Peninsula in 1779, that area furnished them a convenient base for attack. Maine also served as a highway for Benedict Arnold in his ill-starred march upon Quebec. Connecticut

---

*Vermont, of course, was not one of the original thirteen states. She declared her independence of Great Britain in 1777 and adopted a constitution, remaining an independent republic until she finally ratified the Constitution in January 1791 and was admitted to the Union on March 4 as the fourteenth state.

A German conception of the burning of British stamps in Boston, engraved by D. Berger, 1784, after D. Chodowiecki. Library of Congress

The gathering in Old South Meetinghouse which preceded the Boston Tea Party. Painting by Charles Hoffbauer, The New England Mutual Life Insurance Company, Boston. Copyright 1943. Murals by Charles Hoffbauer

was attacked at Greenwich, New Haven, Norwalk, New London, and elsewhere, sometimes with great brutality: Arnold (after his treason, which was, if possible, an even greater shock to his native state than it was to the rest of the colonies) commanded the raiders at New London. Though the Tories were strong in Fairfield County, this did not save Ridgefield from an attack in whose aftermath the British lost nearly two hundred men after having inflicted damage which might have been even more serious if they had been less drunk. Bristol, Rhode Island, bombarded in October 1775, paid a tribute of forty sheep, but in May 1778 both she and Warren were pillaged, and the British occupied Newport from December 1776 to October 1779.

Meanwhile American ships were harassing English commerce at sea and menacing and capturing supplies. It has been estimated that about two thousand privateers were out, first and last, nearly half of them from Massachusetts. Connecticut sent out between two and three hundred and took forty-one prizes. David Bushnell of Saybrook even invented a submarine, which met, however, with no great success. And of course New England men participated in many battles not fought on New England soil. Connecticut had 38,000 in service out of a population of 200,000; one-third of Gloucester's able-bodied men were reported killed or missing, and at the end of the war Marblehead counted 458 widows and 966 fatherless children.

We have already seen in other connections that early anti-British feeling was not confined to Boston or to Massachusetts. A mob in Falmouth, Maine, had destroyed tax stamps as early as 1765, and in 1774 the town meeting there declared against taxation without representation. In June 1775 the British ordered lumber from Machias, Maine, to build barracks in Boston. Disagreement appeared as to filling the order, and a meeting was held beside a brook to decide the matter. Benjamin Foster, who was opposed, jumped the brook, inviting all who agreed to follow him, and carried the day; the brook is still called Foster's Rubicon. Shortly after, Machias men captured the British schooner *Margaretta*, whose commander had cut down their Liberty Pole, and two sloops along with it.

Yet the Revolution, like most revolutions, was engineered by a minority. At the beginning at least, there were probably as many loyalists as "patriots" in the colonies and as many indifferentists as either. Nor did the deeds of the patriots always match their professions. Judged by twentieth-century standards, the Revolution was a very unsystematic war. Enlistments were for limited periods; bounties were offered; exemption was often available to those who procured a substitute. Connecticut had the war's most famous hero, Washington's spy, Nathan Hale, who was hanged by the British, September 22, 1776, regretting that he had but one life to give for his country, but about six thousand mili-

Contemporary English conception of the tarring and feathering of an excise man in Boston. Note that the Boston Tea Party is taking place in the background. Library of Congress

tiamen deserted after the disastrous defeat on Long Island. Quotas were assigned for food and clothing for the troops as well as for manpower, but though Connecticut did better than her neighbors, this did not always work. Soldiers from all areas often went unpaid and unclothed, and it was not only at Valley Forge that they experienced great suffering. When the war ended, Massachusetts had only about half her quota in service.

Perhaps the colonies were most like modern warring states in their intolerance toward dissenters. The propaganda machines got under way very quickly with the usual atrocity stories and the usual glorification of self and vilification of the enemy. When Tom Paine could advocate paying for the war by confiscating Tory property and John Adams could boast in retrospect that from 1780 on he had advocated that all "inimical to the cause" be fined, imprisoned, or hanged, and that he himself would have hanged his own brother for taking the English side, one can easily imagine how lesser men

The Bostonians in Distress. Mezzotint, 1774, attributed to Philip Dawe. This English mezzotint, one of a series published by Sayer and Bennett, satirizes the punishment in the form of a blockade meted out to Boston after the Boston Tea Party. Willing representatives from other parts of America are shown handing up fish, symbolic of numerous donations of food, fuel, etc., to the caged, starving Bostonians, who are suspended from the Liberty Tree. British soldiers guard the access route to the town and their cannons encircle the tree trunk. Courtesy of The New-York Historical Society, New York City

Charles Hoffbauer's picture of the reading of the Declaration of Independence from the balcony of the State House in Boston, July 18, 1776. This reproduction is used through the courtesy of The New England Mutual Life Insurance Company. Copyright 1943. Mural by Charles Hoffbauer

Paul Revere gives the alarm to the countryside, by Charles Hoffbauer. This reproduction is used through the courtesy of The New England Mutual Life Insurance Company. Copyright 1943. Murals by Charles Hoffbauer

Charles Hoffbauer's picture of Washington taking command of the Continental Army, under the Washington Elm in Cambridge, July 3, 1775. This reproduction is used through the courtesy of The New England Mutual Life Insurance Company. Copyright 1943. Mural by Charles Hoffbauer

This "Battle of Bunker's Hill" was engraved by John Godfrey after the painting by Alonzo Chappel (1826-1887). FPG

Marker commemorating the stand of the Minute Men on Lexington Common. FPG

Statue of Captain John Parker of the Minute Men, by Henry H. Kitson, on Lexington Common. U.S. Bureau of Public Roads, National Archives

Marker near North Bridge. FPG

Grave of the British soldiers killed in the Revolutionary War at Concord, near North Bridge. The verses are by Lowell. U.S. Bureau of Public Roads, National Archives

Bunkers Hill or America's Head Dress (cartoon). Engraved in 1776. Library of Congress

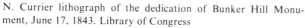

N. Currier lithograph of the dedication of Bunker Hill Monument, June 17, 1843. Library of Congress

Old shot tower used during the Revolution, at West Towerville, Mass. FPG

must have thought and felt. A Massachusetts law of 1778 banished all who refused the oath of allegiance to the new government, threatening them with death should they return, and in Connecticut at least one Tory, Moses Dunbar, lost his life. Moreover, the good old American custom of taxing the poor and allowing the rich to escape was already in operation; consequently many businessmen and speculators made a very good thing out of the war, to the consequent dangerous increase of class feeling.

II

The end of the Revolution found the former colonies in New England operating under a variety of governments old and new. Connecticut did not officially discard the Charter of 1662 until 1818, and Rhode Island kept hers until after the Dorr Rebellion. Samuel Eliot Morison has described the arrangement which Massachusetts adopted in 1780 as "a lawyers' and mer-

The Concord battleground from across the Concord River, from an old lithograph, c. 1836-1874. There was no bridge at this site from 1793 to 1874. This monument was dedicated in 1836. Library of Congress

chants' constitution directed toward something like quarterdeck efficiency in government, and the protection of property against democratic pirates.''

When the Constitutional Convention was called in the spring of 1787, Vermont was not yet eligible to participate and Rhode Island declined. Western and rural areas tended to fear centralized power and the domination of mercantile over agricultural interests. Some also objected to the omission from the original document of a Bill of Rights, yet when this was added, it too met with objections; it is not often remembered that Massachusetts and Connecticut, along with Georgia, did not ratify the Bill of Rights until 1939. The so-called Connecticut Compromise, which gave all states equal representation in the Senate as against proportional representation in the lower House, helped allay some local fears; even so, ratification was secured in Massachusetts only through careful manipulation by John Hancock and others and then only by nineteen votes in the Constitutional Convention. New Hampshire became the ninth and determinative state to ratify, on June 21, 1788, but Rhode Island did not act until May 29, 1790, and then not until the United States had begun to treat her as a foreign power and Newport had threatened to secede from the state. The vote was 34 to 32.

Statue of Colonel William Prescott, by William Wetmore Story, near the Bunker Hill Monument, dedicated 1881. Photo by Katharine Knowles in Walter Muir Whitehill, *Boston Statues,* 1970, courtesy Barre Publishers

The launching of the frigate *Constitution*, architect Joshua Humphreys, at Hart's shipyards on the Charles River, October 21, 1797, by Charles Hoffbauer. The *Constitution* is Oliver Wendell Holmes's "Old Ironsides." This reproduction is used through the courtesy of The New England Mutual Life Insurance Company. Copyright 1943. Mural by Charles Hoffbauer

Most New Englanders, however, must have been much more concerned with crushing postwar economic conditions than with any political considerations. Runaway inflation and the increasing worthlessness of paper money had already become a problem during the war, and peace did not cause it to go away. There were critical shortages of salt, clothing, and much besides; in some localities this had the good effect of stimulating manufacturing, at first largely in homes. New trade restrictions, now that America no longer adhered to the British family, created great difficulties, even though the laws were not always obeyed. There had been some trading with the enemy even during the war, and it continued through the years of peace and the War of 1812. "Many Vermonters in the contraband area near the border," writes Ralph Nading Hill, "did not feel that they were trading with the enemy but with friends and neighbors across the line. The only way most of them could raise any cash to settle their debts and pay taxes was through the sale of potash in Montreal." During the War of 1812 we hear of a raft on Lake Champlain which was half a mile long and which carried a bulletproof fort and between five and six hundred men. Perhaps outlying areas, still in the "Age of Homespun," where people raised their own food and made their own clothes, were better off than those already in the way of developing a more interdependent society. Though New Hampshire acquired her first cotton goods factory at New Ipswich in 1803, trade was still largely by barter, and it took a week to get news from New York. But things were not comfortable anywhere, and when the danger of rebellion in western Massachusetts was at its height, a puzzled Washington inquired why if the grievances were legitimate they had not been redressed, and if not, why the government did not act. After Shays's Rebellion had been crushed, there was considerable resentment over the harsh terms. When the next legislature convened, three-fourths of the members were new, with a number of ex-rebels among them, and ultimately an amnesty act was passed.

Henry Adams called Federalism "a halfway house between the European past and the American future," but the Federalist Party remained dominant in New England for many years after the Revolution. Jonathan Trumbull, Jr., Connecticut politician and statesman, was not alone in his fear of "French atheism." Yet the beginning of the French Revolution in 1789 was celebrated with festivals in Boston and elsewhere; it was not until the coming of the Terror and the Napoleonic dictatorship that American sympathies were altogether alienated. The Federalist backbone was mercantile-legal-capitalist-clerical, and in 1808 John Adams called Connecticut more aristocratic than Great Britain. The influence of merchants on the national government was much stronger than that of the manufacturers, and in 1798 Congress armed merchant ships to defend themselves against the French. In 1800 we very nearly achieved open war with our old ally, and President Adams alienated many Federalists when he dismissed his secretaries of state and war and sent a new envoy to Paris without even consulting his Cabinet. "I desire no other inscription over my gravestone," he later declared, "than: Here lies John Adams, who took upon himself the responsibility of the peace with France in the year 1800."

Like other seemingly well-entrenched groups, however, the Federalists found various ways to alienate their supporters. In Maine the absentee landlordism sponsored by the Massachusetts legislature was resented, and Rhode Island was displeased when the federal government assumed only part of its debt. When, running for reelection in 1804, Jefferson carried every New England state except Connecticut, it seemed a great victory, but New England was soon to be gravely alienated by the embargo which he placed on shipping, though the New Hampshire House and Senate supported it.

III

When "Mr. Madison's War" against England came at last on June 18, 1812, it turned out a foolish and illmanaged affair which brought little satisfaction to anybody. It had been brought on by Republicans, not Federalists, led by such "war hawks" in the Senate as Henry Clay and John C. Calhoun, and inspired less by concern for American shipping than resentment of impressment as an affront to national pride and fear of British influence over the Indians on the western frontier. When it ended, late in 1814, Washington had been burned, the British held part of Maine and were threatening invasion via Lake Champlain, and an expedition against New Orleans was preparing.

Because the struggle against Napoleon had thrown a very large proportion of the world's carrying trade into American ships and because about half of American shipping was New England-owned, New England had a very large stake in this war, but she also led the opposition to it. With France and Great Britain locked in a struggle for survival, there was a wide twilight zone in which the sailing and trading rights of neutrals were only vaguely and imperfectly defined and with reference to which honest differences of opinion might reasonably have been expected to appear. Certainly the British claim that some of the sailors on American ships were British deserters was not wholly inadmissible, but the British refusal to recognize naturalization rights was certainly not helpful.

The governor of New Hampshire drafted thirty-five thousand men for war at the request of President Madison, but even in that state, Daniel Webster, the leading New England statesman of the pre-Civil War period, whom New Hampshire shares with Massachusetts, drew up a public statement opposing the war. Massachusetts, Connecticut, and Rhode Island all denied the federal government the use of state troops (the entire Connecticut delegation had voted against the declaration of war). In Massachusetts the lower house called for "loud and deep" opposition to the war. The Connecticut Assembly also declared the conscription law of 1814 unconstitutional, and the Hartford Common Council prohibited recruiting in that city. Three of Vermont's representatives voted for war, but Martin Chittenden, son of the first governor, collected thousands of signatures from those opposed, and when the threat of invasion from Canada drew Vermonters into the army, he called them home, an order which many disobeyed. In Congress, Chittenden was called a traitor, but Massachusetts pledged him her support, and Canada's governor-general said that two-thirds of the British army in Canada was provisioned by American contractors, drawing upon Vermont and New York supplies. For all that, and whatever the intentions of the Hartford Convention may have been, many New England men did serve in the war. Connecticut contributed eighteen hundred men and eleven privateers. In Maine, despite opposition to the war, fishing and shipbuilding were so hard hit that for some enlistment looked like an economic necessity, and Oliver Hazard Perry, whose inland naval victory gave us control of Lake Erie, was a Rhode Island man.

These were not the only paradoxes which surfaced during the struggle. Though the British knew what was going on well enough to exempt New England ports from their naval blockade, the area did not wholly escape attack. Castine and Bangor were among the sites occupied in Maine. In Massachusetts, raiding parties landed, or attempted to land, at Boston, Annisquam, Wareham, and Scituate, and Provincetown almost became a British naval base. Rhode Island, fearing attack, threw up earthworks at Providence. Having refused to evacuate its inhabitants, Stonington, Connecticut, was bombarded for three days by five British ships. Only one American was wounded, but the British suffered many casualties and nearly lost one vessel.

IV

The disastrous effect of the War of 1812 on foreign trade encouraged native manufacture, with different towns showing a tendency to specialize in particular products. But peace terms were more favorable to the United States than many had expected, and immediately after the cessation of hostilities, there was an influx of foreign goods, often sold at discounts which made competition impossible. In Maine fishing and fur trading flourished (there were more than a half-million inhabitants by 1840), but currency was still in short supply, and various articles were employed as media of exchange. In 1839 the so-called Aroostook War was occasioned by a dispute between Maine and Canada over lumbering rights. General Winfield Scott arranged for a truce and joint occupation, and in 1842, by the Webster-Ashburton Treaty, Maine relinquished about fifty-five hundred square miles of her claim.

Struggles to liberalize state constitutions and widen and bolster human rights went on on many fronts, with varying success, but the trend was upward. The attempts to reform the state constitution in Rhode Island, involving the Dorr Rebellion, have been considered in connection with Providence in Chapter 2. A new constitution was framed in 1842. But victories were not always complete. Connecticut's tax system achieved much needed reform in 1829, but this reduced revenues, and it was education, social welfare, and public improvement that suffered. On the credit side enter the abolition of imprisonment for debt, liberalization of divorce laws, improvement in the position of Jews, and the abolition of the property qualification for voting.

It is interesting that three of the five presidents New England has so far contributed to the nation functioned before the Civil War—John Adams and his son John Quincy Adams, both from Massachusetts, and Hawthorne's friend, Franklin Pierce of Vermont, whom many New Englanders hated for his failure to support abolitionism and the Civil War.* John Quincy Adams helped negotiate the Peace of Ghent at the close of the War of 1812, as Monroe's secretary of state promulgated the Monroe Doctrine, and was important in the establishment of the Smithsonian Institution. He is the only American president who served in Congress after his presidency; during his long term of office there he bore the brunt of Southern fury by sponsoring one antislavery petition after another. Henry F. Howe calls him "probably the last of our presidents whose every decision was made on the merits of the issue."

Unfortunately New England also showed an unhappy hospitality to freak political movements during this period. The Anti-Masonic movement of the 1830s, sparked by the disappearance in 1826 of William Morgan, who had "exposed" the secrets of Freemasonry,

---

*Though devoted to "the grand idea of the irrevocable Union," Pierce opposed the war because he did not believe "aggression by arms" was "a suitable or possible remedy for existing evils." Throughout the war he stood publicly for an immediate armistice and a return to the *status quo ante bellum*. John F. Kennedy of Massachusetts and Calvin Coolidge, whom Massachusetts shares with Vermont, were the only post-Civil War New England presidents. Chester Alan Arthur, who was born in Vermont but became a New Yorker, moved up from the vice-presidency and was never elected president in his own right. Rutherford B. Hayes would have been a Vermonter if he had been born five years earlier, before his parents moved to Ohio.

was not confined to Vermont, but it was in Vermont that Masons were driven from public office and even from pulpits. An Anti-Masonic candidate for governor was elected four years in succession beginning in 1831, and in 1832 Vermont was the only state to choose the Anti-Masonic candidate for president. In the fifties the absurdities of the Know-Nothing Party led to widespread discrimination, and sometimes downright abuse, and against all nonnativists, especially Irish Catholics. In 1854 the Know-Nothings not only elected a governor in Massachusetts but also gained control of both the legislature and Boston's city council.

Quite as remarkable as New England's industrial development during this period, however, was her expansion, especially into the Middle West, which often resulted in the setting up of what were, to all intents and purposes, New England towns, with New England names, governed in the New England manner and by New England principles. Between 1790 and 1810 Vermont experienced the largest population increase of any state, but by 1860, says Ralph Nading Hill, it had lost "to the four points of the compass a larger proportion of its population than any other eastern state, some one hundred and forty-five thousand people—almost half as many as were then living in Vermont itself." There were a number of reasons for this, but the most important was the basic fact that the economic resources of the state, under existing conditions, were simply not adequate to support her expanding population. An amazing number of men and women prominent in various lines of work in other parts of the country hailed from Vermont and neighboring New Hampshire, including such industrialists as Joseph Glidden and Charles H. Deere; Alphonso Taft, founder of an important

John Quincy Adams, from a daguerreotype by Mathew Brady. Library of Congress

This card is from a set of cards used as a teaching aid, probably put up in front of the class. Dimensions: 16 5/8 inches by 13 3/4 inches. Used in New England during the first half of the nineteenth century. Smithsonian Institution Photo No. 56767. The Eleanor and Mabel Van Alstyne American Folk Art Collection

LESSON 26.

GENERAL WASHINGTON

Was once a little child like one of us,
But he would never tell a lie.
His father once gave him a hatchet,
And George went into the garden with it.
In the garden was a beautiful young tree,
And he cut the tree till he spoilt it.
When his father saw it, he was grieved,
And he called all his people before him,
And asked who had ruined his tree!
No one could tell any thing about it.
His son then came in, and his father said,
George, who killed my cherry tree!
And George was silent for a moment,
But he soon wiped the tear from his eye,
And looking at his father, he replied,
I can't tell a lie!....Pa, you know I can't!
It was I did cut it with my hatchet.
     His father held out his hands, and said,
Run to my arms, my dear boy!
You have told the truth, and it is better
Than a thousand, thousand trees,
If all their fruits were silver and gold.

This embroidery was most likely done by Harriet Salter of Massachusetts, early nineteenth century. Smithsonian Institution Photo No. 46973. The Eleanor and Mabel Van Alstyne American Folk Art Collection

Old Slater Mill, 1793, Pawtucket, R.I. Rhode Island Department of Economic Development

Boston town meeting, engraved in John Trumbull *M'Fingal*, 1795. Library of Congress

Friends Meeting House, Newport, 1857; engraving by T. Sinclair. Library of Congress

political family; Long John Wentworth, who became mayor of early Chicago; and even, at a later date, the vaudeville magnate, Benjamin Franklin Keith.

Connecticut was even more expansive, and this tendency was already operative in the seventeenth and eighteenth centuries. She expanded into the Berkshires and into Vermont itself, where land was cheap, taxes low, and life-styles freer than at home. After the Revolution, upper New York State became a magnet (Massachusetts also felt this pull), but Connecticut men were especially important in opening up Ohio and what was then known as the Northwest. When, in 1786, Connecticut yielded the western lands in which her claims had conflicted with Pennsylvania's, she reserved a strip which was called the Western Reserve, and this she governed until 1800. Western Reserve College, now Case Western Reserve University, founded in 1826, was modeled upon Yale and became a powerful center of New England civilization in the West. After the War of 1812 emigration from Connecticut to this area and elsewhere was so great as to raise fears that the state might be drained of the most capable builders of her future.

Scrimshaw, early nineteenth century. Smithsonian Institution Photo No. 62206. The Eleanor and Mabel Van Alstyne American Folk Art Collection

In 1829 the "Yale Band" went to Illinois to set up Congregational churches and found Illinois College, of which Edward Beecher became president; many of the Midwest's clergymen were therefore New England trained. John Brown went from Connecticut to Kansas and Collis P. Huntington, the railroad king, to California. Long Island, New Jersey, even such unlikely areas as Mississippi, South Carolina, and Nova Scotia received Connecticut men, and wherever they went they made themselves felt. According to Charles M. Andrews, Connecticut, during its first half century, "furnished more prominent leaders of government, business, and education" than any other state. In 1831 one-fourth of the members of the House of Representatives and one-third of the senators were Connecticut-born.

Generally speaking, the reform movements of the nineteenth century belong to our last chapter, but abolitionism, already considered in connection with William Lloyd Garrison, is relevant here because it led at last, after years of increasing bitterness and polarization, to the Civil War. It was not until after 1850 that it was "good form" even to discuss slavery in New England; in 1835 Mayor Lyman, Harrison Gray Otis, and others actually appeared at a public meeting in Faneuil Hall

Church of the First Parish (1816), Lancaster, Mass., by Charles Bulfinch. U.S. Office of War Information, National Archives

State House in Newport. Engraving from *The History and Topography of the United States*, 1830, by John H. Hinton. Library of Congress

Northampton, Mass., from illustrations by W. H. Bartlett in *American Scenery* by N. P. Willis, published in London, 1839. U.S. Bureau of Public Roads, National Archives

Daniel Webster, painting by John Neagle, U.S. Capitol. Library of Congress

Theodore Parker, halftone reproduction of illustration by Gaspard, 1907. Library of Congress

to "vindicate the fair name" of Boston, which had been soiled by antislavery agitation. The Mexican War of 1846-48 was unpopular in New England because it was regarded as a war for the extension of slavery, but the record shows no greater consistency than that relating to other human activities. The Connecticut Assembly, for example, opposed both the war and the annexation of Texas yet authorized raising three regiments of volunteers. Vermont's was the first state constitution to outlaw slavery, and her legislature opposed the annexation of Texas and continued to hammer away at slavery down through the years with sufficient persistence to arouse intense anti-Vermont feeling in the South. Stephen A. Douglas of Illinois was a native Vermonter, but in 1860 Lincoln carried Vermont against him four to one. In spite of these considerations, however, some Vermonters served in Mexico with distinction. Blacks were disfranchised in Rhode Island until 1842 and in Connecticut until after the Civil War, and a Hartford church had only peepholes in the Negro pews so that white Christians need not be offended by the sight of their black brothers. Yet Lemuel Hayes, a Negro of illegitimate birth, adopted by a white family, married a Connecticut girl who proposed to him because she knew he would never have the nerve to propose to her, and served as the learned pastor of Rutland West Parish in Vermont for thirty years.

One of the most interesting pre-Civil War New England skirmishes was fought on the issue of segregated education. In 1831 Prudence Crandall, a Quaker, opened a girls' school in Canterbury, Connecticut. When objection was entered to her admitting a Negro girl, she turned it into a school for blacks. The town meeting condemned her, and merchants refused her trade. In May 1833 the Assembly passed a law providing that no black person from outside the state could be admitted into a Connecticut school without the approval of the town involved. Miss Crandall, having disobeyed the law, was arrested and spent a night in jail. Three juries disagreed. Finally the Superior Court convicted her, but the Court of Errors set aside the decree. After her marriage and attacks on her school by vandals, she gave up in 1834. Thirty-two years later, the State of Connecticut acknowledged the wrong she had

Declaration of the Anti-Slavery Convention, December 4, 1833. Library of Congress

Contemporary wood engraving after A. R. Ward of Negro slaves escaping from the South, as pictured in *Harper's Weekly*. Library of Congress

The birthplace of Franklin Pierce, Hillsboro, New Hampshire. From a daguerreotype by Cutting. Library of Congress

suffered and voted her an annuity, sponsored by the chief promoter of the attack against her.*

Once the Civil War had come in 1861, many New Englanders viewed it as a holy crusade, a battle against both slavery and disunion. Though there was some harassment of New England commerce, there was no real fighting on New England soil. On October 19, 1864, however, St. Albans, Vermont, was raided by Captain Bennett Young, CSA, an escapee from a Yankee prison camp; this was the northernmost encounter of the war.

If Massachusetts is the state of which we hear most in the war, this is due largely to the zeal of her war governor, John A. Andrew, who, believing war certain, began readying the militia immediately after his election in 1860 and had three regiments ready to move two days after Lincoln's first call for volunteers. These were the first Union troops ready for battle; some of them were mobbed when they reached Baltimore, where four

*See Elizabeth Yates, *Prudence Crandall, Woman of Courage* (Aladdin Books, 1955).

Franklin Pierce: daguerreotype by Brady. Library of Congress

Banner for Pierce's campaign in 1852. Library of Congress

IN UNION IS STRENGTH

THE UNION MUST AND SHALL BE PRESERVED. Jackson

FOR PRESIDENT   FOR VICE PRESIDENT.

FRANKLIN PIERCE.   WILLIAM R. KING.

THE UNION NOW AND FOREVER.

& PUB. BY N. CURRIER.   Entered according to Act of Congress in the year 1852 by N. Currier, in the Clerks office of the Distr. Court of the Southr. District of N.Y. 152 NASSAU ST. COR. OF SPRUCE

GRAND, NATIONAL, DEMOCRATIC BANNER.
PRESS ONWARD.

NOW I lay me down to sleep,
    I pray the Lord my foul to keep.
If I fhould die before I wake,
I pray the Lord my foul to take.
            Good children muft
Fear God all day,   Love Chrift alway,
Parents obey,   In fecret pray,
No falfe thing fay,   Mind little play,
By no fin ftray,   Make no delay,
            In doing good.
Awake, arife, behold thou haft,
Thy life, a leaf, thy breath, a blaft;
At night lie down prepar'd to have
Thy fleep, thy death, thy bed, thy grave.

A page from the Paisley Edition of *The New England Primer*, 1781. New York Public Library Picture Collection

were killed and thirty-six wounded. All told, Massachusetts sent nearly one hundred and fifty thousand men, more than thirty thousand in excess of her quota, of whom nearly fourteen thousand were killed or died. New Hampshire contributed nearly forty thousand with more than forty-five hundred casualties (it was the Thirty-Ninth New Hampshire that led Union troops into Richmond), and Vermont nearly thirty-five thousand, with over five thousand casualties. Maine had a special problem. Southern businessmen had invested in Maine vessels and mills, and Maine men, in turn, had money in many Southern enterprises. The difficulty was not entirely a matter of vested interests. Marriage, friendship, and other interrelationships had developed, yet Maine put more than 10 percent of her men into uniform, and ex-Governor Hannibal Hamlin, who had gone to Congress as a Democrat but had broken with his party over slavery, was Lincoln's vice-president. Up to the Emancipation Proclamation, he thought Lincoln too conciliatory, and he was to be one of Johnson's enemies after the war.

Connecticut had her war problems. Though she contributed fifty-five thousand men to the struggle and counted twenty thousand casualties, she had raised only about one-third of her assigned quota by October 1863, and in 1864 Lincoln beat McClellan in the state by not much more than two thousand. Some towns raised funds to aid those who wished to escape the draft by hiring a substitute. The Hartford *Times* saw Lincoln es-

John Brown, from a life-sized oil portrait by Nathan B. Onthank, which he painted on an enlarged photograph of John Brown taken in Boston by J. W. Black in May 1859. Boston Athenaeum

John A. Andrew, Massachusetts Civil War governor. Library of Congress

This engraving of the burning *Caleb Cushing* illustrated a story about the cutter's seizure by Confederate raiders. It appeared in *Harper's Weekly* in 1863. Library of Congress

Massachusetts regiment encampment at Concord, Sept. 7, 8, and 9, 1859. Library of Congress

256

Hannibal Hamlin of Maine, Vice-President of the United States during the Civil War. Library of Congress

tablishing a dictatorship and opposed holding the South by force, and in 1863 the Democrats called for an immediate end of the war. But Connecticut's arms industry "boomed," and wartime profits do not often conduce to clearsightedness. "Patriots" wrecked the office of the pacifistic Bridgeport *Evening Farmer* and drove its editor out of the state.

The Currier and Ives interpretation of the attack on Massachusetts troops by a Baltimore mob, April 9, 1861. Library of Congress

Burnside's Rhode Island brigade and the 71st New York Regiment attacking Confederate batteries at Bull Run. Wood engraving in *Harper's Weekly*, August 10, 1861. Library of Congress

The Shoemakers' Strike in Lynn, Mass. Procession, in the midst of a snowstorm, of eight hundred women operatives joining in the strike with banners, inscriptions, and working tools, preceded by the Lynn City guards with music, and followed by four thousand workmen, firemen, &c., March 7, 1860. From *Leslie's Illustrated Newspaper.* Library of Congress

V

Since the Civil War, New England's story and her problems, especially in the southern states, have, like those of most of the rest of America, been involved with increasing industrialization and urbanization. Sometimes, to be sure, industrialization has solved problems; as Henry F. Howe has observed, only the advent of coal saved what was left of New England's forests by Civil War times from being totally destroyed.

Industrialization and other influences destroyed the old, almost, though never quite wholly, exclusively Anglo-Saxon character of New England's population. Some comment has already been made on this matter in connection with the cities and towns specifically considered, but this modification has been general as well as specific. A Moravian colony at Waldoboro, Maine,

dates back to 1739, and coast towns still shelter French Huguenot families, some of which preserve their native speech and customs, dating back to the same period. French Canadians also farmed in Vermont as early as the 1830s, became important in the textile mills of Massachusetts and New Hampshire, and established a "New Canada" around Woonsocket, Rhode Island. Rhode Island received many Italians between 1900 and 1915, and New Hampshire has Poles, Scandinavians, Italians, Germans, Russians, Czechs, Hungarians, and others. Sometimes particular ethnic groups have become important in connection with particular occupations, as the Welsh in Vermont slate mining. Connecticut has many Italians in New Haven, Poles in New Britain and Bridgeport, Lithuanians in Waterbury, and Jews in Hartford and New Haven. Colchester and Lebanon even have Jewish farmers. Hartford also has blacks and Puerto Ricans. By 1910 half Connecticut's population was living in urban areas and about 30 percent were foreign-born. Ten years later more than one-third of the farmers were foreign-born.

Governmentally New England still functions under a variety of arrangements which seem quaint at best to the rest of the country. Connecticut has been called "The State Ruled by Its Uninhabited Country Towns." In 1872 the ten smallest towns (combined population, 5,696) had eleven representatives in the lower house, as against the ten largest cities (191,207), which had eigh-

U.S. Heavy Cavalry Saber and Scabbard, Model 1840. Manufactured by N. P. Ames Manufacturing Co., Cabotville, Mass., 1850. Smithsonian Institution Photo No. 73-3483, Mrs. W. T. Gibb Collection

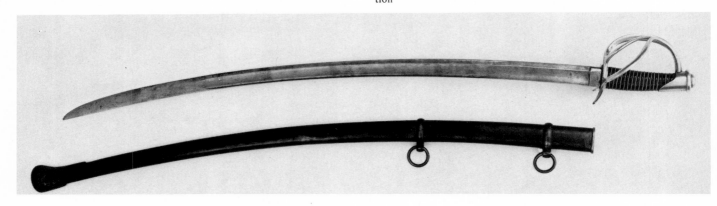

U.S. Pistol, Model 1816, Cal. .54. Made by S. North, Middleton, Conn. Smithsonian Institution Photo No. P63127, H. Hollerith Collection

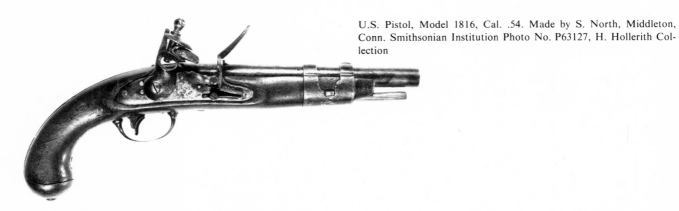

U.S. Spencer Repeating Rifle, Model 1865, Cal. .50. Manufactured by Spencer Repeating Rifle Co., Boston, Mass. Smithsonian Institution Photo No. 45189, War Department Collection

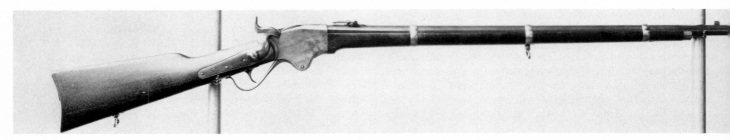

U.S. Hotchkiss Rifle, Model 1878, Cal. .45. Manufactured by Winchester Repeating Arms Co., New Haven, Conn. Smithsonian Institution Photo No. 24189, National Museum Collection

U.S. Winchester Rifle, Model 1873, Cal. .44. Manufactured by Winchester Repeating Arms Co., New Haven, Conn. Smithsonian Institution Photo No. 7302193, Col. Henry May Collection

Faneuil Hall, halftone reproduction of a 1936 drawing by Rafele. Library of Congress

teen, and though county government was abolished in Connecticut during Governor Ribicoff's administration, disproportionate representation was not corrected. Massachusetts, the last state to adopt a written constitution, still functions under the document drawn up in 1780, with later amendments. New Hampshire operates under a constitution only four years younger, with her people voting every seven years on the need to call a constitutional convention to propose amendments. Her lower chamber, the largest in the nation, contains 422 members; every town with 600 inhabitants sends a representative, with additional representatives in proportion to population. In Vermont "town" indicates the village and the surrounding countryside. Barre, Burlington, Montpelier, Newport, Rutland, St. Albans, Vergennes, and Winooski are cities. But Brattleboro is a town, though it is larger than most of the cities, and the country seat is known as the shire town even if it is a city. Republicans have been dominant in Vermont since the Civil War, and until 1904 Republican candidates were nominated in what amounted to a closed party caucus (in 1912 a direct primary law was

achieved). In Connecticut too some towns have boroughs within their borders and some cities.

The Panic of 1873 was felt in New England as elsewhere, especially in industrial areas, and the textile interests were hard hit. In Connecticut, New Haven, which was industrial, tended to be more conservative than Hartford, where financial interests were dominant. The gravitation toward it of the "new" Irish-Americans tended to strengthen the Democratic Party, but Bryanism was too Western and too populist to thrive in New England. The ultraconservative Senator Nelson W. Aldrich of Rhode Island, first elected in 1881, was one of the "Big Four" in the United States Senate from McKinley's administration through Taft's and a frequent thorn in the side of Theodore Roosevelt. Two Maine men were prominent leaders in the later years of the nineteenth century, James G. Blaine, born in Penn-

sylvania, married a Maine girl and moved to Augusta to edit the Kennebec *Journal.* Congressman and speaker of the House, senator, and secretary of state, he was one of the most controversial figures in the political life of his time, who was both adored and deeply mistrusted. Blaine tried several times for the presidential nomination, but when he made it in 1884, the "Mugwumps," who suspected him of involvement in a railroad scandal, defected to the Democratic candidate, Grover Cleveland, and a stupid clerical bigot in New York made Blaine's defeat doubly certain by referring to the Democratic Party as the refuge of "rum, Romanism, and rebellion." Longtime congressman and accomplished parliamentarian, Thomas Brackett Reed, having held a number of political offices in Maine, became speaker of the House in 1889, where he achieved an important revision of the rules governing procedure

As Currier and Ives saw cider making and maple sugaring in New England. Library of Congress

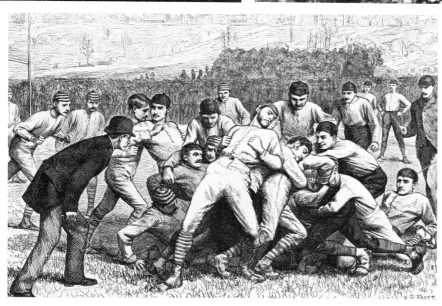

As A. B. Frost pictured the Yale-Princeton game of November 27, 1879, in *Harper's Weekly*, December 20, 1879. Library of Congress

Nelson W. Aldrich, for many years an influential Republican senator from Rhode Island. Library of Congress

U.S. Senator Thomas Brackett Reed, of Maine, outstanding parliamentarian and leading opponent of end-of-the-century imperialism. Library of Congress

and remained a powerful influence until he resigned in 1899 because of his disagreement with McKinley's expansionist policy.

The speech made in the Senate by Senator Redfield Proctor of Vermont, describing conditions in Cuba, has been credited with influencing American opinion in favor of intervention there. Aside from yellow fever and the "embalmed beef" with which the army supplied its recruits, the anguish caused by the "splendid little war" of 1898 was experienced mainly by those whose consciences were outraged (Connecticut, ·for example, called three regiments, but only volunteers and those already in the service saw any action), though the agonies experienced since by every conceivable kind of American from the later development of the policies to which we then committed ourselves are beyond calculation. Vermont's Admiral George Dewey became the great naval hero of the war. Antiwar protest, as noted elsewhere, was strong in Boston. Howells and the Jameses

Governor Roger Wolcott and Spanish-American War memorial by Daniel Chester French in State House, Boston. Library of Congress

Redfield Proctor. Library of Congress

Spring plowing in New England. Photo by George E. Tingley, 1899. Library of Congress

Admiral George Dewey, Vermont-born hero of the Spanish-American War. Library of Congress

Castle Hill Lighthouse, leading into Newport Harbor. Rhode Island Department of Economic Development. Courtesy *Rudder Magazine*

were quite as anti-imperialist as Mark Twain, whose bitterly ironical "Defence of General Funston" in *The North American Review* for his capture of Aguinaldo, in which he argues that Funston was not to blame for what he did, since his nature took to moral slag as inevitably as did Washington's to moral gold, and that his conscience, which leaked out through one of his pores when he was little, was so sickly and puny that he could never have raised it anyway, is one of the bitterest pieces of invective ever penned by an American writer, but the most splendid utterance of the war was that of William Vaughn Moody—Indiana-born, Harvard-trained, and Chicago-based—whose "Ode in Time of Hesitation," one of the narrow handful of great American poetic utterances on public affairs, first published in *The Atlantic Monthly* for May 1900, takes its point of departure from the Saint-Gaudens Civil War memorial to Robert Gould Shaw and his Negro regiment at Beacon and Park streets.

VI

Theodore Roosevelt was in Vermont when informed of the assassination of McKinley and his own accession to the Presidency. T.R. carried Vermont, of course, in 1904, but in 1912, when he made his "Bull Moose" try for another term in the White House, the state remained loyal to Taft, being the only one in the nation except Utah to do so. Massachusetts contributed two hundred thousand men to World War I; Maine, thirty-five thousand; New Hampshire, more than twenty thousand. Intolerance toward dissenters rode high all over America during this conflict; there was much less of this, under much greater peril and provocation, during World War II; and nobody surely needs to be reminded of the boldness of protest during the Korean and Vietnam wars by presidential fiat.

Perhaps Connecticut was the most eager beaver during World War I. She mobilized the National Guard even before the war declaration, and in February 1917 the Assembly passed a bill requiring an inventory of men and materials and sent a questionnaire to every male over sixteen. She was not, to be sure, without vested interest in the war; many Connecticut firms had government contracts, and Winchester made nearly 20 percent of all the rifles used by the army. Bridgeport and Hartford had indeed been enjoying a war boom since 1914; one Bridgeport factory had even been financed by German money, which turned out a bad investment, as the British blockade prevented delivery. Connecticut was efficient in the organization of "American loyalty" programs and other propaganda enterprises, and women went into war work, sometimes for low wages and under dangerous conditions. There were strikes and lockouts too, one of which involved

Mohegan Bluffs, rising 200 feet above the Atlantic for five miles along the coast of Block Island, Rhode Island summer resort, twelve miles off the mainland. In the background is Southeast Point Lighthouse, 1875. Rhode Island Development Council

Scene at Rockport, Mass. FPG

Blockhouse at Wiscasset, Maine. FPG

The elm on Cambridge Common under which Washington took command of the Continental army, already dead, was blown down, October 26, 1923. FPG

President Wilson's personal intervention and the threat of canceling military deferments. In 1916 Connecticut had gone for Hughes; in the 1918 election, the Republicans won again, supporting the war but attacking Wilson's conduct of it.

Connecticut was to pay for her wartime prosperity with much unemployment after the Armistice, and we have already seen that Hartford was one of Attorney-General A. Mitchell Palmer's prime targets in his notorious "Red raids" of 1919-20. The Boston Police Strike and the Sacco-Vanzetti case were the two events that directed the strongest spotlight upon Boston between the two world wars, but these matters too have been considered elsewhere. When President Harding died suddenly in the summer of 1923, Calvin Coolidge's father swore him in, by the light of a kerosene lamp, early in the morning of August 3, at the family home in Plymouth, Vermont; the scene caught the American imagination and bids fair to live as a permanent part of

Smithsonian Institution Photo No. 34546

Interior of the Great Weaving Room, Fall River, Mass. Photo by B. W. Kilburn, 1903. Library of Congress

Calvin Coolidge, Vermont-born, governor of Massachusetts, president of the United States, 1923-29. Engraving by U.S. Bureau of Printing and Engraving. Library of Congress

our legend. As the popular president of a dynamic, comfortable, yet sometimes reckless decade like the twenties, Coolidge was one of the most anomalous figures in history. I am not sure whether the ascription to Alice Roosevelt Longworth of the saying that he looked as if he had been weaned on a pickle is accurate or apocryphal, but nobody has ever claimed that he possessed what is now known as charisma. Perhaps he was trusted because he was so "safe" and because he presided over a government that did not much interfere with anybody. Certainly it did not interfere with business, and in a day when only the "radicals" saw American "prosperity" coming apart at the seams, it may not have occurred to many others that there was any need for the government to interfere in their behalf.

During the twenties and after, in New England as elsewhere, the automobile brought new mobility to Americans except when they were stalled in traffic jams or being killed or maimed in accidents on the expanding highways. The corner grocery languished, interurban trolleys went out of business, in many areas commuter service on the railroads was virtually destroyed, and after World War II the airplane was to come close to doing away with even the great transcontinental trains and the ocean liners, with all their luxuries. The film, stiffer competition than ever for the legitimate theater after it had found its voice in the late twenties, reached the height of its vogue in the thirties, with Hollywood a new sleazy kind of Paris and the land dotted with elaborate movie "palaces" which reproduced every

Drying codfish. Photo by Keystone View Co., 1924. Library of Congress

rococo extravagance, but by now the radio, to be followed by the even more dangerous television, was already beginning to undermine the foundations of the movie empire.

During Prohibition years the area between Boston and Baltimore was called the wettest belt in the nation. The death rate from alcoholism fell during the first three years of Prohibition, then began to climb again, though the liquor interests themselves admitted that the total consumption of liquor had dropped to one-half of the pre-Prohibition level, while milk, candy, ice cream, and soft drinks climbed, that there were fewer arrests, and that children were better dressed.

New England's old political conservatism died hard. Frank B. Brandegee, senator from Connecticut since 1909, one of Wilson's "little group of willful men," irreconcilably opposed to the League of Nations, committed suicide during the 1924 campaign, and his death was a kind of symbol. He had voted not only against the League but also against the income tax, child labor laws, the Federal Reserve system, popular election of senators, and votes for women. When in 1930, a political neophyte, Dean Wilbur L. Cross, was nominated for governor, the political boss, J. Henry Roraback, referred to him as "the dear old gentleman down at Yale who, I understand, is for old-age pensions, and if I were in his place, I'd be too." Before he killed himself in 1937, Roraback had learned to laugh out of the other side of his mouth. Though Cross was sixty-eight when he was elected, he served four two-year terms, sponsored (not always successfully) much progressive legislation, and brought a dignity to his office which has been fortunately sustained by such successors as Chester Bowles and Abraham Ribicoff.

Massachusetts was justly proud of Supreme Court Justice Oliver Wendell Holmes, son of the author of *The Autocrat of the Breakfast Table*. Louis D. Brandeis, a Jew, for whom Brandeis University was to be named, was a native of Kentucky but had long been identified with Boston when Wilson appointed him in 1916; at the time many considered this a daring appointment. In 1939 Franklin D. Roosevelt was to appoint another Jew, the Austrian-born Harvard professor, Felix Frankfurter to the High Court.

The year 1927 brought disastrous floods to Vermont, and in 1936 New Hampshire suffered the greatest flood damage in her history. The same year the Connecticut River climbed to nearly thirty-eight feet, and the tides off the Connecticut coast were ten to seventeen feet above normal. Tornadoes and tropical hurricanes seemed more prone to feel the attraction of New England, and in 1955 Connecticut was again to be plagued by floods. During these years, New England, like the rest of the country, had the Great Depression that began in 1929 to deal with and experienced, first, the resurgence of hope and the partial recovery achieved

Frank Bosworth Brandegee. Library of Congress

Oliver Wendell Holmes, Jr., the son of Dr. Oliver Wendell Holmes and an associate justice of the United States Supreme Court from 1902 to 1932, as much admired in his time for his progressive and forward-looking opinions as William O. Douglas at a later time. Drawing by S. J. Woolf. New York Public Library Picture Collection

during Roosevelt's first administration, followed by the agonies and bitter differences occasioned by the President's shift toward war. New England participated in many WPA and other projects during the Depression, but it was clear that the old spirit was not dead when in 1936 Vermont's voters rejected a Green Mountain Parkway, running the length of the state, to be built by federal funds. When the President ran for reelection that year, Vermont, alone except for Maine, rejected him, thus inspiring the wags to revise the old slogan "As Maine goes, so goes the nation" so as to read "As Maine goes, so goes Vermont," and after World War II, the state, which does not take kindly to bond issues, paid a soldier's bonus out of current funds! In the war itself, Connecticut, an important part of Roosevelt's "arsenal of democracy," had 210,000 in service, as against 550,000 from Massachusetts. Connecticut organized herself much as in World War I, but this time it was Vermont who seemed most eager to jump the gun, for her legislature declared a state of belligerency with Germany three months before Pearl Harbor! It is interesting to recall that she had also anticipated the Declaration of Independence; perhaps she has never quite got over the idea that she is an independent state. Maine, too, called her National Guard into service by June 1941.

VII

Since World War II, New England has generally been regarded as one of the most liberal sections of America. It is hard now to believe the nevertheless undeniable fact that when the Massachusetts volume in the WPA American Guide Series was published in 1937, it was hysterically denounced as Communist-inspired because it gave more space to Sacco and Vanzetti than to the Boston Tea Party or the Boston Massacre! A former governor wanted the book burned on the Common, the now liberal *Globe* thought that "outside" radicals had plotted to discredit the state, and Houghton Mifflin Company were actually asked

to delete all references to the Sacco-Vanzetti case, plus references to every progressive action in the state's history. There was to be no mention of strikes, including the Boston Police and Lawrence strikes, or of child labor laws, welfare legislation, and unions. Labor Day was even to be dropped from the list of official holidays!

Not being idiots, the publishers naturally did none of these things.*

This does not sound much like the Massachusetts of the Kennedys and the only black United States senator,

*See Ray Bearse's account of this matter in his *Massachusetts: A Guide to the Pilgrim State* in The New American Guide Series (pp. vii-viii) and the reference there cited.

Margaret Chase Smith. Library of Congress

Edward M. Brooke (elected 1966) or of Robert F. Drinan, a Jesuit priest and the first Congressman to call publicly for the impeachment of Richard Nixon; the only state which McGovern carried in 1972 and whose legislature actually went on record as opposing the service of her citizens in a war which had not been declared by Congress.

But Massachusetts was not the only state in which new things were being done. After World War II, Vermont elected her first Democratic congressman in more than a century and her first Democratic governor since the Civil War (like Maine, she was to prefer Johnson to Goldwater in 1964). The Republican Margaret Chase Smith, who succeeded her deceased husband in the House of Representatives in 1940, represented Maine in the Senate for years following 1949, but it can hardly be claimed that her voting record was consistently liberal or consistently anything except independent. She supported Selective Service at a time when most Republicans were against it; later Khrushchev was to call her a "devil in the disguise of a woman"! In 1958 a New Hampshire Democrat won a seat in the House of Representatives for the first time in American history. Henry Cabot Lodge, grandson of the senator who, above all others, had engineered President Wilson's defeat on the League of Nations issue, entered the Senate from Massachusetts in 1937, helped bring about the nomination of General Eisenhower in 1952, and was defeated for reelection by John F. Kennedy that same year, partly by the defection of those Republicans who

Ella Grasso, elected governor of Connecticut, in 1974, as the first woman in American history to become governor of a state without inheriting the post from her husband. Wide World Photos

John F. Kennedy. Library of Congress

resented his treatment of the leading rival Republican in the convention, Robert Taft, and ten years later, his son, George Cabot Lodge, was defeated in a Senate race by President Kennedy's youngest brother, Edward M. Kennedy. If "Ted" was regarded with some justice at the time as a Johnny-come-lately riding on his brother's coattails, he soon proved himself a highly capable and extremely hard-working senator, and it is now generally conceded that he can have his party's nomination for the presidency and, very likely, the election along with it, any time he chooses to give the word. After John F. Kennedy had removed the old libel on the loyalty of Catholic Americans, one hopes forever, Maine also sent Edmund S. Muskie, a Roman Catholic of Polish descent, to the Senate and into the forefront of the Democratic party's councils. In the 1972 elections, Maine chose an independent governor, James Longley, and Connecticut elected a Democratic woman, Ella Grasso, after her opponent had, with incredible stupidity, inflamed sexist feeling by proclaiming that Connecticut needed a governor, not a governess, and not Ella but a fella! In Massachusetts the same election brought Michael Dukakis, a progressive young American of Greek ancestry, into the State House. It would have been hard to imagine anybody more different from many of his predecessors.

None of this means that Paradise has been found in New England. Earle Newton can certainly not be accused of a failure to love and appreciate his homeland, yet he writes soberly:

Mental deficiency has increased to the point where statisticians have gloomily calculated the date at which half the population of Vermont would need to be institutionalized and supported by the other half. Emigration has consistently drawn the best stock from isolated, exhausted, back country regions, leaving a series of "tobacco roads," where a pauperized, debilitated and often feeble-minded people multiply faster than the general population.

Massachusetts faces the same problems of suburbanization, loss of community center and community spirit, soaring tax rates, high debts, and welfare costs that plague the nation elsewhere. Nor does she always make the right decisions, legislatively or otherwise. Since World War II her industrial losses in other areas have been rendered tolerable only by her unforeseeable gains in electronics and allied activities. Interestingly enough, her rich educational resources and her rich recreational facilities, once regarded only as occasions of outlay, have proved of startling economic worth. But that part of her story is told in the next chapter.

Chapter 7

Foundations

I

PRESIDENT COOLIDGE is reported to have expressed the opinion that the business of America is business. If business is the only business America has, she is miserable indeed, but any people must find a way to support themselves and satisfy their basic physical needs before they can devote themselves to other things. There may be a world somewhere in which we can exist as pure spirit, but this is not the world we know. Here, as Rufus M. Jones, the Quaker mystic, used to be fond of saying, we are amphibians and must live on two planes simultaneously. In this penultimate chapter of our book, the emphasis will be mainly upon the physical or practical plane, and in what follows upon the other.

When the English colonists came to New England, their first problem was to feed themselves, to provide themselves with clothes and shelter, and to keep, as we say, body and soul together. Food must come from farming and fishing, and trees must be felled for cooking and building. But these things required equipment, and manufacturing and trading began in the attempt to provide them. Sawmills and gristmills were established, and town centers grew up around them. Blacksmiths and tanners opened shops. As life and its needs became more complex, manufacturing became more complicated and trade ranged farther and farther from home.

Though 83 percent of New Hampshire was still in agriculture in 1830, Maine had a tide mill at York as early as 1631 and a good many mills before the Revolution. In 1830 she was leading all other states in forest products; by 1840 she also led in shipbuilding. In 1849 Bangor shipped over five million feet of lumber to California. By 1850 the best of Maine's tall pines were gone, and she was already feeling competition from the Lake states. Yet in 1900 she had thirty-five paper mills, and half the American ships afloat were Maine-built.

When farming got beyond raising food for the family, New England had to find her way by a process of trial and error. Some of the first yields were fantastic, but without proper treatment the soil could not hold up, and what we now think of as farming according to scientific principles necessarily waited upon the establishment of adequate chemical analysis. Massachusetts established an agricultural society in 1792, New Hampshire in 1803, Connecticut in 1817. But Connecticut did not acquire an Agricultural Experiment Station until 1877, and it was not until 1881 that Charles and Augustus Storrs laid the foundation for the agricultural school which ultimately became the University of Connecticut. In 1886 a State Board of Agriculture was set up. Maine, however, had put on an all-state cattle show in 1820, and in the Gardiner Lyceum she ac-

271

Old Stone Mill, Touro Park, Newport. Though legend attributes this erection to the Norsemen, less romantic persons believe that it may have been built by Benedict Arnold, great-grandfather of the traitor and governor of the colony in the late seventeenth century. Rhode Island Department of Economic Development

Lippett Mill, West Warwick, R.I., erected in 1809. New York Public Library Picture Collection

Oriental Powder Mills, South Windham, Maine. New York Public Library Picture Collection

quired, in 1823, the first agricultural school in America. Between 1820 and 1860 much new farm machinery came into being, including the threshing machine built by Hiram and John Pitts in the thirties. Maine's cattle decreased between 1890 and 1900 in the face of western competition, but she has been more fortunate in other lines. In 1890 she shipped out about three million tons of ice, some of it across the seas, and today she is famous for lobsters and seafood of all kinds, especially for sardines (actually small herring), with some coast towns almost economically dependent upon the canning factories, and, when winter approaches, for Christmas trees (the Maine Turnpike State Authority has actually used signs: XMAS TREE TRUCKS USE OUTER LANE). Han-

Old Mill at Durham, New Hampshire. New York Public Library Picture Collection

Gristmill still operated by waterpower near the restored Wayside Inn, Sudbury, Mass. FPG

cock and Washington counties supply a very large proportion of the nation's blueberries, and Aroostook County was making 90 percent of America's starch out of potatoes by Civil War times. Maine has now been passed as a supplier of potatoes by both Idaho and Alaska, but she still remains important.

Aroostook is not the only area that has found it convenient to specialize; among all the specializations Connecticut's tobacco, her Number One product, has been

the least constructive. In colonial times, Rhode Island had large farms, like southern plantations. Rhode Island bred the horse known as the Narragansett Pacer, and Morgan horses, bred in Vermont and New Hampshire, beginning in 1788, became famous as draft horses in the West and cavalry horses in the Civil War. Vermont leads the nation in the production of maple sugar, though this product, famous as it is, provides only 3 percent of her total agricultural income, and one-fourth

Vermont farm. Culver Pictures, Inc.

of all the nation's cranberries come from Carver, Massachusetts.

The coming of the railroads spelled both bane and blessing to New England farmers; on the one hand, it opened up new markets; on the other, it brought in the Middle West as a competitor and helped destroy local village industry. For a time Merino sheep spelled salvation. They were first imported from Spain in 1802, and by 1840 there were two and a quarter million of them in Vermont and New Hampshire, where they brought great prosperity to some farmers. Woolen factories and fulling mills followed as a matter of course, and the sheep remained important, though on a declining curve, until after the Civil War. Emphasis shifted first to cattle; around 1850 New Hampshire herds were being driven to market in Brighton, Massachusetts; during the next ten years the emphasis was upon cereals; the Middle West cut in progressively in both areas. All in all, dairy products have stood up best. Thanks to her nearness to New York and New England cities, Vermont was second only to Iowa as a dairy state by 1894, though economic problems continued until production and marketing codes were established under the New Deal. Vermont cheese is still famous. Milk is still the leading agricultural product of Massachusetts, though poultry, flowers, and vegetables are also important. Rhode Island specializes in dairy products and in those fruits and vegetables which are best sold close to home.*

The "sacred codfish" hanging in the Boston State House has honestly earned his place there, for dried codfish was the colony's first export. New Bedford, which from 1850 until after the Civil War was the whaling capital of the world, now accounts for about half the sea scallops landed. The acres of salted cod formerly seen at Gloucester are no longer there. Today both cod and haddock (never prized until finnan haddie came into vogue in the 1870s) are fished closer to the Grand Banks, and the town deals largely in frozen fish, most of it imported from Canada, Iceland, and Norway; indeed an officer of the Gorton Company once went so far as to declare that the firm might just as well be located in South Dakota.

*During recent years the real threat to New England agriculture has been an insane system of taxation, which has been taxing farmlands as if they were house lots. Vermont and lately Massachusetts have been attempting to grapple with this problem.

Photograph of quintessential New Englander, from *Down on the Farm*, by O. E. Davis, 1898. Library of Congress

Maple sugaring. Photograph by Clyde H. Smith

Pemigewasset House, Plymouth, New Hampshire. Library of Congress

The Lobster Fisherman, by James Chapin. New York Public Library Picture Collection

II

Exports require ships. Between Calais in northern Maine and Stamford on Long Island Sound, New England has about six thousand miles of coastline, and even such places as Hingham, Cohasset, and Quincy became important shipbuilding centers. Until the 1840s nearly all the wood used in shipbuilding was grown in Maine. New Englanders imported coffee from Brazil; wool,

Repairing lobster pots on the New England coast, 1896. The Bettmann Archive

Fishing. Wide World Photo

Fishing. Wide World Photo

sheepskins, and tallow from Argentina; copper and nitrates from Chile. Donald McKay began his work as a shipbuilder at New York in the forties and then came to Boston. The great period of the clipper ships was between 1850 and 1855; after the mid-fifties they ceased to pay. New York built more ships than Massachusetts, but the Massachusetts ships made more records.

In the early days, transportation was largely by water, and ferries, bridges, and canals received early attention. Remains of the Middlesex Canal can still be seen at Medford, Wilmington, and elsewhere, and Lowell is making a park out of its canal system. We are told that at one time Narragansett Bay was "literally criss-crossed with packet and ferry lines." The steamboats on Lake Champlain were large and elegant, some

of them three decks high, and they thrived for almost 150 years; Dickens called the *Burlington* the most luxurious steamer in the world. In the early days of railroading indeed, the roads themselves were often regarded as mere feeders for the steamboats. Competition for steamboat traffic between Boston and Portland was keen enough to induce fierce competition, involving even such a mogul as Commodore Vanderbilt, and at one time the fare from Gardiner to Boston was forced down to twenty-five cents.

The first three important railroads in New England were the Boston and Lowell, the Boston and Providence, and the Boston and Worcester; all date from 1835. Contemporaries were greatly impressed by the comfort and terrific speed they afforded (two and one-

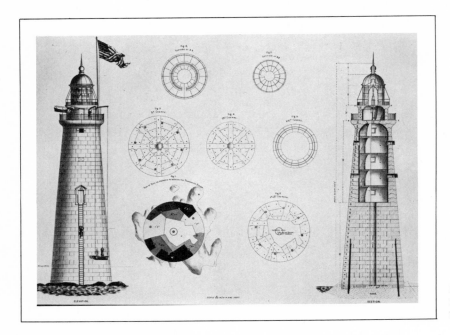

Diagrams for Minot's Ledge Light House, lithograph by E. Burrill, 1860. Library of Congress

half to three hours between Boston and Worcester), but worried about their possibly deleterious effect upon morals. Maine's first was the Bangor and Old Town, 1836. Bangor also had the second trolley line in America, running three and one-half miles in 1889; the first had been built in Richmond the year before.

Massachusetts was comparatively slow in developing rail connections with the West; her first railroads served largely to link her inland towns to Boston. (In 1974 you cannot go from Boston to Chicago by train without first going to New York!) Connecticut's good harbors and rivers delayed her interest in railroading; as a matter of fact, steamboat service on Long Island Sound continued in some form until the Depression. In Vermont chartering began in 1835, but no rails were laid for a decade. In New England as elsewhere, railroad history has been marked by scandal and, during later years, by bankruptcy and declining service; today all eastern railroads function, when they function at all, upon what might be called a system of relief. The New York and New Haven joined with the Hartford and New Haven in the 1870s, and in 1903 the Morgan interests took over. Bankruptcy followed in 1935, and the partial recovery achieved during World War II was only temporary.

The automobile and the airplane have been largely responsible for the decline of the railroads. As for highways, less than 10 percent of Maine's state highways had been macadamized by 1900. Vermont, with over

nine thousand miles of lightly traveled roads, first gave state assistance to road building in 1892, but not much was done before the automotive age. What was done for roads in the early days, beginning in the late eighteenth century, was generally in the form of toll roads, built by private "turnpike" companies; in Connecticut one company collected tolls until 1895. During recent years the turnpike idea has been adopted by the states, and extensive roads have been financed by tolls. With reference to air travel, it must suffice here to record that, though Boston is not generally reputed "the first by whom the new is tried," there was a Boston Aeronautical Club in 1895, that the Harvard Flying Club held a meet in 1911, and that Harvard and M.I.T. were among the first institutions to offer courses in aeronautical engineering.

Many Bostonians still remember nostalgically the no longer available boat trips between Boston and Portland and between Boston and Fall River, and when one reads Louise Dickinson Rich's account of going to summer camp in Maine as a child, it is hard not to wonder whether we have not paid too high a price for "progress."

The trains were locals that proceeded in a leisurely manner from milk stop to whistle stop, where the entire crew—conductor, engineer, fireman and brakeman—got off to carry on long conversations of a personal nature with idlers on the platforms. People would enter the coach, greet acquaintances —and everybody knew everybody except us outlanders—

exchange family news and neighborhood gossip, and then leave the train two or three stations further along. By that time even we knew that the woman with the straw suitcase was going to stay a spell with her sister, who was poorly, and that the man in the plaid shirt and high boots was bound up-country to look over a stand of timber he cal'lated to log off come winter. All the while the lovely Maine scenery unrolled so that we had time to note barns that had been painted since last year, individual apple trees in late bloom, and even the color and breed of cats lying supine on sunny farm doorsteps. When we came to our station, the conductor wished us a happy summer as he handed down our baggage. It was all very folksy and heart-warming.

She adds:

It is [now] possible to fly from Boston to Rockland, Bangor or Bar Harbor in a very short time. It is also possible to spend much of the day flying around and around, only to find yourself back in Boston. The Maine coast is subject to sudden dense fogs that make landing a plane highly inadvisable or downright impossible. I have spent too many hours waiting in fogbound airports for guests who finally arrived the next day by bus to be impressed any longer by "[If you had taken the plane], you'd be there now." . . . Maine is a place where it is wise to keep your feet on the ground.*

It will not do to overidealize the past, however. No modern mode of transportation involves more frightful hazards than those connected with steamboating in the nineteenth century, and if we accept the figures of the National Safety Council on the fatalities suffered in connection with horses and horse-drawn vehicles in 1909, it will be difficult to avoid Henry Howe's conclusion that "horse and buggy travel was more than four times as dangerous as modern travel by auto."

III

About 1790 importation of foreign goods declined heavily in New England on account of home production, then being carried on largely in households. The first cotton thread manufactured in either Europe or America was made at Providence in 1793 by the Englishman Samuel Slater, who had teamed up with Moses

State o' Maine (Harper & Row, 1964).

Woman spinning. Smithsonian Institution

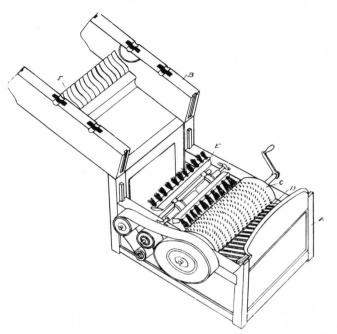

Eli Whitney's original model for the cotton gin. Smithsonian Institution Photo No. 32837-A

Brown. As the emphasis shifted from overseas trade to manufacturing, New Englanders became less foreign-minded and more American-minded, drawing upon the South for raw materials and looking to the West for markets. For many years after the Civil War a very high percentage of the nation's woolens and cottons came from New England; by 1890 Lawrence, Massachusetts, was the third town in the country for cotton manufactures and Lowell the fourth. By 1900 half the shoes Americans were wearing had been made in Massachusetts. Lynn, Brockton, Haverhill, and Worcester were important shoe centers, and other specialties large and small developed elsewhere. Taunton had an ironworks; Dennis on Cape Cod produced salt by evaporating seawater; Sandwich manufactured a now famous glass; even little Rockport produced Anadama Bread, which, legend says, was named from a fisherman's cursing his lazy wife when he had to do his own baking. Crane and Company in Dalton make, along with much else, the paper on which United States currency is printed, and Dennison's, in Framingham, invented gummed labels and Christmas tags and seals.

Up to 1840 Connecticut's economy was still largely agricultural, but by 1850 textiles were being fairly extensively manufactured, and from then on the output increased phenomenally, and the "Yankee Pedlar," with his "notions," became a characteristic American type and ultimately almost a figure of folklore. The ingenuity of the "Connecticut Yankee," as Mark Twain well knew, also became proverbial. From 1790 into the 1930s Connecticut led all states in the number of pat-

ents granted in proportion to population. The brass industry goes back to 1790 in Waterbury, and Eli Whitney's demonstration of the practicability of interchangeable parts stimulated the production of sewing machines, farm machinery, and other useful appliances as well as arms. When Eli Terry applied similar principles to clockmaking, he made it possible for Seth Thomas and others to establish a preeminence in clockmaking which Connecticut has never since quite lost.

In Rhode Island other mills soon followed the establishment of Slater's; by 1860 the little state had 135. Calico printing from wooden blocks got started at East Greenwich in 1790. Woolens and worsteds got under way after 1810.

New England's abundant waterpower probably slowed down and delayed her interest in the development of other kinds of power. In 1840 even the Blackstone River between Worcester and Providence was supplying 150 plants. In Maine not only were the rivers rich in power, but harbors often stretched far inland. The early nineteenth century saw many small mills scattered through the state. In the 1860s a small wood-turning mill began making spools from white birch. Granite was quarried at Vinalhaven as early as 1829, and at one time Maine supplied cobblestones for the most picturesque, one of the most durable (and surely the most uncomfortable) method of street paving ever devised. Her granite, lime, slate, and feldspar quarries are still rich in deposits, much richer than they would be without the increasing use that has been made of steel and concrete in modern construction. In 1929, by popular vote, Maine became the only state in which chartered companies were forbidden to export hydroelectric power. This was done for the purpose of attracting industry to Maine, but it was much more successful in the way of impoverishing the eastern part of the state and bankrupting Eastport when in 1935 it brought about the abandonment of the Passmaquoddy Tidal Power Development Project after much money had been spent on it. A great deal of pulpwood still travels by water in Maine, but private shipbuilding now concentrates on fishing and pleasure boats. The shoe industry found a distinctive line in Bass moccasins and gum boots for hunters and campers, and L. L. Bean built up a worldwide mail-order business in this and other wilderness equipment.

New Hampshire too was rich in waterpower, and she had lumbering, shipbuilding, papermaking, and quarrying, all carried on recklessly at first and without thought of depletion. From 1826 on Abbot and Downing made the famous Concord Coach, which was used for transportation in the West and for carrying the mails; by 1890 their shops covered six acres. These coaches were durably and lovingly made; Potter Palmer ordered a dozen for Chicago's swank Palmer House, and one order from Wells-Fargo was for thirty. The average size of the manufacturing unit in New Hamp-

Amoskeag Manufacturing Company, Manchester, N.H., 1887. New York Public Library Picture Collection

Candle Dip Day, in the early 1800s, was set aside for thrifty Vermont households to make up the entire year's supply of tallow dips and candles. Culver Pictures

shire tended to be small, the brilliantly disastrous exception being the Amoskeag Mills, with forty-five acres of buildings along the banks of the Merrimack at Manchester, which controlled all the waterpower between Manchester and Concord and employed up to seventeen thousand persons. Its beginnings reach back to the first decade of the nineteenth century; its collapse, beginning with labor troubles in the early 1920s and culminating in 1936, all but paralyzed a community of over eighty thousand people. Natural disasters and changing conditions (notably the growing displacement of gingham by rayon) contributed to the calamity, but few doubted that the management had protected the interests of the stockholders in serene disregard of the needs of either the hands or the town. The machine tool industry has also been important in New Hampshire economy. Asahel Hubbard established the National Hydraulic Company, and it is said that more than one-twentieth of all the machines used to produce equipment for World War II came from Springfield and Windsor. Today Nashua is an electronics center.

Vermont remained largely an agricultural state for the first hundred years, but there were many contributing industries. The wool business in Vermont began before the Revolution, and there are said to have been fifteen thousand hand looms by 1809. The first boom in wool and cotton collapsed after the War of 1812 and was revived through the coming of Merino sheep, but ran into the doldrums again in the 1840s, when sheep were outnumbering men in Vermont six to one. In 1841 Albert E. Dewey began the production of "shoddy," or reworked wool. In the 1820s Alvin Adams began operating the Adams Express between Windsor and Woodstock; more importantly, Thaddeus Fairbanks and his brothers got to work. At first they made wagons, stoves, and plows, but from the beginning of the thirties they were making scales and coming into great prosperity. They endowed the St. Johnsbury Academy, Athenaeum, Music Hall, and Museum of

Science. After the Chicago Fire, one of their salesmen, Charles H. Morse, established Fairbanks, Morse and Company in Chicago; in 1910 he was to buy out the parent company. The Howe Scale Company began in 1856; between them, Howe and Fairbanks make three-quarters of American scales. Vermont also claims an astonishing number of inventions: the steam calliope, the horsedrawn hayrake, laughing gas, the railroad refrigerator car, and Thomas Davenport's electric motor. Davenport also constructed an electric telegraph before Samuel F. B. Morse, but failed to secure the necessary backing and returned to blacksmithing. Samuel Morey invented an internal combustion engine, but this too came to nothing; Morey always believed that Robert Fulton had stolen his ideas from him. Lemuel Hedge invented a machine for ruling paper. Hides, clippers, and fertilizers became other factors in Vermont economy, and Brattleboro, like Burlington and Concord, New Hampshire, became a printing center. Today Burlington, with General Electric, IBM, four colleges, and much besides, has the heaviest concentration of population and industry in the state. Barre produces one-third of all the granite used in American public and private memorials, though during later years it has often been displaced by marble, which is cheaper. Redfield Proctor's Vermont Marble Company became one of the state's largest industries; four Proctors and three Fairbankses have occupied the governor's chair. Slate comes from Poultney and Fairhaven, and the state also produces asbestos and soapstone, from which latter talc is made.

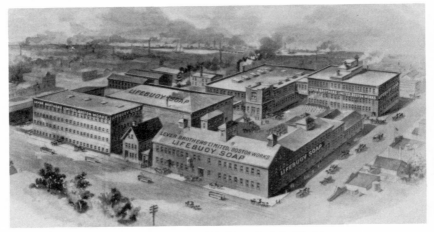

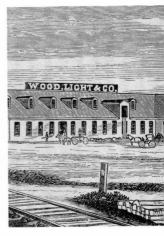

Lever Brothers Limited Boston Works. 1903. New York Public Library Picture Collection

E. and T. Fairbanks Scale Manufactory, St. Johnsbury, Vermont. New York Public Library Picture Collection

L. Candee & Co.'s Rubber Boot and Shoe Works, New Haven. New York Public Library Picture Collection

Wood, Light and Company Machine Factory, Worcester, Mass., 1872. New York Public Library Picture Collection

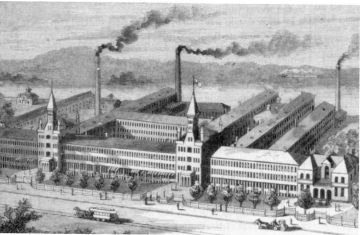

The American Watch Works, Waltham, Mass. New York Public Library Picture Collection

Interior, American Watch Works, Waltham, 1870. The Bettmann Archive

Factory advertisement. New York Public Library Picture Collection

Construction of papermaking mill of the Oxford Paper Company on a turbulent stretch of the Androscoggin River at Rumsford, Maine, 1900. By courtesy of Oxford Paper Division of Ethyl Corporation

The most remarkable thing about New England industry has been the amazing and inspiring way in which, during recent years, she has responded to the challenge of new conditions, involving notably her loss of supremacy in shoes and textiles. In 1880 she had 80 percent of the spindles in America; by 1935 this had shrunk to 30 percent. Reference has been made to the Amoskeag calamity. Within ten years after it had occurred, citizens' committees had brought over one hundred new diversified business establishments into Manchester; the community will never be at the mercy of a single corporation again. The Fall River story is equally remarkable. Between 1919 and 1935, Fall River, Massachusetts, as Howe puts it, "lost half its payroll and three quarters of its spindles." In 1932 one-quarter of its inhabitants were on relief and the city itself was near bankruptcy, but by 1940, 140 new companies had been introduced. Lowell and Lawrence, too, acquired Western Electric, Avoco, and others. Since 1950 an astonishing array of "science-oriented companies" whose very names are as mysterious as Arabic lettering could be to the passing motorists have lined the sixty-five miles of Route 128 around Boston, and in 1960 the first commercial plant in America to make electricity by nuclear power was opened at Rowe. Another remarkable scientific installation was made in Maine. During World War I, Allessandro Fabri discovered that clear radio reception was always available at Otter Creek, Mount Desert Island, after which the Navy proceeded to build there the largest radio station in the world. Later Bell Telephone built its Telstar station at Andover. Mount Desert Island also claims the Jackson Memorial Laboratory, conducting research on cancer, muscular dystrophy, radiation, cell behavior, blood variation, and other important matters. This

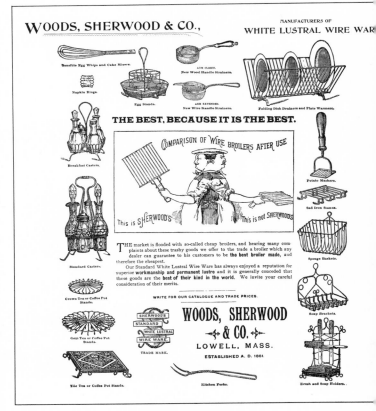

Advertisement of Woods, Sherwood & Co., Lowell, Mass., manufacturers of articles for household use. Culver Pictures, Inc.

The Oxford mill at Rumford today. By courtesy of Oxford Paper Division of Ethyl Corporation

Giant crane at the Bath Iron Works, Bath, Maine. Bath Area Chamber of Commerce

William Stanley, inventor of electrical transformer. The transformer is the device that enables engineers to send electric current for hundreds of miles. Stanley developed the transformer in Great Barrington, Mass., in 1885. New York Public Library Picture Collection

work is supported by such organizations as the American Cancer Society, the Atomic Energy Commission, the Ford Foundation, and the National Hemophilia Foundation. It would be disingenuous, however, to pretend that New England has not suffered, along with the rest of the country, in the economic slump of recent years.

Alexander Graham Bell in his dressing gown, pipe in hand, working in his study. New York Public Library Picture Collection

IV

Industrialism necessarily involved labor problems. Samuel Slater's first employees were children between seven and twelve; in 1801 he had one hundred between four and ten. Josiah Quincy thought "there was an air of dull dejection on the countenances of all of them." So great a lover of Connecticut as Odell Shepard, taking bitter exception, in 1939, to Alexander Johnston's statement that there had always been "a peculiar kindness of relations" between employer and employed in Connecticut, pointed out that in 1831 this was manifested by paying men three dollars a week and women two dollars, while children sometimes received as little as fifty cents a week for a workday which ranged from ten hours in winter to sixteen in summer. Moreover, payment of wages was often late or irregular, and charges for "company board" and "company lodgings" were effective tools for keeping employees under the employer's thumb and in his debt. When Philip Corbin of New Britain began paying weekly wages in 1879, his employees were so amazed that they celebrated by marching with a brass band. Shepard added that "after a struggle of more than a hundred years the situation of organized labor in Connecticut is by no means good and the conditions of labor are in some cases disgracefully bad."

In New England foreigners were often deliberately imported because they would work for lower wages than the Americans and be more subservient to their employers. Labor suffered inevitably in the Panic of 1837, but even after recovery had been achieved, and the mills were paying dividends of 20 percent, the position of labor did not improve, and when wages were not reduced, more work was sometimes demanded. Even in the Lowell mills, conditions deteriorated with the passing of the founders. In 1854 Augusta and Harriet Carter went from Shirley to Lewiston, Maine, to work in the Bates Mill. They began at seventy-five cents and rose to $4.05 for a working week of six days from 5:46 A.M. to 7 P.M., with forty-five minutes for lunch. Board and room in a company building cost $1.25 a week. In the early 1930s Connecticut was still struggling with

Replica of telephone instrument which on October 9, 1876, carried the world's first telephone conversation between Alexander Graham Bell in Boston and Thomas Watson in Cambridgeport, Mass., two miles away. New York Public Library Picture Collection

Thomas A. Watson in 1874. Watson was the recipient of the world's first telephone call. "Come here, Mr. Watson. I want you." New York Public Library Picture Collection

sweatshops, which had fled from New York State's labor laws and were paying $3.00 weekly or less.

Modern labor unions were preceded by such comparatively short-lived and less effective organizations as the New England Association of Farmers, Mechanics, and Other Workingmen and the Knights of Labor. A strike of female workers at Pawtucket, Rhode Island,

in 1824, is called the first example of feminine participation in such activity. In 1825 Boston carpenters
struck for a ten-hour day; this was opposed because it
was feared that the excessive leisure resulting must conduce to vice. This argument was used again and again
in labor disputes, so that it seems the employers·must
at last actually have convinced themselves that they
were grinding the faces of the poor out of sheer humane
consideration for their spiritual well-being. Strikes increased, nevertheless, throughout the nineteenth century, with increasingly bold agitation in favor of an eight-
hour day from the sixties on. In 1902 hatmakers in

Bangor, Maine, in 1837. Culver Pictures, Inc.

Camden, Maine. Culver Pictures, Inc.

Danbury, Connecticut, were judged to have violated the Sherman Act by using the boycott. That same year martial law was declared in Pawtucket during a strike which followed a cut in wages after the passage of a law limiting working hours on the street railways. The streetcar company continued operations under the protection of a state whose law they had defied, and the General Assembly backed down, which led to sufficient indignation so that a Democratic governor was elected in 1906. In 1922 a nine-month textile strike in both New Hampshire and Rhode Island followed reductions in wages which had run up to more than 40 percent and a proposed increase in the workweek. When Rhode Island employers claimed that it was impossible to meet union terms and still earn a profit, the men offered to return to work if this claim were substantiated, but the employers refused to open their books to federal and state inspectors. Connecticut had a serious textile strike in 1934, and two years later there was a disastrous strike involving violence at the Remington-Rand plant. The use of the sit-down technique, first employed in 1937, was opposed by Governor Cross, who was generally friendly toward labor.

As time passed, legislation became a more and more important factor in the labor situation. Labor legislation became more progressive and effective in Massachusetts in the 1870s. New Hampshire claims to be the first state to adopt workmen's compensation and among the first to set up minimum wage laws and legislation affecting unemployment compensation and employment of minors. Rhode Island got workmen's compensation through in 1912, Vermont in 1915. Vermont, which had had ineffective child labor laws in 1904 and 1910, passed a more stringent law in 1912, after an investigation of the mills by the Episcopal Church, and Connecticut achieved much progressive legislation in the 1930s.

V

One interest not obviously connected with trade and industry has become an important factor in the New England economy, especially in the northern states, and this is recreation. Maine now carries "VACATIONLAND" on her automobile license plates, and radio announcers have been known to exhort residents to be kind to the summer visitors. In 1911 Vermont became the first state to establish a publicity bureau; now a part of the Vermont Development Commission, it advertises in the metropolitan papers. The Green Mountain Club began laying out the Long Trail through the mountains in 1910, and by 1949 twenty state forest parks and twenty-five state forests had set up recreational facilities. In 1919, in Maine, Charles W. Eliot and others were instrumental in getting Lafayette (later Acadia) National Park established. The Woodstock Inn, opened in 1892, pioneered in the pro-

Green Animals topiary gardens in Portsmouth, R.I., is famous for its eighty sculptured trees and shrubs shaped in animal forms. Rhode Island Department of Economic Development

Fort Western on Bowman Street in Augusta, Maine, on the east bank of the Kennebec River, just north of the Kennebec River bridge, built in 1754 to defend the Kennebec. Rebuilt and maintained as a museum, the fort now depicts colonial living, includes period rooms, houses crafts, and stages special exhibits. The only fort still standing in Maine which predates the Revolution, it remains an excellent example of a wilderness fort, including stockade and blockhouse. Courtesy, State of Maine

Maine State Capitol, Augusta, a much restored Bulfinch building. Courtesy, State of Maine

Home of James G. Blaine, Augusta, Maine, which serves as Maine's Governor's Mansion. Courtesy, State of Maine

motion of winter sports, and skiing began with an "Outing Club" at Dartmouth in 1909. The first ski tow was started at Woodstock in 1934. The big ski business began in the forties, since which time recreation in Vermont has been on a year-round level.

None of this means that there was nothing of this character in Vermont before the dates indicated. A hotel centered around a water cure was built at Clarendon Springs as early as 1798, and mineral springs flourished at various sites through much of the nineteenth century, when great resort hotels were built in many scenic areas. Manchester's Equinox House antedated the Civil War, and Lake Champlain, Lake Winnipesaukee, and Lake Memphremagog have all been centers of vacation activity. Stowe, now a skiing capital, near Mount Mansfield, acquired a huge, four-storied hotel in 1864, which burned in 1889. But even today skiing is not the only thing people come to Vermont to do, for once-isolated abandoned farms in the hill country are now cherished by outlanders as their summer homes. All this activity has inevitably brought new problems as well as new resources. Some of the outlanders have become Vermont residents, assimilating Vermont traditions and becoming acclimated to Vermont ways, happy to find themselves belonging to a community once again. Elsewhere, however, drugs, disease, and crime have raised their ugly heads, and soaring prices have brought hardship to many along with prosperity to a few.

The influx of new people into the northern states has probably both helped and hurt conservation, for invasion of the wilderness both fosters appreciation of its importance and increases the danger of misuse. Recognition of the need for conservation began early in New England (Thoreau, for one, understood it clearly), and has increased here as elsewhere during recent years in response to increasing need. Unfortunately, however, this consciousness all too often goes unimplemented and therefore does not accomplish very much. In 1867 New Hampshire sold for $26,000 woodlands which the United States paid over $6,000,000 to buy back in 1911. In 1867, too, Vermont provided a Fish Commission to restock depleted streams and replenish water supplies, yet as late as 1947 the state's fish hatcheries were regarded in many quarters as a fit subject for jest. The Weeks Bill established a National Forest in the White Mountains, and Governor Percival Baxter made magnificent gifts of wilderness land in Maine. The Connecticut River flows four hundred miles from the Canadian Border to Long Island Sound, first forming a boundary between New Hampshire and Vermont, then cutting right through the middle of Massachusetts and Connecticut. It has been badly polluted where it flows through industrialized areas, and in the early 1950s a group of Connecticut businessmen formed the Connecticut River Watershed Council, which claims to have made the river 30 percent cleaner in six years. The dams which have been built have also helped to control

Interior of the Blaine House. Courtesy, State of Maine

floods, though there are those who believe they have adversely affected waterlife and lessened the ability of the river to clean itself.*

Certainly the increasing popularity of the three northernmost New England states as recreation areas must inevitably do much to make their inhabitants known to their fellow countrymen as something more than the stock rural characters with which we have been familiarized by plays like *Way Down East*. It has been said that if Vermont were flattened out, it would be as large as Texas. It has more covered bridges than any other state, which were built neither for the convenience of lovers nor to delight connoisseurs of picturesque antiquities but for the purely practical purpose of protecting wooden-planked roadways, and its year comprises

*New England has also greatly progressed in her attitude toward preserving the works of man since the days when she came near losing the Old State House and the Old South Meetinghouse. In addition to the reconstruction of the original settlements at Plymouth and Salem, one may note the achievement of Albert and Joel Cheney Wells, who re-created a nineteenth-century village at Sturbridge, Massachusetts, and of Mr. and Mrs. Watson Webb, with their wonderful museum of New England antiquities at Shelburne, Vermont. See Samuel Chamberlain, *Old Sturbridge Village* (Hastings House, 1951) and Ralph Nading Hill and Lilian Baker Carlisle, *The History of the Shelburne Museum* (Shelburne Museum, 1960).

"nine months winter and three months of damn poor sleddin'," yet it has been claimed that its proverbially frugal, stoical, stubborn, and hard-working inhabitants have achieved more entries in *Who's Who in America*, in proportion to population, than the people of any other state. The inhabitants of what Frederick John Pratson has happily called the "lamb-chop-shaped" state of New Hampshire, "wedged between Vermont and Maine," share some of these characteristics, yet one who knows them so well as Cornelius Weygandt can stress their dramatic quality and appetite for clowning, comparing the. rural auctioneer to "any merry-andrew of Elizabethan times or . . . the vice who attends the Devil in a morality play."

Maine, with over two thousand miles of coastline, counting its inlets, is about as large as all the rest of New England combined. Louise Dickinson Rich calls it a paradise for cats, a statement one is inclined to doubt when she records calmly, and without the appropriate shudder of horror at such depravity, that stray cats are captured and cut up for fox bait. In any event, Maine seems to have every variety of feline, including the coon cat, reputedly descended from a Chinese cat brought in by Captain Samuel Clough in 1793, which was crossed with the common house cat, and "money cats," said to be always female, who are mottled black, white, and orange. This same Clough once planned to bring Marie Antoinette to Maine, and some of her possessions were actually sent there, but she was arrested in time to prevent her from becoming a Yankee. Some of her treasures remain in Maine while others have gone to the Metropolitan Museum in New York. Louise Rich calls "Down-Easterners" "shrewd, cautious, industrious, hard-headed, tight-fisted, strait-laced and well endowed with common sense," and I do not know how their independence could be better attested than by the story she tells of what happened in 1860 on Louds Island, which lies one and one-half miles off Round Pound Village in the town of Bristol. Louds Islanders vote in Bristol, but in 1860 they voted Democratic, and Bristol threw out their votes so that the town might be counted as solidly Republican. They thereupon withdrew from Bristol and set up the independent Republic of Muscongus. When conscripts were drawn for the Bristol draft, nine Louds Island men were included, but the women drove off the recruiter by bombarding him with potatoes. Thereupon the Louds Islanders proceeded to conduct their own draft; they had no quarrel with the United States, but they were not going to submit to dictation and chicanery from Bristol.

VI

With whatever accent one may choose to read "recreation business," however, New England has a number of recreation areas, each of which has a distinctive character of its own. In 1724 Massachusetts men bought about one-quarter of Berkshire County in the western part of the state for £460, three barrels of cider, and thirty quarts of rum. This beautiful region is certainly not a backwater, but during more than their first century all the Connecticut Valley settlements tended to face southward rather than eastward toward Boston. In 1936 Tanglewood, an estate formerly owned by William Aspinwall Tappan, a Boston banker and merchant, was given to Sergea Koussevitzky as a summer home for the Boston Symphony Orchestra, and the Berkshire Music Center was established there, an act which has done much to tie the area to Boston.

Cape Cod, familiarly called "the Cape" by Massachusetts residents, was once a land of clam chowder and clam cakes, with a distinctive sea-based culture, a speech marked by localisms, and a definitely provincial outlook. Fishing began to decline after the Civil War, and by the time the State Pier was built in 1935 to enable fishermen and farmers to get their produce to Boston quickly, the peak of the need had passed. The modern Cape exploits tourism and (now that it is only one and one-half hours from Boston) even commuters. Camp Edwards and Otis Air Force Base have brought in new residents and changed the character of the community. Trade has boomed and population figures have climbed. A large proportion of the population is no longer native-born, and the summer influx resembles a swarm of locusts and includes many persons about as desirable. The establishment of Cape Cod National Seashore in 1966, the country's second (the first was at Cape Hatteras) was a victory for the conservationists, but they have other fights ahead of them. As John Hay remarks in his "Post-Epilogue" to the Second Edition of Henry C. Kittredge's *Cape Cod, Its People and Their History*, conservation faces a "hard sell" in this area.

While salt marshes may be successfully defended, the ponds, swamps and woodlands go. With state aid, some towns have bought large areas of land to be set aside in the public interest; others have lost far more than can be retrieved, but the effort continues, and it is an effort, essentially, to try and reconcile the human world and the natural one, as well as the steady past and the uncertain present. The living *with* has to include all kinds of bedfellows.

Martha's Vineyard and the old-time Quaker whaling center Nantucket have their problems too, but their island status still protects them to a degree. For some strange reason, everybody seems to find it necessary to choose between them. The Vineyard has been loved by many well-known men and women, including the actress Katharine Cornell, who died there in 1974, and it is said that the natives still rejoice in Melville's speaking of Gay Head as a "village . . . which has long supplied the neighboring island of Nantucket with many of her most daring harpooners." Nantucket may have the edge in quaintness, as certainly in remoteness, but the Vineyard has greater variety. If Edgartown is its most aristocratic settlement, Oak Bluffs, once a Methodist campground whose central area is surrounded by an enchanting area of gingerbread houses, still illuminated with paper lanterns one night each summer, is the most picturesque, and there is nothing much more spectacular anywhere than the brilliantly colored clays of Gay Head, illuminated at sunset. One hears rather less today about the Isles of Shoals, lying off New Hampshire's eighteen miles of seacoast, but in 1847 the father of the poet Celia Thaxter built a hotel on Appledore, which not only attracted many distinguished visitors but enjoyed fantastic prosperity during most of what remained of the nineteenth century. Later it declined and burned early during the First World War.

Newport, Rhode Island, became the most famous—and notorious—of the gilded summer colonies, but it was not the only one. The Tappan mansion was one of many erected in the Berkshires (some of them are now living out a useful old age as schools or religious establishments), and by 1900 Bar Harbor, Maine, had attracted rich "rusticators" who sometimes had "cabins" as well as mansions and played at the simple life in the manner of Marie Antoinette at Versailles. Like those of Newport, the people of Bar Harbor had their last great summer in 1914, when the officers of the German liner, *Kronprinzessin Cécile*, which had been interned there, were their guests. Taxes and the "servant problem" cut into all this, and the great estates were closed or sold; in 1947 many of them burned.

Newport, nevertheless, is the magic name. The city has, of course, been much more than a summer resort. As a stronghold of Quakerism, a slave trading and privateering center, a British headquarters, and an Ameri-

Gold Ballroom of the Marble House, W. K. Vanderbilt's "summer cottage," built 1889-92 by Richard Morris Hunt. Rhode Island Department of Economic Development. The Preservation Society of Newport County

Exterior of Marble House. Rhode Island Department of Economic Development

Rosecliff, modeled after the Grand Trianon at Versailles, was designed by McKim, Mead and White for Herman Oelrichs in 1902. The Court of Love, designed by Augustus Saint-Gaudens, is between the two wings. Rhode Island Department of Economic Development

The Valentine-heart-shaped staircase at Rosecliff. Rhode Island Department of Economic Development

The Breakers, Cornelius Vanderbilt's seventy-room Renaissance mansion, overlooking the Cliff Walk, remodeled just before his death by Richard Morris Hunt. Rhode Island Department of Economic Development

can naval base, it has had as varied and anomalous a history as any American city. Southern families summered there early, and at times social affairs seem to have been conducted with courtlike rigidity. After the Civil War, New England intellectuals used Newport as a resort area when they did not go to Nahant. The New York "predators of great wealth"—Astors, Belmonts, Vanderbilts, and others, with their flunkeys, Ward McAllister and Harry Lehr—did not take over until later. These visitors lived on terms of uneasy detente with the townspeople, whom they regarded as their "footstools"; though willing to be gouged by them for necessities, they did not care to associate with them or see them on "their" beach or boulevards. They built "cottages" as ornate as the movie palaces of the twenties to live and entertain in during six or seven weeks each summer and sometimes squandered as much as $100,000 on a single fête. The trouble that these people took over nothing makes heartbreaking reading; one wonders if any unhappier group ever existed upon this earth; indeed two of the most celebrated hostesses literally lost whatever minds they had ever possessed. Apparently it is an even more wearisome business to strive to outdo your competitors in folly than in more constructive pursuits, and such incidents as the extravagant dinner which Harry Lehr gave for dogs and Mrs. Stuyvesant Fish's elaborate affair in honor of a Corsican prince who turned out to be a small monkey shocked all America and contributed to the growth of class feeling. Newport is still a social center, and it still has its

divisions and its follies, but its most lavish period lasted only from about 1890 to 1914, and today summer visitors troop through some of the "cottages."

It would be difficult to think of anything less characteristic of New England, and indeed these people were not New Englanders. Yet Newport has left us two priceless anecdotes. One day Edith Wharton's husband, Edward Wharton, started out down Ocean Walk for an appointment for which he knew he was late. When he saw a milk wagon approaching, it occurred to him that he might save time by climbing in and riding with the driver. Shortly afterwards he encountered an acquaintance whose social position was considerably less secure than his own and who felt obliged to express his displeasure over Wharton's gaffe. "I wouldn't," he said, "do that if I were you." "No," replied Wharton, "I wouldn't do it either if I were you."

The other story relates to Mrs. Potter Palmer, the Chicago society queen who was also a woman of considerable sensitivity and social conscience. Riding one day in her carriage along the boulevard, she noticed a woman staggering along helplessly in the road. Other carriages passed her by in serene disregard on the easy hypothesis that she was drunk. Mrs. Palmer had to find out. She stopped her carriage, found that the woman was sick, invited her into the carriage, and directed the coachman to drive her to her home in another part of the town. Bertha Palmer walked home.

Even in gilded Newport, intelligence and humanity sometimes insisted upon breaking in.

Chapter 8
Mind and Spirit

I

SO MUCH HAS BEEN SAID ABOUT RELIGION in earlier chapters of this volume that less needs to be said here. In early New England history, church and state sometimes almost became one. In early Vermont parsons often served as physicians, lawyers, and teachers, as well as public servants; some went into trade; we know of at least one who became an innkeeper. In 1780 Vermont towns were still collecting taxes for religious purposes, but the law now exempted dissenters from being required to support the establishment. In 1783 a certificate showing that the exemptee was contributing to another church was required, but ten years later the religious test for public office was dropped, and in 1807 religion was left dependent upon voluntary contributions. In New Hampshire, however, the requirement that the governor and other elected officers must be Protestants was not dropped from the state constitution until 1876.

As we have already discovered, Calvinistic orthodoxy was subjected to ingenious modification as far back as the colonial period, and the processes of adaptation were not arrested with the birth of the nation. Though Yale was established to protest the liberalism of Harvard, it was Nathaniel W. Taylor, professor of theology at Yale from 1822 to 1858, who developed the "New

D. L. Moody. New York Public Library Picture Collection

Haven Theology," which, without formally or openly abandoning Calvinism, saw man as depraved only by his own acts and thus essentially responsible for his own salvation. Taylor's friend Lyman Beecher, who was more preacher and reformer than theologian, also undercut Calvinism by entertaining ideas not quite compatible with it.

The intense evangelicalism of the aggressive missionary movement which radiated westward from New England beginning in the 1790s tended to undercut Calvinism also; perhaps its greatest figure was Charles G. Finney, but though Finney was born in Connecticut in 1792, he early removed to New York, and, for forty years beginning in 1835, his base was Oberlin College in Ohio, where his "Oberlin Theology" manifested a distinct inclination toward perfectionism. Late in the century, New England had an important share in the work of another great revivalist, D. L. Moody. Born at Northfield, Massachusetts, in 1837, into a family which, so far as it was anything was Unitarian, Moody was converted while working in a Boston shoe store (a plaque for many years marked its site) and joined the Mount Vernon Congregational Church. Beginning his work in Chicago, he created a sensation in England in collaboration with the Gospel singer, Ira D. Sankey, and returned to the United States to roam far and wide and settle finally in his native Northfield, where he founded two excellent schools. Moody's formal beliefs were antiquated, unsophisticated, and anti-intellectual, but he was a great-hearted and tolerant man who preached far more religion than theology, and he had no difficulty in winning and holding the respect of men like Henry Drummond and Lyman Abbott.

Hartford's Horace Bushnell, a greater figure and a larger influence upon the future, has already been mentioned. In *Christian Nurture* (1847; second edition 1861) he laid foundations for religious education through emphasizing the organic character of the Christian life as a growth in grace rather than a revolutionary change through a startling conversion experience. (The Sunday School movement was well under way in the 1820s; by 1830 there were two hundred schools in Connecticut.) In *Christ and His Salvation* (1864) and other books, Bushnell revived and developed Abelard's "Moral Influence Theory" of the Atonement, arguing that the death of Christ was not a ransom paid to the devil, nor an attempt to placate an angry God by taking upon himself the penalty man must otherwise have suffered, nor yet a token payment to God as governor of the universe, but simply the supreme revelation in time of God's redemptive love for man, which conduces to his salvation through his response to it and consequent dedication of himself to God's service. Through his influence upon Washington Gladden and others, Bushnell also became a force in the "Social Gospel," or application of Christian prin-

A nineteenth-century camp meeting at Oak Bluffs, Martha's Vineyard. New York Public Library Picture Collection

The Cathedral in the Pines, Rindge, N.H., attracts thousands of visitors of every faith. Here, preparations have been made for Jewish religious service. The Altar of the Nation, in background, contains stones from all the states. New York Public Library Picture Collection

The men of the First Congregational Church of Hartland, Vermont,
turn out for one day each year with saws, axes, and wedges to cut
wood to keep the church warm. Wide World Photo

Tiny chapel, Hampton Falls, N.H. Probably the smallest consecrated
chapel in America, it seats twelve persons. Formerly it was an ice-
house. Wide World Photo

St. Mark's Roman Catholic Church, Burlington, Vermont. Wide
World Photo

Modernistic statue of Virgin Mary, St. Mark's Roman Catholic
Church, Burlington, Vermont. Wide World Photo

ciples to corporate life and corporate evils which is so important in the modern church.

The fortunes of other denominations in New England have already been sampled in what has been written about the cities considered in Chapter 2. Episcopalians did well, especially among the "upper" and more fashionable classes, after having recovered from the Revolutionary taint of Toryism. In the later nineteenth century, until he died at fifty-seven in 1893, Phillips Brooks, rector of Trinity Church, Boston, and, at the very end, bishop, was probably his communion's best-known and most influential figure; later Bishop William Lawrence also made a very strong impression. In the early days, Baptists and Methodists were more inclined to rely upon zeal than learning; though both thrived, neither became as strong in New England as in the West. In 1847 the Wesleyan Theological Institute, originally in Newbury, Vermont, moved to Concord, New Hampshire; renamed the Methodist General Biblical Institute, it moved again, this time to Boston, in 1868, where, in 1871, it became the first school in the newly chartered Boston University.

Unitarianism, on the other hand, is distinctively New England; not only did it originate there, but New England has always been the center of its strength. Universalism, now merged with Unitarianism, though much less intellectual and more evangelical in its origins, whose cardinal tenet is universal salvation, achieved its first organized church at Gloucester, Massachusetts, way back in 1779, and by 1793 there was a New England Convention. Though the movement gravitated toward New England (Tufts College and Divinity School in Medford, Massachusetts, were established by the Universalists), it had spread through much of the North before the Civil War. Hosea Ballou, Tufts's first president, was probably its most important early figure.

The fortunes of the Roman Catholic Church in New England have been peculiar. Their missionaries were here in the middle of the seventeenth century, and in Maine they did their work so well that most of the Indians there are still Catholics. But anti-Catholic feeling, in New England and in America at large, began early and lasted long. It is said that Hawthorne at one time considered the possibility of having the Reverend Arthur Dimmesdale in *The Scarlet Letter* confess his sin to a priest but gave up the idea because he was unable to figure out a way to introduce one into Puritan Boston. Later, in *The Marble Faun*, he did have a New England girl confess to a priest in Rome. In modern times, of course, the heavy influx of Irish, Italian, and other Catholic peoples into New England has greatly strengthened the position of the church.

Connecticut recorded the presence of "David the Jew" as early as 1659. Fifteen Sephardic Jews, mainly Spanish and Portuguese, came to Newport from Holland in 1658. In 1763 they dedicated a synagogue, with

Phillips Brooks. New York Public Library Picture Collection

Isaac Touro of Jamaica as their rabbi. The community dwindled during the Revolution, and when the British occupied Newport, some of its adherents fled to Fairfield County in Connecticut. From 1818 to 1883 the synagogue was closed. Still in use today, it is regarded with peculiar veneration as the oldest monument of the Jewish faith in America. Mid-European Ashkenazic Jews, mainly German, became important in America beginning in the 1830s; later they were greatly outnumbered by those of Russian and Polish origin whom they did not often welcome as warmly as coreligionists might have expected or considered their due.

We have glanced elsewhere at some of the off-center religious movements in which New England has had a share. William Miller (1782-1849), who figured out that the world would end in 1844, was born in Pittsfield, Massachusetts, but was moved to Poultney, Vermont, as a small child, and first proclaimed his "revelation" in that state, but he was importantly publicized by a Boston preacher, Joshua V. Hines, and it was in Boston that the Millerite "temple" was situated.

The Shakers were followers of an Englishwoman, Ann Lee, who came to America in 1774; they had communities in New England as well as in New York, and

Touro Synagogue in Newport, interior and exterior. Ground was broken in 1759 and the building dedicated on December 2, 1763. From the synagogue it is only a short walk to the old burial ground, which inspired Longfellow's poem "The Jewish Cemetery at Newport." Photography by John Hopf, Newport

there are still Shakers at Sabbath-Day Lake in Maine and perhaps elsewhere. But in the long run they were doomed by their insistence upon celibacy; aside from proselytizing, their communities could only grow through the children they adopted, and it would have been unreasonable to expect more than a fraction of these to stay. Dickens visited a Shaker community on his first American tour and denounced

that bad spirit, no matter by what class or sect it may be entertained, that would strip life of its healthful graces, rob youth of its innocent pleasures, pluck from maturity and age their pleasant ornaments, and make existence but a narrow path toward the grave: that odious spirit which, if it could have had full scope and sway upon the earth, must have blasted and made barren the imaginations of the greatest men, and left them, in their power of raising up enduring images before their fellow-creatures yet unborn, no better than the beasts. . . .

Within their limitations, however, the achievements of the Shakers were considerable. They were excellent farmers, craftsmen, and businessmen, who established an effective and highly hygienic community organization, and they became famous not only for their seeds and herbs but for their handmade furniture, clothing, candles, baskets, and other products. They also made many inventions, none of which they bothered to patent. At Enfield, New Hampshire, where they built a famous "floating bridge" over Lake Mascoma, they paid over one-fifth of the town taxes during one decade and cared for over a hundred children. Hawthorne dealt with them in "The Canterbury Pilgrims," and Howells seems to have been fascinated by them; they appear in *The Undiscovered Country, The Day of Their Wedding, A Parting and a Meeting*, and *The Vacation of the Kelwyns*.

Mormonism was certainly not a New England phenomenon, but it is worth remembering that both Joseph Smith and Brigham Young were native Vermonters. The really important off-center religious movement of New England origin is Christian Science. Mrs. Mary Baker G. Eddy (1821-1910), a native of Bow, New Hampshire, published *Science and Health* in 1875, and established a monolithic, powerful church organization in Boston, where she built the first "Mother Church" in 1895 and the magnificent edifice whose great dome was for many years about the most conspicuous feature of the Boston skyline in 1906. When *Science and Health* appeared, she seems to have sent copies to all the leading New England writers, but only Bronson Alcott gave her any encouragement to speak of. Longfellow did not bother to acknowledge receipt of the volume until after she had written to inquire about it, and Emerson gave her much shorter shrift than he usually accorded those who sought to interest him in unorthodox ideas. In 1907 Mark Twain launched a furious attack, not so

William Miller. New York Public Library Picture Collection

much against Christian Science as a religion, toward which he was not really unsympathetic, but upon Mrs. Eddy personally for what he regarded as her greed, ignorance, and mendacity, and her attempt to establish a tyranny over men's minds. Subsequent critics and biographers, though less intemperate, are still having considerable difficulty in achieving a meeting of minds concerning her. An interesting by-product of Christian Science was the establishment in 1908 of a distinguished daily newspaper, *The Christian Science Monitor*, now unfortunately reduced to a tabloid, which has attained national circulation and commands universal respect, reaching thousands outside the faith yet never achieving an impressive circulation in Boston itself.

Parenthetically it may perhaps be mentioned here that, as society became less intolerant, New England, like the rest of the country, raised up "infidels," a word of vague connotation not always indicating positive atheism but at least dissent from Christian orthodoxy and churchianity. Boston had a First Society of Free Inquirers and (delightful name!) an Infidel Relief Society, and there were attempts at organization upon a national scale, but they never got very far, perhaps because it is difficult to organize negation. In Boston in 1834 Abner Kneeland, an ex-clergyman, received a sixty-day sentence under an eighteen-century blasphemy law. The case was appealed clear to the Supreme Court, which finally upheld the sentence. Emerson, Channing, and others asked its suspension, not because they sympathized with Kneeland's views or methods, but in the interest of freedom of speech and out of opposition to religious persecution.

Harvard College in 1836. The Second Centennial celebration. New York Public Library Picture Collection

"A Prospect of the Colleges in Cambridge in New England." Harvard. All five Massachusetts signers of the Declaration of Independence had attended Harvard College. New York Public Library Picture Collection

II

About education too a good deal has been said elsewhere in these pages. There is nothing of which New England is more proud than the founding of Harvard College as early as 1636, followed by what was to become another great university, Yale, soon after the turn of the century, and surely there is no place on earth where a richer or wider range of educational institutions is now available to choose from, nor of a higher average quality than those which flourish in New England today. State-supported higher education was much slower getting started in New England than in the Middle and Far West, however, and though considerable progress along this line has been made during recent years, the Northeast still lags behind the hinterland in this respect.

Charles Eliot Norton, professor of the history of art, Harvard (1874-1898). The Bettmann Archive

Yale began at Saybrook in 1701 and moved to New Haven in 1716. It was named for Elihu Yale, from whom it received a bequest of £800; it costs more to get a college named for you today. Alfred E. Perkins's bequest of $10,000 in 1834 was the largest Yale had been offered up to this time; it contrasts interestingly with John W. Sterling's gift of $34,000,000 in our own time. The medical school began in 1810, the divinity school in 1822, the law school in 1826, the Sheffield Scientific School in 1858. The art gallery goes back to John Trumbull's bequest of his paintings in return for an annuity of $1,000 annually for the rest of his life, and the theater school developed rapidly after George Pierce Baker, whose famous playwriting course had begun at Harvard, was lured away from Cambridge in 1925.

An etching by Vernon Howe Bailey showing the Johnston Gate, facing west between Massachusetts and Harvard halls, which has been the main entrance to the Yard since the seventeenth century. New York Public Library Picture Collection

Harvard College. The tower is that of Lowell House. Wide World Photo

Carpenter Center for Visual Arts, Harvard. Designed by Le Corbusier—his first building in the U.S. Wide World Photo

Rector Cutler and the Trustees, from a drawing by Theodore Diedrichsen, Jr., in Edwin Oviatt, *The Beginnings of Yale, 1701-26* (Yale University Press, 1916). New York Public Library Picture Collection

Below, left

Yale College and the State House, ca. 1840. New York Public Library Picture Collection

Below

New Haven, Conn., comprising a view of the Episcopal and Presbyterian churches, State House, and Yale College, ca. 1830. New York Public Library Picture Collection

Yale College and State House, New Haven, drawn by J. A. Davis, nineteenth century. Library of Congress

A snow sculpture at the Dartmouth Winter Carnival, 1947. New York Public Library Picture Collection

Vermont has a right to be proud of having chartered her university in 1791, even though nothing much was done to make it a reality for a decade. The state also boasts the first medical school and the first teacher's training school, under Samuel Hall in 1823 (Massachusetts had the first state-supported one in 1839). Vermont has also been a leading producer of educators (John Dewey came from Burlington), and the Land Grant College Act of 1862 was sponsored by a Vermonter, Justin Morrill. Samuel Reed Hall of Concord brought the blackboard into the classroom, and Philo Stewart, a Congregational minister, invented the Stewart stove and invested the money he made from it to finance Oberlin College.

Bowdoin, founded in 1794, is Maine's oldest college. Among its alumni were Hawthorne, Longfellow (who began his teaching career there), and Franklin Pierce. During recent years, Vermont's Middlebury has not only greatly expanded its regular facilities but has attracted much attention through its summer language school and the Breadloaf School of English. Dartmouth's Hopkins Center and the University of Vermont's Lane Series have both brought many theatrical and musical attractions to areas they could not possibly have reached through commercial channels. Vermont's Bennington College has been mentioned elsewhere, and after 1946 Walter Hendricks, formerly of Chicago, made himself a very controversial figure in Vermont (and American) education by founding and then resigning from three small colleges—Marlboro, Windham, and Mark Hopkins, Marlboro being noted among

Simmons College on the Fenway, Boston. Courtesy of the Boston Public Library, Print Department

A Currier and Ives view of Dartmouth College in the nineteenth century. New York Public Library Picture Collection

At the left is the former headquarters of Boston University, offices and College of Liberal Arts, at the corner of Beacon and Bowdoin streets. Photo, 1870. Courtesy of the Boston Public Library, Print Department

Martha Wilson Dormitory, Smith College. J. W. Ames & E. S. Dodge, architects. New York Public Library Picture Collection

An early view of Amherst College. New York Public Library Picture Collection

An early view of Brown University. New York Public Library Picture Collection

other things for its association with Robert Frost and the musician Rudolf Serkin.

As we have seen elsewhere, the older New England colleges were not particularly receptive to ideas looking toward modifying the old classical-mathematical curriculum. A Dartmouth president once expressed the opinion that a college education was of no use to those engaged in "mercantile, mechanical, or agricultural operations," and when Francis Wayland tried to introduce innovations at Brown, he was removed as president and the public was reassured that the college would continue to devote itself to "educating a sterling class

of citizens" and not to "conferring degrees upon the unfortunate."

The later eighteenth century produced many "academies," dedicated to what we should now call secondary education, and financed by both fees and subsidies. Some admitted girls as well as boys, and there were "seminaries" for girls only. Some of these schools made additions to the classical curriculum and embraced "practical" courses. Such academies as Phillips Andover (Mass.), established in 1778, and Phillips Exeter (N.H.), founded only three years later, have manifested great survival value. Maine opened the

Charleston Female Seminary, between 1836-1841. Lithographer, Thomas Moore. Courtesy of the Boston Public Library, Print Department

Earlier building of the Perkins Institute for the Blind on Broadway in South Boston, Mass. Built in 1837; photo ca. 1860s. Courtesy of the Boston Public Library, Print Department

Samuel Gridley Howe (1801-96), founder of Perkins Institute. The Bettmann Archive

state's first high school for boys, with a classical-mathematical curriculum, but the girls had to wait for their high school until 1850. During the second half of the century high schools multiplied throughout New England; Rhode Island had six by 1870.

At the other end of the educational scale, New Englanders have always been proud of their provision for elementary education. But for all the sentiment which has clustered about the "little red schoolhouse," we cannot but wonder how much of it was mere sentimentality when we read Catharine Beecher's scathing refer-

ence of 1823 to the ordinary school of the time as "a pesthouse fraught with the deadly malaria of both moral and physical disease" and to many teachers as "low, vulgar, obscene, intemperate, and utterly incompetent to teach anything good." Many schools had no sanitary facilities whatever nor any shelter anywhere around them. Women teachers might receive as little as $6.49 per month plus board, as against $23.10 for men, and Negro children were generally excluded. And it was more than a century later that Trinity's Odell Shepard recorded more in sorrow than in anger that if he might have an opportunity to show Timothy Dwight, who really put Yale on the educational map, around modern Connecticut, he would "not volunteer the information that although Connecticut is one of the wealthier states of the Union, her expenditure for public education, figured on a *per capita* basis, is about the lowest in the land."

Boston Farm School at Thompson's Island, Boston Harbor, 1852 wood engraving. Artist, John P. Mallory; lithographer, Joshua H. Peirce. Appeared in *Boston*, Sat. July 31, 1852, *F. Gleason.* Courtesy of the Boston Public Library, Print Department

Odell Shepard. New York Public Library Picture Collection

In the early days the difficulty was not that the vision was lacking nor even the will to translate it into law, but in far too many cases nothing was done to implement it. Theoretically Vermont, for example, provided a complete system of education from 1777. In 1867 she became the second state in the Union to pass a compulsory attendance law and in 1880 the second to add a kindergarten to her system, but consolidation of her multitudinous school districts did not begin until 1870 and was not required until 1892, and state aid to common schools did not begin until 1890. In 1870 only about 50 percent of Maine's children were attending school. An attendance law was passed in 1875, but the minimum school term was still only twelve weeks, and though a normal school had been established at Farmington nine years before, almost half the teachers had not themselves gone beyond the eighth grade. By 1900 most children were in school, but still for only fifteen to thirty weeks out of the year, and many schools were ungraded, with forty to sixty pupils on all levels herded together.

Rhode Island tried unsuccessfully to establish a public school system in 1768, and her first free public school state law, early in the nineteenth century, was soon repealed. In Connecticut the dedication to education in 1795 of the moneys received from the sale of land in the Western Reserve had the unhappy effect of lessening a feeling of responsibility for local appropriations. There were many private schools, good and bad, of course, for those who could afford them, and both the schools established by Samuel Slater at Pawtucket for his child employees in the mills and the many other schools which bloomed in the wake of the establishment of the American Sunday School Union in 1824 had considerable significance for general as well as religious education.

Samuel Slater's Mill at Pawtucket, Rhode Island. Photograph by Samuel Chamberlain. New York Public Library Picture Collection

Henry Barnard. New York Public Library Picture Collection

In 1837 Massachusetts set up a State Board of Education which registered great progress during the twelve years of Horace Mann's incumbency; the very next year, Connecticut followed, under another great educator, Henry Barnard, later founder of *The American Journal of Education*, president of the University of Wisconsin, and (in 1867) the first United States Commissioner of Education. In 1836 appeared the first of McGuffey's *Readers*, which were destined to make as important a contribution to American education as Noah Webster's speller.

In some areas in modern New England, unfortunately, some of the most effective enemies of education have appeared among spendthrift members of autonomous school committees, who antagonize their constituency and undermine much-needed public support for education when they send the tax rate soaring by erecting unneeded, often badly designed "country club type" school buildings and paying inflated salaries to unneeded administrators who do nothing and are incapable of doing much. Lord Acton's wise saying that all power corrupts and that absolute power corrupts absolutely applies quite as well to big frogs in little puddles as in any other area.

Dublin, New Hampshire, claims the first free public library in America (1822) and Peterborough (1833) the first supported by public funds. Salisbury, Connecticut, however, had a free library for children in 1803. There were fifty bookstores in Boston by the 1770s, and Vermont had twenty-one circulating libraries by 1810. Various college clubs contributed notably toward widening the student's range of interest and supplementing what he learned in the classroom—*The Yale Literary Magazine* goes back to 1836—nor must one overlook the tremendous educational advantages of the Lyceum lecture system, which began in the 1820s and flourished in every self-respecting town for many years. Though commercialized in a measure after the Civil War, when Pond, Redpath, and other professionals took over, it still found a place for a man like Emerson as long as he lived.

III

If the church was importantly tied up with education, so was she with reform, though the abolitionists often judged churchmen backward enough on the slavery issue. Antislavery was the "cause" which made the most noise in the nineteenth century, but there were times when both temperance and "women's rights" came within hailing distance of it. It is hard to realize now that there was ever a time when women readers were not permitted in the Harvard Library or the Boston Athenaeum (it was thought that their presence might embarrass "modest men"). For a time feminism and abolition even showed signs of making common cause, and women won the right to speak in peace meetings and antislavery meetings long before they acquired the vote. The Harvard Medical School admitted its first woman student in 1835, and Connecticut gave married women partial, though not complete, control of their own property in 1845-46. On the other hand, the men of Maine voted against woman suffrage as recently as 1917.

Slavery is gone, and "women's rights" are presumably here to stay, but when, in the 1970s, Massachusetts insanely lowers the legal drinking age in taverns from twenty-one to eighteen and then naïvely wonders why alcoholism is increasing, one can hardly flatter oneself that the other problem has been solved. Early New England was dripping "wet," with alcohol universally consumed by men, women, and children. The inevitable reaction followed. Maine had a Society for the Suppression of Intemperance in 1813, and in 1830 it was noted that more than 150 vessels sailed from Boston with no liquor on board. Maine passed her first prohibition law in 1846, and between then and 1855, when New Hampshire succumbed, all the New England states had gone "dry." Enforcement was, as usual, another matter, and by 1868 repeal had followed everywhere except in Maine, though local option kept many areas officially "dry," as it still does. But even Maine can hardly be described as single-minded. She strengthened the 1846 law in 1851, decided to allow limited sale in 1856, reenacted prohibition two years later, passed a new law in 1871, and enacted a constitutional amendment prohibiting everything except cider in 1874. In 1911 the prohibition forces won on a referendum, but in 1923 they lost, and the prohibition amendment was repealed in 1934.

A pronounced expression of the nineteenth-century reform movement, not peculiar to New England, involved the foundation of various communities. Because of their association with famous writers, George Ripley's Brook Farm, at West Roxbury, Massachusetts, from 1841 to 1847, and Bronson Alcott's more idealistic and much shorter-lived Fruitlands at Harvard were the most famous New England foundations, but Adin Ballou's Hopedale Community at Mendon lasted much longer. John Humphrey Noyes, born at Brattleboro, Vermont, began his community enterprise in his home state, but after the complex and unorthodox sexual arrangements devised, inaccurately stigmatized as "free love," had occasioned scandal, he moved to Oneida, New York, where the society endured until after his death in 1886 and grew prosperous through its silverware and other products.

The War of 1812 stimulated interest in international peace, and the founding of the American Peace Society in New York in 1828 was followed by others in New England. The Peace Society of Massachusetts began in the study of William Ellery Channing. William Ladd, prominent peace advocate of Maine and New Hampshire, anticipated the Hague Tribunal in his *Essay on a Congress of Nations* (1840). A better remembered peace advocate, and one of the most amazing characters in New England history, was the "Learned Blacksmith," Elihu Burritt (1810-1869), of New London,

Congressman (later Senator) Justin S. Morrill of Vermont, sponsor of the Morrill Act, which set aside 13,000,000 acres for the support of higher education in the United States. New York Public Library Picture Collection

Connecticut, and Worcester, Massachusetts. Self-educated and a phenomenal linguist, Burritt published many books, edited *The Christian Citizen* and *The Advocate of Peace and Universal Brotherhood*, and left a twenty-eight-volume manuscript journal. He was prominently identified with peace movements both here and abroad and organized conferences at Brussels (1848) and elsewhere. Despite his opposition to the Civil War, Lincoln gave him a consular appointment at Birmingham.

Many reforms involved no isms except plain humanity; some were necessitated by changing social conditions. It has been estimated that in the 1820s Massachusetts had seventy-five thousand persons in jail for debt, more than half of whom owed less than twenty dollars. Prison conditions were too disgusting to describe, with men, women, and children, hardened criminals and petty or technical offenders herded together indiscriminately in unrelieved filth, misery, and moral degradation. In 1827 Connecticut built a new prison, replacing an ancient atrocity which had been operating in the abandoned shafts of an old copper mine. Massachusetts established a reform school for boys in 1845 and for girls in 1847.

The great heroine of prison reform and humane treatment of the insane was Dorothea Dix (1802-1887); few private persons have ever exercised such influence for good upon public policy. Encouraged by Charles Sumner and by Samuel Gridley Howe, who in 1834 founded the Perkins Institute for the Blind, where his success with the blind deaf-mute Laura Bridgman made her as famous in her time as Helen Keller was afterwards to become, Miss Dix, though herself a semi-invalid, began the long study of jails and asylums which was to carry her across the world. Her 1843 report to the Massachusetts legislature created too great a sensation to be ignored. During the Civil War she became the first United States Superintendent of Nurses. Her younger contemporary, Clara Barton, a native of Oxford, Massachusetts, began her spectacular career as a Civil War nurse. In 1881 she organized the American Red Cross and remained prominently engaged in philanthropic enterprises for the rest of her life.

Charles Sumner. New York Public Library Picture Collection

Dorothea Lynde Dix. Houghton Mifflin Company. New York Public Library Picture Collection

During the remainder of the century the reform tide ebbed and flowed. The McLean Asylum for the Insane was opened in 1818, but there was nothing more in Massachusetts before the opening of the State Asylum at Worcester in 1833. In 1820 selectmen in Connecticut were still being allowed to farm out paupers at public auction. Dr. Eli Todd established the Hartford Retreat in 1824, and Vermont set up the Brattleboro Retreat for the Insane in 1826. Yet Vermont had no State Board of Health until 1886. Though this was one of the early ones, it had little real power, and it was not until 1917 that the state established a Board of Charities and Probation, defining and regulating the obligations of the towns, which, even at that date, was a very controversial measure.

IV

That the nineteenth century in New England and elsewhere was a time of increasing interest in science and in the application of science to "practical" uses, which is technology, nobody can now need to be told. There were those who feared and mistrusted it, first on religious, then on humanistic and social grounds. Russel B. Nye may exaggerate when he writes that "almost to a man, American intellectuals feared technology and its twin industrialism, and searched for strategies to defeat them," but impressive testimonials to support this statement can be gathered, all the way from Hawthorne to Henry Adams, who saw the Dynamo replacing the Virgin and multiplicity taking the place of unity at the World's Columbian Exposition in Chicago in 1893, and who wrote in 1901 that

The present society must break its damn neck in a definite, but remote, time, not exceeding fifty years more. This is an arithmetical calculation from given data, as, for example, from explosives, or electric energy, or control of cosmic power.

Harvard's great zoologist Louis Agassiz, who was capable of drawing five thousand people to hear a scientific lecture in Tremont Temple, her botanist Asa Gray, and Yale's geologist James Dwight Dana and chemist Benjamin Silliman were all important and influential men. The Swiss-born Agassiz, a devout Catholic, refused credence to Darwinism, but Gray failed to find it incompatible with Christian faith and helped ease the way for its acceptance in America. "No one other person understands me so thoroughly as Asa Gray," said Darwin. "If ever I doubt what I mean myself, I think I shall ask him."

Scientific progress was nowhere more striking, and certainly nowhere more beneficent, than in medicine. The pioneering use of anaesthesia from 1846 at Massachusetts General Hospital has already been noted, but in that same state in the fifties, men still had an average life expectancy of 38.7 years and women of 40.9, and here as elsewhere epidemic diseases were rampant, and nobody expected all his children to live to grow up.

Rival medical theories and practices contended for men's allegiance. From the 1840s on many believed in hydropathy, or water cure, a treatment of German origin. This was not peculiar to New England (there was an American Hydropathic Society, later the American Hygienic and Hydropathic Association of Physicians), but many distinguished New Englanders, including Longfellow and Mrs. Stowe were of the faith, and one Dr. Wesselhoeft conducted a well-reputed establishment at Brattleboro, Vermont. Whatever may be thought of hydropathy as medical theory, the treatment contrasted pleasantly with some of the other barbarous medical practices of the period, and the emphasis on diet, exercise, rest, and peace of mind was all to the good. Advocates of dietary reform, of whom the most successful was probably Sylvester Graham (who left us his name with Graham crackers) attracted disciples and served in a measure to counteract the gluttony of an age given to seven-course dinners. More "scientific" were the homeopaths, who cured disease by administering minute doses of drugs which produced conditions similar to those by which the patient was afflicted, thus, or so they believed, stimulating the body to heal itself, and who were strong enough in Boston to draw the fire of the allopath Dr. Oliver Wendell Holmes.

Patent medicines "boomed," of course, as never before, no success being greater than that of Lydia E. Pinkham's Vegetable Compound, which began in Lynn, Massachusetts, in the mid-1870s, and continued to be manufactured there until 1974. Because this medicine contained alcohol, there have been a great many jokes about how "temperance" ladies got their "kicks" from Lydia Pinkham, but if no patent medicine had ever done more harm in the world than her "compound," the record would be much less shameful than it is. The medicine did contain beneficial herbs ("botanic medi-

Louis Agassiz, engraved by J. Sartain from a photograph by Whillpe & Black, Boston. New York Public Library Picture Collection

Sylvester Graham. New York Public Library Picture Collection

Asa Gray. New York Public Library Picture Collection

Lydia E. Pinkham. New York Public Library Picture Collection

Letter from Lydia E. Pinkham. New York Public Library Picture Collection

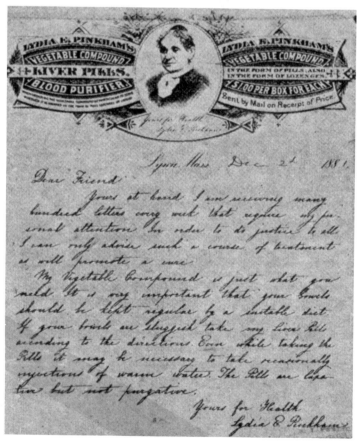

cine," as sponsored by Samuel Thompson of New Hampshire was another interest of the period), and the advice which Mrs. Pinkham gave her thousands of correspondents was, on the whole, surprisingly sensible and, in its application to "female complaints," amazingly and refreshingly frank and honest for its time.

V

If religion has been suspicious of science, she has conducted an off-again, on-again love-hate affair with the arts all down the centuries. All in all, the drama has been traditionally regarded as the most wayward child, though there have been times when fiction has shared in the opprobrium heaped upon her, and not much needs be added here to what has already been recorded concerning the establishment of the theater in various urban centers. Even in New England, however, the story is not quite a blank. Charles M. Thompson has recorded that there was little of what is now known as recreation in the days of his youth; except for whist, fishing, and driving horses, sports were something for boys, not men. Yet even then there were occasional minstrels, ventriloquists, and magicians to be encountered at the town hall. And, of course, when you could tie up entertainment in any form with "culture," it was much easier to defend. Perhaps we have by this time heard enough of how Julia Ward Howe and her friends entertained themselves by translating Mother Goose rhymes into Greek and German, but I still like Thompson's story of how he and some friends stopped at a lonely farmhouse in the eighties or nineties, where they were served an excellent meal for twenty-five cents each, and found the current issues of the *Atlantic*, *Harper's*, and the *Century* on the sitting room table.

Eugene O'Neill, still regarded as probably the foremost American dramatist, was not exactly a New England writer, but he got his first chance at the Wharf Theater in Cape Cod's Provincetown in 1916, used New England materials in *Desire Under the Elms* and elsewhere, and died in what is now Boston University's Shelton Hall. In days gone by, there was some interesting dramatic activity, involving Percy MacKaye, Langdon Mitchell, and others at the summer colony in Cornish, New Hampshire, and of late years the American Shakespeare Festival Theater and Academy at Stratford, Connecticut, has had a remarkable success in its June through September season. "Summer theaters" still flourish in New England, but they seem less creative, and considerably less significant for anything beyond light summer entertainment, than they gave promise of being a quarter of a century ago.

Musicians are cosmopolitan people whom it is hard to pin down, but it is certainly fair to count George W. Chadwick, Charles M. Loeffler, Frederick S. Converse, Horatio W. Parker, and Mrs. H. H. A. Beach as New England composers, and, among contemporaries and

Eugene O'Neill. The Bettmann Archive

near contemporaries, Irving G. Fine, Edward Burlingame Hill, Alan Hohvannes, Charles Ives, and Walter Piston. Reginald De Koven, once famous for *Robin Hood* ("Oh, Promise Me") and other operettas, was born in Middletown, Connecticut. Edward MacDowell (1861-1908) was born and died in New York, but he lived and worked in Boston for a number of years, and the presence of the MacDowell Colony in Peterborough, New Hampshire, long presided over by his widow, where so many creative workers in all the arts have been subsidized and given delightful conditions under which to live and function, seems to make him belong to New England more than he actually did. It is the fashion at present to neglect MacDowell's art songs, and the phonograph companies seem, for some reason, determined not to record them; nevertheless they are the only American works in kind which any sensible person could think of mentioning in the same breath with those of European masters. Today Leonard Bernstein seems more New York than New England, but he was born in Lawrence, Massachusetts, and has had many New England connections, including, at one time, that of assistant to Serge Koussevitzky.

Charles Ives in 1894. New York
Public Library Picture Collection

Charles Ives in 1949. New York
Public Library Picture Collection

Walter Piston. New York Public Library
Picture Collection

Edward MacDowell. New York Public Library
Picture Collection

VI

When Washington Allston, a painter of great range
and vitality, died in 1843, he was generally regarded,
especially by Bostonians, as the greatest American
painter. Today there is much greater interest in the
work of Winslow Homer (1836-1910) and, among contemporaries, in that of Andrew Wyeth. (Whistler was
born in Lowell, but fled from it, and it is hard to think

Winslow Homer at work. Painting by Harry Anderson. New York Public Library Picture Collection

of any artist less allied to New England in his spirit.)

Homer, Boston-born, is most famous for his pictures of Maine and the sea, though he showed equal skill in capturing the lush atmosphere of Florida and the Bahamas. Wyeth, remarkable son of a remarkable father, the great romantic illustrator and muralist N. C. Wyeth (a native of Needham, Massachusetts), calls Chadds Ford, Pennsylvania, home but spends his summers and does much painting in Maine. A superb technician, with an unexcelled gift for finding beauty in common things, Wyeth occasionally makes a friendly gesture in the direction of the avant-garde but is mainly remarkable for his ability to develop in his own orbit, in serene disregard of "tendencies." Like Robert Frost in poetry, he seems to have decided that those who were to accept him must do it absolutely upon his own terms; with both men the challenge has been gladly accepted.

The great John Singer Sargent was not a New Englander, but he did spend considerable time in Boston, where his murals decorate both the Boston Public Library and the Museum of Fine Arts. Across Copley Square from the library, there are murals by John La Farge in Richardson's Trinity Church. William Morris Hunt, Vermont-born, was the most important American painter of the Barbizon school, and Frederick Edwin Church, one of the leading Hudson River painters, was born in Connecticut. Alfred Pinkham Ryder, who hailed from New Bedford, looked at the sea and other things with the eyes of a mystic. Childe Hassam had associations with both Boston and Old Lyme, Connecticut, and the Vermont landscapes of the Italian-born Luigi Lucioni have an admirable clarity and individuality that is all their own.

Ships' figureheads provided an early outlet for the carver's art; William Southworth produced more than five hundred of them. After Mount Auburn Cemetery was laid out in Cambridge in 1831, there was an increasing demand for mortuary sculpture. Among sculptors, Connecticut claims Paul W. Bartlett, Bela Pratt, and others. Augustus Saint-Gaudens was born in New Hampshire and died there. Daniel C. French too was a native of New Hampshire, but he was living in Concord, Massachusetts, when he laid the foundations for

Winslow Homer in old age. New York Public Library Picture Collection

John Singer Sargent. Charcoal sketch by R. M. Crosby. New York Public Library Picture Collection

John La Farge. New York Public Library Picture Collection

his fame with *The Minute Man.* Between 1830 and 1860 both painting and sculpture found generous patronage in America. About 1825 Horatio Greenough led the exodus to Rome which involved such highly talented people as Thomas Crawford, William Wetmore Story, Larkin Mead, and Harriet Hosmer. In spite of what many regard as the prudery of our New England forebears, *The Greek Slave* of Powers and *The White Captive* of Erastus Dow Palmer were both immensely admired. Mrs. Longfellow, who found the *Captive* beautiful but "uncomfortably nude," notes having heard that the head was taken from "a Pittsfield damsel's" and the body from that of "a sempstress of the family" ("Can you imagine a Yankee girl brought to that!"), but it has also been stated that Palmer's model was his own daughter. It is difficult to believe that those who loved these frank, though idealized, nudes, read into them all the metaphysical subtleties ("trust . . . in a Divine Providence," etc.) which Powers hypothesized; many, surely, must simply have enjoyed the rare opportunity of looking at a beautiful naked girl without feeling obliged to be ashamed of their enjoyment. High-minded they may have been, but these sculptors were not squeamish nor much given to fig leaves; Greenough's *Cupid Bound* is surely a small masterpiece of its kind.

A word should be added about "popular" art and artists, whatever that rather glib term may mean. In the mid-nineteenth century, George Henry Durrie, a Connecticut painter who specialized in winter landscapes, gained very wide exposure through the work he did for Currier and Ives prints, while the sculptor John Rogers turned out a great variety of genre groups, always ex-

Daniel Chester French, from the bust by Margaret French Cresson in the Hall of American Artists, New York University. New York Public Library Picture Collection

Harriet Hosmer. New York Public Library Picture Collection

ecuted with great skill, and often of great charm, which were widely circulated throughout America. In the early twentieth century, by all means the most popular American painter was Maxfield Parrish, a Philadelphian, who spent many of his ninety-five years at Cornish, New Hampshire, where he died in 1966, and who created a kind of enchanted fairy world that is all his own. It is too bad to be so intoxicated by "Maxfield Parrish blue" that one fails to recognize his excellent draftsmanship, delicate fancy, and delightful, playful humor. After years of neglect, Parrish is now being rediscovered, oddly enough sometimes by the kind of "modernists" he despised. Though such works as his *Yankee Doodle* show that he is capable of it, there is less romance in Norman Rockwell, though there is even more humor, more "genre," and more delighted observation of everyday American activities, especially those involving children. Though born in New York, Rockwell too has lived much in New England. Through many years his incomparable showcase was the cover of *The Saturday Evening Post*.

The art lover is, of course, dependent upon museums, though during recent years these have been notably aided and supplemented by the wonderfully fine reproductions in many of the art books which constitute one of the main triumphs and services of contemporary publishing. Besides the great Boston Museum of Fine Arts, the Isabella Stewart Gardner Museum in the Fenway, and the Fogg at Harvard, New England has many fine smaller museums, including the Worcester Museum, the Smith College Art Museum, the Addison Gallery of American Art at Andover, and the Sterling and Francine Clark Institute in Williamstown, founded by an heir to the Singer sewing machine fortune, who bequeathed to it half his estate and his fine collection of fourteenth- to twentieth-century paintings.

Childe Hassam. New York Public Library Picture Collection

VII

Literature is the most democratic of the arts and certainly the easiest to circulate and reproduce. New England literature did not end with the "Golden Age" which has already been surveyed, though perhaps there has been no other period since when it was quite so dominant or so redolent of its section. The three great

Maxfield Parrish at seventeen. New York Public Library Picture Collection

Maxfield Parrish, drawing by Kenyon Cox, 1904. New York Public Library Picture Collection

Norman Rockwell, painting from models. New York Public Library Picture Collection

Portrait of Andrew Wyeth by James Wyeth. Copyright © 1969, 1970 by James Wyeth. Photograph courtesy of the Brandywine River Museum. Private collection

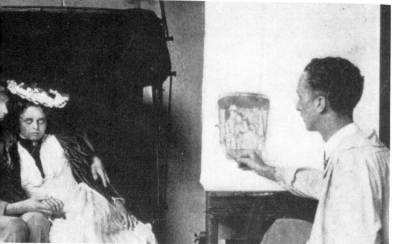

fiction writers of the late nineteenth and early twentieth centuries—Mark Twain (1835-1910), William Dean Howells (1837-1920), and Henry James (1843-1916)—all had a connection with New England, but though both Howells and James are buried in the Cambridge Cemetery, none really belonged to it.

James, born in New York, spent a good deal of his early life in Cambridge, but became a cosmopolitan of cosmopolitans and, at the very end, a British subject. Nevertheless, he found much literary material in New England, and the use he made of it in his fiction shows his understanding of the region, as what he wrote of it directly in *The American Scene*, the fruit of his last visit there, shows his affection for it. Mark Twain and Howells both came from what was then "the West," the first from Missouri, the second from Ohio, and Mark Twain seems distinctly western or southwestern in the spirit of his work. *A Connecticut Yankee in King Arthur's Court* is his only long fiction with a distinctly New England hero, but many short pieces show his understanding of New England character. He was reared on southwestern Calvinism, a somewhat vulgarized New England importation, and for all his rebellions, he never really got over it; even his famous determinism shows its influence. Some of his best writing years were spent in Hartford, and he died in Redding. Howells came closer to being a real New Englander than either of the others, for he was in the Boston area from 1866 until near the end of the eighties; as James T. Fields's assistant on the *Atlantic* for five years and himself its editor for ten more, he found in New England abundant materials for his fiction. For all that, neither Howells himself nor any native New Englander ever thought of him as quite belonging to the inner circle, and when he left Houghton Mifflin for Harpers he transferred himself to the New York area and stayed there the rest of his life.

The credentials of the New England local writers as representatives of their area are, of course, unimpeachable. Thomas Bailey Aldrich, like Howells an *Atlantic* editor, was born in Portsmouth, spent part of his boyhood in New Orleans, and began his literary career in New York journalism, but once having come to Boston in 1866, he remained there until he died in 1907. *The Story of a Bad Boy* preceded *Tom Sawyer*, but Aldrich's finest work went into the carefully chiseled lyrics of his later years which have caused him not unreasonably to be compared to Robert Herrick. Edward Bellamy's famous and influential utopia *Looking Backward* (1888) has a Boston setting (Bellamy was born and died in Chicopee Falls); in *The Duke of Stockbridge* he wrote about Shays's Rebellion; Howells thought his fantasies good enough to entitle him to rank ahead of all other American romancers except Hawthorne.

Modern writers of fiction (as of every other type of literature) in New England are like autumn leaves in Vallombrosa; only a few token names can be mentioned here, and these must be mainly those of writers who have found their inspiration in the New England scene. One of the best known was J. P. Marquand, who, though his reputation seems now to have faded, was, until his death in 1960, generally regarded as the foremost contemporary American practitioner of the novel of manners. Though Marquand was born in Delaware, he was related to Margaret Fuller, and he had a long and successful career as a "popular" writer before

Henry James. New York Public Library Picture Collection

William Dean Howells in later life. Photograph by Zaida Ben-Yusuf. New York Public Library Picture Collection

Sarah Orne Jewett. New York Public Library Picture Collection

Thomas Bailey Aldrich. New York Public Library Picture Collection →

John P. Marquand, 1963. Wide World Photo

Mary Ellen Chase. New York Public Library Picture Collection

he caught the Boston Brahmin so unerringly in *The Late George Apley* (1937). Dorothy Canfield too had her cosmopolitan aspects, but her roots in New England were very deep, and during her later years, she was probably better known as an exponent of the Vermont spirit than as the author of such once popular novels as *The Brimming Cup* (1921). Among contemporary New England novelists, Gerald Warner Brace (*The Garretson Chronicle*, etc.), Mary Ellen Chase (*Mary Peters*, etc.), and Gladys Hasty Carroll (*As the Earth Turns*, etc.) have been well to the fore. Among those specializing in history, Kenneth Roberts, who was famous for his authenticity and minute documentation, had the courage to present the Loyalist cause in the Revolution in *Oliver Wiswell* and to give us the unfallen Benedict Arnold in his heroic early aspect in *Arundel* and *Rabble in Arms*, and Esther Forbes, of Worcester, illuminated early New England in many aspects, perhaps most notably in connection with Salem in *The Running of the Tide*. It is also worth remembering that for five years (1892-97), after he had married a New England girl, the great Rudyard Kipling lived at Brattleboro, Vermont, and there wrote *Captains Courageous*, the *Jungle Books*, and other works.

New England was well and brilliantly represented in the so-called "New Poetry" renaissance which began well before the First World War, outstandingly by Edwin Arlington Robinson, Robert Frost, Amy Lowell, Josephine Preston Peabody, and Edna St. Vincent Millay. Robinson, who was related to Anne Bradstreet and admired Hawthorne, Emerson, and Emily Dickinson, was born in Head Tide, Maine, but removed to Gardiner while still very young. He entered Harvard, but financial stringency compelled him to withdraw. He

324

Rudyard Kipling. New York Public Library Picture Collection

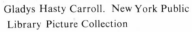

Gladys Hasty Carroll. New York Public Library Picture Collection

Kenneth Roberts. New York Public Library Picture Collection

worked as an inspector on the New York subway while it was under construction and wrote advertising copy for a Boston department store. After *Captain Craig* was published in 1902, he experienced the unique distinction of being "boomed" by a president of the United States. Theodore Roosevelt, who, having learned of his difficult circumstances, almost begged him to accept a government appointment. Robinson finally agreed but relinquished the post as soon as he found reasonable certainty that he was going to be able to keep body and soul together through his writing; he later spent much time in the MacDowell Colony. During his lifetime, which ended in 1935, Robinson was generally regarded as the most important of the "new poets" (Frost did not achieve the height of his vogue until a little later), and won three Pulitzer Prizes. Like Browning, he was primarily a psychologist and a student of human behavior, but his greatest popularity began in 1927 with the publication of what was for him the unusually full-throated and richly emotional *Tristram*, the final member of an Arthurian trilogy. Robinson worked always with traditional verse forms, and his use of colloquial language and avoidance of many of the ornaments customarily associated with poetry helped him to achieve a distinctively individual utterance whose very "dryness" contributed to the desired effect.

Robert Frost was born in San Francisco in 1875 (he had a Copperhead father whose dislike of New England in wartime had driven him west) and defiantly named, after the great leader of the Confederacy, Robert Lee Frost. After his father died in 1885, he came with his

Esther Forbes. New York Public Library Picture Collection

Robert Frost, ca. 1915. The Bettmann Archive

Robert Frost reciting his poem "The Gift Outright" at the inauguration of President Kennedy. New York Public Library Picture Collection

mother and sister to Lawrence, Massachusetts, and in 1892 he was graduated from high school there, covaledictorian of his class with the girl he was to marry. Two years later *The Independent* printed the first of his poems to be accepted by a magazine with a national circulation, but this was a false dawn; up to 1912 he had only been able to repeat this success a dozen more times. In that year he left for England with his wife and family. There his first book, *A Boy's Will*, was published, and when the war drove the Frosts back to America in 1915, one of the first things he saw was a long and enthusiastic article about his work in a new magazine called *The New Republic.*

Frost received almost every honor that can be bestowed upon an American writer. During the early years he taught and farmed on occasion; later he often served as a poet-in-residence—or "poetic radiator," as he called it—at many colleges and universities; he also met with great success as a public reader of his own work. He had connections with several New England states. One book is called *New Hampshire*, another *West-Running Brook*, still another *North of Boston*. All three titles are characteristic.

Frost was one of the strongest individualists among American writers. Neither almost complete neglect nor overwhelming success ever swerved him for one moment out of his chosen path. It must have been a shock to many to learn when he appeared at Kennedy's inauguration that, for all his New Hampshire-Vermont atmosphere, he was a Democrat. As a man he was not without his neurotic aspects; as a writer, he always gave the impression of being an optimist who blinked nothing, one who faced life foursquare and built his house upon a rock. He was a selective realist who did not think it necessary to offer dirt with his potato to show that it was a real potato, a "synecdochist" who preferred to deal in indirection and mean two things where he could only say one. His style is a conversational style, in which we seem to hear real people talking, with the rhythm of living speech loosely superimposed upon traditional meters. His philosophical reflections develop directly out of the most exactly and minutely observed fact, and when his deeper meaning is not clear, the reason generally is that life itself is not clear. Though Frost was far from being an Emersonian transcendentalist, there is no writer who gives modern readers a stronger impression of New England character at its best.

Of the three women, Amy Lowell (1874-1925) probably had the widest fame during her lifetime. Essentially an inheritor of the Romantic tradition and an authority on Keats, Miss Lowell owed much of her fame to her eccentricities, her aggressive self-advertising campaigns, and her espousal of free verse, imagism, and "poly-

Amy Lowell. The Bettmann Archive

Josephine Preston Peabody. New York Public Library Picture Collection

phonic prose." Not all her work fell within these confines, however; deliberate in all things, she "made up her mind" to be a poet and spent ten years in study and practice before she began to publish. D. H. Lawrence, who denied that there had ever been such a thing as an imagist "movement," told Glenn Hughes that in everything she did "Amy was a good amateur," and John Livingston Lowes, who admired her, said that, in later years, "I think she had herself ceased to care greatly for what, in effect, were battles long ago." *Pictures of the Floating World* and *Fir-Flower Tablets* brought oriental influences into American poetry, and such narrative poems as "Number 3 on the Docket" and "The Rosebud Wallpaper" show as great insight into humble New England lives as that of some of the writers who have made this their whole stock in trade. The ambitious *Can Grande's Castle* shows the influence of Carlyle's *French* Revolution, of Hardy's *Dynasts*, of the Boston historians, of the cyclic theories of history expounded by Henry and Brooks Adams, and of D. W. Griffith's film, *Intolerance*. Though Miss Lowell's fame has faded since her death, "Lilacs" is rich in the New England spirit, and "Patterns" is a moving indictment of war. At its best, her poetry is as full of light and color and shifting shapes as the Russian ballet.

Josephine Preston Peabody was a very different proposition. Born in New York, she was educated at the Girls' Latin School in Boston and at Radcliffe and taught for a little while at Wellesley. In 1908 she married Harvard Professor Lionel S. Marks, and from then until her death, at forty-eight, in 1922, she lived on Brattle Street as an admired member of the community.

She began publishing verses in her teens and "made" the *Atlantic* before she was twenty. The other great magazines of the time swiftly capitulated in its wake; she attracted the love of readers and the friendliness of editors and critics. Her first collection, *The Wayfarers*, had a brilliant press, and E. C. Stedman chose nine poems from it for his *American Anthology*, a great compliment to a young writer. When *Fortune and Men's Eyes* appeared in 1900, Richard Henry Stoddard called her one of the foremost living poets.

Her fame was greatly increased when in 1910 her play, *The Piper*, a reworking in terms of modern Christian social consciousness of the old legend of the Pied Piper of Hamelin, won a contest sponsored by the Shakespeare Memorial Theatre at Stratford-upon-Avon. Acted in Stratford by Sir Frank Benson and in America by Edith Wynne Matthison, it still remains eloquent and passionate, one of the best American verse plays. Her last collection, *Harvest Moon* (1916), was a woman's protest against war.

Edna St. Vincent Millay (1892-1950) was born in Rockland, Maine, was graduated from Vassar in 1917, gravitated toward Greenwich Village, and became the first voice in American poetry of the "flaming youth" of the twenties. Though there is still division of opinion as to whether Miss Millay was one of the finest of all women lyric poets or merely a gifted sophomore who never quite grew up, there is no denying the beauty of the metaphysical "Renascence"; the tenderness and hatred of cruelty and violence expressed in "The Buck in the Snow"; the sympathetic understanding of "Prayer to Persephone"; or the power of such sonnets as "To Jesus on His Birthday," that stern indictment of our paganized, commercialized Christmas and the society which makes it inevitable. In 1927 she wrote the libretto for Deems Taylor's successful opera, *The King's Henchman*. Her involvement in the Sacco-Vanzetti case showed her capacity for social concern. In her later years she wrote much about World War II, under whose influence she tended, for the first time, toward the freer forms of verse, but what she wrote about the war is not generally rated with her best work. All in all, it seems fair to say that as long as there are people who love Mrs. Browning's *Sonnets from the Portuguese*, there will also be those who, in spite of all her faults, love Edna Millay.

If I have given only samplings of later New England writers of fiction and poetry, I can give only suggestions under the heading of general literature. Henry Adams (1838-1910), born in Boston, though not permanently resident there, owes his reputation as an historian to his history of the United States under Jefferson and Madison, though the general reader knows him better for *Mont-Saint-Michel and Chartres*, and his posthumous semiautobiography, *The Education of Henry Adams*. The New England historian who reached the widest audience, however, was John Fiske, who was born at Hartford in 1842, settled in Cambridge, and died at Gloucester in 1904. Later scholars have had no difficulty in pointing out some of Fiske's limitations, but most of them might do well to envy his literary gifts. A philosopher as well as an historian, he popularized Darwin and Herbert Spencer in America and helped reconcile science and religion for many of his contemporaries.

Charles Eliot Norton (1827-1908), son of Andrews Norton, "the Unitarian Pope," was primarily an art critic and historian; he also sustained close relations with a number of his older contemporaries of the "Golden Age," notably Lowell. The poet and critic George Edward Woodberry spent the most important part of his career at Columbia, but he was born at Beverly, Massachusetts, of colonial stock, and educated at Phillips Andover and Harvard, where he came into close contact with Norton and Henry Adams. The later leaders of the "New Humanists" were New Englanders only by a certain extension. Irving Babbitt was born in Ohio, Paul Elmer More in St. Louis. Having come to Harvard, Babbitt stayed there as Professor of French until his death in 1933, but More departed for *The Nation* and Princeton. He had studied at Harvard, however, and taught Sanskrit there and at Bryn Mawr, and he named his long and impressive collection of critical studies *Shelburne Essays* (begun in 1904) from his farm at Shelburne, New Hampshire. Their younger contemporary, Stuart P. Sherman, who joined them in their

Edna St. Vincent Millay. New York Public Library Picture Collection

Henry Adams in his study. Photograph by his wife. The Bettmann Archive

fight against naturalistic tendencies, was born in Iowa, taught at Northwestern and the University of Illinois, and left teaching to edit the New York *Herald-Tribune Books*, but he had come of New England ancestry and been trained at Williams and Harvard.

Among the essayists none is more of a figure than Thomas Wentworth Higginson (1823-1911), who, like Norton, was a younger contemporary of the "Schoolroom Poets." Higginson was clergyman, abolitionist, feminist, peace and physical culture propagandist, pioneer discoverer of Negro spirituals and of Emily Dickinson. He attempted many different kinds of writing and contributed more material to the *Atlantic* during its first twenty years than anyone else except Lowell and Holmes. His abolitionism led him into activities that would be considered "subversive" today (he admired John Brown), but he commanded a black regiment during the Civil War. His *Cheerful Yesterdays* is still a delightful book, and there have been two full-length studies of him during recent years. Charles Dudley Warner, Mark Twain's collaborator on *The Gilded Age*, born at Plainfield, Massachusetts, was educated outside of New England and had professional experience in Chicago and Missouri before newspaper work brought him to Hartford, where he remained. *Being a Boy* and *My Summer in a Garden* are still charming reading. Later came Samuel McChord Crothers (1857-1927), born in the Middle West, and of varied experience before he settled in Cambridge in 1894, as pastor of the wooden Gothic First Unitarian Church, across from the Harvard Yard. As a humorist, Crothers had a decided resemblance to Oliver Wendell Holmes and was certainly quite as good. The Philadelphian Agnes Repplier was his only rival as the leading *Atlantic* essayist during the years when that periodical was famous for a type of writing which has since unhappily fallen into desuetude.

One of the most original writers of his time was Gamaliel Bradford (1863-1932), a semi-invalid who lived in Wellesley Hills. Passionately eager for literary fame, Bradford wrote everything—poems, novels, plays, even book reviews and editorials for *The Youth's Companion* and the Boston *Herald*—but he owed his reputation to a new form of biographical writing which, following Sainte-Beuve, he called psychography. Psychography has nothing to do with psychoanalysis (Bradford was allergic to Freud); it is simply character writing, organized topically, not chronologically, and focusing on the subject's character and personality rather than the events of his life. Bradford made his first success with *Lee the American* in 1912, which was followed by *Damaged Souls*, *Wives*, *The Quick and the Dead*, *Daughters of Eve*, *Saints and Sinners*, and other volumes. His "portraits" appeared frequently in the *Atlantic*, *Harper's*, and almost all the other leading American magazines of his time until his death. In the twenties, when interest in biography "boomed," he was

Thomas Wentworth Higginson. New York Public Library Picture Collection

Gamaliel Bradford VI (1863-1932); distinguished biographer and descendant of the Pilgrim governor.

often mentioned along with the Englishman Lytton Strachey, the Frenchman André Maurois, and the German Emil Ludwig. None of the others, however, were so innovative in form as he.

VIII

New England's sons have never thought it necessary to claim that mother was quite perfect. Whittier used to speculate about whether it might not have been better if the *Mayflower* had drifted around the Horn and landed at Santa Barbara, and the elder Henry Cabot Lodge, who was a charming and accomplished man of letters, whether one likes his politics or not, summed it up well when he wrote: "New England has a harsh climate, a barren soil, a rough and stormy coast, and yet we love it, even with a love passing that of dwellers in more favored regions."

These men were born here. But my book is a tribute to New England from an adopted son, who was born in Chicago (which gave him another book) and spent nearly two decades of his life on the Pacific Coast.

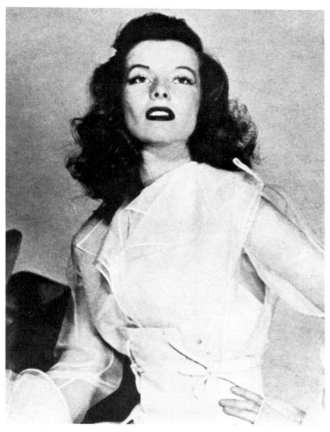

Hartford's Katharine Hepburn. New York Public Library Picture Collection

Whatever faults or virtues it may have, it certainly cannot claim either omniscience or exhaustiveness. But I have tried to hold the balance even, to record accomplishments generously and shortcomings, when they had to be noted, with love.

I first saw Boston and the Boston area in 1926, when I came there to visit Gamaliel Bradford and to confer with Ellery Sedgwick about a literary career which, as it turned out, was destined to be developed through other agencies than *The Atlantic Monthly*. I was strongly attracted by both the city and the New England countryside; even if I had never seen it again, I am sure I should not have forgotten the purple sheen of the loosestrife, as I saw it from the bridge at Concord, growing in the river meadows. But it was not until 1947 that I was free, after two intervening visits, to come here to live. And though I did not relish any of the changes that had been made in the city itself since 1926 (and was to relish those which would rapidly follow even less), there was no doubt in my mind that this was still where I desired to be.

My first-hand knowledge of New England and New Englanders is, therefore, Boston-based, but I did have one encounter in Maine with the old-time Yankee which, out of fairness to him, deserves to be recorded.

About thirty years ago, my wife and I were driving home on the Maine turnpike with three then small children. Suddenly we saw a white liquid being sprayed over the windshield from inside the hood of the car.

Since we neither of us knew anything about mechanics, this was not a sight calculated to fill us with elation. But one of my wife's most amiable characteristics is a touching faith in the combined efficiency and goodwill of truck drivers. And after she had driven the car to the edge of the road and flagged one of these down, her faith proved, in this instance, abundantly justified.

The truck driver found that the liquid was coming out of a rubber hose which had rotted away and needed to be replaced. "I have some adhesive tape in my truck," he said, "and I will tape it up for you. At the end of the turnpike there is a service station. That is about fifteen miles away. If you drive carefully and not too fast, you ought to make it."

We did. And at the service station we were greeted by a white-haired gentleman (and I do mean gentleman) with a gift for silence and what seemed to me a decidedly frosty gleam in his eye.

"What seems to be the trouble?"

In my imbecilic way, I tried to tell him. He examined the car with all the solemnity of a great surgeon examining a patient.

Still silence. I broke the suspense by asking, "Can you fix it?"

He seemed to think the question improper. But I was encouraged by his answer. He said, "Yes, I can fix it," thus actually using two or three more words than would have been strictly necessary.

"Very well," I said. "I wish you would."

He summoned an assistant, and they went to work. After a little while, he beckoned me over from where I was standing with what was more like the flicker of an eyelash than a gesture.

"There is another hose just like this on the other side," he said. "It is rotting too. Do you want me to replace them both?"

I did, but since I had not brought my bank account with me, I thought I had better find out what I was in for. So I asked him what it would cost.

He gave me, if possible, a more penetrating glance than before. "Well," he said, "it will be fifty cents for each hose and fifty cents for my work. Do you think that's too much?"

By the time we left a great cordiality had been established.

Such was the man of old New England. I wonder how many of him are left. When the breed dies out, the world will be poorer.

Suggestions for Further Reading

Adams, Charles Francis. *Charles Francis Adams, 1835-1915: An Autobiography* (Houghton Mifflin, 1916).

Adams, James Truslow. *The Founding of New England; Revolutionary New England, 1691-1776; New England in the Republic, 1776-1850* (Little, Brown, 1921, 1923, 1926).

Addison, Daniel Dulany. *Lucy Larcom: Life, Letters, and Diary* (Houghton Mifflin, 1894).

Ahlstrom, Sydney E. *A Religious History of the American People* (Yale University Press, 1972).

Aldrich, Thomas Bailey. *An Old Town by the Sea* (Houghton Mifflin, 1893).

Allen, Gay Wilson. *William James, A Biography* (Viking Press, 1967).

Andrews, Charles M. *The Colonial Period of American History* (Yale University Press, 4 vols., 1934-38).

Ballou, Ellen B. *The Building of the House: Houghton Mifflin's Formative Years* (Houghton Mifflin, 1970).

Bearse, Ray. *Maine: A Guide to the Vacation State; Massachusetts: A Guide to the Pilgrim State; Vermont: A Guide to the Green Mountain State* (Houghton Mifflin, 1969, 1971, 1966).

Birdsall, Richard D. *Berkshire County: A Cultural History* (Yale University Press, 1959).

Bixby, William. *Connecticut: A New Guide* (Scribners, 1974).

Brennan, Bernard F. *William James* (Twayne Publishers, 1966).

Bridenbaugh, Carl. *Cities in the Wilderness; The First Century of Urban Life in America, 1625-1742; Cities in Revolt; Urban Life in America, 1743-1776* (Knopf, 1955).

Brooks, Van Wyck. *The Flowering of New England; New England: Indian Summer, 1865-1915* (Dutton, 1936, 1940).

Brown, Charles H. *William Cullen Bryant* (Scribners, 1971).

Clifford, Harold B. *Maine and Her People* (The Bond Wheelwright Company, 1958).

Craven, Wesley Frank. *The Colonies in Transition, 1660-1713* (Harper & Row, 1968).

Crockett, Walter Hill. *Vermont: The Green Mountain State* (The Century History Company, 4 vols., 1921).

Crofut, Florence S. Marcy. *Guide to the History and the Historic Sites of Connecticut* (Yale University Press, 2 vols., 1937).

Cutler, John Henry. *Cardinal Cushing of Boston* (Hawthorn Books, 1970).

Dibner, Michael, editor. *Portland* (Greater Portland Landmarks, 1972).

Fisher, Dorothy Canfield. *Vermont Tradition: The Biography of an Outlook on Life* (Little, Brown, 1953).

Fiske, John. *The Beginnings of New England; New France and New England* (Houghton Mifflin, 1899, 1902).

Flexner, James T. *American Painting: First Flowers of the Wilderness* (Houghton Mifflin, 1947).

French, Allen. *Old Concord*, illustrated by Lester G. Hornby (Little, Brown, 1915).

Goold, William. *Portland in the Past* (B. Thurston & Co., 1886).

Green, Samuel M. *American Art: A Historical Survey* (Ronald Press Co., 1966).

Harding, Walter. *The Days of Henry Thoreau* (Knopf, 1965).

Hart, Albert Bushnell, editor. *The Commonwealth History of Massachusetts* (The States History Company, 6 vols., 1927 ff.).

Hill, Ralph Nading. *Yankee Kingdom: Vermont and New Hampshire* (Harper & Row, Updated Edition, 1973).

Howe, Henry F. *Massachusetts: There She Is—Behold Her* (Harper & Row, 1960).

Howe, M. A. DeWolfe. *Boston: The Place and the People* (Macmillan, 1903).

Hughes, Glenn. *A History of the American Theatre* (Samuel French, 1951).

James, Henry. *Charles W. Eliot, President of Harvard University, 1869-1909* (Houghton Mifflin, 2 vols., 1930).

Johnson, Thomas H. *Emily Dickinson: An Interpretive Biography* (Harvard University Press, 1955).

Jones, Herbert G. *Old Portland Town* (Machigonne Press, 1938).

Jones, Howard Mumford, and Bessie Zaban Jones, editors, *The Many Voices of Boston: A Historical Anthology, 1630-1975* (Atlantic-Little, Brown, 1975).

Kimball, Gertrude Selwyn. *Providence in Colonial Times* (Houghton Mifflin, 1912).

Kirk, William, editor. *A Modern City: Providence, Rhode Island, and Its Activities* (The University of Chicago Press, 1909).

Kirker, Harold, and James Kirker. *Bulfinch's Boston, 1787-1817* (Oxford University Press, 1964).

Kirkland, Edward Chase. *Charles Francis Adams, Jr., 1835-1915: The Patrician at Bay* (Harvard University Press, 1965).

Kittredge, George Lyman. *Witchcraft in Old and New England* (Harvard University Press, 1929).

Kittredge, Henry C. *Cape Cod, Its People and Their History* (Houghton Mifflin, Second Edition, 1968).

Levin, David. *History as Romantic Art: Bancroft, Prescott, Motley, and Parkman* (Stanford University Press, 1959).

May, Ralph. *Early Portsmouth History* (C. E. Goodspeed & Co., 1926).

Merrill, John V. D. S., and Caroline R. *Sketches of Historic Bennington* (Cambridge, privately printed, 1908).

Merrill, Walter M. *Against Wind and Tide: A Biography of Wm. Lloyd Garrison* (Harvard University Press, 1963).

Middlekauff, Robert. *The Mathers: Three Generations of Puritan Intellectuals, 1596-1728* (Oxford University Press, 1971).

Miller, Perry. *Jonathan Edwards* (William Sloane Associates, 1949).

——— *Roger Williams: His Contribution to the American Tradition* (Bobbs-Merrill, 1953).

——— *The New England Mind: The Seventeenth Century* (Macmillan, 1939).

——— *The New England Mind: From Colony to Province* (Harvard University Press, 1953).

Miller, Perry, and Thomas H. Johnson, editors. *The Puritans* (American Book Company, 1938).

Morison, Samuel Eliot. *Builders of the Bay Colony* (Houghton Mifflin, 1930).

——— *The Intellectual Life of Colonial New England* (New York University Press, 1956).

——— *The Maritime History of Massachusetts, 1783-1921* (Houghton Mifflin, 1921).

Moulton, Augustus F. *Portland by the Sea: An Historical Treatise* (Katahdin Publishing Co., 1926).

Neilson, William Allan, editor. *Charles W. Eliot, The Man and His Beliefs* (Harpers, 2 vols., 1926).

Newton, Earle. *The Vermont Story: A History of the People of the Green Mountain State, 1749-1949* (Vermont Historical Society, 1949).

Niles, Grace Greylock. *The Hoosac Valley, Its Legends and Its History* (Putnam, 1912).

Nye, Russel B. *The Cultural Life of the New Nation; Society and Culture in America, 1830-1860* (Harper & Row, 1960, 1974).

O'Connor, Richard. *The Golden Summers: An Antic History of Newport* (Putnam, 1974).

Osborn, Norris Galpin, editor. *History of Connecticut* (The States History Company, 5 vols., 1925).

Palfrey, John Gorham. *History of New England* (Little, Brown, 5 vols., 1858 ff.).

Palmer, George Herbert. *The Life of Alice Freeman Palmer* (Houghton Mifflin, 1908).

———— *An Academic Courtship: Letters of Alice Freeman Palmer and George Herbert Palmer* (Harvard University Press, 1940).

Phillips, James Duncan. *Salem in the Seventeenth Century; Salem in the Eighteenth Century; Salem and the Indies* (Houghton Mifflin, 1933, 1937, 1947).

Pomfret, John M., with Lloyd M. Shumway. *Founding the American Colonies, 1583-1660* (Harper & Row, 1970).

Pratson, Frederick John. *New Hampshire* (The Stephen Greene Press, 1974).

Rich, Louis Dickinson. *State o' Maine* (Harper & Row, 1964).

Richman, Irving B. *Rhode Island: A Study in Separatism* (Houghton Mifflin, 1905).

Roberts, Kenneth. *Trending into Maine*, illustrated by N. C. Wyeth (Little, Brown, 1938).

Robinson, Rowland E. *Vermont: A Study in Independence* (Houghton Mifflin, 1892).

Rutman, Darrett B. *Winthrop's Boston: Portrait of a Puritan Town, 1630-1649* (University of North Carolina Press, 1965).

Sablosky, Irving. *American Music* (The University of Chicago Press, 1969).

Sanborn, Frank B. *New Hampshire: An Epitome of Popular Government* (Houghton Mifflin, 1904).

Scudder, Townsend. *Concord, American Town* (Little, Brown, 1947).

Seaburg, Carl. *Boston Observed* (Beacon Press, 1971).

Shepard, Odell. *Connecticut, Past and Present* (Knopf, 1939).

———— *Pedlar's Progress: The Life of Bronson Alcott* (Little, Brown, 1937).

Swayne, Josephine Latham. *The Story of Concord* (Meador Publishing Co., 1939).

Thomas, John L. *The Liberator: William Lloyd Garrison, A Biography* (Little, Brown, 1963).

Tilton, Eleanor M. *Amiable Autocrat: A Biography of Dr. Oliver Wendell Holmes* (Henry Schuman, 1947).

Trumbull, J. Hammond, editor. *The Memorial History of Hartford County, Connecticut, 1663-1884* (Edward L. Osgood, 1886).

Vanderpoel, Emily Noyes. *More Chronicles of a Pioneer School . . .* (The Cadmus Book Shop, 1927).

————, and Elizabeth C. Barnet Burt. *Chronicles of a Pioneer School from 1792 to 1832 . . .* (Cambridge, privately printed, 1903).

Van Dusen, Albert E. *Connecticut* (Random House, 1931).

Wade, Mason. *Margaret Fuller, Whetstone of Genius* (The Viking Press, 1940).

Wagenknecht, Edward. *Cavalcade of the American Novel . . .* (Holt, Rinehart & Winston, 1952).

———— *Harriet Beecher Stowe, The Known and the Unknown* (Oxford University Press, 1965).

———— *Henry Wadsworth Longfellow: Portrait of an American Humanist* (Oxford, 1966).

———— *James Russell Lowell: Portrait of a Many-Sided Man* (Oxford, 1971).

———— *John Greenleaf Whittier: A Portrait in Paradox* (Oxford, 1967).

———— *Mark Twain, The Man and His Work* (University of Oklahoma Press, Third Edition . . . , 1967).

———— *Nathaniel Hawthorne, Man and Writer* (Oxford, 1961).

———— *Ralph Waldo Emerson: Portrait of a Balanced Soul* (Oxford, 1961).

———— *William Dean Howells: The Friendly Eye* (Oxford, 1969).

Warfel, Harry R. *Noah Webster: Schoolmaster to America* (Macmillan, 1936).

Wendell, Barrett. *Cotton Mather, The Puritan Priest* (Dodd, Mead, 1891).

Wertenbacker, Thomas J. *The Golden Age of Colonial Culture* (New York University Press, 1949).

———— *The Puritan Oligarchy: The Founding of American Civilization* (Scribners, 1969).

Weston, George F., Jr. *Boston Ways, High, By, and Folk* (Beacon Press, Revised Edition, 1967).

Weygandt, Cornelius. *The Heart of New Hampshire: Things Held Dear by Folks of the Old Stocks* (Putnam, 1944).

Wheeler, Ruth R. *Concord: Climate for Freedom* (The Concord Antiquarian Society, 1967).

White, Alain C. *The History of the Town of Litchfield, Connecticut, 1720-1920* (Enquirer Print, 1920).

Whitehill, Walter Muir. *Boston, A Topographical History* (Harvard University Press, 1959).

———— *Boston in the Age of John Fitzgerald Kennedy* (University of Oklahoma Press, 1966).

Williams, Hermann Warner, Jr. *Mirror to the American Past: A Survey of American Genre Painting, 1750-1900* (New York Graphic Society, 1973).

Willis, William. *The History of Portland, From 1632 to 1854 . . .* (Bailey & Noyes, Second Edition, Revised and Enlarged, 1865).

Willison, George F. *Saints and Strangers* (Reynal & Hitchcock, 1945).

Winslow, Ola Elizabeth. *A Destroying Angel: The Conquest of Smallpox in Colonial Boston* (Houghton Mifflin, 1974).

———— *Jonathan Edwards, 1703-1758, A Biography* (Macmillan, 1940).

———— *John Eliot, "Apostle to the Indians"* (Houghton Mifflin, 1968).

———— *Master Roger Williams* (Macmillan, 1957).

———— *Meetinghouse Hill, 1630-1783* (Macmillan, 1952).

———— *Portsmouth: The Life of a Town* (Macmillan, 1966).

———— *Samuel Sewall of Boston* (Macmillan, 1964).

Winwar, Frances. *Puritan City: The Story of Salem* (McBride, 1938).

WPA American Guide Series. *Connecticut: A Guide to Its Roads, Lore, and People; New Hampshire: A Guide to the Granite State; Rhode Island: A Guide to the Smallest State* (Houghton Mifflin, 1938, 1938, 1937).

WPA, Writers Program—Maine. *Portland City Guide* (The Forest City Printing Company, 1940).

Wright, Louis B. *The American Heritage History of the Thirteen Colonies* (Simon and Schuster, 1967).

———— *The Cultural Life of the American Colonies, 1607-1763* (Harper & Row, 1957).

Index